The Faces of Buddhism in America

The Faces of
Buddhism
in America

EDITED BY CHARLES S. PREBISH
AND KENNETH K. TANAKA

University of California Press
Berkeley   Los Angeles   London

University of California Press
Berkeley and Los Angeles, California

University of California Press, Ltd.
London, England

Part of chapter 2 appeared in much abbreviated form as "The
Western Pure Land: Shin Buddhism in America," *Tricycle* 4, no. 4
(summer 1995).

Library of Congress Cataloging-in-Publication Data

The faces of Buddhism in America / Charles S. Prebish and Kenneth
K. Tanaka, editors.
    p.   cm.
    Includes bibliographical references and index.
    ISBN 0-520-20460-3 (alk. paper). — ISBN 0-520-21301-7
(pbk. : alk. paper)
    1. Buddhism—United States.   I. Prebish, Charles S.
II. Tanaka, Kenneth Ken'ichi.
  BQ746.F35 1998
  294.3'0973—dc21   97-38769
                                      CIP

Printed in the United States of America
9 8 7 6 5 4 3 2 1

Contents

In Memoriam:
Reverend Dr. Yehan Numata
(1897–1994)

Yehan Numata's propagation of the Buddha Dharma has been on such a vast scale that one can only be reminded of such figures from Buddhist history as King Aśoka, the model that Numata had taken for himself.

While a student at the University of California, Berkeley, he established a journal called *Pacific World*, intended as a vehicle for communicating Buddhism to the English-speaking community. The initial version of *Pacific World* was published from June 1925 to December 1928, but finally failed for lack of financial support. It was at this time that Numata determined to become a businessman, establishing Mitutoyo Company. Today, Mitutoyo is one of the world's leaders in the manufacture of precision measuring instruments.

The success of Mitutoyo allowed Numata to initiate a variety of projects in support of Buddhist propagation. In 1962, on the model of the Gideon Society, he began to distribute *The Teaching of the Buddha*, an abridged translation of *Shinyaku Bukkyo Seiten*, a collection of sayings from the Buddhist canon which had been compiled by Japanese scholars and published in 1925. In December 1965 he established the Bukkyo Dendo Kyokai (BDK, Buddhist Promoting Foundation), which carried on the revising, publication, and distribution of *The Teaching of the Buddha*. A variety of other propagation efforts, including reestablishing *Pacific World* as the journal of the Institute of Buddhist Studies in spring 1982, are supported by BDK. Also, each year the foundation presents the Cultural Service Award to individuals who have made a major contribution to the promotion of Buddhism.

To commemorate the fiftieth anniversary of the establishment of Mitutoyo, Numata initiated two new major projects of the BDK. One was the translation into English of the entirety of the Chinese Buddhist canon, and the other was the establishment of endowed chairs of Buddhist studies at major universities around the world. An editorial committee for the translation project was established in July 1982, headed by Shoyu Hanayama. The base of operations for the translation project was established as the Numata Center for Buddhist Translation and Research in Berkeley, California, in November 1984, under the direction of Reverend Seishin Yamashita.

Several universities have received endowments for the Numata Chairs, including the University of California at Berkeley, Harvard University, and the University of Chicago. The Institute of Buddhist Studies also benefits from an endowment for a Numata Chair. In most cases these chairs are used for visiting professors to give courses in their areas of expertise, thereby supplementing the resources available for the study of Buddhism. At the Institute of Buddhist Studies, the chair is used to sponsor an annual series of lectures, and it is out of the 1994 lecture series that this collection of essays has developed. Buddhism in the West has benefited greatly from the generosity of Yehan Numata, and it is therefore appropriate that this collection of essays on Buddhism in North America be dedicated to his memory. It is also fortunate for the future growth of Buddhism in the West that Numata's heirs have indicated their intent to carry on the projects he initiated.

Richard K. Payne, Dean
Institute of Buddhist Studies, Graduate Theological Union

Introduction

CHARLES S. PREBISH

Between the months of June and November 1994, features on American Buddhism appeared in such popular print media as the *Wall Street Journal, USA Today, Newsweek, New York Magazine,* and *Christianity Today.* The *Newsweek* article, titled "800,000 Hands Clapping," focused on a varied group of American Buddhists that included John Daido Loori, the abbot of Zen Mountain Monastery in upstate New York, well-known actor Richard Gere, Mitchell Kapor of Lotus Development Corporation, Phil Jackson, coach of the world champion Chicago Bulls professional basketball team, and even rock group The Beastie Boys, who recorded "The Bodhisattva Vow," a rap tribute to the Buddhist path. *New York Magazine* went even further, categorizing American Buddhists as "Beat Buddhists" (such as Gary Snyder, Allen Ginsberg, Philip Whalen, and Lawrence Ferlinghetti), "Celluloid Buddhists" (including Willem Dafoe, Oliver Stone, and Ellen Burstyn, along with Gere), "Art Buddhists" (Milton Glaser, Robert Moscowitz, Roy Lichtenstein, and Robert Rauschenberg, among others), "Power Buddhists" (Jerry Brown), and "Benefit Buddhists" (like Porter McCray and Bokara Legendre).

Also in 1994, American Buddhism was presented as a major feature on the *ABC Nightly News with Peter Jennings* (with scholar-Buddhists Robert Thurman and me serving as scholarly consultants) as well as on *Talk of the Nation* on National Public Radio (with Helen Tworkov and Kenneth Tanaka fielding questions from a national audience). Peter Jennings's researchers estimated the American Buddhist population to be between four and six million individuals, composed of both Asian American and Euro-American ethnic groups, making American Buddhism a religious movement significantly larger than many Protestant denominations.

The flurry of national media attention devoted to American Buddhism has continued almost nonstop since. And it's expanding. The *Utne Reader* ran a short feature titled "Buddhism American Style" in the issue for January–February 1995, and the *New York Times* ran an article on October 15, 1995, on apartments that were being turned into would-be *zendōs* for informal meditation sessions. Moreover, American youngsters are even being identified as incarnations of famous Buddhist teachers. On January 25, 1996, *USA Today* ran the story of Sonam Wangdu, a young boy born in Seattle to an American mother and Tibetan father who was identified as the incarnation of Lama Deshung Rinpoche III, a Tibetan teacher who died in Seattle in 1987.

Rodger Kamenetz, author of *The Jew in the Lotus,* a best-selling book on the Jewish-Buddhist dialogue, wrote a popular article titled "Robert Thurman Doesn't *Look* Buddhist" (*New York Times Magazine,* May 5, 1996), highlighting Thurman's role as one of the most visible members of a new breed of scholar-Buddhists, or well-credentialed academic investigators of the Buddhist religion who also happen to be Buddhist practitioners. Thurman is especially visible as one of the Dalai Lama's chief American translators, as well as being the father of noted actress Uma Thurman. Even the newspaper layout of news on American Buddhism foreshadows its growing normative status in mainline American religion. On June 26, 1996, the *New York Times* juxtaposed an article on the construction of Odiyan, a Tibetan Buddhist temple in northern California, alongside an article on the suspected Unabomber's not-guilty plea. And the cover story of *Time* magazine's October 13, 1997, edition was titled, "America's Fascination with Buddhism."

Although there is little consensus on an explanation for the growing popularity of American Buddhism in the latter half of the twentieth century, Peter Berger's perceptive comment of more than thirty years ago still seems applicable today: "Secularization brings about a demonopolization of religious traditions and thus, *ipso facto,* leads to a pluralistic situation." Berger goes on to say that "the key characteristic of all pluralistic situations, whatever the details of their historical background, is that the monopolies can no longer take for granted the allegiance of their client populations. . . . The pluralistic situation is, above all, a *market situation.*"[1] That Buddhism was able to exploit this "market situation" is now widely acknowledged. Robert Bellah, for example, has noted: "In many ways Asian spirituality provided a more thorough contrast to the rejected utilitarian individualism than did biblical religion. To external achievement it posed inner experience; to the exploitation of nature, harmony with nature; to impersonal organization, an intense relation to a guru."[2] In this complex social situation, in addition to its Asian American constituents, the Buddhist movement in America has been especially attractive to individuals from

Jewish backgrounds, as Rodger Kamenetz has pointed out;[3] to many African Americans, following the highly visible Buddhist involvement of Tina Turner and bell hooks;[4] to those steeped in the new language of the wellness movement, conversant with the works of Jon Kabat-Zinn,[5] Mark Epstein,[6] and others; and to a small but continually growing portion of the highly literate, socially and politically active Euro-American urban elite.

Not all of the attention highlighting American Buddhism has occurred in the popular press and print media. Following a profusion of scholarly publications, Syracuse University sponsored a major conference in spring 1977 with the exuberant and perhaps presumptuous title, "The Flowering of Buddhism in America." The trend has continued, expanding to include panels at professional meetings, doctoral dissertations, and even university courses.

More recently, the Institute of Buddhist Studies in Berkeley, California, with funding from the Bukkyo Dendo Kyokai (founded by Reverend Dr. Yehan Numata in Japan), sponsored a twelve-week lecture series organized by Kenneth Tanaka and entitled "Buddhisms in America: An Expanding Frontier" during the fall of 1994. Many of the presentations from that lecture series have been included in this volume. In January 1997, the most ambitious conference of its kind on the topic, titled "Buddhism in America: A Landmark Conference of the Future of Buddhist Meditative Practice in the West," was held in Boston, and in May 1997, Harvard University's Harvard Buddhist Studies Forum sponsored a highly comprehensive conference on the academic investigation of American Buddhism called "Scholarly Contributions to the Study of Buddhism in America."

Historical Concerns

Although it is now rather common to refer to Oriental influences in the writings of such prominent American literary figures as Henry David Thoreau, Ralph Waldo Emerson, and Walt Whitman, and to point to the impact of the Theosophists on the Oriental movement in America, the more specific beginnings of Buddhism in America can be traced to the Chinese immigrants who began to appear on the West Coast in the 1840s.[7] Prior to the discovery of gold at Sutter's Mill, the number of Chinese immigrants was small, but with the news of the golden wealth in the land, the figure increased exponentially. Rick Fields, author of *How the Swans Came to the Lake: A Narrative History of Buddhism in America,* has suggested that by 1852, twenty thousand Chinese were present in California, and within a decade, nearly one-tenth of the California population was Chinese.[8] In the Chinese temples that dotted the California coastline and began to appear in the Chinatown section of San Francisco, the religious practice was an eclectic blend of Buddhism, Taoism, and Confucianism, and although there were many Buddhist priests in residence, a distinctly Chinese Buddhism on the North American continent did not develop until much later.

The Japanese presence in America developed more slowly than the Chinese, but had much greater impact. By 1890, when the Chinese presence was already quite apparent, the Japanese population was barely two thousand. The World Parliament of Religions, however, held in conjunction with the Chicago World's Fair in 1893, radically changed the entire landscape for Japanese Buddhism in America. Among the participants at the parliament was Shaku Sōen, a Rōshi who was to return to America a decade later and promote the school of Rinzai Zen (one of the two major branches of Japanese Zen Buddhism). Sōen Rōshi returned to America in 1905, lecturing in several cities and establishing a basic ground for the entry of Zen. Upon his return to Japan in 1906, three of his students were selected to promote the Rinzai lineage in America.

The first of Sōen Rōshi's students, Nyōgen Senzaki, came to California in the first decade of the twentieth century, but delayed his teaching mission until 1922. Sōen Rōshi's second disciple, Shaku Sōkatsu, lived in America from 1906 to 1908, and again from 1909 to 1910, but eventually returned to Japan without having made much impact. By far Sōen Rōshi's most noted disciple, and the man who made the most impact on the early growth of Buddhism in America, was Daisetz Teitaro Suzuki. Suzuki worked for Open Court Publishing Company in LaSalle, Illinois, from 1897 to 1909, but returned to Japan to pursue a career in Buddhist Studies. He visited America again from 1936 until the beginning of World War II, and eventually returned for a final time from 1950 to 1958, lecturing frequently in American universities and cities.

Nonetheless, the Rinzai lineage was not the only one to develop in America. The Sōtō tradition (the other major branch of Japanese Zen) began to appear in America in the 1950s. By the mid-1950s, Soyu Matsuoka Rōshi had established the Chicago Buddhist Temple, and Shunryu Suzuki Rōshi arrived in San Francisco in 1959, founding the San Francisco Zen Center shortly thereafter. The Dharma successors to Suzuki Rōshi have continued the Sōtō lineage, while other teachers in this lineage (including one of the few female rōshis, Jiyu Kennett) have also appeared.

In addition to the traditional forms of Rinzai and Sōtō Zen, still another form of Zen has appeared in America, one that attempts to harmonize the major doctrines and practices of each school into a unified whole. This movement owes its American origins to Sogaku Harada, although he never visited the United States himself. Proponents of this approach included Taizan Maezumi Rōshi (arriving in 1956), Hakuun Yasutani Rōshi (who visited the United States first in 1962, and who visited regularly until his death in 1973), and Philip Kapleau, an American by birth who first learned about Japanese religion and culture while serving as a court reporter in 1946 during the War Crimes Trials held in Tokyo. Maezumi Rōshi and Kapleau Rōshi have been enormously successful. Maezumi Rōshi established the Zen Center of Los Angeles, where he resided until his death in 1995. He left a dozen Dharma heirs, many of whom have developed their own vital, creative communities. Kapleau Rōshi too was quite successful, having built a stable Zen community in Rochester, New York, that was notable for its attempt to develop an American style for Zen practice; it recently celebrated its thirtieth anniversary. Other significant teachers are Robert Aitken Rōshi, who founded the Diamond Sangha in Hawaii in 1959, Eidō Shimano Rōshi, who first came to the United States as a translator for Yasutani Rōshi, and Joshu Sasaki Rōshi, who founded the Cimarron Zen Center in Los Angeles in 1966 and the Mount Baldy Zen Center five years later.

Zen was surely not the only Japanese Buddhist tradition to make an appearance in America before the turn of the twentieth century. In 1898 two Japanese missionaries, Shuye Sonoda and Kakuryo Nishijima, were sent to San Francisco to establish the Buddhist Mission of North America, an organization associated with a Pure Land school of Japanese Buddhism. Although their formation was seriously hampered by the Japanese Immigration Exclusion Act of 1924, thirty-three main temples were active by 1931. With the outbreak of World War II, more than one hundred thousand Japanese Americans (more than half of whom were Buddhist and two-thirds American born) were relocated to internment camps. In 1944, the name Buddhist Mission of North America was changed to Buddhist Churches of America. With headquarters in San Francisco, this Buddhist organization remains one of the most stable Buddhist communities in North America.

In the 1960s, another form of Japanese Buddhism appeared on the American landscape. It was known as Nichiren Shōshū of America, and by 1974 it boasted 258 chapters and over 200,000 members (although these figures were highly suspect). This group grew out of the Sōka Gakkai movement in Japan, a nonmeditative form of Buddhism that based its teachings on the thirteenth-century figure Nichiren (1222–82) and his emphasis on the doctrines and practices focusing on or deriving from the famous *Lotus Sūtra*. Brought to this country by Masayasa Sadanaga (who changed his name to George Williams), the organization set up headquarters in Santa Monica, California, where it began an active program of proselytizing. Although the group has recently splintered, it remains a formidable Buddhist presence in America, having become extremely attractive among Euro-American and African American Buddhists.

The Chinese are once again making their presence visible in American Buddhism. Although not nearly so visible as the Japanese Buddhist groups, several Chinese Buddhist organizations have appeared in the last half-century. Perhaps the most notable of these is a largely monastic group originally known as the Sino-American Buddhist Association which, until his recent death, was under the direction of a venerable monk named Hsüan-Hua. Established in 1959, this organization has developed a huge monastery in Talmage, California, known as the "City of Ten Thousand Buddhas," which serves as the headquarters of what is now identified as the Dharma Realm Buddhist Association. Of even larger size (and quite possibly importance) is the Hsi Lai Temple outside Los Angeles, founded in 1978, and now offering a wide variety of Buddhist teachings and services. Other Chinese Buddhist groups can be found in virtually every major metropolitan area. There are approximately 125 Chinese Buddhist organizations in the United States, more than half of which are in California and one-fifth of which are in New York. The religious practice of the Chinese Buddhist groups in America is largely an eclectic combination of various Buddhist schools, combining Ch'an, Vinaya, T'ien-t'ai, Tantra, and Pure Land practices. Most of these practices are Mahāyāna-based, and a similar kind of approach is followed by the Vietnamese Buddhist groups that have begun to appear in urban areas, mostly as a result of a large influx of Vietnamese immigrants following the termination of the United States' involvement in Vietnam. To some degree, this eclectic approach can also be seen in the various Korean Buddhist groups that began appearing in the United States in the latter half of the twentieth century.

The Buddhist culture to enter America most recently is the Tibetan. Although a few Buddhist groups appeared in the West prior to 1960, the majority came after the Tibetan holocaust, during which the Communist Chinese made every effort to extinguish religion in Tibet. Following an immediate exile in India, Bhutan, Nepal, and Sikkim, the diaspora has widened, with many Tibetans seeking to reestablish their sacred lineages on American soil. Communities from each of the four major Tibetan sects can now be found in America, with those founded by Tarthang Tulku and Chögyam Trungpa Rinpoche being especially popular and visible. The Tibetan groups are the most colorful of all the Buddhist groups now prospering in America, possessing a rich tradition of Buddhist art and a powerful psychological approach to mental health. They continue to grow rapidly, being very attractive to Euro-American Buddhists. It is no wonder, then, that they quote the thousand-year-old saying attributed to the sage Padmasambhava to explain their rapid growth: "When the iron bird flies, and horses run on wheels, the Tibetan people will be scattered like ants across the World, and the Dharma will come to the land of the Red Man."

The final sectarian tradition to be considered is that of the Theravāda, which permeated South Asia following the missionary tradition of the Indian King Aśoka in the third century B.C.E., and which continues today.

Until quite recently, most Theravāda groups in the United States were similar to the Buddhist Vihāra Society in Washington, D.C., an organization founded in 1965 under the direction of the Venerable Bope Vinita from Sri Lanka, and appealing to the large diplomatic community in the nation's capital. Now, however, as many Buddhists from Laos, Cambodia, Thailand, and Burma have migrated to the United States to escape the economic and political uncertainty of their native homes, there is a vigorous new infusion of Theravāda Buddhism into America. Temples are appearing in major cities, as these immigrant groups have tended to settle in ethnic communities not unlike the Chinese and Japanese communities of the early decades of the twentieth century.

Developmental Issues

Outlining the historical details of the Buddhist movement in America tells but a small part of the story, for the growth of American Buddhism is far more than its history. Rather, it presents a struggle to acculturate and accommodate on the part of a religious tradition that initially appeared to be wholly foreign to the American mindset. It is important to realize that two different groups were primarily responsible for Buddhism's earliest growth in America. On the one hand, Buddhism is the native religion of a significant number of Asian immigrants. On the other hand, it became the religion, or at least the subject of serious personal interest, for an ever-increasing group of (mostly) Euro-Americans who embraced Buddhism primarily out of intellectual attraction and interest in spiritual practice. This latter circumstance has created its own Buddhist subculture that is literate, urban, upwardly mobile, perhaps even elite in its life orientation. That bifurcation makes even the issue of Buddhist identity and membership a murky problem, further exacerbated with confusion about various Buddhist positions on ethical issues, sexuality, gender roles, and the like. This developmental pattern and the issues associated with it need to be explored alongside a careful consideration of each of the Buddhist traditions now present on American soil.

Thomas Tweed's important and influential book *The American Encounter with Buddhism 1844–1912: Victorian Culture and the Limits of Dissent* suggests a variety of reasons for late-Victorian America's fascination with Buddhism.[9] Clearly, there was a growing dissatisfaction with the answers provided by the traditional religions of the time, and apologists, such as Paul Carus, were quick to suggest that imported Asian religions might well offer more satisfactory answers to the religious needs of Americans. Additionally, several Asian teachers, such as Anagarika Dharmapala and D. T. Suzuki, had sufficient personal charisma to advance that cause. Few Asian Buddhist teachers took up residence in America, however, and the two primary Buddhist organizations—the American Maha Bodhi Society and the Dharma Sangha of Buddha—were institutionally weak. Tweed notes well that while Buddhist sympathizers resonated favorably with the mid-Victorian period's emphasis on optimism and activism as important cultural values, on the whole, Buddhism's presumed characterization as pessimistic and passive made a much more compelling argument for its detractors. Tweed's insightful postscript[10] suggests that, because they were also faced with the serious lack of accurate textual translations, most Victorians, however disillusioned they may have been, looked elsewhere for potential resolutions to their spiritual crises.

That American Buddhism in the late twentieth century seems to be far more extensive than it had at the end of the previous century, and far more visible in American culture, suggests that many of Tweed's postulates for the failure of Victorian Buddhism in America have been remedied. And indeed they have—especially so in the last half of the century.

By 1970, virtually the full extent of Asian Buddhist sects was represented in America, and there was a plethora of Asian Buddhist teachers in permanent residence in the growing number of American Buddhist centers. The growth of these centers has been so staggering in the second half of the twentieth century that in 1988 Don Morreale was able to catalogue nearly 350 pages of listings for these groups in *Buddhist America: Centers, Retreats, Practices.* A new edition has now appeared, aided by a register service posted on the World Wide Web. Dozens of rōshis, along with their Dharma heirs, many Tibetan *tulkus,* Chinese monks and nuns, and an increasing number of Theravāda monks from various South and Southeast Asian cultures are now visibly active on American soil. The presence of a growing number of Asian Buddhist teachers in America has been complemented and augmented by regular visits from global Buddhist leaders such as the Dalai Lama and Thich Nhat Hanh.

Further, these Asian Buddhist teachers, and the gradually increasing number of American Buddhist masters, are beginning to establish an institutional foundation that is stable, solid, and even ecumenical. In 1987 the "World Buddhism in North America" conference was held at the University of Michigan,[11] during which a statement of consensus was promulgated (1) "to create the conditions necessary for tolerance and understanding among Buddhists and non-Buddhists alike," (2) "to initiate a dialogue among Buddhists in North America in order to further mutual understanding, growth in understanding, and cooperation," (3) "to increase our sense of community by recognizing and understanding our differences as well as our common beliefs and practices," and (4) "to cultivate thoughts and actions of friendliness towards others, whether they accept our beliefs or not, and in so doing approach the world as the proper field of Dharma, not as a sphere of conduct irreconcilable with the practice of Dharma."

Geographically organized organizations, like the Sangha Council of Southern California, and associations of the students of famous Buddhist masters, such as the White Plum Sangha, linking the Dharma heirs of Taizan Maezumi Rōshi, are now becoming commonplace in the American Buddhist movement.

The availability of accurate primary and secondary literature has expanded almost exponentially in the latter half of the twentieth century. Several university presses, such as the State University of New York Press, University of Hawaii Press, University of California Press, and Princeton University Press have been leaders in publishing scholarly books devoted to the study of Buddhism, and a variety of trade publishers has emerged as well, such as Snow Lion and Wisdom Publications, that emphasize Buddhism specifically. Reliable translations of the entire Pāli canon are now readily available throughout the world, and a project to publish translations of the entire Chinese Buddhist canon is currently under way, sponsored by the Bukkyo Dendo Kyokai. This translation endeavor represents a significant step forward in the American Buddhist movement because it requires extensive language training in Sanskrit, Pāli, Chinese, Japanese, and Tibetan. This training is usually, although not exclusively, obtained in American universities. As of 1994, nearly two dozen North American universities could boast at least two full-time faculty devoted to the academic discipline of Buddhist Studies, and nearly 150 academic scholars of Buddhism are located on the North American continent, many of whom can best be identified as "scholar-*practitioners.*" Moreover, the American Buddhist movement is aided by the presence of a growing number of individuals who have traveled to Asia for extensive training and then returned to the United States to share their approach with Americans. One of the most successful enterprises of this kind is the Insight Meditation Society in Barre, Massachusetts, initially guided by Joseph Goldstein, Jack Kornfield, Sharon Salzberg, and Christina Feldman, each of whom received extensive *vipassanā* training in Asia.

Certainly, the issue of social and religious anomie is no less critical in the latter years of the twentieth century than it was in the previous century. A quick perusal of Theodore Roszak's *Making of a Counter Culture,* Harvey Cox's *Secular City,* or Peter Berger's *Sacred Canopy* shows how the pervasive influence of secularism and pluralism created the same kind of religious crisis as witnessed prior to the World Parliament of Religions, held in Chicago in 1893.[12] Roszak even argued that the counterculture of the 1960s was, "essentially, an exploration of the politics of consciousness."[13] The counterculture of the twentieth century differed from that of the preceding century, however, in that it was no longer either passive or pessimistic, and this was clearly obvious in the American Buddhist movement.

Quite apart from issues relating to the specificity with which American

Buddhist life is manifested (lay versus monastic ideals; urban versus rural lifestyle), a distinct and unique application of Buddhist ethics, creatively called "socially engaged Buddhism," is emerging that demonstrates in dramatic fashion both the *active* and the *optimistic* approach of today's American Buddhism. The overarching approach of socially engaged Buddhism is clearly portrayed in Ken Jones's useful book *The Social Face of Buddhism*, and summarized extremely well in Kenneth Kraft's introduction to his edited volume *Inner Peace, World Peace*.[14] Organizations like the Buddhist Peace Fellowship, founded in 1978, aggressively demonstrate how to strike a careful balance between meditational training and political activism. Their task in bringing this activism and optimism to the American Buddhist public is aided by a strong new Buddhist journalism in America that has fostered exciting publications such as *Tricycle: The Buddhist Quarterly*, the *Shambhala Sun*, and *Turning Wheel: Journal of the Buddhist Peace Fellowship*, as well as many publications of individual Buddhist centers. In addition, the useful and productive development of the Internet has allowed American Buddhism to expand its sphere of influence to a *sangha* not necessarily limited to a given geographic space. The electronic *Journal of Buddhist Ethics*, for example, in its "Global Resources for Buddhist Studies" component, has created links to literally hundreds of American Buddhist *sanghas* across the totality of North America.

Thus the faces of Buddhism in America are many. They are diverse, and enthusiastic, and active, and forward looking in their optimism. In the chapters that follow, both the various American Buddhist traditions and the issues impacting on those traditions are explored in an interesting and comprehensive way.

Part One

AMERICAN BUDDHIST TRADITIONS

IN TRANSITION

Chinese Buddhism in America: Identity and Practice

STUART CHANDLER

O ne rarely hears about the practice of Chinese Buddhism in the United States. Even specialists in the American forms of Buddhism have difficulty estimating the number of Chinese Buddhist associations in our country or identifying the group's major characteristics. This lack of knowledge is understandable, considering the small size and general insularity of the community. Nonetheless, the evolution of Chinese Buddhism in America is worthy of greater attention, if for no other reasons than its relatively long history in the United States and the fact that one Chinese organization, the International Buddhist Progress Society, has constructed in Hacienda Heights, California, what is arguably the largest Buddhist monastery in the Western hemisphere, Hsi Lai Temple. In order to introduce the Chinese Buddhist community to a wider audience, this chapter will provide a brief history, describe the principal activities of Chinese Buddhist organizations, and consider issues of identity for those who regard themselves as Chinese, American, and Buddhist.

Soon after I began conducting research on Chinese Buddhism in the United States, several recent immigrants from Taiwan assured me that the history of this phenomenon dates back to the year 458, when a Buddhist monk landed somewhere on the western coast of Mexico. Later, I discovered that this theory was not the invention of a few American Chinese Buddhists but, rather, originally had been raised and debated within the European scholarly community. The theory was first proposed in 1761 by Joseph de Guignes, who cited a memorial found in the Chinese imperial archives that cryptically described the sea route taken by a Buddhist monk named Hui Shan to the land of Fu-sang.[1] On the basis of an analysis of the lands and distances described along the journey, de Guignes concluded that Fu-sang was very probably Mexico. Reaction to the hypothesis was mixed. J. Klaproth thought de Guignes's reasoning and evidence both far-fetched. For one thing, the mention of horses and grape vines in the me-morial proved that the land could not have been America, since both of these were introduced by the Spanish in the fifteenth century. Fu-sang, argued Klaproth, was more likely an early name for Japan.[2]

Other scholars rose to de Guignes's defense. Chevalier de Paravey main-tained that horses may have already been present in America before the Spanish arrival and, even if they hadn't been, Hui Shan may have used the Chinese term for horse, *ma*, loosely to describe the South American llamas and alpacas. Furthermore, the presence of what looked to be Buddhist architectural designs in certain Yucatan temples could only be explained by the presence of Buddhist monks to direct construction.[3] The German scholar Karl Eugen Neumann and his student, the American folklorist Charles G. Leland, also found such architectural and iconographic parallels too striking to be mere coincidence. Especially noteworthy, exclaimed Le-land, was the statuary found in Mexico and Central America that resembled the Buddha in the pose of meditation. In his opinion, not only the artistic styles and crude images of the Buddha, but even the gentle temperament of the mound-builders of Central and North America had been greatly influenced by the teachings of Buddhist missionaries.[4]

The most detailed study in a Western language identifying Fu-sang with America is Edward P. Vining's eight-hundred-page book, *An Inglorious Co-lumbus; or, Evidence that Hwui Shan and a Party of Buddhist Monks from Af-ghanistan Discovered America in the Fifth Century A.D.* Vining's compendium, written in 1885, not only summarizes the arguments on the subject given by some fifty scholars and provides an exhaustive list of parallels in the customs, arts, and religious beliefs of Buddhists, but includes a chapter devoted to demonstrating that the Chinese and Mexicans translated key names and terms from each other's language: the graphs for "Fu-san-guo," for instance, in the seventh century may have sounded similar to Mixteca, the coeval pronunciation for "Mexico"; in the same vane, Wixipecocha, the name given in Aztec stories to a mysterious, light-skinned pilgrim who had visited the region in the remote past, may have been a transliteration of "Hui-Shan, bhikshu" and the name Guatemala may have originally referred to the Buddha's clan name, that is, "Gautama-tlan, the Place of Gautama."[5]

Ironically, the publication of Vining's massive work marked the end of interest in the subject among the American and European scholarly com-munity, although a smattering of articles and books have continued to appear over the years.[6] Chinese scholars, however, picked up where West-ern academics left off. Professor Wei Chu-hsien has devoted virtually his entire career to cataloguing archaeological, anthropological, and historical evidence for early contacts between Chinese and American peoples. In his opinion, Hui Shan's expedition represents a relatively late interaction: some one thousand years earlier Confucius may have already made references to the North American hummingbird![7] It is from the work of Wei Chu-hsien and other such scholars that the Chinese Buddhist community in the United States has learned of Hui Shan's voyage to Fu-sang.

Whether or not Fu-sang was a Chinese name for the continent of America will probably never be known definitively. Most of the evidence cited to substantiate the theory is tentative at best, fanciful at worst. The various monographs on the subject give the sense that the issue has much greater symbolic than historical import. Attributing the "discovery" of America to an Asian Buddhist rather than to a European Christian inverts the rhetoric of forebear and newcomer, thereby radically transforming the notions of national heritage and identity. Most Euro-Americans will continue to draw strength from their own mythology. For Chinese Buddhists who come to America, however, to regard this land as Fu-sang is to place themselves within an ancient and noble missionary adventure.

Historical Concerns

Even if Hui Shan did not "discover America" the Chinese were still the earliest Asian group to come to the United States in any great numbers. The first ship of Chinese arrived in California in 1849, one year after gold had been discovered at John Sutter's sawmill. By 1854, over 13,000 Chinese, virtually all men, had come in hopes of unearthing a fortune in "Gold Mountain," as California was called.[8] Sixteen years later, the census bureau recorded 63,199 Chinese in the United States, composing 10 percent of the population in California and Montana, and 29 percent of the population in Idaho (excluding Native Americans). The early Chinese population reached its peak in the 1880s, numbering slightly over 100,000.[9]

Not surprisingly, as the Chinese community grew, it established places of worship. The first Chinese temples to be constructed in the continental United States were the Tin Hou Temple and Kong Chow Temple, built in San Francisco around 1853.[10] By 1875 the number of temples in that city had grown to at least eight, and by the turn of the century there were hundreds of "joss houses," as Chinese temples and shrines were called, throughout the Western United States. One cannot characterize such structures as strictly "Buddhist," however, since in most cases a variety of Chinese Taoist, folk, and Buddhist figures received shelter and homage together. The vast majority of these dwellings which once dotted the West Coast were abandoned soon after they were built. With the passage of anti-Chinese legislation, starting with the Chinese Exclusion Act of 1882, the number of Chinese in the United States steadily declined, until 1920 when there were only 61,639 left, most of whom were elderly men. The younger generation that remarried, however, tended to have large families, so for the next forty-five years, the population stabilized and gradually increased in numbers. Despite this growth, because the second-generation Chinese Americans were not particularly interested in their religious heritage the various temples in the Chinatowns received ever fewer devotees, until, one by one, they were abandoned. In fact, most news accounts of such temples in the 1930s and 1940s were announcements of their foreclosure due to failure to make rental, mortgage, or tax payments.

As with all Asian groups, the Chinese benefited greatly from the Immigration Act of 1965. In the twenty years following the passage of this act, 420,000 Chinese came to the United States. By 1990, the Chinese population had surpassed 921,000.[11] It is difficult to say how many of these Chinese Americans consider themselves to be Buddhists—probably not as many as those who consider themselves Christian, and certainly not nearly as many as those with no religious affiliation whatsoever. There are approximately 125 Chinese Buddhist organizations in the United States, 68 of which are in California, 25 in New York, and the rest scattered from Colorado to Massachusetts, from Louisiana to Wisconsin.[12] On the most important holidays, such as Chinese New Year and Buddha's Birthday, thousands of Chinese spend at least part of the day at one of these temples. The rest of the year, however, attendance is much smaller, with most of the organizations having only one or two dozen members who regularly participate.

Two characteristics of Chinese immigration have been especially important in shaping the general nature of the Chinese Buddhist experience in the United States. First, the vast majority of Chinese Buddhists have not been forced to seek asylum in America from political upheaval; they have usually come either to further their education or to find employment. In this regard they are more similar to Buddhists from Japan, Korea, Thailand, and Sri Lanka than to those from Cambodia, Laos, Vietnam, and Tibet (although Chinese who came as part of the exodus from Vietnam are an important exception to this). Although the Chinese have not been forced to America from their homeland by war and therefore have not had to contend with the financial and psychological hardships inevitably accompanying such flight, many of the Chinese arriving from Hong Kong or Taiwan either fled from Communist China or are the offspring of those who fled, so they do exhibit traces of the refugee mentality.

Second, because so many Chinese have come to the United States for postgraduate education, there are a great many highly educated individuals within the community. As of 1990, 30 percent of those who have come to the United States from Mainland China, 47 percent of those who have come from Hong Kong, and 62 percent of those from Taiwan have at least a college degree. Given the relative numbers of sojourners and immigrants from these three places, the overall number comes to 40 percent, an extremely high percentage (for the sake of comparison, 19 percent of those who have come from Germany, 23 percent of those from the United Kingdom, and 32 percent of those from France can claim this level of education).[13] This fact should not be overemphasized, however. As Ronald Takaki has observed, there is a bipolar Chinese American community divided between an undereducated working class and a sophisticated, entrepreneurial middle class.[14] Although the percentage of educated Chinese entering this country may be higher than from most other nations, the majority of Chinese in America are nonetheless without any higher education, 27 percent lacking even a high school diploma.

Faint repercussions of the division between working-class and professional-class immigrants may be found in the Buddhist community. Across the United States, *nien-fo* (devotional recitation), especially chanting the name and attributes of O-mi-t'uo Fo (Amitābha Buddha) and Chi-le Shih-chieh (Sukhāvatī), is the principal form of religious activity in Chinese Buddhist organizations, regardless of the socioeconomic status of the members. Less evident in the weekly activities of Chinese organizations is training in meditation. When lessons in Ch'an practice are offered, they tend to attract one of two types of audiences. Most often, meditation classes will be designed for non-Chinese. Hsi Lai Temple and Chuang Yen Monastery, for instance, have weekly classes on meditation conducted in English, but not in Chinese. Nearly all of the participants in each case are Euro-Americans. More important for the current discussion is the fact that, when organizations do offer meditation instruction in Chinese, there will invariably be a high number of well-educated members in the group as a whole and participating in the meditation sessions.

Organizations with many well-educated members may be marked by three other characteristics as well. First, several such groups emphasize the study of Buddhist scriptures. In the Buddhist Study Group of Huntsville (Alabama) which, as its name indicates, focuses on the discussion of Buddhist scriptures and commentaries, all of the approximately twenty members have college diplomas and several are either working toward or already have acquired a doctoral degree. The Mahābodhi Society of U.S.A., another group with high educational credentials, meets two Saturdays each month in Saratoga, California, to examine "the original ideas of Buddhism," especially as they are revealed by early *sūtras*. According to Mr. Loo, who is the group's teacher, the goal is to find the right path for living, not simply engage in religious rituals. The association periodically publishes the results of its studies, most recently an impressive commentary on the Āgamas.

Since many of the scholars sent from Taiwan, Hong Kong, and Mainland China are young men studying engineering, business, or one of the sciences, much attention in meditation or study groups is given to the compatibility of Buddhist practice with a scientific, technological worldview. C. T. Shen, well known in Chinese Buddhist circles for his patronage of Chuang Yen Monastery, has spoken and written extensively on the subject of parallels between Buddhist philosophy and the recent discoveries in physics and astronomy. Similarly, Mr. Loo, of the Mahābodhi Society of U.S.A., has written in his booklet *Fo-fa Tsai Yuan-tse Shih-tai* (Buddhism in the Atomic Age) that the Buddhist doctrine of dependent co-origination is much more closely aligned with quantum physics than with any religious notion of God. Members of the Massachusetts Buddhist Association would agree: along with strengthening people's minds through the peacefulness afforded by meditation, relieving stress and worries through chanting, and disseminating Buddhist teachings so as to improve people's wisdom, the by-laws of this organization state that one of its primary goals is "to help college students to further their understanding of state-of-the-art technology."

Third, groups with a highly educated membership are less likely to seek the guidance of a monk or nun, preferring to "come and see for themselves." Hence, the Buddhist Study Group of Huntsville, the Mahābodhi Society of U.S.A., the Massachusetts Buddhist Association, and the Buddhist Association of Wisdom and Compassion of Akron, Ohio (another organization with impressive credentials), all have lay leadership. The formation of such lay Buddhist societies is by no means novel, of course; the first such societies may have formed in China as early as the fifth century. What is noteworthy about the American context is that it is primarily the more highly educated who have tapped into this tradition.

Two caveats need to be mentioned in attempting to discern correspondences between socioeconomic class and forms of practice. First of all, the relationship between socioeconomic level and preferred form of Buddhist practice is by no means straightforward, since many, probably most, well-educated Chinese participate in recitation as a primary form of practice. This is not simply a case where the working class practices recitation under the guidance of a monk or nun while white-collar professionals engage in meditation and *sūtra* study through lay organizations. Recitation, meditation, and *sūtra* study may be found in all Chinese Buddhist organizations, with the great majority emphasizing recitation. Where meditation or *sūtra* study come more to the fore, however, one will find a high number of either Chinese intellectuals or Euro-American converts.

Chinese Buddhist Practice

One should also be chary of making too much of the distinction between Pure Land and Ch'an practice. Unlike Japanese Buddhism, in which strong institutional boundaries differentiate Pure Land (Shinshū and Jōdo

Shinshū) from Zen Buddhism, this division has remained much more tenuous in Chinese Buddhism. At least since the tenth century, Chinese Buddhists have regarded recitation and meditation as complementary and even analogous methods for achieving enlightenment. Recitation is often considered to be a particular form of meditation that serves to concentrate one's mind and purify one's thoughts. Hence, at the Ch'an Meditation Center in Elmhurst, New York, Master Chang Sheng-yen not only provides instruction in Ts'ao-tung (Sōtō in Japan) and Lin-chi (Rinzai in Japan) practice, but also leads his congregation in various recitation sessions. Each Sunday morning, for instance, starts with group meditation from 10:00 to 11:00 a.m., followed by a short talk, then group recitation from 11:30 to 12:30. Such a schedule is typical of centers specializing in Ch'an. Most Chinese Buddhists, whether they practice in Taiwan, Hong Kong, Mainland China, or the United States, regard recitation as an extremely effective form of meditational practice, given the distractions and hardships of twentieth-century existence.

In addition to recitation, meditation, and *sūtra* study, there is one other activity that not only plays an important part in the life of Chinese Buddhist organizations, but also serves as a common thread joining together the other three practices. For practitioners of Chinese Buddhism, O-mi-t'o Fo (Amitābha Buddha) and Kuan-yin (Avalokiteśvara) are not only the focus of study and meditational devotion, but are also exemplars for the community.[15] Just as O-mi-t'o Fo, the Buddha of Blissful Light, made forty-eight vows aimed at alleviating the suffering and aiding the spiritual progression of all sentient beings, Chinese Buddhists are expected to make a similar commitment. In fact, displaying such *pei (karuṇā)*, or compassion, is one of the primary signs that a person has gained the absolute faith necessary for rebirth in the Western Pure Land. Chinese Buddhists express compassion in a variety of ways. As with many other Buddhists, one of the most basic has been to become a vegetarian, a lifestyle expected of all who have taken the Bodhisattva Vows. An extension of vegetarianism is the practice of releasing animals, birds, or aquatic life otherwise destined for the butcher's block or a life of captivity. Although other Buddhist ethnic traditions also engage in this activity, it plays a more prominent role in Chinese communities. Ding Gong Temple in Massachusetts has an annual outing during which dozens of lobsters, crabs, turtles, and shellfish are freed in Boston Harbor. Even more impressive is the International Buddhist Association in El Cerrito, California, which over the past two decades has set free more than 250,000 fish, crabs, frogs, turtles, and doves.

Chinese Buddhists also devote energy to ameliorating the suffering of fellow humans. Jade Buddha Temple, the 1,200-member association in Houston, Texas, frequently works with local churches to aid people displaced by natural disasters. The Buddhist Association of Wisdom and Compassion organizes the distribution of furniture, clothing, and money to the needy, as well as sponsoring health fairs in which medically trained members of the organization provide free physical examinations. Believing that the greatest ill suffered by most people arises from their own undisciplined mind, many Chinese organizations provide training in meditation not only to Buddhists, but to the general public. Hsi Lai Temple, for example, sends a member of the *sangha* to teach Ch'an practice at a nearby correctional facility and to a hospital for recovering substance abusers. For these audiences, Buddhist terminology is kept to a minimum, much as it is in the Tibetan Vajrayāna-inspired program of Shambhala Training.

Although meditation is regarded as efficacious whether or not a person becomes a Buddhist, overcoming suffering ultimately requires not only right concentration, but right understanding as well. For this reason, the translation and dissemination of Buddhist texts is considered to be one of the highest expressions of compassion. The work of the Buddhist Text Translation Institute, located at the City of Ten Thousand Buddhas (near Talmage, California), the project under way at Chuang Yen Monastery in Kent, New York, to store Buddhist scriptures on CD-ROM, and the distribution of pamphlets on Buddha Dharma at railroad stations by the International Buddhist Association are all undertaken with the conviction that gaining a greater appreciation for Buddhist teaching is the most direct path to overcoming the limitations and hardships of the human condition.

Since this world is still very far from being a Pure Land, our own efforts are not sufficient to overcome the myriad sources of suffering. Liberation requires that one be reborn in a Ching-t'u (Pure Land) such as Chi-le Shih-chieh, which can only occur through receiving the compassion of O-mi-t'o Fo, who from his infinite store of merit transfers the necessary amount of merit to an individual. Not only a great Buddha like O-mi-t'o Fo, but anyone with a store of good deeds can transfer that merit to benefit others. Ironically, by transferring merit, a person is much more likely to receive blessings from O-mi-t'o Fo. When Ding Gong Monastery and other Pure Land organizations send out reminders of upcoming festivals, the notice invariably states that, through the transferal of merit, the group's activity will benefit all sentient beings. Merit can be transferred to both the living and the dead. For this reason, the International Buddhist Association has prayed on behalf of more than 3.5 million souls in seventy cemeteries.

Whether by maintaining a vegetarian diet, freeing animals, providing disaster relief and medical care, distributing Buddhist literature, or chanting for the benefit of others, the activities of Chinese Buddhists are geared to improve the conditions of this world so that all people can attain enlightenment. Ideally, these compassionate acts will make this world a Pure Land and obviate the need for rebirth in Chi-le Shih-chieh. While most Chinese Buddhist organizations have not explicitly stated the transformation of this world into a Pure Land as an aim, Master Hsing Yun, the founder of Fo Kuang Buddhism (which is headquartered in Taiwan, but has numerous temples and associations in the United States, including Hsi Lai Temple), considers this both a reasonable and an attainable goal. Citing the great progress humankind has made in material comfort and political rights, Master Hsing Yun sees the distinct possibility of creating a fully ethical society in the near future. By participating in this process of transformation a person may receive from O-mi-t'o Fo the necessary merit for rebirth in Chi-le Shih-chieh. The cumulative effects of such compassionate acts will eventually allow people to attain enlightenment without first going to Chi-le Shih-chieh.

The degree to which meditation, study, and scientific and technological endeavor are valued as means to liberation from suffering points to the age-old Buddhist dilemma of whether one can rely on one's own efforts or if one must depend solely on the saving grace of O-mi-t'o Fo, Yao-shih (Bhaiṣajyaguru, the Medicine Buddha), or some other Buddha. How a person resolves this issue significantly affects his or her understanding of what it means to be a Buddhist. For Chinese Buddhists, the line of reasoning behind each of these conflicting attitudes toward the world and human effort has developed through centuries of debate. With the importation of the tradition into the United States, more immediate environmental pressures have given a novel imprint on how the debate is progressing. With this in mind, I now turn to the highly complex issue of the interrelationship between the adjectives *Buddhist, Chinese,* and *American.* I first consider the theoretical models for the changing religious landscape in the United States that have been developed by Will Herberg, Charles Prebish, and Jan Nattier. Then I offer an alternative way of analyzing the material.

Buddhist Chinese American or American Chinese Buddhist?

In his penetrating analysis of trends within the Protestant, Catholic, and Jewish communities over the course of the first half of the twentieth century, Herberg noted that the first three generations of new Americans differed in their attitudes toward their inherited religion. The immigrant generation gained strength from their imported religious beliefs and practices because these maintained "something of the old life," thereby providing continuity and order in what was otherwise a confusing new land.[16] For the American-bred generation, however, the vestiges of the old country were seen as a source of confusion and disadvantage. Herberg observed: "To them religion, along with the language of the home, seemed to be part and parcel of the immigrant baggage of foreignness they were so eager to

abandon. To the dismay of their parents, and to the distaste of better acculturated Americans, many of the second generation tended to draw away
from the religion of their fathers, and from religion altogether."[17] The third
generation, fully assimilated into the American way of life and therefore
much more secure than their parents, recognized that, while the language
and many of the customs of their grandparents could not be perpetuated
on these shores, not only could the religion of one's forebears be maintained, but an important element of American identity was precisely the
preservation of one's religious legacy. For this and later generations, then,
religion "has become the differentiating element and the context of self-
identification and social location."[18]

Herberg did not regard his model as accurate for the Buddhism of Chinese and Japanese immigrants. He thought this tradition simply too alien,
so that the Americanization of East Asian immigrants required "dropping
the non-American faith and becoming a Catholic or Protestant, usually the
latter."[19] Perhaps making such an exception seemed accurate in the 1950s;
half a century later it appears that the general thrust of the three-
generation model works as well for Buddhists as for Protestants, Catholics,
and Jews. The shifts in nomenclature and practice within the Japanese
American Jōdo Shinshū community are a case in point. From 1899 to 1942,
this organization was known as the Buddhist Mission of North America.
Hoping to demonstrate its full loyalty to the United States government and
fidelity to the American way of life, during World War II the community
changed its name to the Buddhist Church of America (BCA), added pews
and an organ to its places of worship, and adopted Christian-style hymns
and responsive readings as part of its services. As members in recent years
have more openly recognized that being Buddhist and American are not
antinomic, a growing number of BCA chapters—such as Senshin Buddhist
Temple (Los Angeles) and Midwest Buddhist Temple (Chicago)—have
returned to the more traditional terminology and service.

The Chinese case introduces a different set of dynamics into the equa-
tion. Chinese immigrants have not necessarily brought Buddhist beliefs and
practices to America as part of their "cultural baggage." Dr. Ted T'ang of
the Buddhist Association of Compassion and Wisdom estimates that over
half of the Chinese who actively participate in Buddhist associations took
the Five Precepts Vow only *after* arriving in America. Although no systematic
study has been conducted on the matter, a sampling of the membership
in several typical organizations indicates that at least a significant minority
of Chinese American Buddhists, and probably a majority, had negligible
knowledge of Buddhist teachings before reaching the United States. In
other words, these first-generation immigrants are returning to Buddhism,
much as third-generation practitioners have in other communities. The
parents of these Chinese had already distanced themselves from much of

their Chinese heritage in the intellectual and political iconoclastic movements of the past seventy-five years, so that even in the first Sinic world[20] there is widespread questioning of cultural identity. For those who come abroad, this uncertainty reaches a point of crisis. It is time to return to one's roots, at least to selective aspects of those roots. First-generation Chinese Americans who become Buddhist are not maintaining a directly inherited identity so much as reconstructing one. Given these unique dynamics at play for the first-generation immigrants, and the greater acceptance of Buddhism as compatible with the American way of life, one can only wonder how this scenario will evolve in the next generation. The current trend suggests that, instead of exaggerating their American citizenship over their Chinese ancestry, they may increasingly regard themselves first and foremost as Buddhists, averring that the universal message of Buddhism transcends all cultural or ethnic dualism.

The fact that so many Chinese American Buddhists are discovering their religious heritage only after arriving in America places an interesting twist on Charles Prebish's distinction between "ethnic" and "elite" Buddhism. Prebish postulates that while "ethnic" forms of Buddhism serve to preserve immigrant cultural identity, "elite Buddhism" concerns itself more with the transformation of American society. The former tends toward conservatism while the latter serves as a catalyst for change.[21] In this model, Chinese Buddhist communities obviously fall under the rubric "ethnic Buddhism." They differ from others in the category, however, in that the Buddhist symbols and practices have not been learned as an integral part of the cultural matrix; rather, the Chinese have consciously reappropriated these symbols and practices. This difference accentuates a dynamic that most likely is at play in all ethnic Buddhist organizations. Just as practitioners of elite Buddhism employ Buddhist criteria to critique American society, members of ethnic Buddhist groups often take advantage of their transitional status to reform certain aspects of their Buddhist heritage. Despite the role Buddhism plays in affirming ethnic identity, for many its arrival in America is seen as an opportunity to purge the tradition of cultural accretions and superstitions. When asked about the advantages of coming to America to spread the Dharma, several nuns at Hsi Lai Temple cited the very lack of a Buddhist legacy in this country as a seminal opportunity to pass on the teaching in its pristine form, shorn of the myriad customs that have appended themselves to it over the centuries in China. A more radical example is that of the Buddhist Association of Wisdom and Compassion, which neither supports a member of the *sangha* nor has a temple, considering both of these unnecessary and an aberration from the Buddha's original message, which was one of compassionate service within society. No longer in China, and yet not indigenous to the United States, the tradition is viewed as neither Chinese nor American Buddhism, but rather as pure and simple Buddhism. Of course, the opposite is really the case; what is being practiced at Hsi Lai Temple and in the Association of Wisdom and Compassion are variant forms of Chinese American Buddhism, the former modeled on the Pure Land and Ch'an traditions, the latter perpetuating the archetype of the lay Buddhist Vimalakīrti.

Both elite and ethnic Buddhist communities are tapping into the new confluence of multiple cultural systems to reform at least one of the systems: elite Buddhism employs various Buddhist criteria to critique American culture; ethnic Buddhist communities utilize their new American surroundings to better recognize the specifically ethnic character of their particular brand of Buddhism. The focus of reform may differ, but the underlying process is remarkably similar. Hence, designating one type of Buddhism as conservative and the other as transformative may be misleading.

Jan Nattier, who deems Prebish's model too simplistic to adequately describe the current situation of Buddhism in the United States, adds the category "Evangelistic" or "Missionary" Buddhism as a third type. In this "export" model, exemplified by the Sōka Gakkai leader George M. Williams, Buddhism has been brought unsolicited by missionaries from Asia, whose message—due to their aggressive techniques of evangelism—reaches members of a wide range of socioeconomic groups.[22] Chinese Buddhism may also be said to have been brought to the United States through the missionary activity of charismatic members of the *sangha*. Unlike their Sōka Gakkai counterparts, however, these missionaries direct their attention primarily to (re)introducing Buddhist teachings to specifically the Chinese American community. Most monks and nuns who have come to the United States devote themselves to tending to the needs of Chinese expatriates who have only recently taken the Three Refuges Vow. Even Master Hsüan Hua, spiritual leader of the Dharma Realm Buddhist Association (headquartered at the City of Ten Thousand Buddhas), which in the 1970s was essentially a Euro-American organization, originally came to serve a fledgling Chinese American community. Only after he had been here for a decade did the religious experimentalism of late 1960s California impel Euro-Americans to tap the wisdom of this master. Subsequently, the organization has once again drawn a large Chinese American membership, leading to the ironic situation in which Euro-American monks and nuns provide instruction in Chinese Buddhism for Chinese American laity.

Conclusion

The unique dynamics at the Dharma Realm Buddhist Association highlight the difficulty of understanding the interrelationship between the various factors shaping self-identity. The title of this chapter points to two possible constellations of identity for those who are ethnically Chinese, American residents or citizens, and followers of the Buddhist path. Certain individuals may consider themselves first and foremost American citizens. Secondarily, their ancestors hail from China, just as the ancestors of other Americans lived in England, Italy, Saudi Arabia, or Zaire. Finally, these Chinese Americans express their heritage and fulfill spiritual needs through participating in the Buddhist faith, although this participation remains minimal, essentially confined to visiting the local temple for Chinese New Year, the birthday of Kuan-Yin, and perhaps a few other major holidays. One may classify the self-identify of such people as "Buddhist Chinese American." Other individuals may experience their self-identity in precisely the reverse order: they think and experience the world as Buddhists; beyond that, they are of Chinese heritage; and, least important, they happen to live in the United States. Such people are "American Chinese Buddhists." The two types of individuals draw on the same three symbolic systems to define and express their identity, but they differ from one another in the ranking that they give to these systems. (For the current discussion, I have indicated the variant rankings through word order, placing the dominant category of identity in the final position, and qualifying it with the other two; hence, the word order goes from least to most important category of self-identity.)

In addition to the above two options, there are four other possible constellations. First-generation immigrants who only visit temples to celebrate the essentially non-Buddhist festivals of Chinese New Year and Mid-Autumn Festival may be thought of as "Buddhist American Chinese." Other first-generation immigrants either were already practicing Buddhists before coming to the United States or have delved deeply into Buddhist practice since arriving; these individuals are "American Buddhist Chinese." The category "Chinese Buddhist Americans," in contrast, designates those who have grown up in the United States, speak English as their first and perhaps only language, and yet have become deeply committed to Buddhist practice. Such individuals may not necessarily even participate in a specifically *Chinese* Buddhist community. Finally, there are "Chinese American Buddhists." As with Chinese Buddhist Americans, these individuals consider themselves thoroughly American, only incidentally of Chinese heritage. Beyond this, however, their commitment to the Buddhist way of life is so deep that even their identity as Americans seems insignificant: they are Buddhists who happen to reside in America. As mentioned in the discussion of Herberg, a growing number of second-generation Chinese Americans who have returned to the Buddhist faith appear to think of themselves in this way.

I have enumerated these six options to highlight the intrinsically fluid character of self-identity. As Buddhists have long acknowledged, what we think of as the self is in constant flux, continually evolving with changes in the environment and adjustments in personal goals. The situation is, in fact, even more complex than the foregoing typology of identity patterns indicates. For one thing, other sources of identity enter the picture, such as a person's occupation. Furthermore, the offspring of intermarriage will not simply be Chinese Buddhist Americans or Chinese American Buddhists. They may be Chinese European Buddhist Americans, or African Chinese American Buddhists. Finally, although the term *Chinese* as it has thus far been employed here can be understood as referring to ethnic identity, it may be more fruitful to think of it as a cultural designation, hence parallel to the category "American." A person need not necessarily be ethnically Chinese to be a Chinese Buddhist American; many of the monks at the City of Ten Thousand Buddhas and the vast majority of those participating in the meditation classes at Chuang Yen Monastery and Hsi Lai Temple, for instance, are not. Such individuals practice the Buddhist teachings as they have developed in and been mediated through Chinese culture. To the degree that Chinese elements come to the fore in the manner in which a person experiences the Buddhist teachings, that individual "becomes" Chinese, regardless of his or her ethnic background. The assumption of Chinese identity may even find explicit symbolic expression through the donning of traditional Chinese garb or the adoption of a Chinese name. All Euro-Americans who join the Dharma Realm Buddhist Association, for example, receive a Chinese Dharma name. Those who have taken the Five Precepts Vows, thereby becoming lay members, assume the surname *Kuo*. For those who have gone on to take the Bodhisattva Vows, *Kuo* is replaced by the name *Heng*. Finally, those who have undergone a Complete Precept Platform ordination to become monks gain the surname *Shih*, the first graph of Shih-chia Mou-ni, Śākyamuni's name as it is written in Chinese.

Other scholars have also called for an expanded definition of cultural China. The New Confucianist Tu Wei-ming argues for a conceptualization incorporating three overlapping symbolic universes. First, there are the societies in which ethnic Chinese constitute a majority: China, Taiwan, Hong Kong, and Singapore. The second symbolic world consists of the Chinese "diaspora"—those Chinese communities scattered throughout the world from Malaysia to the United States. Third, there are the individuals who seek to comprehend China intellectually and bring this understanding to their own communities. This final category includes teachers, scholars, journalists, industrialists, and writers of a variety of linguistic backgrounds. Ironically, states Tu, "For the last four decades the international discourse on cultural China has unquestionably been shaped by the third symbolic universe more than by the first two combined."[23] Although Tu does not explicitly state that such individuals need not be ethnically Chinese, his model strongly implies that participation in the Chinese worldview both as receptor and contributor, extends far beyond not only geopolitical but also ethnic definitions of the Sinic world. Tu emphasizes the effect such people have on Chinese society. My emphasis, in contrast, is the profound influence the Chinese worldview can have on those who sympathetically delve into its value system. Thus employing "Chinese" as a primarily cultural rather than ethnic designation serves to provide nuance to the discussion of self-identity. So long as the analysis of the dynamics between Chinese and American identity remains couched in ethnic terms, it perpetuates the assumption that the issue is mainly sociological. In fact, however, the tensions and interplay of Chinese and American identity are as much psychological as sociological. The "culture war" occurs not only between groups, but within each individual.

Just as the designations of "Chinese" and "American" refer to cultural symbolic systems, the label "Buddhist" names yet another such system.[24] The issue before us, then, when considering the dynamics of self-understanding for those who practice a Chinese form of Buddhism in America, is one essentially concerned with the tensions and transformations that occur with the internalization of three cultural complexes whose practices and values often conflict. The American preoccupation with rugged individualism, for example, clashes with the Chinese emphasis on filial piety and reverence for authorities. Similarly, many of the Christian elements that underlie the assumptions shaping mainstream American values radically differ from the Buddhist worldview: the notions of sin and an eternal soul, for instance, versus those of k'u (duḥkha) and k'ung (śūnyatā).

Beyond these tensions, analogous incompatibilities may be found between Chinese and Buddhist values. The Chinese cultural complex is an ever-transforming amalgamation of political, social, and religious elements. Buddhism, therefore, has constituted one facet of Chinese civilization, while simultaneously remaining a somewhat independent entity with its own trajectory. The semiautonomous nature of these two intimately interrelated cultural systems points to a subtle irony in the utilization of Buddhist symbols to express one's Chinese heritage. Although Chinese Buddhist organizations in the United States emphasize the harmonious interpenetration of the Sinic and Buddhist cultures, historically the foreign origins of Buddhism have caused Chinese to regard it with a certain uneasiness and ambivalence. From the time Buddhism first entered China in the first century, Confucian scholars warned that its institutionalized monasticism posed a serious threat to familial and civic loyalties. Such Buddhist practices as shaving the head of monks and nuns upon ordination and enforcing strict celibacy thereafter were especially anathema to traditional sensibilities. The discomfiture over Buddhism's cultural invasion did not lessen with time. In the eighth century, the Confucian Han Yu lambasted the tradition as a "cult of barbarian peoples" which was corrupting China's high culture and violating its venerable customs. The Buddha, Han

Yu continued, neither spoke Chinese nor understood the duties and affection that bind sovereign and subject, father and son.[25] This ongoing cultural tension toward Buddhism's alien system of values periodically rose to feverish heights, providing the emotional turbulence that fueled violent political outbursts. Another twelve hundred years of assimilation has not completely dispelled the disjunction between the Buddhist and autochthonous value systems. In 1937 the scholar Hu Shih blamed the otherworldliness of Buddhism for truncating the humane, rational, and protoscientific culture of China, causing it to fall behind the West. To remedy this, he argued, would require China to liberate itself from the pernicious "Indianization" that had adulterated Sinic culture for nearly two thousand years.[26]

The paradox of employing Buddhist symbolism to express Chinese heritage lies much deeper than merely the fact that Buddhism is not indigenous to Chinese culture; the same point could be made of all of the Buddhist communities found in the United States: not long before Buddhism was introduced into China in the first century, it had already spread from North India into Burma, Thailand, Laos, and Sri Lanka. Subsequently, the tradition spread via China to Korea and Japan and, around the same time, through both China and India into Tibet. What makes the Chinese case distinct is the fact that, when Buddhist missionaries arrived on the scene, the "Middle Kingdom," although weakened by civil wars and foreign invasions, already possessed a highly evolved civilization with a massive political apparatus legitimated by sophisticated religious and philosophical symbols. Unlike elsewhere in Asia, therefore, in China Buddhism never enjoyed long-term imperial patronage.[27] In fact, because Buddhist monasteries had early on secured for themselves a fair degree of autonomy from government control, and with time gradually acquired extensive landholdings and assets (all of which were tax exempt), Chinese royal houses were, at best, uneasy with their presence and, at worst, determined to eradicate them. Anti-Buddhist campaigns led to the defrocking of thousands of monks and nuns and the destruction of innumerable temples in 446, 574, and 844, the last of these signaling, according to some historians, the decline of Buddhism as a dominant cultural and intellectual force in China.

Given the paradoxical relation between Buddhist and Chinese culture—so intimately intertwined and yet constantly in tension—one may wonder why Chinese Americans have been more apt to appropriate Buddhism rather than Confucianism or Taoism as a primary mechanism for reasserting their Chinese heritage. Theoretically, the latter two would better serve to symbolize Chinese culture.[28] Political circumstances, however, have dictated otherwise. Chinese scholars since the May Fourth Movement of the 1920s certainly have been critical of Buddhism, but they have saved their most potent censure for the superstitions associated with Taoism and Chinese folk religion and for the stultifying ritualism of "Confucius and Sons."

For many, both Confucianism and Taoism have come to represent traditional China at its worst: parochial, superstitious, and backward. To symbolize one's allegiance to Chinese culture through these religions would be tantamount to binding oneself to the vanquished Middle Kingdom of yesteryear.

The intellectual and political movements of the early twentieth century left Chinese Buddhism relatively unscathed, although in Mainland China the subsequent attacks by the Communist Party have proved devastating. In Hong Kong, Taiwan, Singapore, and Malaysia such Buddhist masters as Yin Hsun, Hsing Yun, and Sheng Yen have actually benefited from this situation, successfully sparking a Buddhist resurgence by marketing themselves as representing all that was wholesome in precommunist China. With the growing disillusionment toward Communist ideology in Mainland China, interest in religion has returned even there. For some who come to the United States, joining a Buddhist organization is seen as the best means to fulfill spiritual needs while reasserting one's Chinese heritage. To participate in a Buddhist temple in America, then, is to associate oneself with an ongoing and dynamic aspect of Chinese culture, an association evident in the dual residency of many monks and nuns in both the United States and either Hong Kong or Taiwan.

In closing, I would like to make a few observations about the Chinese Buddhist tradition in the United States. First, while the Chinese have the longest history of any Asian Americans and were the first to build temples in the United States, the present Chinese Buddhist organizations are quite young; the vast majority have been established only within the past twenty-five years. Second, partially as a function of their relatively short history, Chinese American Buddhist organizations have very few non-Chinese participants or masters. One can say that, as a whole, the tradition is American Chinese rather than Chinese American. Third, the emphasis on "Chinese" is a conscious choice. Many of the people who participate in these organizations became active Buddhists only after having come to the United States. The Buddhist groups act as an important link back to cultural China. Fourth, while the Buddhist tradition serves as a source of stability for a community whose members are undergoing a radical shift in their sense of identity, its transplantation to fresh soil is also regarded as an opportunity for the renewal of the authentic Buddhist message. The apparent opposites of stability and transformation are occurring in tandem, indicating that Chinese Buddhism will enjoy a long-lasting and fruitful life in the United States.[29]

Shin Buddhism in America:
A Social Perspective

ALFRED BLOOM

As mentioned in the introduction to this volume, Buddhism initially became known during the nineteenth century to the American intellectual and literary world through such persons as Ralph Waldo Emerson, Henry David Thoreau, Walt Whitman, Helena P. Blavatsky and her associate Col. Henry Steel Olcott. While an awareness of Buddhism was growing among the more cultured classes, Japanese workers migrating to Hawaii and North America were bringing with them their Buddhist traditions and diverse denominations. By far the largest and best organized were the Honganji branches of the Jōdo Shinshū sect, commonly called Shin Buddhism in English.[1] Though Shin Buddhism has been a major religious institution in Japan, it has remained a virtually unknown tradition in the West in comparison to the recent prominence of the Zen, Tibetan, or Theravādin traditions.

The Buddhist Churches of America, the mainland United States branch of the Shin Buddhist Honganji (there are also branches in Hawaii, Canada, and Brazil), will celebrate its centennial in 1999. As it approaches this significant occasion, this institution encounters problems of decreasing membership, shrinking ministry, ambivalence to opening the faith to the wider community, and of interpreting the teaching in a way that is meaningful to modern, well-educated temple members, as well as inquirers from outside.

An Overview of the History of Shin Buddhism in America

Due to economic conditions in Japan, Japanese farmers and laborers sought their fortunes abroad. The first Japanese immigrants arrived in

Hawaii as contract laborers to work on sugar plantations in June 1868, the first year of the Meiji era. As a result of agreements between the Japanese and the Hawaiian kingdom, those immigrants who followed were referred to as *kanyaku-imin* (contract labor immigrants).

The first group to settle in California arrived in June 1869 and established what was to become known as the Wakamatsu Tea and Silk Colony at Gold Hill in Eldorado County. Available data indicate there were only some 55 Japanese in the United States in 1870. By 1900, the number reached over 10,000.[2] According to Wilson and Hosokawa, the cumulative total of Japanese immigrants to mainland America through 1919 was 237,121. Nevertheless, the 1920 census showed 110,010 "Japanese" in the U.S. mainland, including the 29,672 Nisei who were American citizens by birth.[3]

Shin Buddhism, as well as other Buddhist denominations, followed the immigrants to America, arriving in the Hawaiian islands in 1889 and on the U.S. mainland in 1899. As a minority group experiencing various forms of discrimination and pressures, the immigrants needed to hold on to the customs, faith, and loyalties that they brought with them. Buddhist temples became social centers and the teaching a source of consolation for those who underwent the hard life of the plantations, farms, or cities. Government-sponsored immigration, however, allowed the formation of a more defined community. The social and religious basis for the development of Shin Buddhism in Hawaii took shape when wives were brought from Japan to establish families.

In 1889, the first Jōdo Shinshū priest came to establish Shin Buddhism in the Christian-oriented islands. Reverend Soryu Kagahi set up a small temple in Hawaii and then returned to Japan. Laypeople carried on services until the next missionaries came in 1897. Reverend Hoji Satomi established a Shin Buddhist temple on Fort Street in Honolulu. He was accompanied by Reverend Yemyo Imamura, who served the Honpa Honganji Mission as bishop until his death in 1932. Bishop Imamura was a forceful leader and was held in high respect by the entire community as a religious and social leader through his activities in connection with the sugar strikes. His creative leadership established Shin Buddhism as a significant religious community in the islands. Although hostility toward Buddhism was particularly strong in Hawaii (where most Shin Buddhists lived in the early years), Bishop Imamura remained undaunted by anti-Japanese sentiments and upheld the ideal of uniting Japanese and Western culture and "Americanizing" the Japanese, meaning that they would be loyal citizens in their adopted country. He organized Boy Scout troops and worked to universalize Buddhism through the development of hymns, sermons in English, Sunday school programs, and used pews and pulpits in temples. Bishop Imamura articulated his ideal clearly: "The true religion ought to rise above and be applicable to any country and nationality and so assimilate with every state and nation. The final object of Hongwanji is to plant the gospel of Buddha Amita in the true spirit of every nation in the corner of the world."[4]

Bishop Imamura's ideal was admired by many, but for financial and religious reasons, the English program initiated by Imamura in the International Buddhist Institute was eventually terminated after his death. English services were continued, however, and English-speaking Japanese scholars visited. According to Ruth Tabrah, "In the eight years since Yemyo Imamura's death his idea of a cosmopolitan, American Buddhism as the focus of the Hawaii Mission had not been carried forward. The ideal, like his vision of worldwide propagation, was to become a temporary casualty of the war years ahead, and to remain dormant for at least a decade following the deep emotional wounds of World War II."[5]

In spite of the dominant Christian society, Buddhist temples in Hawaii developed their educational and cultural programs. They also attempted to adapt their services to meet the needs of the new environment, manifesting the flexibility that had characterized the spread of Buddhism through Asia.

Buddhist efforts to pacify laborers and encourage adaptation were initially welcomed by the planters. The support given sugar strikers by Bishop Imamura and other Buddhist leaders, however, aroused strong opposition and criticism in the general community. In addition, Japanese-language schools came to be viewed as a threat to the American way of life. Christians also resented Buddhist resistance to conversion. With the onset of World War II, the patriotism and loyalty of Buddhists fell under suspicion, because of association with Japan and a confusion of Buddhism with Shinto, which was employed in Japan as a cult of patriotism. Temples were shut down and ministers arrested. Christian evangelists frequently stressed that Buddhism and Americanism were contradictory.[6]

Great efforts were made by Buddhist missionaries to give immigrants spiritual direction and consolation in their many problems as a minority people, although the social environment in America placed Buddhism on the defensive. It had to help maintain an awareness of, and respect for, Japanese tradition among people who were not permitted to become American citizens, while encouraging followers to be good citizens in their adopted land.

On the mainland in this same period, other Shin Buddhist teachers had arrived as early as 1872, resulting in the formation of the Young Men's Buddhist Association (Bukkyō Seinen Kai) in San Francisco. This organization, formally established on July 30, 1898, was the precursor of what is now the Buddhist Church of San Francisco. The initial visitors recommended that the head temple initiate missionary activity in America.

Consequently, Reverend Dr. Shuye Sonoda and Reverend Kakuryo Nishijima were the first Jōdo Shinshū ministers sent as official missionaries to the United States, arriving in San Francisco on September 1, 1899. They set about laying the foundation for what became the Buddhist Mission of North America (BMNA) in 1914 and is now the Buddhist Churches of America (BCA). During his tenure, Reverend Sonoda together with Dr. Norman, a physician, established the first non-Asian Buddhist organization, the Dharma Sangha of Buddha.[7] Their efforts and those of later Jōdo Shinshū ministers were nevertheless directed primarily toward serving the religious and social needs and interests of the Japanese immigrants who were already (at least nominally) Buddhists and preponderantly followers of Shin Buddhism.

Coincidentally with the enlargement of Shin Buddhist activities in North America, anti-Japanese attitudes and actions by Americans (particularly those with vested economic interests in states on the West Coast) intensified to the point that further immigration from Japan was stopped by the Japanese Exclusion Act of 1924. Alien land laws in California, Oregon, and Washington prevented the acquisition of land by Japanese and complicated the possession of property for use as churches or temples.

In the 1920s and 1930s, activities designed to meet the needs of the English-speaking Nisei members of the temples were established and expanded. Sunday schools (now called Dharma schools) became an essential feature of the temples for imparting Dharma lessons in English to school-age children. Various kinds of youth organizations, such as the Young Men's Buddhist Associations and Young Women's Buddhist Associations (YMBAs and YWBAs), also provided young people with devotional opportunities as well as social and athletic outlets. Their activities encouraged intracommunity networking by young people in their respective locales.

Also in this period there was increasing awareness of the need for English-speaking ministers. In 1929, delegates to the meeting of the ministers and lay representatives (of the Buddhist Mission of North America) in San Francisco approved the establishment of a foundation whose objectives were to support the propagation of Buddhism in America and provide for training ministers. By 1931, there were thirty-three churches and several branches affiliated with the BMNA, but few of the ministers were fully proficient in English. Consequently, in 1930 Reverend Kenju Masuyama, formerly a professor of the Honganji Ryukoku University, became the bishop, or Sōchō. He placed great emphasis on finding suitable candidates among the Nisei (second-generation youth) to become Buddhist ministers. Ministerial aspirants went to Japan to receive formal training that would qualify them for ordination by the Honpa Honganji. Ironically, the necessary proficiency in the Japanese language limited the use of English.

The instructional program begun in San Francisco by Bishop Masuyama might have become more firmly rooted had it not been for the advent of World War II. During this time all persons of Japanese ancestry (including United States citizens) and their ministers living on the West Coast were removed from their homes by the U.S. government and interned in concentration camps called "relocation centers." Since the Japanese American residents of San Francisco were incarcerated in the Topaz Relocation Center in Utah, the headquarters of the BMNA was established in that camp. In April 1944, it was decided to rename the BMNA as the Buddhist Churches of America (BCA) and to incorporate the entity in the state of California.

Bishop Ryotai Matsukage returned to San Francisco in August 1945 and reopened the headquarters of what had become the Buddhist Churches of America. In many cases, the temples and any affiliated Japanese-language school buildings had to be used as temporary shelters for the returning evacuees. By the mid-1950s, however, most of the temples were nearing recovery from the setbacks of the war years and looking to the future with plans for refurbishing old facilities as well as building new ones.

Significant numbers of Japanese Americans from the various relocation centers had migrated to areas east of the Mississippi during the war years, and they established new temples. In 1941, there were forty-four temples affiliated with the BMNA, and by 1989, there were sixty-one temples and seven *sanghas* (fellowships) affiliated with its successor, the BCA.

Although the initiation of any concerted program for training English-speaking Jōdo Shinshū ministers was forestalled by World War II, in 1949 Bishop Enryo Shigefuji began conducting study classes in Berkeley, California. Reverend Kanmo Imamura, resident minister of the Berkeley Buddhist Temple, further developed the study class and established the BCA Study Center. In 1956 the BCA established the Special Projects Fund to support the center and expenses of ministerial students who attended. In 1966, the BCA National Council decided to establish what is now the Institute of Buddhist Studies (IBS) and to purchase a suitable property in Berkeley for that purpose. It eventually became affiliated with the Graduate Theological Union (GTU) as a graduate school and seminary in 1985. Following its affiliation with GTU, in 1987 the institute acquired its present facility and enlarged its library and program.

The institute now functions within a Jewish and Christian community as the only non-Western religious school of higher learning, participating in an ongoing academic and multireligious environment and stimulated by Buddhist-Christian dialogue. The hopes of the early missionaries to integrate Shin Buddhism within the mainstream American religious environment have made great progress toward realization.

Japanese Cultural Background of
Shin Buddhism in Modern Context

Historically, Shin Buddhism was initiated by Shinran (1173–1263) during the Kamakura era (1185–1332). The movement is known in Japan as Jōdo Shinshū (True Sect [Teaching] of the Pure Land). In polemical dispute with other interpreters of Pure Land teaching, Shinran claimed that he only followed the teaching of his master, Hōnen (1143–1212). While not regarding himself as the founder of a new movement, Shinran laid the doctrinal foundations of the teaching, drawing on earlier Chinese and Japanese Pure Land sources, which he adroitly reinterpreted in conformity with his own religious experience.

The eighth successor, Rennyo (1415–99), who is sometimes regarded as the second founder, established the movement as a major, popular religious and social force with its base in the peasant class. It became closely allied with the feudal structure that solidified during the 250 years of Tokugawa rule (1600–1868). Eventually a complex, hereditary ecclesiastical structure—centered on the abbot, who was a direct descendant of Shinran—evolved with formalized doctrinal and scholastic traditions. This monarchical structure, however, continued to rely on a broadbased popular faith and piety among the adherents.

With its deep roots in peasant society, Japanese Shin was suited to the needs of a rural community in that it offered ordinary laypeople a simple way to spiritual deliverance. According to Shin, a practitioner need only have faith and recite the name of Amida Buddha (*Namu-amida-butsu*) with gratitude in order to reach the Pure Land. Moreover, Shin was particularly suited to lay life since it departed decisively from the traditional forms of celibate monastic Buddhism. Shinran himself married and fathered six children. Since that time the abbacy and later the priesthood have been hereditary.

The basic teaching of Shin, grounded in ancient Pure Land myth, derives from the belief that Amida Buddha, the Buddha of Eternal Life and Infinite Light, has taken the form of the bodhisattva Dharmākara, who made forty-eight vows or promises for the salvation of all beings. He pledged to create an ideal spiritual world, the Western Pure Land (also called Sukhāvatī), into which all beings, regardless of social, intellectual, or moral capacities, can be reborn and attain final liberation and enlightenment. Essentially, Shin teaches salvation through trusting faith (*shinjin*).

It was Shinran's distinctive view that faith or trust is endowed by the Buddha, being his true mind of wisdom and compassion. As a consequence, salvation is assured and no special practices or meritorious good deeds are required for birth into the Pure Land. After trust in Amida's primal vow has arisen, all religious activities are viewed as expressions of gratitude and self-righteousness is negated. Further, awareness of the obligation one owes to the compassion of the Buddha is the foundation of ethics and morality. In the context of Japanese society, in which ancestor reverence has been a focal point for ethics and morality, Shin thought viewed the obligation to ancestors as an aspect of Buddha's compassion and the basis for good citizenship, stressing duty and obedience to superiors. Through emphasis on filial observances and respect for authority, Shin Buddhism became intertwined with the Japanese family system within the hierarchical society.

In the immigrant situation, the family system and its coordinate respect for authority supported the cohesiveness of the family and the ethnic community as a whole, stressing social responsibility and obedience to the law. The concepts of *on* or *giri*—obligation or duty—which had been central to Japanese society, operated among the Japanese Americans as the ethical foundation for human relations. The *on-giri* relationship is essentially conservative and can be stultifying for the individual, especially in the context of a status society and within a close family situation. The psychosocial functioning of these principles is that individuals tend to be more conscious of their external relations than their own inner promptings. There is, consequently, a disposition to be conformist, unquestioning, and prudent. This tendency has given rise to the terms *quiet Americans* or *model minority*, which, though seemingly positive, have negative implications and undermine Japanese American critique of American society.

In addition to ethical values, there are other cultural attitudes that have been transferred from Japan. These are *shikata-ga-nai*, which means to accept those things over which one has no control; *mottainai*, which generally suggests modesty, conveying a sense of unworthiness; *gaman*, which means to endure and persevere in the face of difficulty; *enryō*, which is a nonassertive restraint or reserve; and finally *okage-sama-de* and *arigatai*, which express gratitude and appreciation to all those factors supporting our lives, though unseen. These cultural attitudes have contributed to the seemingly closed character of the Japanese American Buddhist community. They have been conducive to more introspective and less aggressive personality formation, but also a flexibility in adapting to the changing conditions of society, while lessening tension with traditional values.

The Japanese community, like most ethnic groups, attained a measure of solidarity through ethnocentrism, highlighting its own cultural attitudes and mores. Consequently, the transmission of such particularistic attitudes through family relationships thwarts the universalism of Buddhism. Despite the popularity and seeming interest in and attraction to Buddhism by non-Japanese, Buddhist temples established by the immigrants have few members of other races. In such circumstances racial homogeneity, reinforced by language and culture, has made it difficult for outsiders to enter the heart of the Buddhist tradition. This situation persists because many Buddhist ministers are recruited from Japan or are second- or third-generation Japanese Americans who have spent many years of training in Japan and are deeply imbued with Japanese cultural attitudes. A fair number have problems speaking English and are often ill at ease outside the Japanese community.

Ryo M. Imamura has made a detailed study of the psychological types among temple ministers and nontemple ministers. According to his study, Protestant and Catholic ministers are generally more extroverted, while Buddhists tend to be introverted, and more "introspective, persevering, hard to convince or change, quiet, caring, concerned about deep and enduring values and spend energy in making people happy and in bringing harmony into relationships." He states: "Jōdo Shin Buddhism and the Japanese culture stress harmony and interrelatedness, quiet reflection, patience, appreciation and humility."[8] Differences in personality formation among religious leaders influence the stance of the group vis-à-vis the dominant society and any effort to reach out.

Amid the many vicissitudes experienced in the process of transplanting its spiritual and cultural heritage to the new American environment, Shin Buddhism has struggled seriously to discover its role in the changing, modern society. When the immigrant Japanese were excluded from and demeaned by the dominant society, their ethnic character and the values and attitudes transmitted from Japan were effective in providing a rallying point for a community under siege. As the Buddhist Churches of America celebrates its centennial in 1999, it now faces the challenge of transcending its ethnic character to become more universal as a Buddhist tradition and thereby fulfill the meaning and potentiality of Shinran's teaching.

There have been efforts, particularly among younger members, to distinguish the specifically Buddhist element in Shin teaching and temple life from elements that are carryovers from Japanese culture. For example, Buddhism is egalitarian, while Japanese culture is hierarchical; hierarchy is not essential to Buddhism. A problem remains that while the teaching is universal, the organization functions to a significant degree according to Japanese cultural assumptions. However, Shin Buddhists have been Americans for several generations and educated in the American system. For all intents and purposes they are Westerners who happen to be Japanese and who pursue the same goals as others in society. Temples need to change to meet the spiritual and intellectual needs of these individuals, whether or not the organization seeks to reach out beyond the ethnic community. In any case, Shin has to look beyond limited ethnic boundaries for adherents, because Buddhism itself is a world religion. The appeal to be Shin Buddhist simply because one is Japanese or out of some family loyalty has proven inadequate to stem the loss of adherents or to maintain the vitality of the community. Consequently, in contemporary America, Shin Buddhism is attempting, through such facilities as the Institute of Buddhist Studies, gradually to develop its own well-defined form and position within the religious environment of Western culture. Moreover, younger Shin members—who have higher education and greater social mobility compared to members in the earlier years—desire to participate in working toward the solutions to contemporary problems in social concerns committees and special seminars. Shin Buddhists are constantly asked the Shin view about women, abortion, race, ecological issues, and political questions. Their responses require consideration on a more universal plane. Further, Shin, as a facet of Mahāyāna Buddhism, has a clear mandate to reach out to all people in the ideal of the bodhisattva and in Shinran's teaching. The translation of Shin texts has reinforced this obligation, because Shinran clearly expressed a universal ideal. Because the teachings are now more easily accessible to members, more questions are being raised concerning the deeper meaning of Shin in society.

Shin Buddhism in American Society: Problems and Prospects

The background of discrimination, war, incarceration, and cultural transition has given rise to numerous problems and tensions within the Shin Buddhist community. In the absence of solutions, however, there continues to be an attrition of members and ministers which is reaching crisis proportions. Various issues are significant for the future development of Shin Buddhism in the West, but we should note that many aspects of the current crisis are influenced by problems and conditions affecting other religions as well in Western societies. The small size of BCA, perhaps, intensifies the significance of the crisis.

As the figures cited here show, the Shin community faces a crisis, particularly on the mainland. This is evident in the obvious decline in the number of general memberships and ministers.[9] According to one study, the Buddhist Churches of America reached its peak in 1930 with 123 ministers; by 1981 there were 71. In 1977 the general membership stood at 21,600 families (approximately 65,000 persons).[10] According to the 1995 report, memberships have dropped officially to 16,925 (about 50,775 persons).[11] Clearly, gradual attrition has been going on for many years. It is also well known that in recent years "outmarriage" (that is, marriages with individuals of a different ethnic background) by Japanese American youth is more than 50 percent. Yet few of the children of mixed marriages, or their parents, are active in the temples.

Dharma schools are usually viewed as the seedbed for the future development of the temples. Hence, temple education programs focus on the children, while little attention is paid to adult education. The peak of Dharma school enrollment for which there are records was 7,500 students in 1940. In 1972, the number had declined to 6,209.[12] By 1983–84 the total was approximately 2,550 students. Since that time the number has risen to 3,045 in 1992–93. Though the numbers have risen and fallen over the years, since 1990 there has been an increase, which may be due to better organization and efforts of Dharma school parents and the encouragement of the ministers.[13] With the improvement of teaching materials, methods, and personnel, the downward trend may be reversed, and the Dharma schools can once again assure the future of the temples.

A major factor in the deepening crisis is the attrition of clergy who are aging and retiring. Many a minister serves two or three temples, while some retired ministers are pressed into service. Altogether there are some sixty-two ministers in service, with additional retirements every year. The number of replacements has not kept pace with the number who have retired or left the ministry.

In the early years of Shin presence in America the ministers were enlisted in Japan. Because of the large numbers of first-generation Japanese in the community, this arrangement was optimal. Japanese priests who make the trip now, however, have great difficulty culturally and linguistically in relating to the younger generations. In addition to problems of adapting to another culture, life for the priest is better in Japan than it is in the United States. Priests in Japan are more or less in control of their temples, whereas in America priests are considered employees of the congregation, and they may receive lower wages than in Japan. It should be pointed out that the *sangha* is making efforts to upgrade salaries and provide better retirement benefits.

Another aspect of the crisis is the difficulty in recruiting ministers among Japanese American youth. It is evident that such youth, observing Shin's emphasis on death, are not greatly attracted to becoming ministers, especially when there are many other options in society for fulfilling themselves. In line with the general character of Buddhism in Japan, a major function of Shin temples is holding funerals and memorializing the dead. Shin, with its belief in rebirth in the Pure Land after death, is generally regarded as an otherworldly religion and, like other Buddhist sects, dubbed "Funeral Buddhism." This has not changed much in its transfer to the West and has contributed to the lack of appeal for young people. They are also aware of the difficult working conditions and low remuneration of the ministers.

There are non-Japanese individuals who have entered the ministry at various times through its history. They have generally encountered Buddhism in its various forms through exposure to Asian spiritual and religious traditions in their own quest for meaning. They may have studied Buddhism in its more ideal forms or may have practiced other forms of discipline. For deeply personal reasons, they turn to Shin Buddhism as the way to cultivate Buddhist experience and values. They have not been subjected in their early lives to the emphasis on rituals associated with the dead, but have been drawn by the character of Buddhist teaching itself. Shin welcomes those who make such a commitment and are willing to undergo the requisite training. There are presently five non-Japanese clergy, two of whom have become chief ministers in important temples.

While progress has been made in the area of ministerial education, the life of the temples remains generally what it has been for decades. The focus of the temple remains the traditional nuclear family, and it provides few specialized programs or activities for new styles of family life such as single-parent families, blended families, divorcés, singles, or nontraditional gender orientations.

Further, although a school has been created to train English-speaking ministers, trainees still go to Japan for several years to imbibe the traditional teaching and learn Japanese. Since the teaching given in Japan is shaped by issues of Japanese history and culture, the ministers who return may have difficulty interpreting the teaching culturally to interested inquirers. There is little discussion of Buddhism in relation to contemporary issues in sermons. Although doctrinal themes may be addressed, the further philosophical implications and meanings are seldom explored. Lay members generally desire rather simple presentations. The great emphasis on ceremony and ritual results from Japanese cultural heritage, and much of the ritual is performed in Sino-Japanese language and understood by few members. As a result, the ideals embodied in the text are not communicated. The future development of Shin Buddhism requires a more balanced approach, highlighting education and understanding of the teaching.

While external, historical circumstances are partially responsible for attrition in Shin, it is also due to a lack of dynamic leadership within the tradition. An important element contributing to this problem is the high degree of professionalism of Japanese Americans, which encourages the young people to become doctors, lawyers, dentists, scientists, engineers, and businesspeople. It has been pointed out that only 6 percent of Japanese American students in doctoral-level graduate study take up the humanities,[14] which involve traditional academic disciplines that might lead to consideration of ministry. As a consequence, Shin lacks a vibrant, intellectual core of members, despite the professionalization of its members. Few members have training in religious and philosophical studies to explore these issues critically and move the community in a more positive direction.

The broader dispersion of Japanese Americans throughout American society after the war, higher education, and greater professional mobility have supported the acculturation of the younger generations and loss of contact with the temples. At the same time, many young people have a growing interest in Japanese heritage, which is encouraged by the larger society's emphasis on diversity and pluralism as well as by the persistence of racism in America. Nevertheless, these factors have not been sufficient to alter the trend of attrition within the temples.

Some of the younger Japanese American ministers also have become aware of the richness of their ethnic and religious heritage, as a result of studying in Japan. Their religious and educational experience of the traditional religion sometimes leads them to appear to reinforce the conservative tendencies of the community, which wishes to return to former times when temple life seemed more vital and cohesive. Hence, both ministers and community members can be ambivalent about developing practical programs for outreach. The traditional definition of ministry as focused on the temple also limits development of more specialized ministries, such as hospital chaplains, campus ministers, or ministers of education.

There is a tension within the denomination between the responsibility not to abandon the cultural heritage of one's parents—particularly the first-generation immigrants, who sacrificed so much to establish the teaching in America—and efforts to extend to the wider society. The problem of seeking non-Japanese members lies in the latent anxiety of losing control over the institutions developed by the first-generation (Issei) forebears. On one occasion, a long-standing member informed me that many members did not want white, black, Chinese, Korean, or other non-Japanese members in the temples because large numbers of non-Japanese would take control of the organization. His view is borne out when we see that there has been no policy, personnel, or financial provision established within the BCA to carry out a concerted or organized effort of outreach.

Another major area of concern for the BCA is the problem of religious education. There have been several attempts to upgrade and improve the educational resources in the temple over the years. Dharma school teachers are usually all volunteers, and there are few programs that offer systematic training for teachers. They tend to rely instead on the knowledge they received when they attended Dharma school. The teachers are, however, to be commended for the efforts they make.

The young student is introduced to basic Buddhist teaching, such as the Four Noble Truths, the Eightfold Path, and many stories about Śākyamuni and models of Buddhist piety, as well as ritual. The appeal is more to the affective aspect that conveys the feeling of being Buddhist. Young people frequently leave the temple at adolescence or when they go to college. Their exposure to the basic principles of Shin Buddhism is very limited, leaving them with many questions. They may not return to the temple until middle age when they have their own families, if they return at all. When they do return in later life, there are very few classes designed for adults that address contemporary problems of religion and modern life. Sermons and occasional lecture programs are the main source of information.

The availability of literature on Shin Buddhism in English has increased, but members are not noted for reading such materials. Consequently, the laypeople, who should be taking the lead in sharing the teaching with others, have themselves only a hazy understanding of the relation of early Buddhism to Shin Buddhism or of the content of Shin Buddhism itself. Laypeople often state that it is the responsibility of the priest to know the religion, thereby discounting their own responsibility to study and become knowledgeable about their faith.

When we look at the problem of education, we can also observe that Shin Buddhism has an element of anti-intellectualism which derives in some degree from Japanese religious tradition generally, and because the founder and the successors emphasized that one should not try to rationalize the mystery of faith or exhibit faith openly to flaunt one's spiritual superiority. Related to this issue is the stress laid on models of Shin piety called *myōkōnin*, wondrously good people, who are constantly held up for admiration in sermons and lectures. Stories about them reinforce the affective appeal of Shin Buddhism and tend to devalue intellectual issues.

These factors fed into an important philosophical distinction between absolute and conventional truth. This distinction generally designates the two spheres of Buddha Dharma (Buddhist truth or religious truth) and the Royal or Imperial Dharma (secular truth or morality). The religious realm stresses the way to be born into the Pure Land through faith in one's mind or heart, while the secular realm requires the person, as a member of society, to obey superiors and maintain order, an approach largely based on Confucian ethics. This dual perspective has unconsciously shaped the basic social understanding of the teaching among the members. An implication of the theory has been to disconnect spiritual concerns from the social arena. Even today it is difficult for the temples and the leadership to take up social issues as a matter of religious concern and commitment. With the decline in active belief in the afterlife, the relevance of the religion is at stake.

Because of these conditions, Shin Buddhism still remains relatively isolated in American society, where even after one hundred years it appears to be a foreign religion. Recently, Kimi Yonemura Hisatsune, a leading laywoman and writer, has written: "Yet, our temples operate as if Jōdo Shinshū is basically a Japanese religion, and some followers of Shinran Shōnin even believe that it is vitally important or necessary to maintain or transmit the Japanese character of the Shin tradition."[15]

Charles Prebish, in his volume *American Buddhism*, notes the ambivalence within BCA, commenting: "As the issei (first generation) members of the congregation die, Buddhist Churches of America cannot seem to decide whether to follow the general wishes of the nisei members (second generation) and Americanize more fully, or honor the wishes of the clergy (and many young members) and reassert their Japanese heritage."[16] He might also have noted that BCA not only has the longest history in America, but is the best organized, and endowed with human and financial resources. Yet it has not been able to make the transition to America easily. The issue is not one merely of statistics and sociology or history. Although Prebish indicates that Shin Buddhism has the best opportunity to become transnational because of its similarities with Western religion, it has not realized this potential.

So far we have discussed internal factors that, despite its important presence in the American scene, have restricted the emergence of Shin Buddhism as a significant participant in the process of the permeation of Buddhism within American society. The appeal of Shin Buddhism has also been limited, however, by the perceptions of outside observers. Some scholars have questioned its authenticity as Buddhism. Christmas Humphreys is highly critical when he declares that Shin Buddhism "is a form of Buddhism which on the face of it discards three-quarters of Buddhism. Compared with the Teaching of the Pali Canon it is but Buddhism and water." He ends his discussion of Shin Buddhism by stating: "It was therefore immediately popular, and it may be better than no religion at all. But is it Buddhism?"[17] Shin is presented as a degenerate form of Buddhism, designed merely for the spiritually ineffectual masses. It has also been called a "do nothing" religion with a cheap form of salvation.

A similar question has been posed more recently by Paul Williams in his analysis of Shin teaching.[18] Though he acknowledges the features of Mahāyāna Buddhism that shape Shin Buddhist teaching, and its effectiveness and influcncc in the lives of followers, he states that it is de facto Buddhism, though it is rooted in the history and development of Mahāyāna tradition and cannot be defined in such a way as to exclude it from Buddhism. Nevertheless, the tenor of the discussion leaves the subtle impression that its status remains unclear. Even though his presentation of Shin Buddhism is quite positive, the ambiguity of its status as Buddhism would naturally reduce interest in it by seekers.

It is true that Shin Buddhism rejects traditional disciplines such as meditation and precepts, which have been the core of Buddhist practice as the way to enlightenment. Shin views those practices as compassionate means given by the Buddha to lead practitioners to insight into the depth of egocentrism and its attachments. Humphreys overlooks the understanding of human nature underlying Shin and instead focuses on the issue of difficult versus easy practice, which has been used in the Buddhist tradition to distinguish Pure Land teaching from other schools. Shinran went further than this simple distinction in probing human experience, as a result of his twenty-year religious experience in the monastery on Mount Hiei. While the Shin Buddhist view may not be without its problems, it is an outgrowth of the logic of Mahāyāna Buddhist historical development and is, therefore, a serious interpretation of Mahāyāna Buddhism.

Further, the emphasis on the evil, defiled character of human life appears throughout Shinran's writings and in his confessions. This feature of Shin appears negative and would hardly appeal to Westerners who have already given up belief in original sin, a term Humphreys uses to describe the basis of Shin teaching.[19] What seems negative at first glance, however, may be a realistic recognition of the passion-ridden character of human existence. This understanding led Shinran to the positive insight that if salvation is possible, its source is not in his own finite, unstable mind and actions, but in Amida Buddha, which symbolizes the reality that embraces and sustains his life. Shinran gained insight into the complexity of the motivation and sincerity that underlie all spiritual human efforts, no matter how demanding in difficulty or quantity. According to Shinran, Amida Buddha is perceived as the absolute Other Power, a power beyond but not apart from the empirical self. It is the dynamic essence of life, which is expressed in the mythic structure of Amida Buddha's Primal Vows. Shinran's so-called negative insight opens the way to a positive approach to life and hope.

Another feature that distracts seekers is the apparent otherworldly character of Shin Buddhism. Occasionally Shinran employed the symbolism of the Pure Land to console grieving disciples with the hope of reunion in the Pure Land. Such statements imply a more concrete, literal, or personal understanding of the Pure Land. In his major scholarly text *Kyōgyōshinshō*, however, Shinran describes birth into the Pure Land as the birth of non-birth, or nirvana, and beyond conceivability. He also connects it to the ideal of the bodhisattva who returns to this world to save all beings, as well as immediate attainment of Buddhahood, which has the same fundamental intention. We should note that there is no necessary contradiction between the literal, personalistic expressions and the more abstract, philosophical concepts. It is a question of the contexts in which the idea is being asserted, since it is common to adjust religious expressions to the needs of the particular listener.

Finally, the apparent similarity of Shin Buddhism to Christianity also deflects interest for those who want something clearly different from what they had in Western religion. However, the similarities between the two religions indicate their universality in dealing with common human problems and aspirations. Similarities are not to be completely discounted, even though differences among faiths are more decisive in evaluating their meaning.

Conclusion

In our presentation we have tried to offer a perspective on why Shin Buddhism, despite its prominence in Japan and its history in America, remains a relatively unknown and misunderstood Buddhist teaching. Part of the reason is due to the historical conditions that Shin Buddhists have encountered; part is due to the reluctance of Shin Buddhists themselves to address the larger society; another part is the result of somewhat biased presentations in popular texts on Buddhism.

A ray of hope for better understanding is emerging from wider scholarly interest in Shin Buddhism and Buddhist-Christian dialogue, which grapple seriously with the historical and dharmological principles and issues presented by Shinran and Shin Buddhism. Comparative studies are helping to demonstrate the similarities and differences between Christianity and Shin Buddhism and to clarify the position of the latter among the world's religions. As this process continues, it is challenging and stimulating Shin teachers to interact more seriously with Western culture and through this effort to discover Shin Buddhism's meaning and mission within modern society.

Japanese Zen in America: Americanizing the Face in the Mirror

G. VICTOR SŌGEN HORI

I s the practice of Zen in America like the observance of Valentine's Day in Japan? Any set of practices that has originated in one culture takes on a different significance when transplanted to another. Valentine's Day is now celebrated in Japan in the following way: Through skillful sales promotion, the chocolate manufacturers of Japan have spread the impression that in the West, Valentine's Day is marked by sending a gift of chocolate to the person who is the object of one's romantic affections. Chocolate sales around Valentine's Day have now become so large that chocolate manufacturers do most of the year's business in the month of February. Also in February, one can often find newspaper articles with the results of yet another survey showing that among Japanese people buying chocolate, young women outnumber men by a huge percentage. The newspaper article may reveal too that a young woman will buy chocolate for several men, persons to whom she stands in a position of social obligation (*osewa ni natte iru*). These may include her supervisor at work, a senior colleague, or a teacher in some capacity, among others. Sometimes in a reversal of hierarchy, older women will buy chocolate for their students, mothers for their sons. In a small minority of cases, the woman may even give a gift of chocolate to a man for whom she feels romantic affection (and to whom she may also, coincidentally, be socially obligated—like her husband). The chocolate companies, sensing a chance to increase sales, have tried to encourage even more chocolate buying by creating White Day on March 14, one month after Valentine's Day. On White Day, men who have received chocolate on Valentine's Day are enjoined to return the favor (*okaeshi*) by buying a gift of white chocolate for the young lady. Men give white chocolate in contrast to the dark chocolate which the women gave.

The example of Valentine's Day in Japan reveals how a practice transplanted from one culture to another culture acquires a different meaning. As anthropologists have pointed out, Japan is a gift culture. Despite the advertising that utilizes the symbols and rhetoric of love and romance, on Valentine's Day, the giving of chocolates reflects traditional Japanese gift-giving that expresses the intertwined feelings of gratitude and obligation which arise out of social role as much as the personal affection of one individual for another. In such a gift culture, a man is likely to give a gift of white chocolate as much from the feeling of obligation to return a favor as from a feeling of personal affection (sometimes those two feelings are not so easily distinguishable). A scholar of religion and culture might want to generalize and say that Valentine's Day chocolate-giving in Japan expresses a pattern of social relations defined not by individual romantic affection but by Confucian ideas of social hierarchy, reciprocity, and obligation. Such a scholar might also notice that the creation of White Day chocolate-giving can be seen as a yin-yang separation and pairing of complementary opposites. As in Western culture, women in Japan seem to keep up the social forms more than do men, but chocolate manufacturers have exploited some traditional Asian ideas about gender separation and difference to get men to do likewise. At a deeper level, the scholar might also notice that love, the theme of Valentine's Day, has a different connotation in Japanese society. The word for love in Japanese is *ai*, and *ai* is the same word that expresses the Buddhist notion of attachment, or self-centered clinging, which is a source of suffering in human existence. I once saw a television program in which a marriage expert said that in *mukashi*, "the old days" (whenever that was), one sought in a marriage partner not someone to love for the rest of one's life but someone who would share one's suffering in life. While some Japanese cultural practices, such as a culture and economy of gift-giving, have made possible the easy transplantation of Valentine's Day, these and other cultural practices and assumptions, such as about the relative importance of social obligation vis-à-vis love, have changed the day's significance. Of course, one should not think that the background context of Japanese culture is fixed and unchangeable. The very introduction of Valentine's Day strengthens the position of romantic love in relation to social obligation in Japanese culture, changing Japanese culture even as Japanese culture changes the significance of Valentine's Day. All this occurs not quite at the level of awareness. One lives in one's own culture without necessarily making it an explicit object of examination. Only belatedly have Japanese people begun to realize that in the West, Valentine's Day has little to do with buying chocolate.

One can thus see the point in wondering whether Valentine's Day in Japan—gift-culture commercialized, Confucianized, yin-yangized, seen through a Buddhist perspective on romantic love—is the same custom with the same meaning as Valentine's Day in the West. Now, is Zen in America the same as Valentine's Day in Japan?

A century has passed since the first Japanese Zen monk, Shaku Sōen, came to North America in 1893. Though there was some literary and academic interest in Zen in the first half of the twentieth century, the first of the serious Zen practice communities did not open in North America until 1959. The late start, however, sparked a surge: by 1975 there were more than a hundred such centers.[1] Then just as suddenly, the tide turned. In the early 1980s, several of the Zen centers in North America developed a new institutional rite of passage—scandal that exposed the sexual involvement of the revered Zen master with his students. A series of one crisis after another triggered criticism of the "autocracy of the Zen master"[2] and, more generally, of the authoritarianism of the entire "samurai," "Confucian," or "Asian" tradition.[3] The problem and its solution, it seems, are cultural: voices all around agree that Zen needs to be Americanized or Westernized. The blanket call for Americanization, however, tends to reduce the complex issue of the cultural understanding of Zen to a few simpleminded labels like "autocracy," "authoritarianism," and "samurai." Further, it encourages people to lay the blame on the perceived other before understanding the complexity of the issues. Before rushing to judgment, we should first comprehend clearly this thing called Zen in America. When we do, I believe that we will see that, like Valentine's Day in Japan, Zen in America, as a historical entity, has been shaped as much by its present American cultural context as by its Asian history. Americanization of Zen started long ago, the very first time any American heard or read anything about Zen and said, "Hah!"

In what follows, I propose to look at several different features of Zen in America—ritual life, methods of teaching and learning, social organization, and meditation practice—and contrast the Japanese and the American versions. Or perhaps I should say "a Japanese and an American version," for I am not implying that there is a single Japanese version of, say, Zen ritual, or a single American version of the same. As in the case of Valentine's Day in Japan, however, surrounding the particular examples are complex nets of traditional patterns, expectations, moral standards, social roles, images of self, and even economic forces (remember those chocolate manufacturers) which mold the particular Zen practice I talk about and which are shared much more widely than any particular example.

I write from my personal experience in Zen and scholarship practiced in different cultures. I originally started out specializing in Western philosophy assuming I would have a career in academic teaching. In Japan to study Japanese philosophy, I instead found myself gravitating more toward

Zen meditation and *kōan* practice, which quickly became more important to me than academic study. After completing the doctorate degree and several years of preliminary Zen practice, I asked to be ordained and admitted to the Zen monastery. During the following thirteen years, the *kōan* practice put me under five different rōshi in several Zen temples, monasteries and training schools. Once back in North America, I discovered that although it was possible to continue *kōan* training under a Zen rōshi at a North American Zen center, I did not feel at home in the Zen center itself. This chapter is the result of my reflections on the cultural habits and influences that have already reshaped Zen in America and have already Americanized Zen. The attempt to understand Zen in a Western context has helped me understand Zen in the original Japanese context in which I first experienced it. I have come to see that Japanese Zen is just as uniquely shaped by Japanese tradition and culture, but that Japan has had the advantage of many more years to meld meditation practices, social relations, ritual, language, and so forth to create a seamless total environment which is both Japanese and Zen. This has not yet happened in America.

My background is in Rinzai Zen; it differs in significant ways from the Sōtō lineage and from the mixed Sōtō-Rinzai tradition of the Yasutani-Harada lineage, which has influenced much American Zen. While many readers may not be familiar or sympathetic with Rinzai Zen practices, I cannot write about anything beyond my personal experience. I hope such readers may derive some benefit from my discussion of more general issues of cultural shaping.

Ritual

I did my early training at Ryōshōji, the main *sōdō* or monastery for the Daitokuji line of Rinzai Zen temples in Japan. It is located on the compound of the headquarters temple in Kyoto, the only monastery among twenty-five sub-temples. Since the Meiji Restoration in 1868, the number of active monasteries in Japan has declined steadily, indicating the gradual loss of institutional vitality of Japanese temple Buddhism. Those remaining house fewer and fewer monks, who come for shorter and shorter periods of time. Today there are about fifteen to twenty monks in active training at any time at Daitokuji.[4] About half of the monks at any given time, in my experience, are the sons of temple priests, most of whom will leave after two or three years of *sōdō* training to return to their temples, eventually to succeed their fathers. Historically "sons of temple priests" are a recent phenomenon, since before the Meiji Restoration, there were no officially married priests in Zen and therefore no sons. The *sōdō* population is quite uniform compared to the membership of an American Zen center. The monks are all male, all ordained, usually in their early twenties, usually single, and usually all looking forward to a similar life afterward as a temple priest.

The ABC Zen Center in the United States was founded twenty-five years ago by a Japanese Rinzai Zen priest. The present community consists of the rōshi, a small number of monks (four or five), and an always changing, larger number of ordained, lay-ordained, and unordained students and trainees, both men and women, young and old, totally committed and just testing. There are two ninety-day practice periods a year, one each in summer and winter. During these practice periods, the Zen Center holds several *sesshin*, weeks of intense *zazen* practice, to which an additional thirty or more people come. The *sesshin* is considered the quintessential Zen practice combining long hours of *zazen* with four *sanzen* a day (*sanzen*, or *dokusan*, is a one-to-one meeting with the rōshi in which the practitioner offers a response to a *kōan*). The rōshi maintains an extremely full schedule, conducting up to fifteen major *sesshin* a year, which frequently draw forty or more people. By contrast, in Japan an average rōshi conducts only six or seven major *sesshin* a year in monasteries with often fewer than fifteen monks.

ABC Zen Center chants all its *sūtras* in Japanese rather than in English; the terminology for the daily schedule is Rinzai monastic vocabulary; the feeling of Japanese origin hangs in the air. But though the center tries consciously to transmit Japanese monasticism, it has developed ritual "traditions" never practiced in Japan. What ideas and attitudes shape those new rituals?

Ritual Time

Both ABC Zen Center and Ryōshōji mark periods of *zazen* using the same traditional signals: one clap from the wooden blocks followed by four slow rings of a handbell starts a period of *zazen*; a single ring followed by two claps of the blocks ends the period. ABC also has introduced a new "tradition": a candle on the altar is lit whenever *zazen* is in progress. The new custom is also a new rule: no *zazen* allowed if the candle is not burning. When the candle is blown out every night, *zazen* ends. When it is lit the next day, *zazen* begins again.

In the Daitokuji monastery, *zazen* is not just another activity in the monastery's daily schedule; in a ritual sense, *zazen* is the only activity of the monastery. At the end of the day, the *jikijitsu* (head of the *zendō*, or meditation hall) leaves everyone in sitting position and walks out of the *zendō* without formally ending the period of *zazen*. That period of *zazen* continues through the night. When he reenters the next morning, everyone is sitting in place as if unmoved from the night before. The *jikijitsu* starts the morning by ringing once and clapping twice, thus ending the period of *zazen* started the night before. Ritually speaking, everyone has slept the night within *zazen*.

Meals begin and end in the *zendō* in *zazen*. After the *jikijitsu* begins a period of *zazen* with the appropriate claps and rings, the monks proceed from the *zendō* to the dining hall. Ritually speaking, the monks are still in *zazen* while eating. Posture and concentration while eating should thus be the same as while sitting in *zazen*. After returning to the *zendō*, the *jikijitsu* deliberately does not end the period of *zazen*. Instead, he walks out of the *zendō* leaving everyone sitting in position. *Zazen* never ends.

In traditional monastery vocabulary, monastery activities are classified as either *hajū*, literally "holding on and residing," or *hōgyō*, literally "releasing and going forth." These categories correspond to the classic Mahāyāna distinction, emptiness and form, for *hajū* indicates the realm of the undifferentiated, where there is no separation into host and guest, while *hōgyō* is the realm of the differentiated, where host and guest are separated. *Zazen* is *hajū*, a ritualized instance of emptiness. Other activities are *hōgyō*, ritualized instances of form. The Daitokuji monastery is always in *zazen*, as a monastery should be, and performs all its activities—sleep, meals, work, *sūtra* services, *sanzen*, and so on—from within *zazen*; it ritually resides within *hajū* or emptiness and from within emptiness emerges into *hōgyō* or form.

The ritual at the ABC Zen Center is the reverse. The center employs the traditional signals for beginning and ending a period of *zazen*. There too the *jikijitsu* leaves the *zendō* at night leaving everyone seated in place. But the introduction of the burning candle rule shows that the ABC Zen Center thinks that *zazen* is an activity with a beginning and an end; this reveals a lay or secular, rather than monastic, understanding of *zazen*. It resides first in the realm of daily activity, *hōgyō* or differentiated form, and from there withdraws into *zazen*, *hajū*, or emptiness.

I once asked the rōshi why there was a burning candle rule. His answer was very instructive. He made a series of remarks to the effect that candles are used a lot in the West, that this is probably the influence of Christianity, that candles are used on dinner tables in the West, and that he has even eaten in restaurants where candles were used. At other times, he spoke of how his monks had created many of the traditions at the Zen Center. For him, the burning candle rule was just another example of this. By contrast, the monks say that the rōshi decides everything and they are merely following his instruction. This, I think, exemplifies a general rule: Americanization occurs under the guise of a sincere belief that one is following Japanese Zen tradition.

Ritual Space

At Daitokuji, monks who have no office (the majority) all live together in the communal *zendō;* only the officers have separate rooms. But at the ABC Zen Center, which inherited rooms and cabins from previous owners of the property, no one sleeps in the *zendō* and everyone sleeps in separate rooms. ABC officers usually share a room, two or three together; lay participants are housed seven or eight to a cabin. Nevertheless, every participant has a bed in a room, which, for the week of training, is thought of as "his own." An individual room creates a division in one's mind between a public sphere and a private sphere, between the place of practice and a place to "be oneself" (an anomaly in a tradition that emphasizes no-self). The same ritual classification concerning space can be applied to time. Sleeping communally in the *zendō* ritually represents *hajū*, residing in non-differentiated emptiness. Individuals sleeping in separate rooms ritually represent *hōgyō*, dividing into differentiated form.

Meal Ritual

Of the many aspects of the meal ritual, perhaps the washing of the bowls reveals best the process of implicit Americanization. Hot water is circulated at the end of the meal. Practitioners all wash their bowls in this water and then chant the *Senpatsu Ge* (Verse of Washing the Bowls), also called the *Sessui Ge* (Verse of the Waste Water):

Ga shi sen passui	The water in which I wash the bowls
Nyo ten kanro mi	Tastes like heavenly nectar.
Seyo kijin shu	I offer it to all ghosts and spirits.
Shitsu ryō toku bō man	May all eat and be satisfied.
On ma ku ra sai sowaka.	*On ma ku ra sai sowaka.*

The wash water consists merely of water and leftover particles of the food just eaten. It is just as pure as the food itself. To think it dirty is to be fixated on distinctions that one projects onto the water. Accordingly in traditional monastery practice, one contributes part of the wash water to the "hungry ghosts" and then drinks the remaining "heavenly nectar" while chanting the verse. But the ABC Zen Center follows worldly custom and stipulates that one is not to drink the wash water but instead throw it out.

Other Zen centers in America follow the Japanese ritual much more closely, preserving the ritual of providing for the hungry ghosts and conscientiously teaching its meaning to its members. Some Zen centers depart from Japanese tradition altogether. At one Zen center, when I inquired about the meal ritual, I discovered that the entire practice of washing the bowls had been discarded and instead all the dishes were collected and washed by automatic dishwasher.

These distinctions are not merely quibbles about the "symbolic meaning" of meal practices and other ritual forms. The point of the meal practice is not to eat the food and get out as quickly as possible. The point is to eat the meal cultivating the *samādhi* of nondiscrimination; after all, the meal is part of *zazen*. The "symbolic meaning" is the point and the eating of the food is the skillful means by which it is embodied. Without awareness of the point of meal ritual practices, ritual quickly degenerates into pro forma regimentation. When this happens, the enforcing of strict discipline is in danger of becoming an end in itself rather than a means to encourage the nondiscriminative *samādhi* of the participants.[5]

Teaching and Learning

There were many kinds of teaching and learning conducted in the Rinzai Zen monasteries I experienced: instruction in *sanzen*, instruction in daily ritual and work, instruction in how to instruct, and so on. Over the years, the Japanese Rinzai monastery has evolved a single style of teaching used both inside the *sanzen* room for instruction in the *kōan* and outside the *sanzen* room for instruction in daily work and ritual. It has also fitted together this style of instruction with social organization, and has developed a single language to talk about both *kōan* practice and the activities of daily life.

Teaching without Teaching

As is well known, the rōshi in *sanzen* does not directly teach the point of a *kōan* to his monk. Instead, a monk must seek and search for himself until he comes to a genuine firsthand insight into the *kōan*. It is not necessary here to present again the image we find in Zen literature of the master whose apparently harsh and arbitrary methods turn out to be skillful means by which he brings the student to awakening. What is not well known, however, is that in everyday work situations, senior monks use the same teaching methods with junior monks. Senior monks usually do not directly teach junior monks how to do daily work and ritual. When a monk newly appointed to office makes a mistake, immediately the older monks will scold and humiliate him but they will not offer instruction. If a new *densu* (the officer who chants the dedication after each *sūtra*) makes a mistake in chanting, one of the older monks will shout in a loud voice, "Mistake!" and the *densu* will have to figure out for himself what he did wrong, and then repeat the chant until he gets it right. When a new cook makes a mistake and the monks do not eat what he has prepared, he literally has to eat all the leftovers. This motivates him to learn as quickly as possible how to calculate quantities precisely and what does and does not please the monks. In all these and other cases, the new monk is required to seek and search on his own until he truly understands the work for himself and devises his own efficient way to get the work done. This method of teaching I have called "teaching without teaching" as opposed to "rational" teaching.[6]

Such a method of teaching seems irrational and inhumane by the standards of teaching and learning that predominate in most schools of Western education. It is widely accepted in Western education that teachers should cultivate powers of critical reasoning among their students, that schools ought to be teaching students to think for themselves. This is done in the belief that the enemies of true education are rote learning, ritual formalism, and mere memorization without understanding the reason why. Thus a great deal of emphasis is placed on understanding the reason why and on intellectual comprehension. In the teaching and learning that is common in a Zen monastery, there is a similar desire to break through mere repetition of forms and to arouse authentic understanding, but there is a quite different conception of what constitutes authentic understanding. Intellectual understanding does not constitute authentic understanding, for beyond the ritual form and beyond intellectual understanding is personal experience and insight. Mere intellectual understanding that is not backed up by personal experience and insight is denigrated as *rikutsu*, "intellectualizing," "theorizing," "playing with words." In this context, intellectual understanding is not the cure for rote repetition but its cause. Without genuine personal experience and insight, a person falls back on the intellectual theory and repeats behavior unsuited to the context.

One should not think that ritual formalism has no positive role to play. In fact, in this conception of teaching and learning, ritual formalism is the quickest way to arouse authentic personal experience and insight. In the practice of the *kōan*, the monk repeats and repeats the *kōan* ceaselessly, discarding all intellectual interpretations that inevitably arise, until finally the *kōan* is no longer merely an object of attention, and the monk comes to experience the world from inside the *kōan*. Here the usual division between self and other, subject and object, breaks down. Similarly in work and ritual outside the *sanzen* room, the monk repeats and repeats the assigned task, discarding all preconceptions of how to do the work, until finally the monk no longer thinks about the work to be done as "the work" but just does the work. In such personal experience and insight, there is a breakdown of the division between self and other, subject and object. In chanting, the voices of all the monks come into my ears and go out my mouth. Chopping wood, there is no wood; carrying water, there is no water. But in intellectual understanding, the subject of understanding constantly conceptualizes its object as the work, the wood, the water. That is why ritual formalism, not intellectual understanding, is the more direct route to experience and insight.

Students of Zen in the West are used to the idea that insight into a *kōan* cannot be attained merely through intellectual reasoning; on this basis, they are willing to accept the seemingly arbitrary teaching methods of a Zen teacher, for these are taken to be skillful means for inducing the direct, nonintellectual experience of Zen insight. But there would be a variety of objections to the suggestion that the same teaching methods ought to be applied to all instruction regarding work and ritual activity outside the *sanzen* room: it is wrong to demean and humiliate another person deliberately in public; it is damaging to the learner's self-esteem and therefore counterproductive; "You are not the rōshi"; and so on.

ABC Zen Center has developed several instruction procedures, depending on the person being taught, all of which are straightforward rational methods of teaching. In the simplest form of instruction, a sheet of paper is posted in a room or work area with numbered instructions: (1) Sweep the floor; (2) straighten the benches and tables; (3) beat the cushions and replace neatly; and so forth. At the other end of the instruction spectrum, when a monk is training to take over an office, he is apprenticed to an older monk who already knows the office. They take turns performing the duties of the office, the older monk showing by example what to do one day, coaching the other day. The idea of applying the rōshi's teaching methods to work and ritual outside the *sanzen* room is not considered even as a possibility.

Mutual Polishing

The style of instruction I call teaching without teaching is imbedded in, and made possible by, a social hierarchy. And it is this social hierarchy, wherein one person presumes to be an authority over another person, that Westerners find difficult to accept. For this reason, some Western critics depict the Rinzai Zen monastery as a place of heartless totalitarian control.[7] Each monk occupies a unique place in the monastic hierarchy. He acknowledges the authority of every monk higher in rank and himself has authority over everyone lower in rank. This system of hierarchy, combined with teaching without teaching, means that each monk is involved constantly in correcting the mistakes of any monk lower in rank, while at the same time receiving the criticisms of any monk higher in rank. The Confucian term *sessa takuma*, "cutting, chipping, filing, polishing" (*Analects* I, 15)[8] describes this group dynamic. The assembly of monks is likened to a pile of rough stones placed in a stone mortar and stirred. The abrasive action of stone on stone chips away at rough corners and eventually smoothes and polishes each stone into a gem. Only then does the individual nature of each gem become apparent. No one stone is more important than the others; the newest novice is just as essential as that of the head monk. A higher-ranking monk is obliged to respect and teach the new novice. Teaching too is learning.

This horizontal "mutual polishing" action of monk against monk could not occur unless the monks were ordered into a vertical hierarchy. As in all social groups, a monk feels hesitant to correct another. The explicit hierarchy, however, allows senior monks to make direct criticism of juniors; it also requires them to shoulder unpleasant responsibility without evasion. The explicit hierarchy requires junior monks to listen to correction while at the same time giving them the right to expect leadership and direction from seniors. Though some monks do get carried away by their inch of authority, the hierarchical structure of the monastery does not exist merely so that senior monks can engage in hazing junior monks; it combines with the action of mutual polishing, which is both lateral and reciprocal. Take, for example, that symbol of Zen severity, the *keisaku*, the stick used to wake sleeping sitters and instill discipline. In the usual custom in America, only two or three officers have the authority to carry the *keisaku*. But in the Daitokuji *sōdō*, every monk in the meditation hall takes a turn carrying the *keisaku*. Hierarchy and discipline do not exclude compassion. When I was a monk I heard the story of how a certain well-known rōshi in the previous generation broke his shoulder when he was a *sōdō* monk. As *jikijitsu* during *sesshin*, his job was to challenge all the beginning monks as they returned from *sanzen*, "Did you pass your *kōan*?" He then wrestled with those who had not passed, forcing them to go to *sanzen* one more time. This wrestling took place on a deck several feet above the garden. In one match, the two monks, locked in wrestling holds, teetered on the edge of the deck. When the *jikijitsu* realized they were falling off, he deliberately twisted his body so that the other monk would fall on top. They landed on his shoulder and broke it. He did his duty as the officer with rank. Compassion, hierarchy, authority, discipline, fellowship: in the Zen monastery, these regularly function in ways surprising to a Western perspective. It is a misreading of culture to liken the Zen monastery to "boot camp" and to think that an officer in a Zen monastery acts simply like an army drill sergeant.

I cannot do more than sketch some of the broader features of teaching and learning in the Rinzai monastery. But even this sketch is enough to show that this style of teaching and learning is complex, has a justification in Zen practice, and works in its own cultural context. To dismiss these practices using simplistic labels like "autocratic" and "authoritarian" prevents any understanding of their function in Zen practice. I believe that if people were not so distracted by the "authoritarian" stereotype, Westerners could learn some lessons applicable to another culture. First, the same style of teaching and learning is used both with the *kōan* and with work and ritual in daily life, thus establishing their connection with each other. The question of how Zen practice applies to daily life is easier to answer if the teaching methods are the same both inside and outside the *sanzen* room. Second, the discipline, the support, and the energy that make a successful *sesshin* do not come exclusively from the leadership above but also come laterally from the anonymous people, the true people without rank, who fill up the benches. Mutual polishing, in the Japanese context, skillfully brings ordinary people into contact to help each other in their practice. *Sesshin* is not isolated retreat.

Language

Teaching and learning inside the *sanzen* room is the same as teaching and learning outside the *sanzen* room. So also is the language that is used. When asked, "How does Zen apply to daily life?" the standard Zen answer we have come to expect is, "Just be one with whatever you are doing. When washing dishes, just wash dishes. When driving your car, just drive your car." This is the *hajū* approach, in which there is no differentiation into host and guest. But responses to the *kōan* in the *sanzen* room divide into *hajū* (non-differentiated emptiness) and *hōgyō* (differentiated form). So also do work and daily activity outside the *sanzen* room. And *hōgyō* provides us with another language in which to talk Zen (scholars here might see a connection to the Buddhist notion of twofold truth, but this is not the place to engage in that discussion).

In *hajū*, the task is to *narikiru*, to "become completely one" with whatever one is doing. If one is grappling with a *kōan*, then *hajū* is Mu itself, is the Sound of One Hand itself. If one is doing work, then *hajū* is just to do the work itself without differentiating host and guest, the self that works and the work to be done. There are many ways of not doing the work. Whenever a junior monk is fumbling, or being artificial, or seeks to flee from a situation, or is being too sincere, an older monk will bring him up short with *Bokeru na* (No daydreaming!) or *Mōzō wo kaku na* (No needless thinking!) or *Kyōgai ga warui* (Your spirit is bad!) or *Shikkari shiro* (Get a hold of yourself!). These are also the rōshi's favorite words in the *sanzen* room.

In *hōgyō*, the task is to come forth from nondifferentiated emptiness into the realm of differentiated form. In the *sanzen* room, *hōgyō* is Mu climbing the mountain and rowing on the river, the Sound of One Hand at dinner and at the point of death. In work, *hōgyō* is the doing of work differentiating subject and object, being aware of efficiency, personality, environmental impact, and so on. Concretely, this means that one engages in calculation, evaluation, discrimination, intellectualization, but all from the point of view of bodhisattva compassion. One discriminates, calculates, differentiates, dualizes not for self-advantage but for the purpose of bringing all beings to Buddhahood. Monks are responsible for helping all of the materials and tools that they touch attain Buddhahood by never wasting them and by always finding another rebirth for them. The water used to boil the noodles is not thrown out but instead used again to cook vegetables; the water used in mopping the floors can afterward be used again to scrub the outside stones. This use of materials should not be mistaken for mere thriftiness. The language of work reflects this. To reuse water is to give it "rebirth" (*sairai*), to help it "be reborn" (*umarekawaru*). If water is thrown away, how can it "attain Buddhahood" (*jōbutsu*)? Not even the smallest thing is to be wasted. Thus the rice storage box of Ryōshōji bears the inscription, "Ichi ryūbei shumisen no gotoshi": A grain of rice is like Mount Sumeru—a nice example of the nonduality of big and small together with the compassion of the bodhisattva for a grain of rice.

The bodhisattva activity embodied in work is reciprocal. At the same time that the monk helps his materials and tools attain their Buddhahood, those same materials and tools are helping the monk attain his Buddhahood. For this, the monk is to show gratitude. A monk's underwear is a rectangle of white cotton attached to a waiststring; it is dropped down the back and passed up the front and over the waiststring. I remember a monk who had patched and washed his underwear until finally it started to disintegrate. He washed it one last time and then placed it in the fire while he chanted a *sūtra*—a small funeral, done in gratitude, for a piece of underwear. There was an old priest who was also a schoolteacher. After he died, relatives discovered a desk drawer full of one-inch pencil stubs. Though the stubs were unusable, he never threw them away because, it was explained, *empitsu ni mōshiwakenai:* To the pencil, he would have no apology. Work conceptualized in this way shows how all sentient beings interrelate by mutually performing bodhisattva activity for each other and gives concrete meaning to the Mahāyāna understanding that all sentient beings are endowed with Buddha-nature.

Retreat Instruction

While teaching without teaching may be tolerated in the *sanzen* room from the rōshi who is acknowledged to have a special position of authority, it will not be tolerated outside the *sanzen* room from other monks. In the vacuum thus created, indigenous American styles of instruction are employed, such as printed instructions, apprenticeships, or the like. Laypeople, who account for the greater proportion at *sesshin*, are at a particular disadvantage. The *sesshin* schedule, though an efficient means of learning for monks in its original Japanese context, is not necessarily an efficient means of learning for laypeople in the American context. During *sesshin*, the laypeople have an intense experience consisting of many continuous hours of *zazen* a day, numerous *sanzen* daily, all in a highly regulated schedule. In the jargon of learning theory, they receive massed practice and frequent, regular reinforcement under invariant conditions. While such intense, invariant practice improves performance on one occasion, retreat-style teaching does not instill long-term retention or the ability to transfer learning to altered conditions. To accomplish that, retreat training should involve a variety of different practices, an intermittent schedule of feedback, and reinforcement under constantly changing conditions. This is, in fact, what is provided by mutual polishing in the Rinzai monastery. For the monk in a Japanese monastery, the intense and highly regulated training of *sesshin* is balanced by the open-ended, informal, less predictable schedule of daily work. But for the layperson attending only intermittent retreats at a Zen center, there is no significant mutual polishing work practice in daily activities to supplement the intense training of the *sanzen* room during *sesshin*. This is somewhat akin to teaching theory in a science course without a lab section, to teaching the theory of swimming without allowing anyone to get into the pool. It is not surprising that people complain they lose the effects of *sesshin* soon after they return home and that they cannot apply Zen to their daily lives. Retreat-style teaching of Buddhism encourages that result.[9]

Full-time residents of a Zen center, of course, get the benefits of being on-site all of the time. Full-time practice means many different things depending on whether the center attempts to run itself like a Japanese monastery, a Christian monastery, a lay center, or a business. Much also depends on how closely the teacher imposes form on daily time, meals, work, relations between people, spending of money, and so on. The important point is that the conduct of daily life can contribute to, or distract from, *kōan* and meditation practice. In her study of religious communes and communities in the United States in the nineteenth century, Rosabeth Moss Kanter tried to identify the factors that distinguished successful communes from those that ultimately failed. One aspect of successful communes was that they conceptualized their everyday activities and social relations as applications of the principles of their central teachings. The failed communes did not do this and allowed their members to conduct their daily lives—their work and play, their social and sexual relations—according to their individual wishes without conceptualizing them as aspects of religious practice.[10] Among other surprising results, Kanter found that religious communities that practiced total abstention from sexual activity and those that practiced "free love," obligating its members to take a variety of sexual partners, were functionally similar; in either case, the community regulated love relations and sexual activity so that they did not compromise the fundamental religious principles of the community.[11] Sitting in *zazen* and working on the job, the *samādhi* of the *kōan* and the *samādhi* of bodhisattva action, Zen for oneself and Zen for others: there needs to be one way of teaching all this and one language to talk about it.

Social Organization

Commenting on social organization is most difficult. In hindsight, it seems clear that in some Zen centers, coherent social organization used to depend significantly on the presence of the charismatic first-generation teacher. When the second-generation teacher took over, the center had to reorganize itself along quite different lines, and in some cases, this reorganization was traumatic. Perhaps eventually someone will peer inside the American Zen center and give us an analysis of its inner workings. Until then, we can only make a few simple comments about the more formal aspects.

Tribe, Family, or Church?

How is the American Zen center to be governed? Is a community based on Buddhist principles inherently democratic? Commentators have implied as much by declaring the early Indian *sangha* "democratic."[12] The early *sangha* did have features that we might loosely call democratic. For example, elders of the *sangha* deliberated major questions and then proposed their answer three times before the entire assembly; if no one disapproved, the proposal passed. This "democracy," however, contained no counterpart to what moderns call "the rights of the minority." Since unanimity was demanded, the only recourse for persons who disagreed with the majority was to form a separate *sangha*. This is why schism is such an important topic for the early *sangha*.[13] It is a mistake, however, to think that Buddhist teachings make necessary any particular form of government. When we are told that society at the time of the Buddha divided people into four castes, we find ourselves wanting to think of the Buddhist *sangha* in terms of a paradigm in which popular democracy struggles to assert itself against an oppressive elite class system. Yet the apparent democracy of the early Indian *sangha* resulted not from putting Buddhist principles into action, but from adopting features of the "tribal council" form of government practiced by the Śākyas, the tribe from which Gautama came.[14] Thus, one should not speak as if the early *sangha* was foreshadowing North American democracy.

The *sangha* in China, as well, reproduced the leading features of an already existing form of social grouping—the extended, hierarchically organized, ancestral family system. In the biographies and stories that comprise the textual basis for Chinese Ch'an, one can see that the head of a temple became the father-priest, his disciples were organized as elder-brother or younger-brother, they all practiced a monastic version of filial piety, the Buddha and patriarchs were ritually revered in ancestor ceremonies, lineages were transmitted, and so on. Again these historical examples show us that the Buddhist *sangha* does not have a particular form of government but adapts a model that the local culture provides.

This principle, that the *sangha* adopts a style of government provided by the local culture, seems to be holding true in North America as well: North American Zen centers seem to be gravitating toward the kind of governing structure found in most Christian churches and Jewish synagogues. Boards in Zen centers have been created in conformity with the law governing the incorporation of religious bodies, and these religious bodies are usually Christian or Jewish in North America. Instead of accepting the authority of a single teacher with overriding powers, increasingly the Zen center is governed by a lay board and a resident Zen teacher, who together share power.

The San Francisco Zen Center now elects its rōshi from a pool of senior students for a four-year term. This experiment, deliberately compounding Zen teaching authority with American-style political authority, looks like a dramatic cultural innovation. But from another point of view, it is merely a variant of the way Christian and Jewish groups in North America have tried to exercise control over their ministers and rabbis. From still another cultural point of view, the San Francisco Zen Center is not the first to elect its chief priest. During the American occupation of Japan after World War II, the law for the incorporation of religious bodies in Japan was revised. Imposing American forms, the new law required that the *kanchō* (chief abbot of a *honzan*, or headquarters) of a line of temples in Japan had to be elected, and in the election, at least two candidates had to stand to ensure fairness of election. Despite the American form, Japanese ideas about seniority, about circulating the office, and so on continue to operate. In one election, which I witnessed, the priest who became *kanchō* was by seniority the logical choice but he hated the job and was forced to stand for election against his will. In another election, which I heard about, the logical candidate for *kanchō* asked his own disciple to stand for election also, so that there would be two candidates and a "fair" election. So, both the San Francisco Zen Center and a Japanese *honzan* elect their chief priest. Are they doing the same thing?

Managerial Zen

The new local conditions of Zen in the West cause American Zen groups to be organized and operated internally in a way not found in the Japanese monastery. In a typical ABC Zen Center *sesshin*, there are two classes of people: a smaller number of ordained monks and a large number of lay practitioners. The ordained monks wear robes, sit at the top end of the *zendō*, share a room with only one or two others, and in general hold all the important offices and give the orders during *sesshin*. They also pay only a token fee to attend *sesshin*. The lay practitioners wear rather plain clothing compared to the robes of the monks, sit in lower positions in the *zendō*, sleep eight or ten to a cabin, and in general are passive participants in running the *sesshin*. They pay several hundred dollars to attend. Although several of the lay practitioners will have jobs like assistant cook or assistant *jikijitsu*, the lay practitioners do not hold offices of important authority. This is a firm distinction: even across long periods of time, so very few people cross the line from lay to ordained (or from ordained back to lay) that when it occurs, it is an occasion of note. In effect, the distinction between ordained and lay divides the people at *sesshin* into two social classes with quite different membership, power, and status. This distinction between monk and layperson looks something like the familiar distinctions between management and worker in an American business corporation, or between hospital staff and patients, or between staff and guest in a hotel, but it does not quite correspond to anything in a Rinzai monastery.

The distinction between monk and layperson is an important distinction in any Asian Buddhist tradition, but the Rinzai Zen monastery does not organize itself into two groups, one monk and one lay. A few laypeople do attend *sesshin* but their numbers are so small that in most monasteries, their presence is barely felt. There is, however, a clear and important distinction between those monks who have office and those who do not have office, although that distinction is not a rigid class distinction dividing monastery membership into two fixed classes with different membership, status, and power, as it is in the American example. First, the officer class is itself divided into two—a very small group of two or three head monks, *yakui*, who are permanent officers and who can be considered an elite, and a larger number of monks who fill their particular office for the half-year term. Some functions of the permanent *yakui* cannot be performed by anyone else, for example, representing the *sōdō* on certain occasions, keeping track of all monies, and setting the calendar schedule. But where possible, the *yakui* delegates authority down the line as part of training. Except for the *yakui*, all other officers trade places with nonofficers every six months so that the officers as a group do not form an elite class. During their tenure in office, monks move into a room, follow a different schedule, and have privileges not shared by nonofficer monks in the communal *zendō*. But once the term is over, the officer monks give up their privileges, return to the communal *zendō*, and let someone else take a turn in office. At any given time, the *muyaku* "no office" assembly of monks contains many monks senior and more experienced than the younger monks then taking their turn in office. If an officer makes a mistake, then those in the *muyaku* who already know that office will immediately shout "Mistake!" and force him to correct it. To be an officer thus does not put a monk in a position of superior authority over the assembly of monks without office. It is often quite the reverse—to be exposed and singled out for their sometimes uncomfortable attention. And although officers are expected to provide active leadership and support, the no-office assembly is not merely the passive recipient of the officers' orders.

Stereotypical labels often come in contrasting pairs. If Asian culture is "autocratic," then America must be democratic. Such labeling prevents us from noticing the action of mutual polishing in Rinzai monastic training, as I have argued, but it also prevents us from seeing the presence of elitist elements of American social organization. Typically distinctions of social class are not called such in American organizations; some other label like "management," or "faculty," or "staff" is used to rationalize the difference in status, power, and privilege. The ABC Zen Center has had many monks who have spent several years in training there and then gone on to head one of the branch centers elsewhere. When they return for *sesshin*, they are given an office even though there is no real work to be done; two monks are appointed to a single office, doubling the number of officer spaces so that these visiting monks can be considered officers, housed with the officers, and considered separate from the lay participants. Although one can justify this custom on the grounds that there is instructional benefit in a senior monk working together with a junior monk, I think the real function is to maintain a distinction of social class.

When the American automobile industry discovered that Japanese manufacturers operated car assembly plants that were more economically efficient and turned out a better product than did American car plants, researchers in business management subjected the Japanese manufacturing plant to intense examination. Many Japanese practices have since been adopted by Western companies, such as just-in-time delivery, which eliminated wasteful warehousing; quality control circles, which combined the roles of worker and quality checker in one person; conceptualizing product manufacture as "value-streaming," and so on. One of the more important lessons learned was that the American-style adversarial relation between management and workers created many problems—such as hostile labor unions, huge grievance backlogs, and just plain disrespect for the other—and that Japanese factories were more efficient and profitable because they involved the plant line workers in the direction and operation of the plant. Driven as much by profit as by cultural pride, American car companies transplanted the Japanese system into the American context. General Motors, through a joint venture with Toyota, transformed its plant in Fremont, California, which had earlier been shut down as inoperable after acquiring a reputation for being "the worst plant in the world."[15] In 1984 Toyota reopened the plant as NUUMI and replaced the old coercive management system, which generated worker contempt, with a worker production team system in which the workers assumed responsibility for the direction and improvement of work on the line. In the revamped plant, the workers worked harder but for the first time felt pride in the product and loyalty to the company; the plant was more bureaucratic but less hierarchical; work procedures were more precisely defined but always under constant improvement by the workers themselves. Management came to think of its role as support staff. This is the industrial version of mutual polishing. An important point in a discussion of cultural perceptions is the fact that the Japanese manufacturing system was itself only a recent development, the Japanese response to the time and work studies of an American, Frederick Winslow Taylor, the original efficiency expert.

There is a lesson here. Distinctions among different groups of people are often class distinctions marking different status, power, and privilege, even though they are rationalized as different abilities or competencies. This is true in all cultures. In the context of American Zen, I am suggesting that the distinction between a privileged group of ordained officers and a not privileged group of laypeople without office, though it looks Asian, is in fact much closer to the status, power, and privilege distinction between American manager and worker. Here again Americanization has been going on in the guise of being faithful to Japanese tradition. Hierarchy in the Japanese monastery merges with mutual polishing, the two together complementing each other in creating a context for Zen practice. But recreating the division between managers and workers, with its institutionalized hostility and disrespect, does not look like a promising strategy for creating a new context for Zen practice.

Zen Master: Person and Office

Zen literature presents us the figure of the Zen master, an enlightened being who resides in awakening where there is no struggling with the strictures of society. Whether he lives alone in the mountains or whether he scratches his big belly in the marketplace, he teaches without intention, is wealthy without money, is free without acquiescing to power. There are several versions of the Zen master. I once met Shunryu Suzuki Rōshi, who immediately struck me as a man of great quietness and humility, the kind of man whose presence calls forth one's respect and perhaps a little shame. But my first *sōdō* rōshi in Japan, Nakamura Sojun, was an intense, fierce, burning furnace of a man, always ready to erupt into a passionate tirade about making constant effort in practice. Some rōshi manage to combine both personalities. Students of Yamada Mumon Rōshi say that outside the *sanzen* room, he looked and acted like a tiny, wispy, immaterial Taoist hermit, but that inside the *sanzen* room, he suddenly turned into a lion. With such examples both in literature and in person, it is hard to believe that Zen master is an office, that one relates to a Zen master not "mind to mind," but through social forms, protocol, and ritual.

I write about the Zen master, of course, because of the several cases of Zen masters in the West who were found to be sexually involved with their students.[16] The string of crises raised the issue of "guru worship"—the fear that both men and women had become so psychologically dependent upon the rōshi that they had lost any sense of independent judgment. This issue is much too complicated to be analyzed here, but since I am dealing with the different cultural incarnations of traditional Buddhist ideas and institutions, I need to comment on how the Zen master is understood in Japan and America.

In Japanese Zen, there is a pronounced rhetoric about the complete intimacy that exists between monk and rōshi. Beyond external words and gestures, the rōshi knows directly the monk's *hara no naka*, the inside of the hara, the seat of heart and mind. In return, the monk is supposed to know his rōshi so well that, to use a typically vulgar Zen expression, he knows the number of hairs around the rōshi's asshole (*ketsu no ana no mawari no ke no kazu*). When I was in the *sōdō*, an older monk once said to me that I could not do proper practice unless I "loved" the rōshi (*rōshi o ai suru*). In enlightenment, one's identification with the entire lineage of masters becomes complete: one sees with the eyes of the Buddhas and ancestors themselves. Here the very distinction between subject and object, self and other, disappears. This colorful language describes an intimacy that seems to be absolute, totally unrestricted, and beyond the influence of any cultural shaping.

The same Zen literature supplies numerous particular examples of masters whose intimacy is quite strange to Westerners. In his "grandmotherly kindness," the master fiercely twists the monk's nose, or cuts off his finger, or slams a door and so breaks the monk's leg. Like the lioness who trains her cubs by pushing them over a cliff, the Zen master's total kindness expresses itself as relentless severity.[17] In return, when the monk finally attains the same enlightenment as the master, he returns the severity of the master, the classic example being master Ōbaku slapping monk Rinzai and Rinzai slapping Ōbaku back. In addition, stories of master-monk relations circulate in the Japanese monastery, which include stories of monks who understood the master's needs without having to ask, or who selflessly cared for the master in his old age. Particularly admired are stories of monks changing the master's diapers when the master's bodily functions started to fail in old age.

These examples of the relations between master and monk show that the concept of intimacy between the two has a particular cultural interpretation. The intimacy presented in these examples is always intimacy between master and monk in the context of Zen practice. In these examples, we see that master and monk always retain their hierarchical status (the story of Rinzai slapping his master is important only because Rinzai is still monk and Ōbaku is still master), and that in general, Zen has absorbed Confucian models of social roles, strict teacher-student relations, and self-sacrificing filial piety. Here it is tempting to think that this is a culturally relative, Asian misinterpretation of Zen which obliterates the absoluteness of intimacy. There is, however, no such thing as an objective or neutral understanding that is untainted with the point of view of any particular culture. In fact, the example of Zen masters in America in sexual relations with their students de facto expresses the way the intimacy of master and monk has been culturally interpreted in America. Despite the antinomian rhetoric, the relationship between master and monk in Japan is so strongly constrained by social conventions in Japan that male teachers do not often get sexually involved with female students. First, monasteries were segregated by sex, so that, in general, only men taught men and only women taught women. That, at least, was the theory. In fact, the monastery system for women has atrophied. The last Rinzai monastery for women closed its doors in the early 1970s; there are still Sōtō monasteries for women. Because there are almost no training halls for women, a woman who wants to do Zen practice with a rōshi must seek out a male rōshi and make an individual arrangement with him. When his monks have *sesshin,* she comes to the temple and sits in a separate room rather than in the *zendō* with the male monks. When they have *sanzen,* she tags along at the end. The rōshi is free to make of this relationship whatever he wishes, but my impression is that there is not much of a problem here simply because the number of women wanting to do *sanzen* is so small (of course, the number is small because the system makes it difficult and unappealing for women to do *sanzen*). So in fact, a male Zen teacher in Japan can have female students, but the numbers are not many.

A second extremely strong distancing factor is the social protocol that structures all interaction between monk and rōshi. Western students of Zen know that on entering and leaving the *sanzen* room, they must make a formal bow. What Western students do not understand is that this ritual formality is actually much more detailed than they realized and also pervades every interaction, formal and informal, between rōshi and monk. As part of the same social protocol, monks in a Japanese monastery also do not look at the face of the rōshi but point their eyes downward. Aside from their proffered response to the *kōan,* they do not actively pose questions and engage in so-called question-and-answer *kōan* dialogue until they have reached a modicum of seniority; they remain passive and do not speak unless spoken to. This formality extends outside the *sanzen* room as well. Monks bow to the floor whenever they enter and leave the rōshi's room even when it is not *sanzen,* keep their eyes pointed downward whenever they are in the rōshi's presence, and never initiate conversation. An American practitioner who had become quite friendly with a Japanese rōshi on the latter's trips to the United States and England was amazed at the way the same rōshi was treated in Japan. In particular, he could not understand the silence of the monks in the presence of the rōshi at what appeared to be a somewhat informal tea in the mornings. For them, even to presume to speak to the rōshi would have been out of place. In addition, Westerners who speak in English to their rōshi do not face the social protocol required in speaking the Japanese language. In Japanese, the choice of every pronoun, the inflection of every verb, and the selection of much vocabulary reflects the social distance (distant-close, above-below, inside-outside) between monk and rōshi.

This social distance, however, is quite compatible with intimacy between master and monk. An attendant monk is supposed to know his rōshi's needs without being told. Before a rōshi reaches for his teacup, some one will fill it. Before he moves toward a door, someone will open it. (Because this ritual protocol is so pervasive, one can make jokes; about a clumsy, incapable person, monks sometimes say, "He can't do anything for himself; he'll have to become a rōshi.") Because there are many stories in the Zen tradition of people who defied social expectation, it is easy to get the impression that in Zen practice one transcends the usual social and moral conventions. It is not so simple. One transcends social conventions by fulfilling them. The quite profound and dynamic intimacy that can develop between rōshi and monk is both a development of Zen "mind to mind" transmission and a complete fulfillment of, not the overcoming of, the social conventions that govern interaction between teacher and student. When Zen gets transplanted to a culture where people believe the teacher-student relation in Zen permits the disregard of social convention and the erasing of social distance, there is no telling what mayhem can occur.

In addition to segregation of sexes and social protocol, Zen monastic practice does not encourage a monk to become dependent on the rōshi as a single authority figure. As I have described, the monastery is a system of mutual polishing where most of the training in work and ritual is done not with the rōshi but with the other monks; all senior monks become one's teacher and all junior monks become one's students. Thus the vertical effect of the rōshi's authority is offset by the lateral effects of mutual polishing. Though one is always learning, one is also always teaching. Though one never forgets one's dependence on others, through teaching others one also forges a sense of competence, of maturity, of independence. All this is done in the eminently public arena with all the other monks. The rōshi contributes to this mutual polishing by delegating decision making as much as possible to his monks, who in turn delegate as much as possible down the line. The rōshi has great authority but does not actually exercise it (scholars might like to see this as an example of Taoist or Asian notions of power, where authority is exercised through its nondisplay). He rarely joins with his own monks in informal activity. Although this secludedness may increase his charisma, he does not become the object of adulation. I myself had been a full-time monk for three years before I ever met the rōshi outside of the *sanzen* room and engaged in a conversation with him. In the years thereafter, I was twice his personal attendant. In many ways, the experience was the most demanding yet fulfilling part of my monastic career, as I had a chance to live day by day with a strong teacher. Yet though I was in constant attendance upon him, we rarely engaged in a conversation that could be called intimate (he once asked some questions about my parents, their age, their health, and so on) and I never had a chance to develop psychological dependence on him.

In America, the relationship between Zen master and student will naturally gravitate toward an indigenous American paradigm. What paradigm? Here is Helen Tworkov's account of the relation of Zen students at the San Francisco Zen Center to Richard Baker Rōshi.

> At Zen Center, *dokusan* became the place where students discussed their marital problems, affairs, unwanted pregnancies, alcoholic parents, abused childhoods, and so on. . . . Baker was told things that people didn't tell each other, contributing to psychological dependencies that he was not trained to handle. He became the sole arbiter of personal decision and what actions did or did not hurt others or the community. Case by case this may have had its merits, but as a strategy for community harmony it became a disaster. In addition to spiritual omniscience and paternalistic jurisdiction, it also invested him with the very potent power of private information. This blocked open communication, making it less accessible by placing Baker on an ever-higher pedestal. The more students invested in him, the more perfect he had to be in their eyes to justify that investment.[18]

The particular causes behind the problem of the Zen master at San Francisco Zen Center may be unique and unduplicated at any other place. But in Tworkov's account, one can see the widely shared assumption that Zen and psychotherapy are in some way similar.[19] The relationship of client to psychotherapist is unusual, for it is supposed to be a formal relationship (service for fee paid) yet one in which the client reveals his or her most private and intimate feelings. The psychotherapist is not one's closest friend but an expert who has training, advanced degrees, authority. Paradoxically such distance and authority encourage rather than discourage intimacy, allowing one to say things that one would not say to one's closest friend. I do not wish to engage here in an attempt to distinguish psychotherapy from Zen. My purpose is just to point out that this assumption is not widely shared in Japan. While Japanese people think that a little Zen practice is admirable and good for building character (so much so that many companies sponsor weekend Zen retreats for their new company employees), psychotherapy is considered an admission of mental illness, a cause for shame. The social stigma attached to psychotherapy discourages people who actually do need psychotherapeutic help from getting it. I recall a Zen scholar in Japan trying to distinguish Zen from psychotherapy by saying that psychotherapy was for those people who were *seishinteki ni nayande iru,* or mentally troubled, while Zen was for those people who were *ningenteki ni nayande iru,* or humanly troubled. Whether this distinction is tenable is not the point. And this is not to deny that psychological dependence on a spiritual authority does take place in Japan—the recent example of the Aum Shinri Kyō clearly shows that it does. The point is that in Japan the relation of Zen master and student is imbedded in a system of social constraints and compensating checks so that developing dependency is very difficult. In such a context, the Zen rhetoric of being of one mind with the master balances the distancing effect of those social constraints. But in America, the relation of Zen master to student comes with no accompanying system of social constraints and is assumed to be similar to the relationship of psychotherapist and client, with all the accompanying dangers of dependence, transference, and projection. Here both rōshi and student are on new ground where both are tempted to exploit the situation to push formalized intimacy to greater extremes.[20]

Meditation and Enlightenment
No Dependence on Words or Letters

Perhaps the majority of practitioners in America believe that Zen practice is meditation and that meditation leads to *satori* or *kenshō,* an ecstatic state of consciousness in which the discriminations of conventional life are obliterated. This state of experience, it is thought, is obtained only by breaking through the accumulated habits, concepts, ideas, and social conditioning which prevent us from seeing the world as it is. Once one experiences *satori* or *kenshō,* one is no longer bothered by the decisions, anxieties, and suffering of life. Instead one will know spontaneously, naturally, "without thinking" what to do: "Sitting quietly, doing nothing, spring comes; grass grows by itself."[21]

In accordance with this vision, Zen practitioners believe that the Zen experience has nothing to do with intellectual study and thought, and they repeat as their justification the Zen slogan "No dependence on words or letters, a separate transmission outside of scripture."[22] Despite this rhetoric, *kōan* training in Japan assumes that the practitioner will eventually be able to devote a great deal of time to literary study, memorizing long passages of text, writing Chinese-style commentary on *kōan*, composing Chinese verses and then writing them in brush. *Kōan* training, in fact, presupposed the culture of the Confucian literati (and this is an example of the influence of Confucianism on the formation of Zen).

Some may urge that the literary and intellectual aspects of *kōan* study be simply dropped; after all, Zen is meditation and enlightenment itself, nothing more. Maybe so. But a full understanding of Zen requires that one knows the Zen within history, language, and culture. More practically speaking, without that literary and intellectual understanding, one is crippled as a teacher no matter how clear and open one's eye of enlightenment. The two Zen phrases *yako zen* and *zen temma* display the interdependence of "beyond words and letters" with "words and letters." One who speaks of Zen with only the secondhand knowledge derived from books and no genuine insight of one's own is said to practice *yako zen*, or "wild fox Zen." One who insists on the personal experience of Zen but has not done the study required to express that personal experience in words and understanding is a Zen *temma*, or "Zen devil." The literary aspect of *kōan* training begins rather early with *jakugo*, "capping phrases."[23] A rōshi investigates the student's first insight into any *kōan* by posing a series of subsidiary questions, called *sassho*, "checking questions." The checking questions for the *kōan* *Mu*, for example, contain two *jakugo* assignments. In *jakugo* practice, the student is required to present a verse that expresses the point of the *kōan* just passed. Several thousand capping phrases have been collected together into a book called the *Zenrin Kushū* (Zen Phrase Collection); monks are required to select their *jakugo* from within that collection.[24] Constantly searching through this verse collection, monks automatically memorize quite large portions of it. Since the verses are drawn from the entire range of Chinese literature and history, monks receive an introduction to the history, literature, and philosophy of China.

Somewhere around the mid-point of a full-time monk's career, he will start to receive assignments: *kakiwake*, or "written explanation," and *nenrō*, which I translate as "deft play." The *kakiwake* is similar to the rōshi's *teishō*, or lecture. It is composed in Japanese and then written in brush. The monk submits his *kakiwake* to the rōshi, who proceeds to grade it with a red pen. Once a *kakiwake* assignment has been completed, the monk advances to *nenrō*, "deft play." The *nenrō* is written not in Japanese but in Chinese, not in prose but in four-line verse of five or seven characters per line. Master Mumon's verse appended to each of the *kōan* in the *Mumonkan* is the model. Together these two sets of written assignments consume all the part of a monk's career, a period of easily more than five years, in which he is engaged in hours of literary study every day.

No one has studied the various *kōan* curricula offered in the different American Zen centers. One center bases its entire curriculum around the *Hekigan-roku* and the *Mumonkan,* which are studied twice. Other places apparently offer the more traditional curriculum right up to the Five Ranks and Ten Precepts. Some centers use "Western" *kōan* specially created for Westerners. So far as I know, however, none of these American curricula includes the traditional monastic literary and intellectual study of the *kōan.*

Satori: *Breaking Out or Breaking In?*

American Zen centers have vigorously created new institutions and practices unlike any seen in Japan—residential communities, farms, businesses, neighborhood foundations, hospices, and so on. But there is disagreement on whether the new Zen organizations distract from Zen practice or are a new form of Zen practice. There is no agreed upon rationale for Buddhist businesses. Bernard Tetsugen Glassman Rōshi at the Zen Center of New York, for example, has created a city center which runs the Greyston Bakery, a full-time business supplying premium quality baked goods to hotels and restaurants in the New York area. The bakery takes homeless people off the streets and trains them to work in the bakery. In addition, the revenue generated by the business is used to purchase and renovate local buildings for low-cost housing. Glassman Rōshi is insistent that such intensive work is Buddhist practice, but many of his people say that the business is, or should be, only a supplement to support Zen practice. Doing business and social work through baking may, or may not be, a Buddhist practice. What makes the difference?

Cooking by itself is not a Zen practice, but cooking in a monastery is, because there one finds a culture of practice in which *sanzen* teaching methods extend into daily life, work itself is seen as bodhisattva activity, and the members in the community all engage in mutual polishing. Under those conditions, the work of cooking helps dissolve our preconceived notions of self and other. In the acts of boiling, slicing, frying, pickling, shining, fermenting, and washing this food and handling these utensils, I help this food and these utensils attain their Buddhahood, and in turn, they help me attain mine. Baking cakes in New York City could be the same.

I believe, however, that North American Zen has not yet reconceptualized social relations, authority in a group, daily work, literary study, and business as Zen practices partly because these activities do not conform to a fixed image of Zen. All of these activities are thought to be irrelevant to, even a hindrance to, the attainment of that ecstatic state called *satori* or *kenshō.* In *satori,* we transcend the ordinary consciousness which categorizes the experienced world into dichotomies; in *kenshō,* we break through the shell of conditioned responses which prevents us from being natural and spontaneous. Although there is a point to talking in this way, this description of *satori* or *kenshō* is fundamentally false.[25] It dichotomizes human experience into two quite opposite states: *satori* or *kenshō* on one side, and ignorance-filled, attachment-ridden ordinary experience on the other. As do all such false dichotomies, this conception reifies *satori* or *kenshō* into a golden idol, a state supposedly devoid of attachment but itself the object of attachment, a state supposedly empty of intellectual activity but itself the object of furious intellectualizing. For beginners, there is some excuse for speaking of *satori* or *kenshō* provisionally in this way, but there can be no genuine Zen practice unless one realizes (makes real) the nonduality of *satori* and ignorance, of *kenshō* and attachment. Form is emptiness and emptiness is form. This means that emptiness never appears as emptiness; it always appears as form. When practitioners assume that *satori* or *kenshō* is only a state of ecstatic consciousness beyond the discriminatory, socially conditioned consciousness of everyday life, they are demanding that emptiness appear as emptiness, dualistically differentiated from form. If *satori* is anything, it is the return from nondiscriminative emptiness back into the conventional world of discrimination, anxiety, and suffering. I remember the title of a recent book in Japanese, *Anshin shite nayamu,* or To worry with peace of mind. That is *satori.*

Bonnō soku bodai: "The delusive passions are at once enlightenment." Engineers are constantly designing tools and utensils to reduce friction between moving parts, and in human relations, we are always seeking to reduce social friction between people. Yet it is a mistake to think that all friction can or ought to be eliminated. Wheels would not turn if there were not friction between tire and road surface. Pens would not write if there were not friction between ballpoint and paper. Planes would not fly without the lift that air resistance creates across the wings. At one and the same time, friction between objects hinders movement and makes it possible. Our individual delusive passions—wants, expectations, self-conceptions, needs, presumptions about right and wrong—create the anxiety and suffering of daily life, but they also create the possibility for living in love and civility, with freedom and peace of mind. Mature Zen is about living freely in this world, finally identified with one's ego, utilizing one's karmic endowments, for the sake of sentient beings. Transcending the mundane world is merely the beginner's goal in Zen.

If one gets fixated on the idea of *satori* as ecstatic consciousness, one will not try to understand community life, love and sexual relations, techniques of teaching and learning, authority in group life, daily work, literary study, and business as fields for Buddhist practice. Instead of grappling with these issues, one will dream of "just being one with the moment" and expect that such problems will spontaneously resolve themselves.

Conclusion

The transplantation of Buddhism to the West cannot be rightly understood by standard metaphors, such as "old wine in new bottles." This image presupposes that the wine stays the same and is unaffected by the bottle. But Zen in America, like Valentine's Day in Japan, is significantly changed by its new environment. Neither does it help to speak of viewing Buddhism through the lens of American culture. This image has the advantage of implying that viewing can be distortion, but it also seems to imply the possibility of undistorted viewing, that we could remove the lens and see Buddhism as it is in itself, free from any cultural point of view.

The call for an Americanization of Buddhism is unnecessary. Every attempt by Americans to comprehend Zen intellectually and to implement it in practice has already contributed to its Americanization. What Americans have been practicing for the last several decades is already Americanized Zen. Pouring wine into a new bottle immediately made it a different wine, although it is an ongoing process. In the long slow process of acculturation, the host culture and the guest religion change each other. The wine changes the bottle into which it is poured; the object changes the lens through which it is viewed. Valentine's Day changes Japanese culture to some extent, just as Japanese culture changes it. So also Buddhism in America influences American culture, just as American culture reshapes Buddhism.

In this process, everything wears different labels. It is said to be Zen but beneath the labels are often American ideas of ritual time, teaching and learning, social organization, enlightenment. Everywhere we need to see that Americanization proceeds under the guise of preserving Buddhist tradition. Hindsight allows us to see some of the errors of the past but there is no accurate predicting of the future. What history does show us is that as Buddhism entered a new culture, in the initial phase, it was interpreted according to familiar ideas provided by the local indigenous culture and that these very same ideas prevented people from understanding just what it is that is unfamiliar about Buddhism. That is the danger in this strident call for Americanization of Zen. In casting out un-American elements, we are in danger of throwing out the "Buddha with the bathwater."[26]

D. T. Suzuki once described the difficulties he encountered translating the *gan* of *hongan*, the Japanese for the Sanskrit *pūrvapraṇidhāna*, an important term in Pure Land Buddhism. *Hon* means "original" or "fundamental" but the two candidates for *gan*, "prayer" and "vow," both imply an activity of the self and are thus not quite accurate. "Prayer" is also so heavily imbued with Christian thought that it would take hundreds of years, said Suzuki, for it to become properly Buddhist. Suzuki also commented that the Chinese too had trouble translating this term and that it was only after a thousand years that the term in Chinese finally became imbued with the meaning it was originally intended to convey.[27] Since Shaku Sōen came to America with Zen, it has been only a hundred years.

Nichiren Shōshū and Soka Gakkai in America: The Pioneer Spirit

JANE HURST

Nichiren Daishōnin's Buddhism was represented at the 1893 World Parliament of Religions held in conjunction with the Columbian Exposition (Chicago World's Fair). A Nichiren priest, Yoshigirai Kawai, was part of a delegation of Japanese Buddhists that came to the parliament. He gave a paper to the assembly and explained "that even ignorant men and women, who cannot read and write, can surely attain the state of the Buddhas, if they sincerely repeat 'Namu-myo-ho-ren-ge-kyo.' "[1] He did not proselytize or seem to have much impact on the delegates, probably in part because he spoke only Japanese. At that time, Buddhism was an exotic religion to most Americans and was practiced almost exclusively by Americans who had emigrated from Buddhist countries.

One hundred years later, the centennial of the World Parliament of Religions was held, again in Chicago. Three delegates of Soka Gakkai International-USA, the largest layperson's organization of Nichiren Buddhists in America, were in attendance. They represented 50,000 to 150,000 American members, largely European American and African American. SGI-USA supports nearly seventy community centers throughout the United States, a weekly newspaper, and the Boston Research Center for the 21st Century located near Harvard University as "a base from which SGI can contribute to the cause of international peace."[2] In February 1996, the Florida Nature and Culture Center opened as a 125-acre retreat center and nature preserve.

Another Nichiren sect, Nichiren Shōshū, has six temples across the United States staffed by Japanese priests with dedicated layperson's groups, called Hokkeko, at each temple. The sect has attracted both Asian and non-Asian members alike since it split from SGI-USA in 1991. A third Nichiren sect, Nichiren Shū, has been thriving among Asian Americans for decades in the western states as the Nichiren Buddhist Church of America. The Buddhism of Nichiren Daishōnin has become firmly established on American soil.

The success of Nichiren Buddhism as an American religion spreading to non-Asians can be traced to three factors. First, Nichiren Buddhism has a strong practice centered on the *Lotus Sūtra* at its core. This practice, with its emphasis on the individual's power to change his or her life for the better, resonates with the ethos of American culture and so is easily accessible to American practitioners. Second, Nichiren Daishōnin's Buddhism was spread in the United States starting in 1960 by an energetic, proselytizing layperson's group Soka Gakkai, later called Soka Gakkai International (SGI). Thus it is also a dynamic social movement. Third, the Buddhism founded in Nichiren's name has always carried the characteristics of its founder: stubborn insistence that its understanding is True Buddhism and that other Buddhist interpretations are wrong, a confrontational response to criticism, and a proud outsider status that attracts the disaffected. We will see how these characteristics are alive and well in the twentieth century and how they have allowed the movement to take hold and prosper in America.

Before discussing these aspects of Nichiren Buddhism in America I would like to make note of the method used in researching this form of Buddhism and the groups that promote it. Because Nichiren Shōshū was part of the influx of Asian religions that had such success in gaining members in the 1960s, it became controversial as well as widespread during that time. To maintain scholarly neutrality, while also trying to understand the experience of members, research was carried out using the sociological tool of *participant observation*. In participant observation, the researcher does not join the group studied, but participates in the same activities members do. The researcher is thus gathering information as both an outsider and an insider.

Although I never became a practicing Nichiren Shōshū Buddhist, I attended weekly Soka Gakkai meetings for nearly three years, the 1976 NSA Bicentennial Convention in New York City, and occasional meetings in the years since. At meetings I engaged in the central practice of chanting *Nam-myōhō-renge-kyō*, though I did not do so as a believer. I never formally joined the group by participating in the initiation ceremony, but I came to be considered "almost a member" in spite of my omnipresent notebook and tape recorder. I have had many conversations with Nichiren Shōshū Temple practitioners, and with members and leaders of SGI-USA. There are aspects of Nichiren Buddhist practice that resonate strongly with me. At the same time, it is not my own spiritual path. Through this process of doing research, I have learned a great deal about honoring ways that are not my own. This is a continual challenge, both personally and professionally, but one that has been a great teacher.

Nichiren Daishōnin's Buddhism

In the interests of scholarly neutrality, the following historical account of Nichiren Daishōnin's Buddhism is told from a believer's point of view. It is not presented as fact but as myth, as the founding story that has inspired believers through the centuries. The lack of contemporary sources on Nichiren outside of his own writings makes it impossible to verify the version of his life presented by his followers in their interpretation of his writings. In this, Nichiren's Buddhism has parallels with Christianity: the historical sources all come from the faithful, outside verifying sources do not exist, and the interpretation of the meaning of the story carries the weight of centuries of believers.

Out of respect for these believers and their tradition, and in the interest of communicating to the reader something of how Nichiren Buddhists experience their religious life, the following historical section is told as if it were true. This does not mean it is objectively so or verifiable, any more than gospel stories about Jesus can be proved true. It does mean that Nichiren Buddhists experience this story as true, and that this makes a difference in how they practice Buddhism.

Another issue concerning Nichiren Buddhism that has been raised by some scholars is whether or not Nichiren's True Buddhism is in fact Buddhism at all. Though it does focus on the *Lotus Sūtra*, one of Buddhism's central texts, missing from its teachings are the story of the Buddha's enlightenment, the Four Noble Truths, the Eightfold Path, and any sort of complex meditative teachings. Nichiren Shōshū, with its focus on the practical efficacy of chanting, is purposely anti-intellectual. It intends to move the practitioner away from mind concerns into the heart of the *Lotus Sūtra* itself. Nichiren Shōshū's attitude and method for doing this are very different from many of the forms of Buddhism found in America today, as comparison with other chapters in this volume will show. The point I want to make is that Nichiren Shōshū's focus on the practical efficacy of ritual has much in common with Buddhism as it is practiced by laypeople throughout Asia. One of my students, born and raised in Canton, China, referred to Buddhism as "that thing my mother does when she makes offerings and prays to the statue of Quan Yin." Raised a Buddhist, she had never been taught meditation. In this context, Nichiren Shōshū looks less like an anomaly except in the highly intellectual American Buddhist milieu.

Nichiren Daishōnin (1222–82) is a unique figure in Buddhist history. This Japanese son of a fisherman became a Buddhist priest of the Tendai school and later a Buddhist prophet who taught his disciples his own understanding of the core of Buddhist truth. His early poverty, in contrast to the princely status of Śākyamuni Buddha, is important to his followers, for Nichiren's Buddhism was to be a "religion of the people" and not of the elite classes.[3] As a student of Buddhism, Nichiren, then known by his priesthood name Zenshobo Rencho, sought a single truth within the multiplicity of Buddhist teachings.

By 1253 at the age of thirty-two, he had discovered it. On April 28, after seven days of seclusion, he climbed a hill overlooking the Pacific Ocean and faced east: "He stood motionless looking toward the East, and as the golden disc of the sun began to break through the haze over the vast expanse of waters, a loud voice, a resounding cry, broke from his lips. It was 'Namu Myōhō-renge-kyō.' "[4] The highest sūtra, the one sūtra that could surpass all other Buddhist teachings, was the Lotus Sūtra, and in its title, Myōhō-renge-kyō, was the essence of that sūtra. As a sign of his new awareness, he adopted the name Nichiren (Sun-Lotus). Nichiren immediately began proselytizing the supremacy of the Truth he had discovered and denounced all other forms of Buddhism as traitorous and leading to the inferno of continuous punishment.[5]

Nichiren Daishōnin's way of teaching set the tone for those who would later take up the mantle of True Buddhism. He alienated other Buddhists by insisting that he had found the Truth and that all other Buddhists, and by inference practitioners of other religions, were wrong. He was intolerant of religious differences because to him compassion would dictate teaching only the highest Truth, the Lotus Sūtra. Nichiren remonstrated the government several times, warning that their current ways would lead to Japan's downfall and that only chanting the Lotus Sūtra would save them.

These attitudes and activities earned him few friends, a death sentence, and periods of exile to Izu Peninsula and Sado Island. Through the years, Nichiren did attract a number of disciples, and fortunately for history communicated with them through writing letters. Nichiren was a calligrapher and inscribed several beautiful mandalas, including the Dai-Gohonzon, a mandala including passages from the Lotus Sūtra. In addition, he left us several major teachings, mostly in the form of scholarly treatises on Buddhism and letters to the faithful, totaling several hundred writings in all, many in his own hand. The Nichiren Shōshū priesthood has identified what it considers the five most important of these teachings for understanding Nichiren Buddhism.

This chart clearly outlines Nichiren's major teachings.[6] In the Kaimoku Shō Nichiren identifies himself as the True Buddha of the age of Mappō, the third and final stage of Buddhism during which Śākyamuni Buddha's transient teachings have fallen away and the True teachings are now available. There are Three Great Secret Laws (sandai hiho) which pertain to the

The Five Major Writings of Nichiren Daishōnin

DATE	WRITING	THESIS
July 16, 1260	*Risshō Ankoku Ron—On Securing the Peace of the Land through True Buddhism*	*stated that practice of a true life-philosophy is the basis for securing happiness and attaining world peace*
February 1272	*Kaimoku Shō—The Opening of the Eyes*	*identified* Honzon *in terms of person—Nichiren Daishōnin, the True Buddha*
April 25, 1273	*Kanjin-no Honzon Shō—On the Supreme Object of Worship*	*declared the establishment of the true object of worship, the Gohonzon, in terms of law*
June 10, 1275	*Senji Shō—The Selection of the Time*	*designated the time for the proper teaching,* Nam-myōhō-renge-kyō, *to be propagated in the time of* Mappō
July 21, 1276	*Hō-on Shō—Requital for the Buddha's Favor*	*stressed the importance of appreciation; clarified the Three Great Secret Laws* (sandai hiho)

age of *Mappō*. One is the true object of worship, the Dai-Gohonzon, the *Hommon-no-Honzon*. The second is the *Hommon-no-Kaidan*, the high sanctuary of True Buddhism, to be built in the age of *Mappō*. The third is the *Hommon-no-Daimoku*, the true invocation, *Nam-myōhō-renge-kyō*.

Nam-myōhō-renge-kyō is translated by English-speaking Nichiren Buddhist practitioners as "devotion to the Mystic Law of the *Lotus Sūtra*."[7] This is the phrase repeated as part of the Nichiren Buddhist chanting ritual and is called *daimoku*, or title, being the title of the *Lotus Sūtra*. To the lay members of Soka Gakkai themselves, the phrase has a further explanation. *Nam* represents dedication of one's whole life to the law of the universe, or *Myōhō-renge-kyō*. *Myōhō* is the mystic law of the universe, the underlying principle of duality which is the basis of human life. *Renge* is the lotus flower, which can be understood as a metaphor for the simultaneity of cause and effect (karma) and the pure flower which blooms in a swamp. *Kyō* is the sound or vibration one creates in chanting which attunes the individual to the law of the universe.[8]

The practice of Buddhism as taught by Nichiren Daishōnin includes three aspects: faith, practice, and study. "Faith means to believe in the Gohonzon of the Three Great Secret Laws. Practice means to teach and let others chant the *daimoku* of *Nam-myōhō-renge-kyō* as well as to practice for oneself. Study means to study and understand the Buddhist teachings. Among these three, faith is the most fundamental for the attainment of

Buddhahood. Faith gives rise to practice and study, and practice and study serve to deepen one's faith."⁹ The Nichiren Buddhist practitioner is thus expected to chant to a personally enshrined copy of the Gohonzon every day. The liturgy includes chanting the second chapter (*Hoben*) of the *Lotus Sūtra*, which teaches that Buddha-nature is an inherent potential in all, and the sixteenth chapter (*Juryō*), which teaches that this Buddhahood is not obtained from some outside or divine source, but has existed eternally within the life of each human being, as well as silent prayers of appreciation for these teachings, and *daimoku*.¹⁰

The Nichiren Buddhist practitioner is also expected to work for *kōsen-rufu*, world peace attained through one's personal practice of chanting to the Gohonzon and through one's practice for others by converting them to Nichiren's Buddhism. This should be done through *shakubuku*, literally translated as "break and subdue," a way of assertively converting others to the practice of True Buddhism. Nichiren Daishōnin fully expected that his teachings would spread throughout Japan. Later, his followers would interpret this as the authorization for a worldwide mission to bring others into the era of *kōsen-rufu*.

The year after his death, Nichiren's followers, who added the honorific *Daishōnin* (great sage) to his name, met at Mount Minobu to bring his writings together and decide on what to do next. It seems that an organization was formed, but that within a short time it broke into various schisms. Who had the authority to carry on the Daishōnin's teachings? To make copies of the Dai-Gohonzon? To function as a Nichiren priest? Nikkō Shōnin, an early disciple, left Mount Minobu to found a temple at Mount Fuji, where the Dai-Gohonzon was eventually enshrined. This group later became Nichiren Shōshū, the orthodox sect of Nichiren. Other Nichiren sects also formed, thirty-six of which still exist, each centered around a temple or group of temples.¹¹ Each of these temples had a group of lay members called a *ko*. In medieval times these were called *Hokke-kyō*, after the *Lotus Sūtra (Hokke-kyō)*.¹²

Nichiren's Buddhism as a Social Movement
The Formation of Soka Gakkai

Through the centuries groups of lay members have organized around Nichiren Buddhist temples. These have been mostly small, local groups dedicated to personal practice and support of the priesthood. Soka Gakkai members tell the following story of their founding, which like the story of Nichiren Daishōnin has the status of myth within the group. Tsunesaburo Makiguchi (1871–1944) converted to Nichiren Shōshū Buddhism in 1928 and changed the earlier pattern of practicing Nichiren's Buddhism in the temple setting. Makiguchi, filled with the passion of Nichiren Daishōnin himself, wanted to reform society based on Buddhist principles. In 1930 he founded the Sōka Kyoiku Gakkai (Value Creation Education Society), which was dedicated to this approach. His disciple Josei Toda (1900–1958) became a leader in the group shortly after that. The organization was decimated in 1943 when "Makiguchi, Toda, and other leaders . . . were arrested and imprisoned as 'thought criminals' " for refusing to cooperate with the militaristic government and refusing to take part in state Shinto religious worship.[13]

Makiguchi died in prison, but after the war the renamed Soka Gakkai was reconstituted by Josei Toda, the second president. He began an intense effort to spread Nichiren Daishōnin's teachings to a lay population through *shakubuku*. These seeds fell on fertile ground. In postwar Japan, the old meaning systems that offered an orderly way of life had collapsed. The American occupation, the writing of a new constitution, the new status of the emperor as not divine but merely human, and the vast economic and technological changes of this time left the Japanese people in need of a center for their lives. Many millions found this center in Nichiren Shōshū Buddhism through the recruitment efforts of Soka Gakkai.

After President Toda died, Daisaku Ikeda (1928–   ) took his place as third president of Soka Gakkai. Like President Toda, President Ikeda set goals for the number of members he wanted to add to the Soka Gakkai through *shakubuku*. He understood Nichiren Daishōnin's teachings to apply not only to the conversion of Japan but to the conversion of the world. One of the first places he visited in 1960, a few months after his inauguration, was the United States. He was the first Soka Gakkai president to do so, and it marked an expansion of the organization's mission of *kōsen-rufu*. He visited San Francisco and went to Coit Tower, where, standing near a statue of Christopher Columbus, he said: "We have now made the first footprint on this continent as did Christopher Columbus. Yet we face even a greater task than he in driving home the wedge on this tour. Twenty or fifty years from now, this day will be marked as one of great importance."[14] Soka Gakkai began seriously to recruit American members.

In the early years Soka Gakkai was spread through discussion meetings held by the Japanese-born wives of servicemen returning from the Korean War. These were the Pioneer Women of Soka Gakkai in the United States. Under their guidance as early Soka Gakkai leaders, Nichiren's Buddhism became the first successful postwar Japanese import. The first English-language meeting was held in 1963, and by 1965, 2,300 members attended the Second General Meeting. By 1968 there was an American General Chapter of Soka Gakkai under the leadership of Korean-born General Director George M. Williams, who had changed his name from Masayasu Sadanaga as a sign of his Americanization.

Here Soka Gakkai was for many years known as Nichiren Shōshū of America, or NSA. NSA grew slowly through the 1960s, relying on techniques of street *shakubuku* and discussion meetings to recruit new members. A district meeting would be planned in a member's home. The district members would then take to the streets to invite people to "a Buddhist meeting." When enough people had been found, the meeting was held complete with songs, chanting *Nam-myōhō-renge-kyō*, an introduction to Nichiren Shōshū Buddhism, and several members' experiences with chanting. In the early years, these meetings were often planned by Japanese women with limited English skills.

In major cities such as Los Angeles, New York, Philadelphia, Boston, and Chicago, chapter houses were rented in a central location and members both lived in them and held NSA meetings there. Leaders were appointed, not elected, and were under the guidance of the central authority of General Director Williams, and after him President Ikeda. The organization was set up from the top down through several layers of leaders to the members. Since the local leaders were themselves community members, this hierarchy was not generally experienced as oppressive by the members, but rather as the appropriate recognition of the leadership qualities of one of their own. In keeping with Japanese custom, members were also divided into the Men's Division, Women's Division, Young Men's Division, and Young Women's Division. Though the first members were Japanese American married women and young, white sixties people seeking religious experience, the group soon expanded to blacks and Hispanics as well.

Because of its social tolerance with "no moral rules" but rather guidance that each person develop his or her relationship with the Gohonzon as a primary standard, NSA was attractive to some participants in the counterculture. Cigarette smoking was common in district and chapter meetings; there were no "rules" against it. NSA also attracted many gay and lesbian members in the early 1970s, and was the first religious group this author knows of to accept without question people who openly participated in such alternate lifestyles. (SGI-USA in 1995 decided to celebrate same-sex "Partnership Ceremonies" when members request them.) NSA attracted refugees from religions with strict moral teachings, especially Roman Catholicism and Judaism, for the same perceived liberal attitude.

NSA developed its own ethos as a religious movement. Its various elements are grouped around the themes of individual power, change, and the mission for world peace. These themes have yielded a group of affective qualities that characterize NSA's ethos. It is confident, positive, and free of anxiety. It is optimistic, hopeful, goal-oriented, extroverted, and energetic. It places the responsibility for each person's life on his or her own shoulders and does not need bad luck or scapegoats to account for reversals of fortune. It is individualistic and conformist at the same time. NSA's ethos is patriotic. These are the qualities that compose the NSA ethos, and these are the qualities early NSA members wanted to experience in their lives.[15]

The enthusiasm of these early days of NSA's success, later known as Phase I, was contagious. Meeting rooms would be packed with members and potential members. NSA members gave their all in their dedication to the *Lotus Sūtra* and Soka Gakkai. They were not expected to devote themselves full time to the group. Even leaders had jobs and were supposed to keep up with their family commitments. But NSA became the center of many people's lives, making other commitments of time and emotion seem pale by comparison. To be called a "strong member" was a high compliment in NSA.

The intensity of *shakubuku* was off-putting to family and friends, and often not very well-regulated. Potential members would attend a discussion meeting during the week and by the weekend would be taking part in a *Gojukai* ceremony led by priests from Japan to receive a copy of the Gohonzon. The time commitment required, an hour of chanting daily plus evening activities, proved arduous to some converts. The organization was structured on a hierarchical Japanese model and had some features that were not attractive to American members. As a result, NSA had a difficult time keeping members involved. From a reported high of 500,000 members in 1976, there are probably 300,000 members in 1997.

The high point of the NSA year was the National Convention, held in a different city each year. In 1976 the NSA Bicentennial Convention (Thirteenth General Meeting) was held in New York City. All NSA materials for the convention featured the official bicentennial logo. To participate in the national bicentennial celebration, NSA members staged an illuminated night-time parade entitled "Toward the Dawn of World Peace." During the break between the two baseball games at Shea Stadium on July 4, NSA members put on a "Spirit of '76" show, tracing America's glorious history in song and dance. This show covered the expected patriotic themes with two exceptions. First, although the Revolutionary War, the Civil War, and World War I were highlighted, America's participation in World War II was completely omitted. Second, when George Washington was shown at Valley Forge, discouraged and on his knees in prayer, he held his body in the active lotus position, the posture NSA members take to do their daily chanting ritual. NSA members on July 4, 1976, could feel like proud Americans and dedicated Buddhists at the same time.

The Bicentennial Convention concluded with a gathering of 10,000 NSA members in colonial costumes at Louis Armstrong Stadium, Flushing Meadows. The stadium was decorated with scenes from American history, including Paul Revere's ride and Washington crossing the Delaware. Members did not chant together, since the group does not do its sacred ritual in a public setting. But they did sing NSA songs, shout "A-A-O" (Hip, Hip,

Hooray!), and enjoy a culture presentation complete with hula dancers and a simulated volcano. This convention epitomized the spirit of NSA in Phase I.

During Phase I, American Nichiren Buddhists paid little attention to behind-the-scenes power struggles in Japan. In 1979, some organizational changes were made. This was in part due to conflicts between Soka Gakkai and the Nichiren Shōshū priesthood, and in part due to internal Soka Gakkai politics, which have been only vaguely discussed in public. President Ikeda was made Honorary President of Soka Gakkai and was moved to the full-time presidency of Soka Gakkai International, which he had founded in 1975. His picture was removed from meeting rooms, though it reappeared the next year. Hiroshi Hojo became the fourth Soka Gakkai president and served until 1981, when Einosuke Akiya, the fifth and current president, was chosen.

More important to members was the Jonestown mass suicide/murder in late 1978. It seemed that Soka Gakkai, still called NSA in America, became frightened of its own power, at least as regular members saw it. During this time, Phase II of the Soka Gakkai movement was begun. Nightly activities were scaled back. Big national conventions became regional meetings. Street *shakubuku* was discontinued. In America, and probably in other countries outside Japan, the movement began to lose members in increasing numbers.

By the mid-1980s, an attempt was made to revive the energy and enthusiasm of Phase I. Then this effort, too, was abandoned, and a more person-to-person approach was tried. Recruitment would now take place within one's existing social networks. This did enable the membership to stabilize, but with a different mix from before. The group has become increasingly less Asian and white and increasingly older. It is the only Buddhist group in America to attract African American and Hispanic members in any sizable numbers, between 25 and 30 percent of the overall membership. In some communities such as Washington, D.C., minorities are the majority of members. This is a big change from the days when the faces at NSA conventions, though always multicultural, were mostly those of white, middle-class young people.

The strong minority membership today in Soka Gakkai, especially in larger cities, is in keeping with Nichiren Daishōnin's teachings and Soka Gakkai history. Nichiren sought to appeal to people outside the mainstream by rejecting the religious and political status quo of his times. His years in exile were the result of his antiestablishment activities. In prewar Japan, Soka Gakkai sought to promote values opposed to the imperial militarism that led to World War II, and after the war it appealed to people whose meaning systems were destroyed by the loss of the war and the collapse of the imperial cult.

In late-twentieth-century America we have seen a similar collapse of meaning systems. Our economic and social systems are increasingly divided between the "haves" and the "have-nots." The promise of the American dream has not been kept for many Americans, and this is especially so for urban minorities. Soka Gakkai's teaching of Nichiren Buddhism offers hope for individuals through accessing the power of the Gohonzon by chanting *Nam-myōhō-renge-kyō.* Thus minority Soka Gakkai members can experience its ethos of individual power, the freedom to change one's life no matter what one's circumstances, and the support of the mission for world peace. Nichiren Buddhism's ethos is enlightened self-interest. As a practitioner improves his or her own karma and creates positive cause for positive effects, the world itself can become more peaceful and "a better place." These are very American values experienced by minority Nichiren Buddhists in a nontraditional way. It makes sense that Nichiren Buddhism's unusual approach to these values should be embraced by minority groups often ignored or rejected by mainstream American society.

In Japan in the 1980s, Soka Gakkai was also changing. The movement had stabilized at 5 to 8.5 million families (these are official statistics and are very difficult to verify) in 115 countries and had become, instead of an upstart "new religion," rather mainstream. Nichiren Daishōnin himself was an outsider of humble origins who challenged the ruling priestly and governmental elite and was met with hostility. When his twentieth-century lay followers in Japan, themselves largely drawn from the lower classes, did the same, they met with a similar response. In the early days of Soka Gakkai, its *shakubuku* techniques had been heavy-handed, though these techniques were later modified in a parallel to the changes made in American *shakubuku* techniques. The group's political party, Kōmeitō, had to be formally separated from the religious entity, though it is still supported by Soka Gakkai members. Kōmeitō has proved a continuing political force and has moved from being "a fringe element to a more accepted and trusted member of Japan's political establishment."[16] Moderation seemed to be the key as Soka Gakkai moved into its middle age.

President Ikeda, too, changed as time passed. As a young man, he had carried on the fight for *kōsen-rufu* with dedication and reenvisioned Soka Gakkai's mission as international in scope. Under his leadership, the third Great Secret Law was fulfilled with the construction of the Sho-Hondo (*Hommon-no-Kaidan*) at Taiseki-ji at the base of Mount Fuji. The Dai-Gohonzon is now enshrined there. A charismatic man, a skillful leader, and a gifted photographer and poet, Ikeda came to be much feared outside the Soka Gakkai membership. He was addressed as *Sensei* (honored teacher) by members, but was seen as too powerful by outsiders. Japan had seen what total devotion to a leader could lead to, and many Japanese were wary of anyone with too much personal and political power.

All this changed when Ikeda was ousted from the presidency of Soka Gakkai in 1979 and he assumed his role as president of Soka Gakkai International, which had seemed to be an essentially honorary position with little real power. The situation leading up to this shift is confusing, but the 1991 split between the Soka Gakkai and the Nichiren Shōshū priesthood seemed to indicate that Ikeda's powerful leadership was challenged by the high priest and vice versa. Tensions were building in what had been a difficult but workable relationship up to that point.

The Soka Gakkai–Nichiren Shōshū Priesthood Split

When Josei Toda rebuilt Soka Gakkai after World War II, he gained the cooperation of the Nichiren Shōshū priests by ceding ritual authority to them in all ceremonial functions, such as bestowing the Gohonzon to new Nichiren Shōshū believers, weddings, funerals, and the keeping of the Head Temple Taiseki-ji. In return, the priesthood began to prosper as never before in its history, due to the pilgrimages to the Dai-Gohonzon encouraged for all lay believers and the financial support of the growing Soka Gakkai movement. In return, the "new religion" Soka Gakkai was given legitimate status through its association with an established religious group.

In 1991 this cooperation came to an end when High Priest Nikken Shōnin excommunicated all Soka Gakkai members. This meant that Soka Gakkai members (including leaders) were denied access to the ritual functions performed by Nichiren Shōshū priests, to the Dai-Gohonzon at the head temple, and to all other Nichiren Shōshū temples, including the six in the United States. The temples in turn organized Hokkeko, the pre–Soka Gakkai model of lay believers' groups associated with local temples. These groups do not do *shakubuku* in the Soka Gakkai fashion and have largely attracted disaffected former Soka Gakkai members. They do not have leaders, but prefer to call those who are in positions of responsibility "communicators."

The split between Soka Gakkai and the priesthood was shocking and upsetting to all concerned. The major causes of the split were conflicting claims to authority between the Soka Gakkai and priesthood leaders, their relative positions of power, disagreements over the interpretation of Nichiren Daishōnin's teachings, and certain financial issues. Discerning the truth of what actually led to the breakup is difficult due to the passions on both sides.

From a historical view, the most compelling explanation of the split is that Nichiren Shōshū High Priest Nikken Shōnin and Soka Gakkai International President Ikeda were each regarded by separate groups of followers as carriers of Nichiren Daishōnin's charisma, and perhaps were even seen as his reincarnation. This obviously led to factionalism. Earlier we described Nichiren Daishōnin's stubborn defense of his perception of the Truth and his confrontational style. For his Buddhist descendants these character traits have made communication between the two sides difficult.

From the priesthood side, Soka Gakkai members and leaders did not show appropriate respect for the High Priest and put the authority of SGI President Ikeda above him. Soka Gakkai members would study President Ikeda's writings more than those of Nichiren. This is a violation of the heritage of Nichiren Shōshū, which derives its authority from Nichiren himself passing to High Priest Nikko Shōnin and from him to the current, sixty-seventh High Priest, Nikken Shōnin. As one Hokkeko member told me, "Our differences are based on a different understanding of the Three Treasures of Buddhism: the Law, the Priest, and the Buddha. These are all important to us (in Hokkeko) but the Priests are not valued by the Gakkai."[17] Nikken Shōnin is inheritor of the Law transmitted by Nichiren Daishōnin, the Buddha of the Latter Day of the Law. To challenge the authority of the High Priest is to rebel against the Truth. There is only one way to *kōsen-rufu.*

A publication distributed by Nichiren Shōshū in English, which attempts to convince Soka Gakkai members that they are practicing a false religion, states, "Though their religion may seem the same as ours, they lack the single, unbroken line of heritage of the Law received directly from Nichiren Daishōnin. If one's faith is not based on this line of inheritance, it is worthless to embrace the Gohonzon, for no benefit will be forthcoming." This broadside goes on to challenge the fund-raising practices of Soka Gakkai, accuses the group of making money through a "crass attitude toward the Gohonzon," and threatens that the "counterfeit Gohonzons" being distributed by the Soka Gakkai and former Nichiren Shōshū priests associated with them "will be nothing but a source of unhappiness."[18]

Former Soka Gakkai members of the temple Hokkeko groups are deeply upset by the appropriation of Nichiren Daishōnin's True Buddhism by a group they consider to be distasteful, slanderous, materialistic, and heretical. These former SGI members report being harassed by Soka Gakkai after they began practicing at the temples. In early 1992, this author was unable to interview any Hokkeko leaders or Nichiren Shōshū priests because of their suspicions of me, though I clearly stated that I was not now nor had I ever been a member of Soka Gakkai. I personally met a couple of members who would talk to me about the split and its causes, but I could not arrange a visit to a Hokkeko meeting. One member wrote me an impassioned letter in defense of Nichiren Shōshū and detailed the offenses of Soka Gakkai.

Nearly four years after the split, Hokkeko members are still quite suspicious of outsiders. A phone call to the Seiganzan Myoshinji Temple in

Pinole, California, reputedly the head temple in America, was quite frustrating. When I introduced myself as a scholar and asked if Reverend Takahashi was still the leader of Nichiren Shōshū in America, I was told, "We can't give out that type of information. . . . We can't answer these questions because we don't know if you are with the Soka Gakkai."

To the Hokkeko members and Nichiren Shōshū priests, this split is of major proportions. They have lost millions of lay members and the financial support that they provided to the priesthood, though they have kept possession of the Soka Gakkai–built Nichiren Shōshū temples in Japan and throughout the world. Their legitimacy has been seriously challenged. It makes sense to draw a parallel with the times of Martin Luther, when a priesthood-laity conflict over the authority to interpret scripture and tradition led to a permanent separation between the Roman Catholic Church and the many denominations of Protestantism.

To Soka Gakkai members, the split with the priesthood seems to be much less upsetting. The only ritual change in the way Soka Gakkai members practice Nichiren's Buddhism is that in their daily silent prayers they offer gratitude to Nikko Shōnin and Nichimoku Shōnin, the first successors to Nichiren, and no longer to the successive Nichiren Shōshū High Priests. Even before the excommunication occurred, Soka Gakkai had begun changing the character of its organization from an authoritarian paradigm with President Ikeda at the head—a lay version of the priestly authority structure—to a more democratic, consensus-based organization. In the United States, this has meant limiting the term of the general director, in 1996 Japanese-born Fred Zaitsu, to three years. The general organization of SGI-USA is now overseen by the SGI-USA Central Executive Council, members of which are appointed for a one-year term. Both men and women serve on this council, several women have served as a vice-general director of SGI-USA, and women are able to become chapter leaders. Women's egalitarian status in the current SGI organization is a major change from the male-dominated hierarchical approach of the earlier Soka Gakkai organization or the male, priesthood-dominated organization of current-day Hokkeko.

When the priesthood excommunicated the Soka Gakkai members, some did leave the group to practice at the temples. The vast majority stayed with SGI. The problem this presented to SGI was how to handle priestly functions. This was solved by creating bonds with former Nichiren Shōshū priests, who had left the Nichiren Shōshū sect with their own objections to that group. Soka Gakkai reproduces Gohonzons for new members to enshrine in their homes based on one that was transcribed by High Priest Nichikan Shōnin at Joen-ji Temple in 1720 and donated to the Soka Gakkai by that temple's incumbent Chief Priest. Each community now appoints "Ministers of Ceremony" to a one-year term. The ministers confer Gohonzons to new members in a New Members Ceremony during which a commitment is made to practice Buddhism. They also handle weddings and funerals for SGI members on a volunteer basis with no financial remuneration. These ceremonies are Buddhist in content. A recent funeral for a long-time SGI member and Korean War veteran held at Arlington National Cemetery featured readings from the *Lotus Sūtra* and chanting *Nam-myōhō-renge-kyō*, all led by a lay SGI leader who was also an old friend of the deceased.

When he left the presidency of Soka Gakkai in 1979 and assumed fulltime responsibility as president of Soka Gakkai International, Daisaku Ikeda made an interesting choice. He did not try to become a guru-type figure by building on his religious authority, though he had long been addressed as *Sensei*, an honorific signifying the master-disciple relationship, by some SGI practitioners. He had plenty of power, religious, political, and financial, within Soka Gakkai International and as honorary Soka Gakkai president in Japan. But President Ikeda decided that he wanted to bring Nichiren's message of how world peace can be achieved to the world. He decided to become a global citizen and bring the organization with him.

As a result of his efforts, SGI is now an official nongovernmental organization (NGO) of the United Nations. Its activities include education through peace projects and cultural exchange. President Ikeda meets with world leaders such as Nelson Mandela, Mikhail Gorbachev, Jacques Chirac, Corazon Aquino, and Elie Wiesel. Soka Gakkai International focuses not on gaining specific numbers of new members through *shakubuku*, but on becoming a force for world peace and attracting members in that fashion. "The SGI aims to realize the happiness of individuals and the prosperity of each country by spreading understanding of the Buddhism of Nichiren Daishōnin (1222–1282). Toward that end, the SGI engages in various activities to promote peace, culture, and education based on Buddhism. . . . The members of the SGI are dedicated to the task of working for a new era based on the universal values of human equality and dignity."[19]

Through President Ikeda SGI has been a consistent voice for ending the threat of nuclear arms and for solving international conflicts by nonmilitary means. For example, on the eve of the Gulf War, President Ikeda sent letters to the leaders of the nations involved in the conflict, pleading with them to find a peaceful alternative to war. SGI has also taken part in the United Nations' fiftieth birthday by sponsoring conferences and cultural presentations.

Some outsiders do not feel that President Ikeda's activities are sincere. Certainly Hokkeko members and Nichiren Shōshū priests do not. In Japan, the political and economic power of Soka Gakkai is not always seen as trustworthy. In a society so respectful of tradition, Soka Gakkai members are seen as lacking respect for the past. In a society that accepts that individuals may have multiple religious affiliations, Soka Gakkai has been insistent that it has the only Truth. There have been accusations of some financial scandals within SGI, although human nature being what it is these are to be expected in such a large and diverse organization.

From the point of view of this observer of Soka Gakkai for more than twenty years, it clearly has changed a great deal in the last twenty years. Persistent, aggressive *shakubuku* has all but disappeared. Recruitment is now based on preexisting relationships or social networks as well as social outreach. *Shakubuku* has been replaced theoretically by propagation based on putting the philosophy and ideals of Buddhism into action through changing one's own life and through secular activities for peace, culture, and education. This is seen by SGI as an expanding circle of compassion based on an interfaith model.

President Ikeda, though still highly honored, has sought an international role and has not based his life on the admiration of SGI members. The organization shows signs of moving toward democracy and consensus decision making, a development not always seen in religious groups. The split with the priesthood is seen as a divorce that was sad but necessary. SGI is confident that it will recover from the trauma of this experience, and already seems to be doing so.

Soka Gakkai has successfully negotiated the process of maturing as a religious movement. In the early days it depended on charismatic leadership and the enthusiasm of new converts to overcome the organizational, doctrinal, and financial obstacles that new movements face. Most movements do not make it past this stage. Then the movement took on a global focus and began to recruit members throughout the world. Despite the crisis created by the split with the priesthood in 1991, the current phase of Soka Gakkai's development is one of comfortable middle age. The identity crises of youth have passed, and skills such as compromise and adaptation to changing times have been developed. This is a creative and dynamic time for the Soka Gakkai as it enters its most productive years for putting faith in Nichiren Daishōnin's Buddhism into practice by working for peace, culture, and education. As they have long taught, SGI members see this as a personal challenge that has global effects.

Hokkeko, in contrast, is still a very young group in America in its current form. It shows all the characteristics of a new movement: a devotion to the leader (the High Priest), intensive defense of the teachings or truth, recruitment of new members, and most important of all a sense of opposition to Soka Gakkai and all that it represents to Hokkeko members. Its numbers are small, estimated to be less than a thousand in America, and much of its identity comes from its self-differentiation from Soka Gakkai. In some ways these Hokkeko members are protesting against a Soka Gakkai that no longer exists since it has begun to institute more democratic organizational paradigms. In other ways, there are irreconcilable differences between Hokkeko and its devotion to the teachings of Nichiren Daishōnin and the way Soka Gakkai seeks to practice these same teachings. Hokkeko as a young movement has yet to find a secure identity and place in the world.

The Future of Nichiren's Buddhism in America

Nichiren's Buddhism has found fertile soil in the United States. It was first carried here by the Asian community, and it has since been firmly established among non-Asians by the pioneers who brought it here with that purpose in mind. Numerically, Nichiren's Buddhism is the most successful of the twentieth-century Buddhisms imported to America. Though like most new religious movements it has lost many members through the years, it has survived with a strong core of believers and a national organization intact.

The priesthood-laity split in Japan has become entrenched in America as well. The two lay organizations that now practice Nichiren's Buddhism, SGI-USA and Hokkeko, seem unable to attain a meeting of the minds and will probably be forever separate. The divorce is final, and too many angry words have been spoken on both sides for a reconciliation. Hokkeko will probably continue to exist as a small organization affiliated with the six Nichiren Shōshū temples in America. Unless it takes up a serious *shakubuku* campaign and develops some economic resources, it will probably not expand.

Soka Gakkai International-USA, with its years of development as a movement, its experienced leaders, and its economic support from Japan, has a better chance to continue as a successful movement. It has entered into a steady state and could possibly become a permanent, widely accepted minority religion like the Mormons. Certainly interfaith efforts by SGI-USA, including working with mainstream Christians and Jews on issues of religious freedom, indicate its intention to be an ongoing part of the American experiment in religious toleration.

Possible future trouble spots that will require attention are issues such as racism and sexism, which of course are problems in society at large. Are there enough minority and women leaders? Are all groups treated equitably in SGI? Another possible problem is that both general directors of SGI-USA have been Asian-born Americans. A potential crisis will have to be dealt with when an American-born leader is appointed, or members think he or she should be appointed. SGI's vision of global cooperation looked idealistic in the sixties; it now looks like a necessity for global survival. This may make it attractive in the next millennium. These and other issues will need to be worked on for SGI to be able to maintain its youthful enthusiasm while enjoying its maturity.

It is remarkable to see how the Buddhist teachings of a thirteenth-century Japanese prophet have such relevance to the lives of contemporary Americans. The teachings of Nichiren Daishōnin, despite his own claim to authority as the one True Buddha for our time, are essentially democratic and nonhierarchical. Anyone who chants the *Lotus Sūtra* and *Nam-myōhō-renge-kyō* to the Gohonzon can become one with the Universal Law of cause and effect and change his or her karma. The stronger one's personal relationship with the Gohonzon through chanting, the more powerful will become one's unity with the Universal Law. In the process, the believer's life is transformed. This is the American dream: success in life through individual effort. That thousands of Americans feel they are achieving this dream through Nichiren Buddhism is a testament to the endurance of Nichiren Daishōnin's teachings.

Tibetan Buddhism in America: The Development of American Vajrayāna

AMY LAVINE

The transmission of Tibetan Buddhism by Tibetan lamas (*bla ma*)[1] to the United States began in earnest in the early 1970s. The primary instigator for this missionary activity was the grave threat placed on the survival of Tibetan culture and religion by the Chinese communist invasion and occupation of Tibet. The West, particularly the United States, was perceived by some as the next open frontier for the introduction and cultivation of the teachings of the Buddha as they had been taught for the previous thirteen hundred years in Tibet. Lamas representing the four main orders[2] of Tibetan Buddhism came to North America to expose a Western audience to the specific practices and teachings as handed down through the centuries by lineages of teachers. Some of these teachers trace their spiritual genealogies to Padmasambhava, the premiere religious figure in the Tibetan landscape, believed to have brought Buddhism from India to Tibet in the eighth century C.E.

This chapter examines how the practitioners of American Vajrayāna are negotiating between the traditional expectations of their Tibetan teachers and their need to introduce elements of their own culture into the Buddhist religion in order to make it fully and authentically their own. When an established religion enters into a new cultural environment there are a host of elements that must concern both its transmitters and its neophytes. The creation of innovations that will translate both the letter and the spirit of its doctrines and practices to this new social, political, cultural, and psychological landscape is among the most challenging tasks for followers of American Vajrayāna. This chapter examines three factors in the transmission of Tibetan Buddhism to the West: (1) the sources of authority in the tradition and the means for securing such authority; (2) continuity between the traditional Tibetan forms of religious practice and the styles and abilities of Western practitioners; and (3) the availability of Tibetan Buddhist teachings across the United States.

Traditionally, religious authority resided in the institutions of two different kinds of religious specialist: the incarnate *tulku* (*sprul sku*)[3] and the *geshe* (*dge bshes*).[4] I discuss here how each of these figures has entered American Vajrayāna in the form of Tibetan persons and recognized Western incarnations. These specialists provided continuity in Tibet as did the institution of monasticism which provided for Tibet's sacred and secular ruling class over a period of four hundred years. In American Vajrayāna, the Buddhist monastery is in embryonic form, and continuity in the new context is only beginning to become visible. American Vajrayāna has thus far proven its ability to make the Buddha's teachings widely available through networks of personal connections with Tibetan teachers and their American successors, educational enterprises, ritual environments, and, now, electronic media. Before I proceed to discuss these transmission factors in full, however, I offer a brief survey to account for how Tibetan Buddhism initially arrived in the United States and to trace the enduring legacies of its pioneering lineage holders.

The Tibetan Transmission of American Vajrayāna

Although the transmission of Tibetan Buddhism to the United States blossomed in the 1970s, its seeds, in the form of a few lamas, arrived on American soil earlier.[5] The first major teacher of Tibetan Buddhism in the United States was Mongolian: Geshe Wangyal settled in New Jersey in 1955. With the blessing and charter from the Dalai Lama (*ta la'i bla ma*), he opened the first Tibetan monastery in this country and named it the Lamaist Buddhist Monastery of America. Geshe Wangyal was a Gelugpa (*dge lugs pa*), a member of the order headed by the Dalai Lama, and had studied at Drepung ('bras spungs) Monastery, one of the important monasteries in Lhasa. He taught courses at Columbia University and from within that academic stronghold laid the foundation of American Vajrayāna. Among his more well-known students are Robert Thurman and Jeffrey Hopkins. Thurman is America's first ordained Tibetan Buddhist monk and currently holds the Jey Tsong Khapa Chair of Indo-Tibetan Buddhist Studies at Columbia. Hopkins is a professor of Indo-Tibetan Buddhist Studies at the University of Virginia, a primary academic center for learning Tibetan language and Gelugpa-style scholastic debate. Hence, the legacy of Geshe Wangyal is mainly felt in the arena of training scholars of Tibetan Buddhism, particularly those who have fluency in Tibetan. Many of them act as translators for Tibetan teachers visiting the United States.

Deshung Rinpoche arrived at the University of Washington in Seattle in 1961. A Sakyapa (*sa skya pa*) who had formerly held the position of abbot at Sakya Tharlan Monastery, Deshung Rinpoche worked closely with some of the West's foundational scholars of Tibetan Buddhism, teaching Tibetan and Buddhist philosophy and helping to compile an English-Tibetan dictionary. It was not until ten years later that he began to teach Vajrayāna Dharma[6] to Western students directly at the request of Kalu Rinpoche, who had by then established his own Buddhist centers in Canada and France. Deshung Rinpoche was, however, primarily concerned that American students learn Tibetan. His enduring legacy, in addition to training scholars in Tibetan language and religion, was to establish an important center in Seattle for the resettlement of ethnic Tibetans, who continue to arrive in North America from India and Nepal.

The two orders thus far represented (Gelugpa and Sakyapa) are traditionally famous in Tibet and now in their current North American incarnations for their emphasis on academic approaches to the study of Buddhism. Two other orders have focused more attention on meditation and contemplation, with particular emphasis on tantric ritual practice. Both foci are of course indispensable in the creation of a truly American Buddhist consciousness. The introduction of Nyingma (*rnying ma*) teachings, those of the oldest Tibetan Buddhist order, was initiated by Tarthang Tulku, who moved to Berkeley, California, in 1969. Within a short time he had founded the Tibetan Nyingma Meditation Center, "the first Vajrayāna congregation in America."[7] Tarthang Tulku prepared his students to undertake the traditional tantric preliminary practices, which commence with one hundred thousand full-body prostrations. The Nyingma order traditionally included a community of families; its lamas were rarely monastics but usually married with children. This noncelibate aspect became part of Tarthang Tulku's teaching style, welcomed by Americans attempting to integrate their normal working lives, complete with familial obligations and occupational constraints, with a rigorous regimen of Buddhist practices. This more or less successful integration of lay livelihood and strict practice is one of the definitional aspects of American Vajrayāna.

The impact of Tarthang Tulku's Nyingma order on the formation of American Vajrayāna has been very interesting and quite unique. The lama himself has not made many public appearances in the past ten years, but many offspring of his teachings have thrived. He started a publishing house for his own writings, Dharma Publishing, which today also publishes selections of translated material from other Tibetan and Sanskrit sources. The Nyingma Institute in Berkeley offers Americans a range of study and practice following Nyingma tradition as taught by Tarthang Tulku's senior Western students. His religious community consists largely of Americans with some ethnic Tibetans. The crowning achievement of his efforts is the recently consecrated retreat and study center called Odiyan in Sonoma County, California. Groundbreaking for this "temple city" began in 1975 and, according to its own sources, is about three-quarters finished at this writing. Surrounding the many temples and shrine rooms is a 144-acre protected reserve and animal sanctuary. The ultimate purpose of the complex is for Tarthang Tulku's students to have a permanent retreat center where they can participate in short- and long-term practice and study sessions.

The last order introduced into American culture was the Kagyupa (*bka' brgyud pa*), represented by Chögyam Trungpa Rinpoche who arrived in North America in 1970. Trungpa Rinpoche, educated at Oxford University (and eventually highly skilled in American idiomatic speech), sought to create a vision of "enlightened society" in North America. The concrete building blocks of that society include: a preschool, an elementary school, an accredited college bestowing undergraduate and graduate degrees, a credit union, bookstores, a "secular" meditation program called Shambhala Training, and numerous for-profit businesses covering a wide range of interests and services. All of these institutions are operated with the idea of encouraging Tibetan Buddhist values. Trungpa Rinpoche's *sangha* may represent the most comprehensive attempt to merge the religious worldview of American Vajrayāna with all other aspects of American life. Once called Vajradhatu, Trungpa Rinpoche's Dharma centers and study groups are now organized under the rubric of Shambhala International and include a large group retreat facility in Barnet, Vermont, and the Rocky Mountain Shambhala Center located in northern Colorado, as well as a solitary retreat center in southern Colorado. Trungpa died in 1987 and today his eldest son, Mipham Rinpoche—recently recognized as the incarnation of a famous Kagyupa teacher and scholar—acts as the spiritual head of Trungpa's large American community.

It is safe to say that the presence of these four representative Tibetan lamas provided the impetus for the development of what is now known as American Vajrayāna. However, it became apparent that the Tibetan lamas themselves needed an authenticating seal of approval for the fledgling child of their own ancient religion. At the invitation of these and other lamas residing in America, the heads of the four main orders eventually visited all of North America's practice centers and bestowed their blessings. The official consecration of the Dharma organizations that were laying the groundwork for American Vajrayāna was a necessary condition that only these foremost leaders, holding the sacred trust of the previous generations, could meet.

The Assertion of Buddhist Authority in America

In traditional Tibetan society, authority was located in the theocratic institution of the monastery (*gompa*) and in the centrally governing aristocracy in Lhasa. As the Tibetan religion moved to the West, it became increasingly clear that the basis for this authority would be challenged by Americans who value individuality, self-reliance, and free expression as demanded by their democratic traditions. These values were virtually nonexistent in Tibet. One of the ways in which American Vajrayāna has molded itself to its new locale is to place senior American practitioners in positions of authority and power within their Buddhist organizations. Once a Tibetan lama establishes a center for practice and study, his students[8] become responsible for its maintenance, upkeep, and general administration. This situation, which always involves fund-raising activities, quickly leads to the creation of boards of directors which determine the vision and policies for the center, usually consisting of American practitioners except for the nominal participation of the founding lama.

Even with an American power base, however, American Vajrayāna still functions under the fundamental authority of Tibet's primary religious specialists: the *geshe* and the *tulku*. It is essential to the endurance of this newest Buddhist incarnation that an authentic lama continue to embody the doctrines and practices that constitute the religion. One of the most important types of lama is the monastic degree holder. In the Kagyupa and Nyingmapa orders, this figure is called *khenpo* (*mkhan po*). A number of *khenpos* teach in the West. The Gelugpa and Sakyapa orders valorize the figure of the *geshe* as the ultimate authority. Traditionally, "the full training for this degree can take from seventeen to twenty years, followed by another eight or nine years for the higher status of *geshe lharampa*."[9] In the United States, the pattern has been for the *geshe* to establish himself[10] at an academic center and to teach, at least initially, through a religious studies or language department. One of the most famous *geshes* in this country is Geshe Sopa, who teaches in the renowned Buddhist Studies program at the University of Wisconsin in Madison, and which is one of the foremost places to learn modern Tibetan. There have not been many Westerners who have received the degree of *geshe;* this is probably because of the serious time commitment involved as well as the fact that one must locate a *gompa* in India or Nepal willing to take on a Western student. Among the better known Western *geshes* are the Swiss Georges Dreyfus (Geshe Sangye Samdup), an Assistant Professor in Indo-Tibetan Studies and Tibetan Language at Williams College in Massachusetts, and Geshe Michael Roach. The latter is a student of Khensur Rinpoche Geshe Lobsang Tharchin, one of the last known *lharampa geshes* to receive his degree in Tibet.[11] Geshe Roach, under the direction of Khen Rinpoche, teaches at the Asian Classics Institute in New York City.

The other primary embodiment of authority is the *tulku*, a presence that has been more pervasive in the development of American Vajrayāna than that of the *geshe*. The role of *tulku* is primarily characteristic of the Nyingmapa and Kagyupa orders. An extremely elaborate system legitimates the recognition of *tulkus* and usually involves a prophecy by the previous lama as well as active searches by his associates for his new incarnation.[12] There were thousands of incarnated *tulkus* in traditional Tibet, many of whom fled their homeland to follow the Dalai Lama in 1959.

The recognition of *tulkus* in Tibet—and, since the exile, in India and Nepal—was a common occurrence, but in the past ten years or so Tibetan teachers have begun recognizing reincarnations of their own lamas in the persons of Westerners. Establishing the future charter of Tibetan Buddhism for authority in American Vajrayāna in the very bodies of Westerners is perhaps the most skillful means that has been developed by Tibetan lamas. The entire system of reincarnation is not an easy concept for the average, well-educated American to understand. Having a fellow "ordinary person" be suddenly recognized, either as an adult or as a child, as the returning figure of an important Tibetan lama is certainly one way for a worldview of karmic activity to take hold in the American imagination. This is not to say that many American followers do not meet this unusual claim to fame with some skepticism. As with all aspects of Buddhism, practitioners are encouraged to test the teachings for themselves rather than to take the word of someone else. *Sangha* members will participate in teachings given by a newly recognized *tulku* (when this person is an adult who is teaching publicly) to see whether what he or she says resonates with their own understanding of the Dharma, as given to them by a previously authenticated Dharma holder. It is probably too early in the development of American Vajrayāna to say how successful American *tulkus* will be in teaching an older generation of Buddhist practitioners while simultaneously attracting new followers to the religion.

There have been a number of Westerners, American and European, who have been recognized as reincarnations of certain lamas by all levels of traditional Tibetan authority. To take one case study briefly as an example, I turn to the life of Catherine Burroughs, who now has the title Jetsunma Ahkön Lhamo.[13] Born and raised in Brooklyn, New York, Burroughs married early and went to live in rural North Carolina. There, isolated from human contact beyond that of her husband, she apparently began spontaneously (with no instruction) to practice Tibetan meditation, including a classical body-awareness technique known as *Chöd*. It was not until some fifteen years or so later that she met Penor Rinpoche, the head of the Palyul Nyingma order, in an airport in Washington, D.C. After making a spontaneous and meaningful connection with this lama, Burroughs visited him at his center in Bylakuppe, India.

It was during Burroughs's first trip to India that Penor Rinpoche told her that she was the incarnation of a *yoginī* from the seventeenth century, the first Genyenma Ahkön Lhamo. The *yoginī* is an important figure in Tibetan Buddhism, especially for the Nyingmapa and Kagyupa orders. The female version of the more well-known *yogin* (sometimes referred to as a *mahāsiddha*, or great saint), the *yoginī* is usually a solitary wandering meditator who lives primarily in caves or charnel grounds, spending most of her time performing elaborate tantric rituals. According to Penor Rinpoche, Genyenma was known for her wild demeanor, for spending decades alone in caves, and occasionally for offering some kind of healing to those who sought her out. Although Burroughs's memories of her predecessor are admittedly "pretty Swiss Cheesy," she claims to have "some awareness of [being connected to her]."[14] The fact that Burroughs already had a community of students in Maryland who considered her a reliable teacher helped moderate the shocking idea that this unassuming woman was now to be treated with all of the pomp and circumstance afforded a celebrated religious figure. She did lose some followers during the transition, but has retained a core group who have chosen to remain with her.

Today, Burroughs (known simply as Jetsunma) presides over a large American Vajrayāna practice and study center in Poolesville, Maryland. She was officially enthroned by Penor Rinpoche in 1988, and the ceremony attracted national media attention as the first of its kind in the United States. The center, called Kunzang Palyul Chöling (KPC), includes a teaching room, an elementary school, a children's center, a kitchen, a sixty-five-acre wildlife refuge, and twenty-eight *stūpas* (including a thirty-eight-foot Migyur Dorje *stūpa*). KPC also houses a traditional seven-year Buddhist institute of academic study and intensive practice called the Migyur Dorje Institute. The newly discovered lama lives there with her husband and two children. Catherine Burroughs's story is one of the more dramatic examples of a Tibetan lama recognizing a Western adult as being born with the authority of a high lama, more dramatic perhaps because hers is the authority of the *yoginī*, which is unusual even in Tibet. The somewhat more common instances of children (from a wide variety of ethnic backgrounds) being recognized as *tulkus* is discussed here later.

The religious title of *tulku* is an indication of a special kind of accomplishment—albeit one that cannot be achieved merely through effort or excellence—that is realizable through birth and subsequently recognized by a Tibetan lama. Another way in which Tibetan lamas are instilling authority in their American students is by the freer use of traditional Tibetan titles for religious specialists in their American Vajrayāna contexts. For example, before Kalu Rinpoche died, he referred to those students who had completed his extremely demanding three-year retreats as "lamas." He also encouraged them to become teachers in their own right, not as the incarnations of any special persons but rather as people whose own intensive meditation experiences had led them to insights which made them worthy of teaching others. In Trungpa Rinpoche's *sangha*, Mipham Rinpoche recently named nine senior students as *acharyas* (*ācārya*), Sanskrit for teacher.

These nine individuals have been empowered to start meditation and study groups of their own which would exist under the general umbrella of the Shambhala organization. The point of these smaller groups is to allow new practitioners more access to and personal attention from a "recognized," if not reincarnated, teacher. Two of the *acharyas* are women which is a welcome addition to the usually all-male Tibetan lamaist hierarchy. Further, such sub-*sanghas* will place more authority in the hands of Westerners, thus incorporating integrally embodied American cultural experience as part of the transmission of the Buddhist Dharma to America.

The titled roles of *geshe* and *tulku* thus provide American Vajrayāna with authentic and legitimate sources of continuity. These teachers, in their Tibetan and Western guises, present the doctrines and rituals of Tibetan Buddhism in a cohesive and relatively faithful manner. Of course, there are innumerable differences in personal style and approach represented by the four main orders as well as by separate lineages and lineage holders within each of the orders. The highly valued ritual practices that constitute Vajrayāna proper also provide its American branch with an essential vehicle for connecting it to its roots.

Continuity from Tibetan Buddhism to American Vajrayāna

One of the defining aspects of many American Vajrayana communities is what I think of as the inverted style of monastic practice being done by lay followers. In Tibet, householders rarely performed the more intensive tantric practices which circumscribed the lives of monks, nuns, and *yogins* and *yoginīs*. Many Tibetan lamas, particularly those in the Kagyupa and Nyingmapa orders, have taught their senior American students precisely these tantric practices, and the rituals that accompany them, that were practiced for centuries in the homeland. In many Dharma communities in this country, practitioners may spend upwards of four hours a day performing such practices alone or in group settings. In some *sanghas*, there is a formal procedure in which a student must participate to receive instruction and initiation into tantric practices. The Shambhala community, for example, requires students to complete a three-month summer seminary program successfully before they can begin the preliminary practices.

The traditional Tibetan monastery provided the religion with its primary locus of continuity. Approximately 20 percent of the twentieth-century Tibetan population, prior to Chinese occupation, was constituted by monks and nuns.[15] In American Vajrayāna, the monastic institution is still taking shape. The general state of the Tibetan monastery in America involves Tibetan monks, living in monasteries in the United States and Canada, whose physical needs are provided for by Western laypeople. There are some Westerners, both men and women, who have been ordained into a specific Tibetan monastic order, but hardly in sufficient numbers at this time to consider them a vital aspect of American Vajrayāna. Arguably the most important Tibetan monastery in the United States is Namgyal Monastery, established as the Dalai Lama's personal monastery, in Ithaca, New York. Closely associated with it is the Namgyal Institute of Buddhist Studies. The charter monastery is in Dharamsala, India, adjacent to the Dalai Lama's residence. In 1992, His Holiness established the Ithaca branch as the North American seat of Namgyal. It is currently inhabited only by Tibetan monks who were relocated to North America from Dharamsala. The Namgyal Institute, however, provides a traditional Tibetan curriculum of study for Western lay students and is governed jointly by a board of directors (consisting of three Tibetans, one Western geshe, and three Westerners) and an administrative committee of Tibetans in Dharamsala.[16] Thus, Namgyal Institute represents an attempt to merge Tibetan- and American-style authority structures in the formal foundations of a religious center designed to serve the needs of America's developing relationship with the Buddhist Dharma.

Losel Shedrup Ling is a Gelugpa monastery and the North American branch of Drepung Loseling Monastery, one of the foremost monasteries of Tibet. With the creation of the new Tibetan diaspora, it was rebuilt in Karnataka State in South India. In 1989, as a result of the first world tour of the Sacred Music Sacred Dance Group of Tibetan monks, Losel Shedrup Ling was further established in Mineral Bluff, Georgia. It also has monastic affiliates in Tennessee, North Carolina, and Alabama, each of which houses Tibetans from Drepung as well as American adherents.

Kagyu monasticism in North America is represented by two established centers. The first is Karma Triyana Dharmacakra (KTD), the seat of the Karma Kagyu lineage and His Holiness Karmapa. In 1997 there were, again, only Tibetan monks residing there, with Western followers providing financial and material support. The main form such support has taken is in the area of building the facilities for the monks as well as expanding the monastery grounds to house lay practitioners. Currently, KTD is working toward establishing a home for the new Seventeenth Karmapa, His Holiness Urgyen Trinley Dorje, a twelve-year-old Tibetan boy currently living at Tsurphu Monastery in Tibet. The other established monastic center is Gampo Abbey in Cape Breton, Nova Scotia. Under the leadership of an American-born nun, Bhikṣuṇī Pema Chödrön, a senior student of Trungpa Rinpoche and one of the recently named acharyas, Gampo Abbey was established in 1985 explicitly for the use of Western practitioners. The official abbot is Thrangu Rinpoche from Nepal, who is a khenpo.

Continuity in American Vajrayāna is created in part by the nonmonastic intensive retreat, particularly in the Nyingma and Kagyu lineages. This practice arises from the character of the *yogin* or *yoginī*, the noncelibate practitioner who is not affiliated with any *gompa* and who engages in intensive tantric practices for long periods at a time. In America, some Dharma communities have valorized this style of practice to the extent that intensive retreat environments have been established to encourage those students who are able, financially and in terms of life and familial obligations, to emulate it by entering the closed world of the retreatant. The traditional Tibetan yogic retreat lasts for three years, three months, and three days. The American Vajrayāna retreat is done in groups, with participants in their own rooms or cells; part of the practice is done together and the rest is solitary. Such a retreat center exists on the grounds of KTD, with the first group of Western students completing their session in the fall of 1996. According to KTD's *sangha* newsletter, "retreatants train on their own . . . daily practice is performed in Tibetan . . . [they] are getting used to living with less sleep, forsaking conventional beds, and living without coffee. . . . Commitments are reduced. Finances are put in order and on automatic pilot."[17] Until there are more opportunities for Western students to take up the Vajrayāna monastic lifestyle, the intensive retreat is the one place they can go and completely leave the material world of America behind. Some other centers provide for shorter retreats, either in small group settings (often for a month's time, as in the Shambhala community's *dathun*) or in a solitary environment.

I return now to the issue of continuity as it is expressed in the incarnated child *tulku*. It is certainly challenging to American sensibilities to understand and embrace Tibetan metaphysical notions involved in accepting that a Western adult has been recognized as the incarnation of a famous Tibetan lama; it is a far more elaborate task to accept that a small child has been so recognized. On the one hand, it is possible to test for oneself how well an adult reincarnation may teach the Dharma, what his or her "spiritual demeanor" is, and to decide through these empirical tests whether one is able to experience a faith relationship with this figure. These sorts of tests are much more difficult to perform in the case of a child. Since devotion is the principal religious emotion required in Vajrayāna Buddhism, it is necessary for American practitioners to learn to cultivate an attitude of faith toward the reincarnations of their own beloved teachers. In this case, continuity is defined in terms of identity itself. This situation is a relatively new development in American Vajrayāna, because many of the pioneer lamas who first brought the Dharma to the West have died in the past few years and their incarnations are only just beginning to be recognized. Building a personal relationship with these boy lamas (I am not aware of any girl children currently recognized as *tulkus*) represents an increasingly important element in establishing and maintaining the kind of radical continuity required for the survival and prosperity of this Tibetan Buddhism on Western soil.

In many instances, the child *tulku* has not yet visited the United States, either because he is not able to leave Tibet (as with the Seventeenth Karmapa) or because his religious training is so intensive as to preclude him from making such a long journey. Most of these boys live in Tibetan monasteries in India and Nepal, where they are undergoing the rigorous instruction regime that has traditionally formed the cornerstone of *tulku* initiation. This instruction is conducted by a regent or tutor previously appointed by the deceased lama of whom the boy is a *tulku*. One child who made the trip to the United States is Kyab-je Kalu Rinpoche Yansi, the incarnation of the Venerable Kalu Rinpoche, a four-year-old lama who usually resides at the Samdup Thargye Ling Monastery in Sonada, India. Accompanied by five monks, a translator, and his parents, Kyab-je Kalu Rinpoche visited his future North American seat at KTD in 1995. He allegedly "presided" over a number of ceremonies (which were actually led by Bokar Rinpoche, the head of the Shangpa Kagyu lineage), including a children's service. Later, the young lama was present for a special *mahākāla pūja* during which he is said to have fallen asleep twice.[18] These stories show not only how demanding it must be for American practitioners to take the boy lama seriously, but also how difficult it must be for the child himself to act the part. It will be interesting to see over the coming decades how these lamas grow into leadership roles in their communities, and to observe what sorts of adjustments American Vajrayāna as a whole will make to accommodate the radical Tibetan system of belief concerning *tulku* identity, authentication, and faith.

The final issue concerning the continuity of Tibetan Buddhism and American Vajrayāna concerns the relationship between American practitioners and ethnic lay Tibetans. Since their introduction to the religion, this country's Vajrayāna students have almost exclusively encountered Tibetans in the form of celebrated lamas. Starting in 1991, the Tibetan Resettlement Project (TRP) got under way and some one thousand Tibetans (mostly from India and Nepal) were allowed to resettle legally in various host cities in the United States. For many Americans, including Buddhists, this was their first encounter with "ordinary" Tibetan people. Although there were some nonlama Tibetans in this country prior to TRP's official invitation, the 1990s have seen quite a large influx of refugees, including a far greater number of illegal exiles than ever before. Many tightly knit Tibetan communities now exist in the United States, especially in the larger cities, and the interactions between American Vajrayāna students and these ethnic Tibetans generally have been minimal. Only recently have Tibetans started attending public events when a rinpoche comes to town, or occasionally in smaller numbers to attend talks offered by American Vajrayāna teachers. The future of American Vajrayāna may in some ways have to contend with the expectations and assumptions of this new generation of Tibetan Americans as they become more familiar with Western culture. In particular, it will be interesting to see whether the younger generation of Tibetans participates in the rituals and practices of their American counterparts, even if those practices were not necessarily a part of their parents' lives, and conversely whether nonreligious Tibetans might be attracted to their country's native religion as taught to them by non-Tibetans.

Buddhism in an Electronic Frontier

The last topic to be examined here is that of the availability of American Vajrayāna to a large number of people. Personal connections with either a Dharma group or a lama certainly offer the most direct experience. Most talks by lamas or senior students sponsored by various groups are open to the public and tend to be advertised in the alternative newspapers of larger cities or on bulletin boards at "alternative" stores. For more sustained, and often more advanced instruction, weekend meditation workshops with a lama are frequently offered. Longer, more intensive programs are also open to the general public. There are several schools and institutes that concentrate on teaching Tibetan Buddhism. A tremendous amount of information about various American Vajrayāna centers in the United States can be found on the Internet. Quite a few centers have web pages that describe their activities, list schedules of teachings and meditation sessions, and include color pictures of their resident teachers and facilities.

It is important to distinguish between American Vajrayāna religious or meditation centers and those groups that are concerned with Tibetan culture and politics. These arenas do not represent the same foci, and cannot be said to serve the same purposes. The situation concerning the state of Tibetans living under Chinese rule, as well as the status of the many Tibetan refugee populations, has begun to attract attention among certain segments within American culture. There are movies depicting recognizably Tibetan topics: a biography of the Dalai Lama has been made into a film by a major Hollywood studio; popular rock groups write songs about Tibetan Buddhism and present large-scale concert events benefiting Tibetan groups (such as the Free Tibet Concert in San Francisco in the summer of 1996); fashion designers have presented benefit shows dedicated to educating the public about Tibet; and many political groups have emerged in the past ten years that seek to further the aims of the Free Tibet movement. Among the more successful of these groups is Students for a Free Tibet, which has charter groups on dozens of campuses across the country, organizes nonviolent protests at the Chinese Embassy and the United Nations, and generally educates students about Tibetan culture and politics.

This wide range of cultural and political activities should not be confused with the development of American Vajrayāna. It may happen that some of these groups attract American Buddhist practitioners, or that conversely people initially drawn to the Tibetan cause become interested in the American branch of the religion. But much of this crossover is quite recent. It was uncommon that American practitioners had an opportunity to engage with any Tibetans other than their own teachers or visiting lamas. Now that there are thousands of Tibetans in the United States representing the experiences of more than one generation, it is likely that there will be opportunities for meetings between American practitioners and ethnic Tibetans who may or may not participate in similar rituals. My own fieldwork with the Tibetan community living in New York City suggests that most ordinary Tibetans do not meditate, and they consider their own religious practices limited to chanting prayers and caring for a personal shrine. Although these actions are also performed by Americans, the participation in far more elaborate monastic religious practices is more characteristic of American Vajrayānists than of lay ethnic Tibetans.

Many schools that offer courses in Buddhist religion are in close proximity to an American Vajrayāna center, such as the Namgyal Institute in Ithaca, where there is a thriving practice community of both Tibetan monks and American followers. Also in this category is the Naropa Institute in Boulder, Colorado, where a student can learn the philosophical foundations of the religion while also participating in meditation practice. In most of these areas, the Vajrayāna groups sponsor public events to which students are invited. Even within those institutes that were founded by Tibetan teachers, however, students are rarely required or pressured to become members of a particular group or otherwise "convert" to the religion. It is more common that practice communities attract a group of interested people, usually white-collar professionals, who find ways to integrate the teachings and practices into their often very full lives. There is a wide array of study groups, practice centers, retreat environments, and informal classes offered by all four orders, representing many different lineages from each order, in almost every state in the United States as well as many to choose from across Canada. A number of publishing houses specialize in, or in some cases only publish, Tibetan Buddhist texts. Among these are Shambhala Publications, founded by a senior student of Trungpa Rinpoche; Dharma Publishing, the print and translation wing of Tarthang Tulku's organization; Wisdom Publishing; and Snow Lion. There are also several ongoing translation endeavors, including the Nālandā Translation Committee, staffed largely by practitioners dedicated to the creation of accurate and readable translations of texts and liturgies used by American practice communities.

The development of American Vajrayāna is now also being facilitated with increasing access to the Internet frontier where lies a growing number of web pages containing a world of information, graphics, sounds, and representations of exotic landscapes. By simply entering a hypertext address (URL), the computer aficionado can invite into her home beautiful color pictures of Odiyan's vast retreat complex, photos of numerous *tulkus* and *geshes* both Tibetan and American, chants to ensure the long life of the Dalai Lama or to supplicate White Tara, the meditation schedule of the local Dharma center, the itinerary of visiting lamas, texts from recent teachings, the chanting and distinctive tonal melodies of Tibetan monks, and an immense display of other religious indicators that summon up the world of American Vajrayāna. One of the more helpful resource guides to finding these is the Quiet Mountain Tibetan Buddhist Resource Guide. This central storehouse provides links to dozens of sites from all four Tibetan orders, offering directions for negotiating the now intricate labyrinth of Dharma centers in North America. The URL for this guide is http://quietmountain.com. An Internet-wide search of "Tibetan Buddhist monasteries in America" brings up photos of Namgyal's complex as well as information about visiting the southern monastery of Losel Shedrup Ling, including a map and directions for finding its rural locale.

Thus, American Vajrayāna is able to reach countless numbers of interested people in such a way that it may capitalize on the premium placed on the swift retrieval of information and the constantly moving and relocating nature of American culture. The ability to download Tibetan icons, photos of beloved lamas, and the texts of chants creates a level of access and a vicarious experience of participation unheard of in traditional Tibet. With this increased means of access come certain concerns for an emerging Buddhist tradition. What happens to American Vajrayāna if its followers are not making personal, face-to-face contact with a lama or senior student of a teacher? The information one may discover about these teachings from a book or over the Internet cannot supplant the need for more intimate instruction from an embodied teacher or the desire to perform the more demanding practices with an actual group of like-minded people.

As the political situation in Tibet becomes more familiar to an American audience, another question remains as to whether those initially attracted to the politics of colonialism will be inspired to seek out the more spiritual path offered by American Vajrayāna. An influential contingent of famous actors, writers, poets, musicians, designers, and activists is becoming well-educated today about Tibetan culture; however, with several notable exceptions, it remains to be seen whether these people are drawn to its religious doctrines and practices, and if they are, whether their interest will enhance or impair the development of a distinctively American Tibetan Buddhism.

Each of the four orders has added crucial aspects to the composition of American Vajrayāna. The emphasis in the Gelugpa and Sakyapa orders on textual study and translation has strengthened the philosophical material available for practitioners who do not read or speak Tibetan. As with all religious transmission, it is critical that the texts read, prayers chanted, and teachings heard all be translated into English so that American followers are not made to feel alienated from their own religion. It is equally important that many scholars are able to read Tibetan fluently so as to make their translations and interpretations accurate. Kagyu and Nyingma lamas focus more of their teaching on meditation instruction and tantric initiations so as to introduce a new generation of students into the complex rituals of their heritage. Careful attention to the details of these ceremonies can ensure a high level of authenticity for each succeeding generation of American practitioners. It will be interesting to observe over the long run how the presentation of the teachings changes as new cultural and social forces influence practice. Along with senior students, recognized *tulkus*, and American monastics comes a new breed of practitioner, namely the children who are growing up in practice environments that cannot but affect their general worldview. Observers watch to see how meditation practice and the values and orientations of American Vajrayāna provide the ethical and behavioral backdrop for these children's lives, and how this historically unique perspective will influence their attitudes and decisions.

Contact with ordinary ethnic Tibetans will also contribute to the changing face of Tibetan Buddhism as it becomes more familiar in its new home. On the one hand, as Tibetans living in the West move further away from their own cultural roots, many are embracing American culture and adjusting to life in exile by distancing themselves from what they see as the old-fashioned, nonprogressive preoccupations of their ancestors. It should affect the composition of American Vajrayāna if there is a significant ethnic Tibetan population living in the United States which has no relationship to the religion originally brought to this country by its own forebears. On the other hand, if more Tibetans become involved in the practices of American Vajrayāna it will be interesting to see whether the authority structure of various Dharma centers begins to reflect this diversity. Since many Tibetans seem more actively involved in the political struggles of their homeland than in the religious practices of their American patrons, it is also worth watching whether American Dharma centers become more overtly political in an attempt to bridge the gap between these radically different cultures.

The question of child *tulkus* introduces a yet unknown element into the Buddhist faith as it is accepted among Westerners. As these children grow up and take their seats, the nature of power and authority within a given community may undergo significant upheaval. It is too early to know precisely how these communities might change due to the proclivities of their new young leaders. As long as the monastic institutions in India and Nepal (and to some extent those still operating in Tibet) maintain their commitment to the instruction and tutelage of new *tulkus* and future *geshes*, there is every reason to believe that their doctrines and practices will continue to be transmitted faithfully. There is much talk about "preserving" Tibetan culture as lamas bring the Dharma to the West. It might be wiser, however, to consider the ways in which Tibetan culture and religion are able to reconstitute themselves in their new home. The nature of preserving something tends to produce a static picture of what once was a dynamic, constantly evolving tradition. In the process of remaking itself in a new world, Tibetan Buddhism may find that aspects of American culture and the American psyche will contribute perspectives that will ensure its survival well into the next millennium.

Korean Buddhism in America: A New Style of Zen

MU SOENG

Like every subtradition of Buddhism to come to the West, Korean Buddhism in America has its Western and its ethnic aspects. Throughout the 1970s and 1980s, Asian Buddhist teachers teaching in America kept the two aspects separate from each other. In this essay I shall deal almost exclusively with Korean Buddhism as it has been taught to Americans of European descent.

In narrowing the essay's focus in this way it is implied that Korean Buddhism as it has been taught to Americans is vastly different from Buddhism as a cultural, social, and historical phenomenon encountered in Korea itself. This essay seeks to highlight the American phenomenon primarily through the activities of Zen Master Seung Sahn, who has been the first Korean Zen master to live and teach in the West.

Not surprisingly, the "Zen" aspect of Korean Buddhism is what most American Buddhists are most familiar with. It is important, however, to take some care in the use of the words *Ch'an, S'on,* and *Zen.* The average American spiritual seeker encounters Zen primarily in its Japanese forms and is normally unaware that heavy layers of Japanese culture separate this form of Zen from its Chinese and Korean ancestors. Although *Zen* has become a catch-all word for a number of traditions and views, there is almost always an assumption of its association with Japan and things Japanese. What needs to be clarified is the long and distinct history of Ch'an and S'on traditions in contradistinction to the Zen culture of Japan. There may be a number of congruences, and although Buddhism provides an overarching framework, these really are three different religious cultures.

This is to establish, in a broad stroke, the working premise of this essay: that S'on (the Korean word for Zen) is the predominant aspect of Korean Buddhism as taught to persons of European descent in America; that Buddhism in Korea itself is a singular repository of a multidimensional Chinese Sung Buddhism; that this Sung-S'on axis needs to be understood on its own terms and not through the prism of Japanese Zen; and that what passes for Korean Buddhism in America is but a faint glimpse into the Sung-S'on axis.

The S'on Tradition

A brief synopsis of the Korean S'on tradition might be helpful in making the reader familiar with the historical roots of Korean Buddhism in America.[1] S'on is an heir (in form, if not always in spirit) of the Ch'an movement as it evolved in T'ang (617–907) and Sung (970–1279) China. S'on in Korea has never been heavily institutionalized and thus retains some of the freewheeling spirit of the T'ang Ch'an. This Chinese-Korean axis bypasses the Japanese developments, and a lack of understanding of this aspect of Ch'an history presents American Zen students with serious difficulties of historical interpretation.

Ch'an—as inspired by Hui-neng, and the only form to survive down to our own time, albeit in highly transformed ways—began in southern China during the T'ang dynasty as a rural, economically self-reliant (through farming), anti-intellectual, and iconoclastic movement. Its most original form is a creative synthesis of Taoist naturalism and Indian Buddhist metaphysics. Even though it came to be co-opted by the Sung dynasty as a state religion, with all its attendant ills, Ch'an has always sought to define itself through its core organizing principles form T'ang China.

Korean Buddhism developed along lines quite different from its Chinese ancestor. Almost from the very beginning (late fourth century), Buddhism was embraced wholeheartedly by the Korean rulers and did not face the same obstacles as it did in China. The Silla dynasty (668–935) unified Korea into one kingdom and adopted Buddhism as a state religion. Buddhism thus exerted a great influence on the destiny of the nation. More than in most countries of East Asia, Buddhism in Korea has played the twin role of a propagator of state cult and a protector of popular Buddhism with excessive zeal.

Buddhism's hold on Korea became even more pronounced during the succeeding Koryŏ dynasty (936–1392). During the period of both dynasties, Buddhism in Korea consciously modeled itself after the multisystem schools of T'ien-t'ai and Hua-yen in China.[2] This syncretistic approach was championed most notably by the monk Wŏnhyo (616–86), who is considered the most influential personality in Korean Buddhist history, and later by Chinul (1158–1210), who brought about a basic reconciliation between the Kyo (Sūtra) and S'on (Zen) schools and became the founder of a native tradition of S'on in Korea.

In ninth-century Korea, this syncretistic approach was interrupted most rudely by some of the monks returning from China who had trained in the Hung-chou school of southern Ch'an under the disciples of Ma-tsu (709–88), the originator of the Ch'an "shock tactics." Between 828 and 931, a total of nine "Mountain Schools" of S'on were established in a burst of creative enterprise. The unruliness and the combativeness the S'on monks brought from China in their approach to Buddhism did not sit well with their non-S'on peers, nor did it sit well with the succeeding generations of Confucian bureaucrats who controlled the administrative machinery of the country throughout Korean history. The unfolding of Buddhism in Korea mirrored as well the one dominant theme in Chinese Buddhist history: the unceasing efforts of Confucian bureaucrats to stamp out the influence of Buddhism in the affairs of the state. The nature and duration of this conflict have implications for Korean Buddhism in America, as we shall see in this essay.

Between 828 and 1392, Korean Buddhism was a history of confrontation and periodic reconciliation between the S'on (Zen) and the Kyo (Sūtra) schools. Despite this confrontational history, S'on in Korea never became an independent and powerful institution as it did in Japan.

As with Ch'an in China after the 845–47 persecutions, S'on in Korea survived with great fortitude in the mountains after neo-Confucian orthodoxy took control of the state bureaucracy under the Chosŏn dynasty (1392–1910) and launched a series of persecutions against the Buddhists. The net effect of these persecutions was to reduce Buddhism to a mere skeleton of its former glory and power; for 272 years, until 1895, the Buddhist monks were not even allowed to enter the city gates.[3] Only in the last two decades of the nineteenth century did Buddhism begin to revive in Korea.

Ironically, Buddhism was brought out of its mountain hermitages and back into public life through the interference of Japanese military adventurers who had begun making inroads into Korean territories in the 1880s and 1890s.[4] After the Japanese formally annexed Korea in 1910, they demanded of its Buddhists that they reorganize themselves along the lines of Sōtō Zen in Japan, which by this time had become the parish religion of Japan. The most destabilizing of Japanese demands, at least to the Korean *sangha*, was that its members give up the traditional rule of celibacy and marry if they were to be appointed abbots of any temple.

In 1935, the celibate S'on monks, under assault from the occupying Japanese, merged themselves with the disparate Kyo (Sūtra) schools into a single unit, the Chogye order. As a result, today each of the temples under the Chogye control is an integrated unit, without distinction between a S'on or a Kyo temple. Large monastic complexes may consist of several buildings, each one serving a different function for the needs of the lay as well as the monastic community. The 1935 unification was in many ways a fulfillment of Wŏnhyo's and Chinul's syncretic dreams. While there are as many as seventeen other sects calling themselves Buddhist, they are of more recent origin (almost all of them in this century) and of a more modest pedigree. The Chogye order is thus the descendant and a repository of a 1,500-year-old historical process.

At the time of Korea's independence from Japan in 1945, there were only a handful of celibate monks (about six hundred) among an estimated seven thousand monks and nuns in the country.[5] In the 1950s, the celibate monks of the Chogye order engaged in a furious struggle to reestablish their leadership role in Korean Buddhism, which meant expelling the married monks, who then formed their separate Tae'go order. Zen Master Seung Sahn's personality especially was shaped by these ecclesiastical skirmishes of the 1950s and 1960s, and his personality in turn shaped the culture of Buddhism he brought to America in 1972.

Korean American Zen

The Providence Zen Center, in the small town of Cumberland in the northern part of the tiny state of Rhode Island, is the head "temple" of a network of meditation groups and centers founded by Seung Sahn, the first Korean Zen master to live and teach in the West.[6] This network was centrally organized in 1983 and is now called the Kwan Um Zen School ("Perceive Sound" School of Zen), and its activities are coordinated by offices at the Providence Zen Center.

Here, in an isolated part of the town, residents of the center, both monks and laypeople, men and women, get up at 4:30 a.m. and start their morning meditation session with 108 vigorous prostrations in the large hall. The prostrations are followed by the chanting of morning liturgy, which is then followed by a half-hour of quiet sitting. The entire ritual is reenacted, in a somewhat modified form, in the evening as well. During the day, many residents drive to nearby towns to their places of employment; the smaller number of staff residents caretake the offices, buildings, and grounds.

The style of Kwan Um Zen School is a unique product of Seung Sahn's experiments with Korean Buddhism in America. It fits neither the S'on model in Korea nor the Zen model in Japan. It is a blending of traditional Korean temple Buddhism with normative Japanese Zen forms. Intentionally or not, it follows the religious culture of an urban temple in the Sung-S'on axis.

Although the Kwan Um Zen School proclaims it is a center for the training of Zen, the actual practices at the centers and groups, such as the morning and evening liturgy (an amalgam of Pure Land, Hua-yen, and Ch'an sentiments) and occasional chanting of the name of Kwan Se Um Bosal (the bodhisattva of compassion), are replications of Korean popular

folk Buddhist practices. The practice of vigorous prostrations is likewise peculiar to Korean folk Buddhist tradition; Seung Sahn just made it uniquely
his own in adapting Korean Buddhism for Americans.

What is the actual practice of Zen within Kwan Um Zen School? It is a
unique version of "Action Zen" as envisaged by Seung Sahn. He has never
placed a high premium on *zazen*, the backbone of both Rinzai and Sōtō
forms of Japanese Zen. Here we must not fall into the temptation of defining Zen through its Japanese context; it might even be useful to keep in
mind the unstructured culture of southern Ch'an under Ma-tsu and his
successors. Although Kwan Um Zen School has evolved its own form of
sitting practice, it developed without being a main focus of Seung Sahn's
interest. Some of his early students had practiced with Shunryu Suzuki
Rōshi at the San Francisco Zen Center and convinced Seung Sahn that in
order to succeed in America as a Zen master, he had to incorporate sitting
practice as part of the package of Korean Buddhism he was offering.

When Seung Sahn first arrived in America in 1972, American Zen was
still in its formative stage; no one knew precisely what "Zen" meant. It was
a freewheeling enterprise, capable of being grafted onto any trend and
experiment. Seung Sahn turned out to be a very different kind of Zen
master from what had been the norm up until that time. Other Zen masters
created an aura of stillness around them; Seung Sahn was in perpetual
motion, even while sitting. He created vibrations wherever he went; the
molecules moved differently with his energy in the room. With him it was
not about quiet and stillness any more; it was about *retailing* Zen like it had
never been done before, and, by explicit association, retailing Korean Buddhism.

Seung Sahn's modus operandi has been to travel all over the world, give
public talks in numerous cities and towns, and encourage the local folks
who come to these talks to start a "Zen center." There have been many
takers. His perspective is that the Kwan Um Zen School central office exists
to provide information about the "style" of the school, and if local people
are interested in learning more about Korean Buddhism they can come up
to larger temples for "serious training." He has always chosen to call his
American centers and groups, whether residential or nonresidential, "temples."[7] Unbeknownst to many of the American students, it is a replication
of the Korean monastic model, reflecting the relationship of rural, small-
town temples to large regional head temples.

Seung Sahn's teaching role has focused more on proselytizing than on
leading meditation retreats. Shen-hui, the impresario of Hui-neng's Zen,
would have embraced him as a brother-in-arms. Seung Sahn's exhortation
to his American students has been to live together in meditation centers
in what he calls "together action"—"potatoes rubbing against each [other]

and getting cleaned." There is an overt gilding of Confucian societal mores in this model,[8] and it veers sharply from the rugged iconoclastic individualism of Ch'an, to which it pays nominal homage. A case has been made that the culture of Kwan Um Zen School is hardly anything more than an expression of Seung Sahn's personality as it has been shaped by the Confucian-Buddhist amalgam in Korea during the last thousand years.[9]

Seung Sahn's "Action Zen" consists of four elements that have since become synonymous with "Kwan Um Zen School style":

1. it displays his genius in translating classic Ch'an insights into sound bites: his phrases "only don't know," "put it all down," "don't make anything," and "just do it" have become popular parts of American Zen culture;
2. it has shifted the emphasis from striving for liberation to "together action," a more socially engaged format, encapsulated by his phrase, "How can I help you?" which he exhorts his students to use as a rallying cry for their "Zen bodhisattva" practice;
3. his emphasis on "bodhisattva action" replicates in America the pastor-parishioner relationship in Korean Buddhism;
4. his use of either a *kōan* or a mantra as a practice tool for Zen training, while confusing for many of his American students, is but a continuation of the mix of Pure Land and Ch'an practices that have dominated Korean Buddhism for the last several hundred years.

It is one of the conflicts of Seung Sahn's approach to Zen practice that although he proclaims himself a Zen master, he has always seen his role as an evangelist in the service of Korean Buddhism, and of his own interpretation of it. This contrast is seen most notably through the lives and activities of other Korean Zen masters in this century.[10] To this approach Seung Sahn has brought his immense charisma, a dynamic personality, and an engaging style that often tends to obfuscate the line between *zazen* practice and popular Korean Buddhism. Some of the results of Seung Sahn's version of Korean Buddhism in America include the following.

1. Lay students are permitted to wear the traditional Korean monk's robes. Until quite recently, almost as a matter of routine, a person who had been around for a few months was made a "Dharma teacher" and was given a monk's robe to wear. At times it has seemed more like a sop to the practitioner's ego and to the need for identity-confirmation through a uniform than an authentication of the person's immersion in practice.
2. Although considering himself as acting on behalf of the Chogye order of Korean Buddhism, an association of celibate monks and nuns,

Seung Sahn started ordaining lay American students as monks and nuns—the "bodhisattva monks." This has roused the ire of many of his compatriots in Korea.

3. Seung Sahn insists that a highly formulaic approach to *kōan* interviews during retreats is followed without deviation.

4. His approach to the bodhisattva path is reflective of the popular Korean Buddhist culture where all middle-aged women working in the monasteries are addressed as "bosal nim" (the Korean word for bodhisattva), and it pays no heed to the doctrinal foundations of the bodhisattva path as articulated in the great Mahāyāna *sūtras,* where bodhisattvahood is the culminating experience of a lifetime (or several) of rigorous perfection of the pāramitās.

A number of Zen centers have appeared and disappeared in Seung Sahn's firmament with great rapidity. One example that captures the hilarious aspect of this approach is the case of a young Russian musician who appeared at the Providence Zen Center in the late 1980s without any familiarity with Zen or Buddhism. After a stay of about six months he returned to St. Petersburg, his home town, where, at Seung Sahn's urging, he started a Zen center.[11] He used the address of his parents' apartment for the fledgling center. The interesting thing was that his parents were die-hard communists and he was not even welcome in his parents' apartment! In the literature distributed by Kwan Um Zen School this young man was consistently identified as the "Abbot of St. Petersburg Zen Center." Within a few months, however, he disappeared, never to be heard from again; the St. Petersburg Zen Center followed suit.

This example has been replicated several times in America on a less dramatic scale. The establishment of the Diamond Hill Zen Monastery, on the grounds of Providence Zen Center, is a case in point. The monastery was built in 1983–84 for the express purpose of serious training for the ordained monks. But from the very beginning Seung Sahn never took a personal interest in the training program at the monastery. He did not even insist that all his ordained American students make the monastery their home and contribute to its growth as a monastic center. To this day, the Diamond Hill Zen Monastery remains a minor footnote to Seung Sahn's missionary activities in America.

Seung Sahn's argument has been that he has trained many American students who are now capable of teaching on their own. These students are called Ji Do Poep Sa Nim (Korean for "One Who Shows the Way"), and yet Seung Sahn has never been personally involved in the training of these students, save for one or two in the very early days of his time in America. There has been no prerequisite that these teachers be well versed in the Buddhist tradition or even have a working knowledge of the Korean Buddhist tradition. The only requirement is that they be able and willing to replicate faithfully Kwan Um Zen School's teaching style—use of prostrations, chanting, and formulaic *kōan* interviews—and a missionary approach. In this approach there is much greater emphasis on recruiting people to live in a Zen center or to become members of the organization than on their spiritual training.

Some of the people who have spent years in Seung Sahn's organization have a palpable impression that he is most interested in gaining a large number of students, even if they turn out to be short-term catches. This striving for numbers for numbers' sake has left a parallel impression that Seung Sahn has been remarkably unconcerned with the spiritual training of those who might come into contact with the groups within his organization. As a result the culture of Kwan Um Zen School has been an uneasy commingling of the preternaturally American with the Sung-S'on Buddhist monastic model—a tribe of individual nomads trying to fit into a mold of clan loyalty and group identity. Seung Sahn, through his immense charisma and willpower, has overwhelmed his students, even dominated them at times, but the attrition has been alarming.

Conclusion

American Buddhism is driven, for the most part, more by the actual practice of meditation than by a deeply imbibed Buddhist worldview. Korean Buddhism in America is no exception to this rule. While Seung Sahn has made heroic efforts in translating his version of the urban Sung-S'on monastic model to the inner-city environs in America, he has made little effort in articulating the Sung-S'on Buddhist worldview and its doctrinal foundations to his American students.

Overall, Seung Sahn's approach to Korean Buddhism in America has been that of a missionary, the emphasis being on a "storefront" presentation of Korean Buddhism. Some have conjectured that he seems to be inspired by the Japanese models of charismatic Buddhism he encountered while living in Japan from 1966 to 1972. Although he disparages the Japanese models, he embraces wholeheartedly the tone and approach of Japan's New Buddhism: aggressive, confrontational, and missionary. The nonseparation of Confucian societal mores from a striving for liberation remains at the heart of Seung Sahn's legacy in America.

These observations, I must acknowledge, derive from my personal involvement with Kwan Um Zen School. I was a student of Seung Sahn for some fifteen years, of which eleven years were spent as a monk. I had the opportunity to look intimately at the model he created, work with it, and reflect on it from the perspective of day-to-day immersion. My observations are thus not a sociological field-study but an intensely lived experience. I found Seung Sahn to be a wise and charismatic leader, yet found him lacking as a meditation teacher. His presence and his organization were of enormous benefit to myself and many others. Yet I, and many others like me, ran into some difficulties concerning the motivation and interpretation in Seung Sahn's approach to Korean Buddhism in America. I must also acknowledge that many students who remain within Kwan Um Zen School will have an altogether different perspective from what I have articulated here.

Furthermore, it may be true that the grafting of Korean Buddhism onto American culture, as evidenced by Seung Sahn's efforts, shares many characteristics with similar efforts by Asian Buddhist teachers in America, in all the subtraditions of Mahāyāna, Zen, Vajrayāna, Theravāda, and *vipassanā*. As a contemporary Buddhist scholar has pointed out,

> Rapid growth [in North American Buddhist culture] has led many Dharma centres on this continent to focus so much attention on establishing a physical presence in the form of monasteries, churches and schools, and on financing all this physical expansion, that very little time has been left over for people to sit down and study the history, literature and culture of the religious tradition that they have adopted. As a consequence, too many North American Buddhists, despite an abundance of energy and zeal and inspiration, have remained virtually unschooled in Buddhist culture and, as is always the case when ignorance is widespread, there has been much room for myth and fallacy to take root in the place of the true Dharma. In some respects this situation is particularly acute among North American Zen circles, where there has too often been a disdain for bookish activity or indeed any activity aside from manual labour and *zazen*.[12]

In the last few years, as Seung Sahn's health has waned, his American students have been doing their own experimentation with Seung Sahn's experimentation with Korean Buddhism in America, while remaining nominally affiliated with the Kwan Um Zen School. Some of these students, with financial resources of their own, have started their own "monasteries," including one in Kentucky and one in the San Bernardino mountains outside of Palm Springs, California. In these and other places, in an ironic twist, T'ang China's "thousand experiments on a thousand peaks" are being carried on, changing the contours of Kwan Um Zen School's legacy in America. As the school's teaching is presently so closely calibrated to Seung Sahn's personal preferences, it is hard to say what shape his legacy will take as it finds itself increasingly in the midst of an aging population of American practitioners.

The Kwan Um Zen School, in addition to its headquarters at the Providence Zen Center in Rhode Island, has urban centers in New York, Los Angeles, Boston, and New Haven, as well as satellite groups in other towns and cities.

In addition to Zen Master Seung Sahn, Samu Sunim has been another prominent Korean monk to live and teach in the West. Born in Korea in 1941, he arrived in Montreal in 1968 and moved to Toronto in 1972.[13] He also started teaching Zen and presented an aesthetically somewhat more elegant version of it than Seung Sahn's.

Lacking Seung Sahn's pedigree of a lineage transmission, Samu Sunim proclaimed in 1977 that he had received transmission from his old Zen teacher, dead for many years, in a vision.[14] As a result of this visionary transmission Samu Sunim formally started calling himself a Zen master. In addition to his main center in Toronto, Samu Sunim has branch centers in Ann Arbor and Chicago. His students recently purchased an old Methodist church on Chicago's Northside, and for the first few months were doing *zazen*, prostrations, and devotional offerings in front of a huge cross.

Samu Sunim is extremely devoted to spreading Buddhism throughout North America and demonstrates a tireless energy in getting the word out through press releases, free talks, tours, classes, "interreligious" conferences, and so on. By and large, Samu Sunim has shown a greater willingness to engage in cross-cultural exchanges and has sponsored artistic events through his center to highlight traditional Korean Buddhist arts and their relevance to contemporary arts in the West.[15]

Like most Asian Buddhist teachers, both Seung Sahn and Samu Sunim have tempered their presentation of S'on and Korean Buddhism to suit American audiences. Both of them have encountered difficulties in translating a monastic model nestled in the mountains of Korea to the inner-city environs of America. These mountain temples were the training ground for both of them, and their compatriot monks provided a system of checks and balances. Lacking both a physical monastery and other ordained monks to work with, the efforts of both Seung Sahn and Samu Sunim have been creative at best. Both have found American students who are willing to make only a short-term commitment to a teacher and are only too willing and eager to sample the range of other Buddhist traditions, teachings, and teachers. The shape of Korean Buddhism in America bears the unmistakable imprints of these transactions between Seung Sahn and Samu Sunim and their American students. Again, these transactions have been no different from the difficulties faced by other Asian Buddhist teachers in similar situations.

Among the other Korean monastics who have had some contact with Americans, two are worth mentioning. Kyung-bo Sunim, a highly regarded spiritual head of the Chogye order in Korea in the 1960s, made several trips to America in the 1970s but never stayed. Several Americans who came in contact with him started their own centers in different parts of the country—one in Walnut Creek, outside of San Francisco, one in Arkansas, among others—but it is unclear what the level or content of their training has been. Kyung-bo Sunim himself never learned English. In the early

1990s, an American woman started a Korean "temple" in Crestone, Colorado, to further the work of a charismatic Korean nun, Dae Haeng Sunim. The nun spoke no English and did not stay in America, and it is difficult to say what it means to have a Korean "temple" in Crestone, Colorado.

On the other side of the spectrum, a number of Korean monks and nuns have come to America for shorter or longer periods of time and have had no interaction with students of European descent. In a normal pattern, a middle-aged Korean American couple will invite a monk or a nun from Korea at the behest of their aging matriarch and provide a house or a portion of a house for the use of the monastic. An unstated agenda in such an invitation might be to reconnect their teenage children with the values of their inherited culture through a living "saint." In such a situation, a shrine room will be set up on the first floor of the house and will serve as a congregation point for the local ethnic Korean Buddhist community. In most cases, the monastic is unable or unwilling to learn English and remains isolated from Western Buddhists. These "temples" function as a Sunday church gathering for the Korean community and allow them to hold on to the vestiges of their heritage. The number of ethnic Koreans in America who consider themselves Buddhist seems to be minuscule compared to those who consider themselves Christian. The activities of ethnic Korean Buddhism in America are quite limited.

The proliferation of Korean Buddhism in America has thus taken place largely through the activities of Seung Sahn and Samu Sunim among persons of European descent and faces the same demographic issues as other Buddhist groups in the country.

Vietnamese Buddhism in North America: Tradition and Acculturation

CUONG TU NGUYEN

A. W. BARBER

This essay offers an overview of the general features of modern Vietnamese Buddhism, the process of the institution's acculturation in North America, and its awareness (or lack of awareness) of this process. The essay concludes with some speculation on the nature of Vietnamese Buddhism in North America. Although both Theravāda and Mahāyāna Buddhism exist in Vietnam, the predominant tradition is Mahāyāna Buddhism as filtered through China.[1] In this essay when we refer to "Vietnamese Buddhism," we mean this form of Buddhism. We will delineate the main doctrines and practices, as well as the prejudices and imagined realities, that constitute the rationale for the behavior and aspirations of modern Vietnamese Buddhists. These elements influence the way Vietnamese Buddhists view themselves and the future of their tradition in North America.[2]

In preparing this essay we have worked closely with the abbots of two temples. The first is the Venerable Thích Trí Tuệ, abbot of Vạn Hạnh Temple in Centreville, Virginia. There are three Vietnamese Buddhist temples in northern Virginia. The Centreville temple was selected because it has a permanent abbot. His opinions represent the view of a current monastic leader of a Vietnamese Buddhist community. The second is the Venerable Tiên Quang, abbot of Chùa Bát Nhã Pagoda in Calgary, Alberta. This is the largest Buddhist congregation in southern Alberta, a traditional stronghold of Buddhism in North America.[3]

Venerable Trí Tuệ is fifty years old and has been a monk for almost forty years. He received a traditional monastic education at the Huệ Nghiêm Buddhist Institute in South Vietnam. Vạn Hạnh Temple is located on a ten-acre tract of land and consists of two small buildings: the main hall (*chính điện*) and the residential hall, which includes a living room, kitchen, and the abbot's room. Vạn Hạnh Temple has its own congregation and operates independently. This is not an uncommon pattern in Vietnamese Buddhism.

Venerable Tiên Quang is in his mid-forties. He completed two master's degrees in Vietnam. In addition to being a well-educated monk he claims to be a Ch'an meditation master as well as a *vipaśyanā* and *śamatha* instructor. Chùa Bát Nhã is located in the Vietnamese neighborhood in the southeast section of Calgary. It is a three-floor structure. Although from the outside three floors are evident, from the inside the second and third floors are open and constitute a two-story temple area. The partially submerged first floor holds a large general-use room, a kitchen, offices, and living quarters for the several monks.[4] Three nuns live in housing off the property.

A Brief Note on the History of Vietnamese Buddhism in North America

Vietnamese Buddhism is one of the newcomers among the Buddhist traditions that have arrived in North America in the last few decades. The first Vietnamese Buddhist community appeared in America after 1975, in the wake of the fall of South Vietnam. In the last two decades Vietnamese Buddhism in North America has been growing by leaps and bounds. By 1995 there were around 160 Vietnamese Buddhist temples and centers in North America.[5]

In his book *How the Swans Came to the Lake*, Rick Fields mentions two Vietnamese Buddhist teachers, Thích Thiên Ân and Thích Nhất Hạnh, as the pioneers of Vietnamese Buddhism in North America.[6] However, whether or not these two represent Vietnamese Buddhism is questionable. As Fields points out, Thích Thiên Ân was trained as a Zen master in the Rinzai tradition of Japanese Buddhism.[7] Thích Nhất Hạnh, although he does not reside in North America, makes frequent lecture tours there and has become one of the two most visible and influential Buddhist teachers in the West, alongside the Tibetan Dalai Lama, according to Fields.[8]

Thích Thiên Ân died in 1980. Since he did not have a specific teaching to make a lasting impact on the Vietnamese Buddhist community, his memory has faded away. In contrast, Thích Nhất Hạnh, though he was never known as a Ch'an master in Vietnam, has become a famous master in the West. He oversees several retreat centers in America and Europe where his Western and Vietnamese disciples engage in the practice of a "New Age"–style Zen and rituals created by him[9] that do not have any affinity with or any foundation in traditional Vietnamese Buddhist practices.

Modern Vietnamese Buddhism: An Overview

It is the popular opinion that Buddhism is the spiritual tradition[10] of 80 percent of the Vietnamese population and that Buddhism has deep roots in the Vietnamese culture. Some modern Western scholars have expressed doubt about this opinion. The French scholar Léopold Cadière, for instance, stated that in the final analysis the Vietnamese are not really Buddhist.[11] This remark is not completely incorrect, but it reflects the lack of a deeper investigation into the nature of Vietnamese Buddhism. It is true that on closer analysis the Vietnamese Buddhists are not Buddhist in the same way the Khmer or Thai Buddhists are, and the Buddhism in Vietnam never had the kind of *sangha*, institutions, hierarchy, or organizations found in Sri Lankan Buddhism.

Nevertheless, Vietnamese Buddhists are Buddhist in the sense that they define their spiritual needs and satisfactions in the context of the Buddhist worldview. It is not an exaggeration to say that Buddhism is the tradition for the majority of the Vietnamese people. Vietnamese Buddhism fulfilled the spiritual needs of the majority of the Vietnamese population, whether they are officially Buddhist or not (except of course for the Vietnamese Christians). However, Vietnamese Buddhism has lived in a symbiotic relationship with Taoism, Chinese spirituality, and the indigenous Vietnamese religion. Having once been part of China, and usually having friendly relations with the various imperial governments, Vietnam has participated in high culture from early in its history. Obviously, Buddhism would function differently in such an environment from how it would in a society where it was the main transmitter of high culture as in the Southeast Asian countries.

Vietnamese Buddhism is basically acephalous and nonsectarian. Buddhism spread to Vietnam around the first century c.e. Yet it was not until the middle of the tenth century, when Vietnam gained independence from Chinese hegemony, that Vietnamese Buddhism began to search for an identity. Even during its heyday, however, there was never a unified, state-consecrated *sangha*. Nor was there sufficient state support to institutionalize a scholastic tradition or to establish any lasting sectarian schools.

During the French domination, several revival movements within Vietnamese Buddhism occurred. These movements, however, took place in the form of discrete Buddhist organizations in the three parts of Vietnam. Although there were some communications between them, the situation was still not conducive to the formation of a unified, institutionalized *sangha*.

It was not until after the fall of the Ngô Đình Diệm regime that the Vietnamese Unified Buddhist Church[12] was founded in South Vietnam. The senior monk, Venerable Thích Tịnh Khiết, became general supervisor of monks (*tăng thống*). It would be misleading, however, to present the Vietnamese Unified Buddhist Church as a tightly knit, hierarchical religious organization. As a newly created church that lacked both tradition and experience, it could not function the way one would expect an institutionalized church to function. Most temples and monks supported the political view of the Vietnamese Unified Buddhist Church, but they still operated quite independently. This pattern existed before the founding of the Unified Buddhist Church and continued to exist afterward.

The same pattern carries over to Vietnamese Buddhism in North America. Temples are built and supported by separate groups of Buddhists. Although there are a few "Overseas Buddhist Churches" and nominal leaders, the common pattern is that a certain monk is invited to become the abbot of a temple by a certain Buddhist congregation that deems him qualified. Such an abbot is in no way appointed by or responsible to any central or higher power. For example, Chùa Bát Nhã belongs to the World Vietnamese Buddhist Association and to the Canadian Vietnamese Buddhist Association. These affiliations are voluntary and do not establish Chùa Bát Nhã as being subordinate to any organization. The temple was established by the local community and is under the direction of the executive board. All decisions pertaining to the running of the temple, doctrine, and activities are made locally.[13]

The Main Features

Vietnamese Buddhism (both in Vietnam before 1975 and in North America after 1975) functions on the basis of semi-independent Buddhist temples and groups. Yet Vietnamese Buddhist teaching and practice have been homogenous and stabilized for centuries. For the lay followers, this is partially due to the paucity of scriptures and other Buddhist literature accessible to the general population. For the monastics it is primarily due to the inherited traditions from China and perhaps to the lack of education. The renewal of Buddhism that began in the early part of this century in China does not seem to have reached Vietnam before World War II. Chinese is the main canonical language. Basic Mahāyāna *sūtras*, such as the *Lotus Sūtra*, the *Diamond Sūtra*, the *Vimalakīrti Sūtra*, the *Complete Enlightenment Sūtra*, the *Śūraṅgama Sūtra*, the *Amitābha Sūtra*, and so forth, have been translated into Vietnamese. But most of these translations are stilted and unintelligible to the average Vietnamese Buddhist since they teem with Sino-Vietnamese technical terms. Among these *sūtras*, the *Lotus Sūtra* and the *Amitābha Sūtra* are the more often used. There are standard liturgical texts containing material from a host of *sūtras* and some *dhāraṇīs*, following the Chinese model.

Vietnamese Buddhism is closely related to Chinese Buddhism in general and reflects the post–Sung dynasty formation. Thus one finds various Chinese teachings being offered. The *Vinaya* transmission comes from the Dharmaguptaka sect.[14] The bodhisattva precepts are transmitted originating with the T'ien-t'ai tradition,[15] but presently coming through the Ch'an heritage along with the Ch'an rules.[16] The overall doctrinal position is the inclusive system of T'ien-t'ai, with the higher metaphysics being informed by Hua-yen. However, most Vietnamese Buddhists are unaware of this.

Although there were a few monastic colleges in Vietnam before 1975, not all monks were trained there. It was not even a requirement that monks receive monastic education at those colleges.[17] Some studied at their temples or went to public schools; few went on to receive any higher education. Since Vietnamese Buddhism has always been nonsectarian, there have never been sectarian schools with their own colleges, doctrinal systems, training programs, and so forth, as in Tibetan Buddhism. Monks who went to monastic colleges received some education in Buddhist history and doctrine, but the extent that this knowledge was of use to them is undetermined.

The Practice

A Vietnamese monk's intellectual background does not have much to do with his actual practice. Vietnamese monks would follow the same program of practice, regardless of their intellectual disparities. This program consists of chanting the *sūtras*, reciting Buddhas' names (mostly Amitābha), doing repentance, and praying for rebirth in Amitābha's Pure Land. It is true that monks and lay followers sit in meditation occasionally, and some regularly, but meditation is not a principal element in Vietnamese Buddhist practice. Not every Vietnamese Buddhist monk is an adept in meditation.

The most essential practice in Vietnamese Buddhism is to gain merit (*puṇya*). Most Vietnamese Buddhists, including intellectual ones, do not believe that they could attain awakening or liberation on their own by practicing meditation. For the masses liberation means to be assisted by the Buddhas and bodhisattvas. Most adhere to the popular belief that the merit accumulated in this life, if not good enough to earn one a place in Amitābha's Pure Land, at least guarantees a better rebirth in one's next life or a better future in this life. The modern Vietnamese Buddhist practice a composite form of Buddhism that is utterly eclectic. It includes elements from Ch'an, Pure Land, T'ien-t'ai, and popular Vajrayāna.

The generally held opinion by most Vietnamese Buddhists is that Vietnamese Buddhism is a combination of Ch'an and Pure Land. Venerable Trí Tuệ explains that all teachings are one, but it is necessary to master all teachings as a skillful means to guide sentient beings with different spiritual abilities. We will not consider here the misconceptions presented in most English-language materials regarding the distinctness of these schools and the strong inclination for "syncretism" found in Chinese and Vietnamese Buddhism. Much has been said about the incompatibility of different schools and their difficulty in successfully communicating with each other and combining their doctrines. None of these theories reflects realities in Vietnam (or China) past or present. The followers have no problem practicing the various teachings at the same time. Although some masters hold that one needs to use a combined Ch'an and Pure Land approach, others do not.[18] Venerable Trí Tuệ vehemently rejects the idea that it is possible to attain liberation relying on meditation alone.[19] In contrast, Venerable Tiên Quang accepts the idea of meditation by itself being efficacious; he adds, however, that this is a more difficult path than the Pure Land or the combined Ch'an and Pure Land approach.[20]

Although meditation is not the predominant element, it is an integral part of the Buddhist program of practice. But sitting quietly contemplating the magnificence of Amitābha's paradise or the auspicious marks of the Buddha, or mentally reciting Amitābha's name, is also a legitimate form of meditation. As mentioned before, the emphasis for most Vietnamese Buddhists is gaining merit (puṇya) and this becomes a critical concept in Vietnamese Buddhism. The goal of the accumulation of merit is to gain rebirth in Amitābha's Pure Land. Despite the fact that Vietnamese Buddhism has a decentralized organizational form, its practice is almost uniform. One can learn almost everything about the general pattern of Vietnamese Buddhist practice by visiting any temple.

Vietnamese Buddhist practice consists of three intervals of service performed regularly at dawn, noon, and dusk. These three sessions of service consist mainly of chanting sūtras, reciting dhāraṇīs and Buddha's name, and circumambulation. Some of the principal Mahāyāna sūtras have been translated into Vietnamese, but not every sūtra is chanted. In most cases only devotional sūtras, or more specifically chapters from them, are chanted. The three most chanted sūtras are the Heart Sūtra, Lotus Sūtra,[21] and Amitābha Sūtra.

1. Morning service: The morning service takes place early, from around 4:00 to 5:00 a.m. First the large bells are struck. Then the monks chant the Śūraṅgama Dhāraṇī and the Heart Sūtra. Afterward they circumambulate while reciting the name of Amitābha Buddha.

2. Noon service: The noon service takes place from around 11:00 a.m. to 1:00 p.m. The monks chant the Heart Sūtra. Then they perform the rice-offering ritual. Between the full moon of the fourth month to the full moon of the seventh month (lunar calendar), the monks circumambulate and recite Amitābha Buddha's name after lunch.

3. Evening service: The evening service takes place from around 6:00 to 7:00 p.m. First the monks chant the *Amitābha Sūtra* and the *Heart Sūtra.* Then they circumambulate and recite Amitābha Buddha's name.

Laypeople can participate in these services if they choose to. It is not uncommon to see quite a few laypeople come to the temple and join the monks in these three services, especially the evening one. Devout Buddhists can perform these daily services at home. They do not have to be done three times a day, seven days a week, though some do keep to this schedule faithfully. For example, in Chùa Bát Nhã active participation on a daily basis seems dominated by the senior members of the congregation. Elderly women are the most prevalent of this group. Many members of the congregation have taken refuge and hold bodhisattva vows. This allows them to wear the traditional black robes and red-brown outer robe, although most members do not exercise this option; the seniors, however, seem to prefer it. Generally the senior members, determined by age, will occupy the front of any assembly just behind the monks and nuns.

Besides the daily service, there are also special services. The most popular and regular of these is the repentance liturgy. This liturgy takes place in the evening twice a month at the full moon and new moon. It is referred to in Vietnamese as *sám hối* (repentance) or *hồng danh sám hối* (to repent by reciting the names of Buddhas). In this liturgy the Buddhists recite aloud the names of 108 Buddhas and bow each time a Buddha's name is recited. Then they chant the *Heart Sūtra* and recite Amitābha Buddha's name.[22]

Venerable Trí Tuệ explains that repentance is a useful and practical practice. The goal of repentance is to be mindful of the bad karma that one might commit by actions of body, speech, or mind. It is also a way to face the Buddha and make a confession. Chanting the names of the Buddhas is a way to purify one's bad karma through their sustaining powers.

The Role of the Temple

In medieval and colonial times, some temples were built by royal decree and supported by the state. In modern times, most temples have been built mainly because certain Buddhist congregations felt the need for a place of focus in order to continue to live as Buddhist. Such a group would invite a monk to come and then build a temple. Sometimes a temple was built first and a search for a monk was launched afterward.

The same pattern continues in North America. Vietnamese Buddhists believe that the temple is where they come to carry out their spiritual activities. Yet the temple also assumes an important social role: it is the place where traditional and cultural values are preserved, where Vietnamese children come not just for Dharma but to learn something about the customs and habits of their ancestral homeland. Some temples give Vietnamese-language lessons on weekends. Some also offer children's Dharma classes in addition to whatever adult education may take place.

Buddhists contribute to the upkeep of the temple; contributions are on a voluntary basis. At every temple there is a "merit box" (*phước sương*), that is, donation box. When there is a special pressing need, the abbot makes a public announcement either in a letter or directly to the laypeople after a Dharma talk and requests donations. But contributions are always voluntary.

At Chùa Bát Nhã, for example, not only was the money for building the temple collected, but on an ongoing basis members support the monks and nuns with donations. In addition to giving money, many members send food and other items to help further support the monks and nuns. Some members volunteer their time to help in temple activities. During special holidays there are often large ceremonies followed by a vegetarian meal. People can help in a variety of ways from cooking to audio- and video-taping the ceremonies. The temple also needs to be maintained and people volunteer to help with the yard work, snow removal, and other such tasks.

Vietnamese Buddhism centers around rituals, and one of the main functions of the temple is to perform these rituals. Among the most important rituals is the commemoration of the *vía*-day of Buddhas. *Vía* literally means "spirit," but in this context it denotes either the birthday or the awakening day of a particular Buddha or bodhisattva. The Buddhist calendar figures twenty-four such days, including Śākyamuni's birthday and awakening day. It also includes the *vía*-day of some Chinese spirits and deified heros like Kuan Kung.[23]

In Vietnam most temples commemorate all of these *vía*-days. In North America, due to new circumstances, only the main *vía*-days are commemorated. These are Maitreya's Day (which is also Tết, the Vietnamese New Year's Day), the Full Moon of the First Month (*Răm Tháng Giêng*), Avalokiteśvara's Day, Śākyamuni's Birthday, Ullambana (*Vu Lan*),[24] Amitābha's Day, and Śākyamuni's Awakening Day.

Vietnamese Buddhists celebrate these days by chanting *sūtras*, making offerings to Buddha, praying for peace (*cầu an*), and praying for rebirth in Amitābha's Pure Land (*cầu siêu*). Praying for peace can be communal or individual, and it can be praying for peace of the country and the world.

More popular is the praying for the well-being of family members who are still alive. This is based on the doctrine of transference of merit (*hồi hướng*) and confidence in the powers of Buddhas and bodhisattvas. According to this concept, people can transfer the merit they earn by performing a rite dedicated to their loved ones. Praying for rebirth, or *cầu siêu*, is a ritual that a person or a family performs to pray for a deceased member in the family so that he or she might gain a better rebirth or if possible a rebirth in Amitābha's Pure Land.

The Concept of Merit

Gaining merit is the focal point of modern Vietnamese Buddhist practice. There are numerous ways for a person to gain merit: contributing to the building of temples or to the printing of Buddhist books, supporting (*cúng dường*) monks and nuns, and so forth. The most common form of merit making is perhaps making contributions for the printing of Buddhist books. These books range from multivolume translations into Vietnamese of large *sūtras* such as the *Hua-yen Sūtra*, the collections of short *sūtras* and *dhāraṇīs* for daily service, to small booklets containing *dhāraṇīs*, the most chanted among which is the *Chú Đại Bi* (Great Compassion *Dhāraṇī*). Visitors can pick up one of these booklets at any Vietnamese Buddhist temple and find on its last page a list of names of the contributors. Laypeople believe that this is a meritorious act because by contributing to the printing of Buddhist books they help make the Buddha Dharma accessible to other sentient beings.

Another way of earning merit is the practice of *phóng sinh*, or setting free living creatures. On certain occasions (such as *vía*-days) a Buddhist buys living animals, mostly birds and fish, and sets them free. Venerable Trí Tuệ explains that *phóng sinh* has a triple objective: to show compassion to humans and other living beings, to reduce greed because *phóng sinh* is a form of giving (*dāna*), and to reduce one's bad karma.

Acculturation and Change

Vietnamese refugees began to come to North America in 1975 in the aftermath of the Vietnam War. Since then more Vietnamese have immigrated to Canada and the United States under various circumstances. Buddhists make up the majority of the Vietnamese diaspora. Like other groups of Indochinese immigrants, the Vietnamese have had to experience culture shock, adaptation, and acculturation. The Vietnamese did not suffer the same level of trauma that the Cambodians did.[25] The Vietnamese Buddhists who are scattered throughout Canada and the United States build temples with the intention to continue to live as Vietnamese Buddhists and to preserve their faith and cultural values not only during their own time, but for the generations to come.

The temple plays a central role in Vietnamese Buddhist activities. In Vietnam the temple is more or less the "property" of the abbot. In medieval and premodern times some temples were built by royal decree with financial support from the court. In modern times, a temple is usually built by a particular Buddhist group, sometimes headed by a monk. The money comes mainly from donations collected before the temple is erected. The abbot is the spiritual leader, but it is not uncommon that he also serves as president of the congregation and of its various administrative boards.

Milada Kalab wrote in her study of Cambodian Buddhist monasteries in Paris:

> Administratively, the organization of monasteries in resettlement countries depends to some degree on the laws of the country. In France and probably in most western countries, these religious institutions are run by duly constituted charitable associations with elected presidents, secretaries, and treasurers, and with proper bookkeeping and audits. . . . Also in Cambodia, the committee managing the monastery was composed of laymen separated from the monastic organization, although they often held meetings together. In France, however, a monk is often president or secretary of the association.[26]

Vietnamese Buddhism in North America tends to follow this organizational pattern. For instance, Vạn Hạnh Temple functions as a nonprofit organization with its attendant administrative boards. Since most temples in Vietnam were self-governed, this represents less of a change than it does for Cambodian Buddhists in the West, since in Cambodia the community of monks was organized and supervised by the state. Even in Vietnam before 1975, in most cases each temple had its own governing board with the abbot as the president, although this was not required by the government.

One problem Vietnamese Buddhist temples face in North America is the zoning of land. In Vietnam no one would complain—let alone sue a temple—simply because the monks strike a big bell early in the morning or because they turn on the loudspeakers and send a cacophony of chanting into the neighborhood. But in North America it is not so simple. Quite a few Vietnamese temples in California and Texas have been involuntarily caught in legal wrangles with their neighbors.[27] Venerable Trí Tuệ also receives complaints from his neighbors that there are too many cars on Buddhist holidays.

Although the main role of the temple (both in Vietnam and in North America) is to perform services, the Buddhist spiritual tradition is not just a matter of Sunday mornings. The devotees can come to the temple to make offerings, pray, chant the *sūtras*, and so on whenever they like. In Vietnam, Buddhists would normally go to a temple in their neighborhood. Only on special occasions would they go to a bigger or more prestigious temple. In North America most temples are located away from residential areas, and public transportation is quite limited, except in very big cities. Since most temple-goers are older people, this has created some serious transportation difficulties.

In Vietnam monks do not have to work, so there are always some monks or nuns around in the temple to talk to or help laypeople with domestic, personal rituals. It is quite a different situation in the West. Most temples have only one resident monk, and some temples do not even have a permanent resident monk. Some of the monks have to work, like the abbot of a temple in Washington, D.C., who works full time as a television repairman. Venerable Trí Tuệ works part time to get health benefits. The fact that some monks have to work to support themselves has disturbed the traditional "division of labor" and altered the relationship between the cleric and the laity. There are temples that are exceptions, like Chùa Bát Nhã, where four young monks and three nuns are being trained by Venerable Tiên Quang.

For all these reasons, most temples in North America are closed weekdays and only open on Buddhist holidays and for Sunday services. Sunday services consist of observance of service and a Dharma talk by the abbot. At some larger temples, especially in California, there are activities by the Buddhist youth groups (*gia đình Phật tử*) and Vietnamese-language lessons.

Vạn Hạnh is a small temple. According to Venerable Trí Tuệ, the temple has around two thousand members, that is, two thousand people on its mailing list. However, only a few dozen typically show up for Sunday services. A funeral might be attended by one hundred people. Buddha's Birthday and Ullambana attract four to five hundred people. On the Vietnamese New Year's Day seven or eight hundred people might come to the temple.

Chùa Bát Nhã has a membership of around three thousand adults who are formal members, and an informal membership (those who occasionally come) between one and two thousand. Although the new temple has 17,000 square feet of floor space it is usually filled beyond capacity on holidays (weather permitting).

In sum, people only come to the temple when they need to. The temple still serves mainly as a place for performing rituals, especially funerals. Although most educated men and young lay Buddhists are not very keen on rituals, they still come to the temple and participate in rituals that are relevant to them personally. In recent years, even in Vietnam, temples have begun to hold wedding ceremonies, but most monks still feel a bit uncomfortable with this. (Weddings used to be done at home before the ancestral altar, in a "nonreligious" ceremony.) In Vietnam the Buddhists come to temples not only to make offerings and practice, but also to study the Dharma. Even here in North America some temples occasionally offer courses on Buddhist doctrine, although this may be becoming less frequent.

According to Venerable Trí Tuệ, there are many reasons why most temples are no longer able to offer classes on Buddhist doctrine. First of all, facilities, competent teachers, and material resources are all lacking. Above all, nowadays lay Buddhists can listen to Dharma talks on cassette tapes, so they do not deem it necessary to come to the temple to participate in Dharma classes. Most Buddhists seem to think that it is more convenient to buy a cassette tape and listen to it whenever they want, than to drive half an hour to the temple to listen to a Dharma talk. Venerable Trí Tuệ does not think that this is a good idea, since by listening to the tape the lay Buddhists would have no one to explain further to them if there are things they do not quite understand. For the Vietnamese Buddhist, however, acquiring merit is the most important activity. It matters not whether they understand the teachings, because the way they see it, listening to a Dharma talk is in itself a meritorious act.[28]

Vietnamese Buddhism and North Americans

Vietnamese Buddhism is perhaps the least popular form of Buddhism among North Americans. Observing the services at a Vietnamese temple, one hardly sees any Westerners. The main reason for this may be the lack of a rigorous intellectual tradition and a well-articulated philosophy. More important, Vietnamese Buddhist practice is deeply rooted in Vietnamese culture and does not particularly emphasize meditation, which is the main feature that attracts Westerners to Buddhism. It is difficult for a Westerner to find anything interesting or exciting about participating in the Ullambana rites or the repentance liturgy.

Further, most Vietnamese Buddhist monks feel more comfortable guiding their Vietnamese followers than having to exert the considerable effort required to win over the Western sympathizers and the curious. Some Westerners do come to the temples for other than intellectual and meditative reasons. They come mainly because they are moved by the friendliness of the monks and the lay followers and for the homey atmosphere at the temple. Venerable Trí Tuệ is not concerned about this. He explains that although the Buddha was not indifferent to missionary work, right now it may be more important to create favorable conditions, and not impose anything on anybody. He added that to proselytize aggressively is to create affliction.

Chùa Bát Nhã offers a counter-example. Dharma classes are a weekly feature. The Venerable Tiên Quang makes considerable effort to educate both his monastic following and his lay followers. He has also sponsored English-language Dharma classes that were well attended. Further, being a meditation master, he has attracted a number of Western students over the years. Although the Western students come and go, there is regularly a group associated with the temple. They generally are not interested in the various rituals but do attend some of the larger holiday functions.

Some Challenges and Speculation on the Future

An educated Vietnamese nun once confided to Cuong T. Nguyen her pessimism about the future of Vietnamese Buddhism both in Vietnam and overseas. She was concerned that once the United States normalizes diplomatic relations with Vietnam, Vietnamese Buddhism would be hard-pressed to withstand the onslaught of American popular culture. She was uncertain how the traditional Buddhist worldview and ethics would respond to the challenges of modern ideas and technology. Above all, she was acutely aware of the most immediate practical challenge: how Vietnamese Buddhism would respond to the aggressive activities of Protestant Christian denominations that have already initiated missionary works in Vietnam.

When Cuong Nguyen related these worries to Venerable Trí Tuệ, he did not seem to be concerned. He explained that it is not important what religion people choose to embrace. It is just a matter of karma and of the spiritual maturity of sentient beings. If they are not ready "to become the vessels of the Dharma," it is useless to try to impose anything on them. To support his view, he recalled a story in the *Lotus Sūtra:* when the Buddha first started to expound the Mahāyāna, five hundred arhats, who were not spiritually mature enough to hear it, stood up and left the assembly.[29] Besides, he said, is it not true that Buddhism is making inroads in the West?[30]

When an argument was ventured that if Buddhism declines, does it not mean that the Buddhists, particularly the Buddhist leaders, are failing in their responsibility to preserve the Dharma, Venerable Trí Tuệ said that there might be some truth in that viewpoint. He went on to invoke the two truths theory, asserting that the argument makes sense only at the level of conventional truth and from a social perspective, but it does not apply at the level of ultimate truth and from a doctrinal perspective. Did the Buddha not prophesy in many scriptures the inevitable degeneration of the Dharma at some point in the future?[31] Besides, he continued, it is one of the Buddhist truths that all things must necessarily go through the four phases of *thành* (origination), *trụ* (subsistence), *hoại* (degeneration), and *diệt* (extinction). Therefore, if Vietnamese Buddhism, or for that matter Buddhism as a whole, should disappear from this world, it will of course not be a happy turn of events, but after all it will only verify the Buddha's prophecy and the Buddhist truth.

Professor Nguyen mentioned to Venerable Trí Tuệ that when he first met him more than fifteen years ago, he was deeply pessimistic about the future of Vietnamese Buddhism in America; thus it was fair to wonder whether he had after all these years seen any reason to feel more encouraged. He said that he has become a bit less pessimistic because he has some hope for the young generation. However, most Vietnamese parents seem to be more concerned with their children's material success than with their loyalty to and faith in Buddhism.

When Professor A. W. Barber discussed this topic with Venerable Tiên Quang, however, the latter agreed with the general statements but was somewhat more optimistic. He pointed out his Buddhist youth groups with children from many age groups, the Dharma classes he holds weekly, and the training of young monks and nuns under his guidance. He also pointed out the well-attended class in English on Buddhism that was held and attended by both Vietnamese and Canadians as well as the meditation students he has taught over the years. Although he recognizes the vast challenge that is facing Vietnamese Buddhism and Buddhism in general, he seems to be trying to face it head on.

The most serious problem is the lack of facilities to provide an education in Buddhism to monks and nuns. Venerable Trí Tuệ blamed this on the latitudinarian atmosphere of the Vietnamese Buddhist community. There are too many temples and organizations operating independently without a charismatic leader to unite them. Venerable Thích Hạnh Tuấn, a doctoral candidate in Buddhist Studies at the University of California at Berkeley, currently a resident monk at Từ Quang Temple in San Francisco, also expressed the same pessimism. He elaborated some of the challenges facing Vietnamese Buddhism in North America along the following lines. For the last twenty years Vietnamese Buddhism in North America has not been able to train more capable monks and nuns. Most monks and nuns have to teach themselves, and they do not have any sustained, systematic support from any Buddhist organization. As a result many have abandoned their monastic vocation. In Vietnam itself, not many monks and nuns are highly learned in Buddhist doctrine. But this has never been a problem, since most lay Buddhists prefer monks who are keen on organizing large ceremonies and officiating at domestic rituals and worship. A monk is considered a *punya-kṣetra*, or field of merit (*phước điền*): simply to support a monk is a meritorious act. Consequently, lay Buddhists respect monks almost unconditionally, but they are inclined to turn them into "pet monks"—specialists in religious rituals and worships who assist them in fulfilling their religious needs and serve as a means for them to accumulate merit, but who do not challenge them spiritually or intellectually.

The situation is different in North America, since monks have to deal with a younger generation of Buddhists who have grown up in a completely different cultural and linguistic atmosphere. To get their messages across to these younger audiences, a Vietnamese monk not only has to be well versed in Buddhist doctrine and fluent in English, but also must be aware of various dilemmas of modernity.

Venerable Hạnh Tuấn remarked that the main problem, as he sees it, is how to keep the younger generation within Buddhism. According to him, there are currently about one hundred Buddhist youth groups throughout the United States and even more in Canada. Each of these groups has between 50 and 150 members. Many among these young and educated Buddhists are going through some kind of a (cultural) identity crisis and they are searching for a way to return to their cultural roots (*về nguồn*).

In these circumstances, Venerable Hạnh Tuấn emphasizes, the main difficulties are the lack of capable monks and the language barrier. The majority of these educated Vietnamese youths growing up in North America do not know Vietnamese well enough to understand Dharma talks or to read books on Buddhism in Vietnamese, which are rife with unintelligible Sino-Vietnamese Buddhist jargon. Monks who are well versed in Buddhist doctrine, Western civilization, and North American popular culture, and who are fluent in English are a rare, if nonexistent species. Needless to say, as Venerable Hạnh Tuấn points out, a Buddhist teacher has to understand these young Vietnamese Americans' and Vietnamese Canadians' way of thinking to command their respect and to teach them. Otherwise we will continue to witness the discouraging phenomenon in which most of these youths will leave their groups as soon as they reach college age or go to graduate school. Some will eventually forget about Buddhism, while others will remain Buddhist only superficially.

The lack of an elite class of lay followers also makes it difficult to initiate and spread the awareness of the new challenges that Vietnamese Buddhism is facing. In the last few years, there has been only one Buddhist group in southern California—the Giao Điểm Buddhist Foundation—that extends its efforts to matters beyond the purely religious. Besides undertaking charity works in Vietnam, the group publishes a quarterly magazine. This group consists mainly of politically minded professionals whose intention is to arouse an awareness of the issues of modernity and to engage Buddhism in interreligious dialogue.

The *Giao Điểm* magazine is a mixed offering. It contains short essays on Buddhism, mostly at a very popular level, which contain terribly outdated ideas and clichés. It also publishes a regular bilingual article on basic Buddhist teachings. The article is usually an excerpt from a popular book on Buddhism printed in parallel with a Vietnamese translation. According to the publishers, this is intended to help younger Vietnamese who are more comfortable with English not only to learn about Buddhism but also to improve their Vietnamese. One cannot say that the publishers have achieved their goal, since most of the excerpts are from books that are completely outdated, and the translation is as usual in a kind of unintelligible Buddhist-hybrid Vietnamese. Besides, there is an abundance of books on Buddhism in English and they are easily accessible to these North American–educated Vietnamese youths.

The writing in this magazine does not reflect any knowledge of the current scholarship in Buddhism, comparative religion, or interreligious dialogue. On the contrary, it only reiterates attitudes carried over from South Vietnam before 1975: the West-bashing, pseudo-Zen Oriental mysticism movement that originated during the mid-sixties after the Ngô Đình Diệm regime was overthrown, with the attendant revival of Buddhism. The main idea is that Western civilization is inferior to Asian culture and is on the decline, as supposedly evidenced by the popularity of Buddhism and other Asian religions in the West. The claim is that Buddhism is scientific and more suitable to modernity than are Western philosophies and religions.

Thus, what originally was supposed to be a cool, logical effort at reassessing traditional Buddhist values and engaging in a dialogue with modernity with a view to modernizing Buddhism ends up as a mass of defensive, apologetic, and emotional self-assertion, wedded to a complacent fantasy of cultural superiority. To borrow Arthur Wright's words, these Buddhists believe that "Buddhist metaphysicians had anticipated Einsteinian physics, that Buddhist organizations had been pioneers in the application of the principles of equality and democracy to group life, that Buddhist psychologists had been more perceptive—and a millennium earlier—than Freud and Jung, and so on."[32]

V. S. Naipaul once wrote about a typical Indian mentality that he observed: "Out of a superficial reading of the past, then, out of the sentimental conviction that India is eternal and forever revives, there comes not a fear for further defeat and destruction, but an indifference to it. India will somehow look after itself; the individual is free of all responsibility."[33]

It seems true that out of a superficial reading of the past and thus out of the sentimental convictions, most educated Buddhists think that (Vietnamese) Buddhism will take care of itself. Only a handful of monks, nuns, and lay followers with a modern Western education seem to be aware of the challenges that Vietnamese Buddhism is facing and conscious of the obstacles that it has to overcome if it is to have any future in North America.

The main concern of Vietnamese Buddhists seems to be to re-create an atmosphere and environment in which they could continue their religious life as it was in Vietnam before 1975. It is interesting to note that despite a total historical dislocation brought about by the Vietnam War and its aftermath, with some minor adaptations and modifications, most older Vietnamese monks and nuns are able to continue their clerical lifestyle, first-generation lay Buddhists are able to carry on their traditional services, and most educated Buddhists are able to indulge in their nostalgic version of Buddhism.

If the Vietnamese Buddhist community can find ways to support the existing young monastics and recruit new ones from the younger generation and provide material support for their education, it will benefit greatly in the future from the exposure and experiences gained in foreign countries. North America and Europe offer facilities and resources undreamed of in Vietnam. In Vietnam before 1975, in most cases, to enter monastic life was a way to escape economic hardship. This may explain the lack of intellectual interests among the typical monastics. In North America and Europe there are young, educated Vietnamese who wish to take up the monastic life but are unable to do so because there are insufficient facilities to accommodate them. If the current situation continues for a few more decades, Vietnamese Buddhism will be reduced to an insignificant relic, a fossil of a vanished time, relevant only for a small number of people isolated within an ethnic ghetto.

Theravāda Buddhism in America: Prospects for the Sangha

PAUL DAVID NUMRICH

In a June 1974 talk at the London Buddhist Vihara, noted Sinhalese scholar-monk Venerable Walpola Rahula discussed the establishment of Buddhism in Western countries. At that time only two Theravāda temples existed in the United States, the Sinhalese Washington, D.C., Buddhist Vihara and Wat Thai of Los Angeles. Over twenty years later, with approximately 150 such temples—Sinhalese, Thai, Kampuchean, Lao, and Burmese—now dotting the American religious landscape,[1] we do well to consider Venerable Rahula's topic afresh, paying special attention to its American context: as he phrased it, "The Problem of the Prospect of the Saṅgha in the West."[2]

Sangha

Venerable Rahula rightly linked the establishment of Buddhism, particularly its Theravāda expression, with the establishment of the *sangha*. This important term requires careful explication at the outset of our discussion. *Sangha* literally means "comprising," that is, an "assembly" of some kind.[3] The Pali texts often compound this term to specify the kind of assembly being described. The *sāvaka-sangha* (assembly of hearers or disciples) or *ariya-sangha* (assembly of noble ones) comprises all those persons, whether lay or monastic, who have reached the higher spiritual levels on the path to *nibbāna*, or liberation.[4] Scholars variously render this the "Spiritual Sangha," the "ideal Sangha," the "doctrinal sangha," or the "invisible community of the enlightened,"[5] distinguishing it from the more narrow terms *bhikkhu-sangha* and *bhikkhunī-sangha*. These terms refer to the assemblies of monks (*bhikkhus*) and nuns (*bhikkhunīs*), the orders of the Buddha's monastic followers, sometimes collectively called the *ubhato-sangha*, or twofold assembly.

Traditional Theravāda, that expression of Theravāda Buddhism which took shape and dominated in the period from Aśoka (third century B.C.E.) to modern times,[6] functionally narrowed the usage of the general term *sangha* to refer exclusively to the *bhikkhu-sangha*, or order of monks.[7] This is quite understandable given the roles played by the monks in the perpetuation of the tradition, as both exemplars of its ideal renunciatory lifestyle (living according to the *Vinaya* or disciplinary code) and conveyors of its teachings (the *Dhamma*). "The history of Theravāda Buddhism," Richard Gombrich summarizes, "seen from the point of view taken by the tradition itself . . . is the history of the [*bhikkhu-*]Sangha."[8] Gombrich goes on to observe that this "virtual identification of the fortunes of a religion with those of its professionals is alien to most religious traditions. . . . But in our view it constitutes the very core of Theravāda Buddhism." Today, when Theravāda Buddhists recite the Three Refuges, they typically understand the third refuge, the *sangha*, to be the *bhikkhu-sangha*.[9]

Clearly, then, the establishment of traditional Theravāda Buddhism in any country depends on the establishment of the order of monks there. Various passages in the Theravāda literature recount a conversation between the Thera (Elder) Mahinda and King Devanampiya-Tissa of Ceylon concerning the progress of Buddhism's establishment on the island. "When, Venerable Sir, will the [religion's] roots indeed be deep?" the King asks. Venerable Mahinda replies: "When a young man, born of Ceylonese parents on the island of Ceylon, having gone forth on the island of Ceylon and learned the monastic discipline in this same island of Ceylon, when he will recite that discipline on the island of Ceylon—then, Great King, will the roots of the religion indeed be deep."[10] In other words, the firm establishment of the religion requires indigenous monks (*bhikkhu-sangha*) who uphold the monastic discipline (*Vinaya*) through recitation of its precepts (*pātimokkha sikkhāpada*).[11] As Michael Carrithers succinctly puts it, "no Buddhism without the [*bhikkhu-*]Sangha, and no [*bhikkhu-*]Sangha without the Discipline."[12]

"American Buddhism," that predominantly Euro-American, lay-oriented, meditation-centered new religious movement which includes some Theravāda groups, typically democratizes the term *sangha* to refer to all Buddhists regardless of status (lay or monastic) or progress along the path to liberation.[13] Such usage represents a significant departure from the Pali texts, which never use the term *sangha* when referring to lay followers per se.[14]

Cultivating an Indigenous Theravāda *Bhikkhu-Sangha*

If we estimate the number of ethnic Asian or immigrant[15] Theravāda Buddhist temples in the United States today to be about 150, and if we further estimate the average number of resident monks in each of these temples to be 3 or 4, we derive a present total of between 450 and 600 Theravāda Buddhist monks in America.[16] The vast majority of these monks are Asian nationals, often possessing only minimal English-language proficiency and a passing acquaintance with American culture, who have been imported from the home countries to staff the immigrant temples. My monastic consultants report no new permanent monks[17] from the ranks of the American-born second generation of immigrants, and can identify only about ten non-Asian monks (one African American, the rest Caucasian) in United States temples.

The lack of interest in the monastic life among second-generation Asians appears straightforward enough: both they and their immigrant parents value other vocational choices in America. In fact, at times the first generation wonders whether their offspring will wish even to carry on lay leadership of the temples when that day arrives.

A more complex picture presents itself when we inquire as to why so few non-Asian, American monks can be found in United States Theravāda temples. To begin with, consider Theravāda's location within the larger phenomenon of Buddhism in America. The Zen and Tibetan schools have always been more popular among American converts, which leaves a relatively small pool of candidates for Theravāda monasticism. Moreover, generally speaking, "American Buddhism" (see earlier) has tended to be a lay movement. American interest in Theravāda has largely confined itself to that school's distinctive form of meditation—*vipassanā*, or insight meditation. For some American Buddhists, in fact, Theravāda monasticism epitomizes those aspects of traditional Asian Buddhism that should be abandoned in the construction of a new, nonhierarchical, nonauthoritarian, and nonsexist Western vehicle of the Buddha's teachings.

As some observers point out, the monastic lifestyle simply goes against the grain of mainstream American culture. In contrast to Asian Buddhist countries, monasticism is not portrayed as a viable option in this society, much less as a spiritual ideal. The married Protestant minister provides the model for clergy in America, which has negatively affected the recruitment of Roman Catholic priests, whose vows include monastic elements. As a noted leader in the American *vipassanā* movement put it, to Western people "the monastic life is an oddity rather than a common occurrence."[18] The difficulties inherent in being a cultural oddity often compel American Theravāda monks either to leave the robes or to relocate to temples in Asia.

The number of Americans taking the Theravāda robes, even for a short period, remains very small. Many American Theravāda Buddhists see monasticism as irrelevant to the practice of Buddhism in America. Some may express a wish to enter the monastic order but quickly admit that they cannot adopt the required renunciatory lifestyle. Families, homes and other property, careers, interests—a variety of "worldly" attachments make the monastic commitment impractical in their minds. These individuals sometimes promise to take the robes at retirement. One of my consultants dubbed such an eventuality a "Geritol *sangha*"; another saw it as "disastrous." Such an approach to the spiritual life resembles the Hindu *ashrama* (stages of life) scheme more than it does the Buddha's movement, which "encouraged people to renounce family life as early as possible."[19]

At least one group of American Theravāda Buddhists made a serious attempt to cultivate an indigenous and, significantly, a culturally "American" Theravāda monastic order. Incorporated in January 1991 as a nonprofit corporation in Denver, Colorado, NAMO TASSA, Inc., sought "to create, develop, maintain and promote in a contemporary American context monastic communities for men and women based upon Theravadan Buddhist principles," and "to invite discussion, [to] explore, to propose and to cautiously implement minor adjustments of the ancient code of discipline, creating, over time a viable American expression of Buddhist monasticism" (articles of incorporation).

The acronym is both ingenious and descriptive: NAMO TASSA, the opening Pali words of the *Buddha vandanā* ("Homage to the Buddha") chant that initiates virtually every Theravāda Buddhist ritual, here stands for New American Monastic Order, Theravada Association for Sangha Support in America. NAMO TASSA's monastic focus distinguished this organization from the preoccupation with *vipassanā* meditation characteristic of other American Theravāda groups. As a statement put it, NAMO TASSA planned to "evolve a neo-monasticism employing insights from renewing contemplative traditions, psychology, etc., while maintaining the basic integrity and commitment of Buddhist monasticism as a tool for Enlightenment . . . [and to] develop ways and means of supporting neo-Theravada Buddhist monastics." Moreover, NAMO TASSA clearly defined the relationship between the many ethnic Asian forms of Buddhism now found in America and the uniquely "American" neo-Theravāda Buddhism it envisioned. A newsletter noted that "national and ethnic expressions of Buddhism abound. As we welcome them to America we have the opportunity to look deeply for guidance among their teachers, their nuns and monks, their best scholars and informed laity." "But," the newsletter continued, "in doing so we must not lose sight of the need to walk a very straight path— our own actual Path of the Dharma."

NAMO TASSA, as originally constituted, lasted less than three years, perhaps due as much to internal conflict as to the difficulties inherent in its mandate. The organization's corporate report to the State of Colorado for 1993 listed only one of the original directors, and its description of NAMO TASSA's purposes said nothing about monasticism. It appears that the organization now serves primarily as a clearinghouse for information about *vipassanā* training opportunities, its newsletter adopting the title "The Newsletter of The Insight Meditation Network and Special Projects of Namo Tassa, Inc."

Before its transformation into an exclusively *vipassanā*-oriented group, NAMO TASSA succeeded in providing support for one American Theravāda "monastic," who now goes by the name of Reverend Anagarika Martha Dharmapali. Significantly, Reverend Dharmapali judges "it highly unlikely [that] North American Buddhism will have a traditional monastic Sangha or even a monastic system at all."[20] Al Reed, one of the original directors of NAMO TASSA, has cofounded a new effort at realizing NAMO TASSA's basic goals, though he, like Reverend Dharmapali, seems chastened by previous experience. Reed and another layman recently launched Theravada Buddhist Ministries (TBM), an organization of trained ministers (called "dhammacariyas") intended "to serve the Ordained Sangha by functioning as a lay auxiliary through which monastic influence may be enhanced for the benefit of all humanity," as TBM's mission statement puts it. The founders also hope that these dhammacariyas will be inspired "to enter into the life of renunciation and contemplation. It is by these expedients that Theravada Buddhist Ministries seeks to vitalize, enhance, and, as circumstances demand, complement the Theravada Ordained Sangha in North America." In Reed's mind, TBM represents the last hope for cultivating a Theravāda monastic *sangha* among non-Asian, American Buddhists.

Reestablishing the Theravāda *Bhikkhunī-Sangha*

Nowhere is the "problem" of the prospects for a Theravāda monastic *sangha* in America more volatile than in the issues surrounding the reestablishment of the *bhikkhunī-sangha*, or order of nuns. As Rita Gross observes, regarding Buddhist canon law generally, "the greatest legal battles facing Buddhist feminists occur over issues of nuns' ordination and nuns' status within the monastic institutions."[21] To Gross and other observers, traditional Theravāda Buddhism constitutes "the form of Buddhism that is least sympathetic to contemporary women's drive for full and dignified participation in their religion."[22]

The well-known story has it that the Buddha allowed the establishment of an order of nuns only after repeated requests from some female postulants and his beloved disciple, Ānanda.[23] Although the Buddha reputedly quipped that now his religion would last only five hundred years rather than a thousand, it appears that his hesitancy stemmed from "social and

practical considerations" about the monastic *sanghas*,[24] not from any doubts
about the spiritual potential of women, whom the Buddha acknowledged
as quite capable of attaining the four levels of the higher path. Consequently, the Buddha stipulated "Eight Important Rules" (*attha garud-
hamma*) for the *bhikkhunī-sangha*, which include showing unconditional def-
erence to every monk, even those junior in ordination age, and receiving
advice from monks without being allowed to reciprocate.[25] The Eight Important Rules present a potential sticking point in any future reestablishment of the Theravāda *bhikkhunī-sangha*. Traditionalist defenders of the
Buddha's pronouncements have difficulty convincing feminist critics that
the Eight Rules reflect anything but the "ecclesiastical submission"[26] or "institutional subordination"[27] of the *bhikkhunī-sangha* to the *bhikkhu-sangha*.
"As such," Gross concludes, the Eight Rules "are not worth fostering any
more."[28]

The *bhikkhunī-sangha* died out in Theravāda lands by the tenth through
the twelfth centuries C.E., although its lineage had been transmitted to
China some centuries earlier. Many women in Theravāda countries today
live a renunciatory, even monastic lifestyle, such as the *mae jis* of Thailand
and the *dasa sil mātāvas* of Sri Lanka,[29] but they have no status within the
official monastic *sangha*. Those occasional attempts by women to claim *bhikkhunī* ordination face either stiff opposition or simple nonrecognition from
ecclesiastical authorities. The *Vinaya* requires that such an ordination be
done by *bhikkhunīs* in the presence of the *ubhato-sangha*, the twofold assembly of both monks and nuns. Since the authorities consider the Theravāda
bhikkhunī line extinct (the Chinese transmission being tainted by Mahāyāna influences), no mechanism exists for the legal ordination of women
today.[30]

Nevertheless, some observers predict the eventual reestablishment (perhaps "rebirth") of the Theravāda *bhikkhunī-sangha* in the West, where resistance, both ecclesiastical and popular, seems minimal.[31] Leading the way
to this end, progressive Sri Lankan monks in two American temples in
particular—the Dharma Vijaya Buddhist Vihara of Los Angeles and the
Bhavana Society of Highview, West Virginia—have ordained several women
as *sāmaṇerīs* since 1987.[32] The story of one such *sāmaṇerī* points out the
parameters of these efforts.

The ordination of a Thai woman, thereafter called Reverend Dhammamitta, took place at Dharma Vijaya during Vesak, 1988. In a letter dated
April 10, 1988, to Venerable Kurunegoda Piyatissa, the president of the Sri
Lanka Sangha Council of North America, Dharma Vijaya's abbot, Venerable Walpola Piyananda, cited the compelling reasons for this "historic
event." First, not only is gender discrimination illegal in America, he
pointed out, but "Attitudes toward women in this country are not and need
not be the same as in Asia." Second, "Strong criticism is being made against

the Theravada form of Buddhism because of the denial of women['s] entry
into the [monastic] order." The increasing number of American women
turning to Mahāyāna schools had begun to jeopardize the Theravāda mission: "If we are going to continue the spread of Theravada in this country,
we need to reexamine our position on the ordination of women." Lastly,
the abbot argued, the atmosphere of ecumenical Buddhist "friendship and
cooperation" in the United States indicates that the time is ripe for such
ordinations, which require a joint assembly of Theravāda monks and Mahāyāna nuns.

Twenty-five Theravāda *bhikkhus* from the Sinhalese and Thai traditions,
and eight Mahāyāna *bhikkhunīs* from the Chinese, Korean, and Vietnamese
traditions participated in the *sāmaṇerī* ordination. Published reports of the
event claimed that it received the "overwhelming support"[33] and "blessings"
of many monks in America, though "some objections [were] raised in Sri
Lanka."[34]

Subsequent to her *sāmaṇerī* ordination, Reverend Dhammamitta opened
a meditation center in Los Angeles. Before making a personal visit to Thailand, however, she turned over her monastic robes to Dharma Vijaya's abbot upon his advice not to cause a stir in Thailand by wearing them. Reverend Dhammamitta has yet to take up the monastic robes again. In fact,
she has since married and entered into a status of lay ministry offered by
Dharma Vijaya.

Venerable Dr. Havanpola Ratanasara of Dharma Vijaya, Reverend Dhammamitta's *upajjhāya* (preceptor, the presiding monk at ordination), once
"expressed the hope that in a few years all of the samaneris can be given
full bhikkhuni ordination."[35] Among women who hope for the reestablishment of the Theravāda *bhikkhunī-sangha* in the West, some envision a slow
but inevitably successful process;[36] others consider the idea "doomed," "an
exercise in frustration"; and still others now call for the establishment of
"An Independent Order of Buddhist Nuns for the West."[37]

Vinaya in America

As the ancient conversation between the Thera Mahinda and King Devanampiya-Tissa of Ceylon indicates, the firm establishment of Theravāda Buddhism in a country requires *bhikkhus* who recite the 227 precepts of the
monastic discipline (*pātimokkha sikkhāpada*).[38] Traditionally, the recitation
ceremony takes place twice monthly as the Theravāda monks within a given
geographical area (usually a village) gather together at a temple with *baddha sīmā*, that is, sacred boundaries consecrated by specific ritual action of
the *bhikkhu-sangha*. In lieu of such a temple, monks may recite the *pātimokkha* within *abaddha sīmā*, that is, "areas whose boundaries have been estab-

lished by the government [e.g., a municipality] or by ancient usage [e.g., a body of water]."[39] A minimum of four *bhikkhus* is required for a legitimate *pātimokkha* ceremony,[40] which reveals "the truly communal dimension of the *pātimokkha* institution," as Gombrich observes.[41] The bimonthly corporate recitation serves as both a "solidarity ritual"[42] and "a kind of 'quality control' "[43] for the *bhikkhu-sangha*.

The situation in America today makes it difficult for many Theravāda monks to perform the *pātimokkha* ceremony in the traditionally prescribed ways. For instance, a temple with fewer than four monks may be the only Theravāda temple in the immediate metropolitan area. Even in cities with several Theravāda temples, distances between temples and differences in ethnic identity can mitigate against frequent joint *pātimokkha* ceremonies. Moreover, only a few temples in the country have consecrated *baddha sīmā*. Although Theravāda monks in America find ways of adjusting to these constraints—such as by carrying out informal confessions or gathering together for the formal *pātimokkha* ceremony less frequently than bimonthly—their sense of communal solidarity and institutional strength may necessarily suffer.

Wijayaratna's comment above about "quality control" within the *bhikkhu-sangha* raises another key issue in evaluating the prospects for the Theravāda *bhikkhu-sangha* in America today—the difficulty in holding to certain ancient *Vinaya* requirements in a modern Western society. Of course, adaptation of the *Vinaya* to new circumstances occurred almost from the beginning of the Buddha's movement: "The Master did not hesitate to modify the rules to make the life of monks and nuns easier in different climatic and social conditions."[44] Before the Buddha died, he granted the *bhikkhu-sangha* permission to make necessary modifications of minor *Vinaya* rules, but the *bhikkhu-sangha* has never been able to determine just which rules the Buddha considered "minor."[45] Consequently, the Theravāda tradition devised a paradoxical hermeneutic of *Vinaya* adaptation which included, on the one hand, strict adherence to the ancient disciplinary code, and, on the other hand, a set of "amendments" or "new rules" standing outside the ancient texts (*pālimuttaka-vinicchaya*) and reached through consensual agreement among the monks (*katikāvatta*). In this way, "without changing the letter of the law, monks discovered ways and means of overcoming the difficulty [of following some rules in their original form] by interpreting the law without compromising themselves."[46] The key here, as in any hermeneutical enterprise, has to do with the point at which one crosses the line of "compromise."

In America that line has been the subject of considerable discussion among both ethnic Asian and American-convert Theravāda *bhikkhus*. The topic took center stage in 1987 at the Conference on World Buddhism in North America, Ann Arbor, Michigan. Venerable Dr. Havanpola

Ratanasara, later that year named executive president of the newly formed American Buddhist Congress, summarized the social realities of *Vinaya* adaptation.[47] *Vinaya*, he said, "is not a static thing because [it concerns] a living group of persons. Living persons will have to adjust to the changing conditions of the society. Monks are not like stones . . . they are living creatures, they have to face changing conditions in the society. So, according to certain conditions, things are changing."[48] Furthermore, Venerable Dr. Ratanasara asserted, the contemporary *bhikkhu-sangha* must take up the challenge of *Vinaya* adaptation in America. "Who can go and make a petition to the Buddha these days?" he asked the conference rhetorically. "Buddha has given permission to the *sangha* . . . therefore, it is with the *sangha* this problem to tackle."

On the other side of the issue, several conference participants spoke against any tampering with the *Vinaya* at all. By pointing out that the *bhikkhus* at the First Buddhist Council considered only a Buddha's wisdom capable of distinguishing "minor" from "major" *Vinaya* rules, Venerable U Silananda, abbot of Dhammananda Vihara, Daly City, California, implicitly challenged today's *bhikkhu-sangha* to show cause that its wisdom matches the Buddha's before tackling this problem. To change the *Vinaya* is to change the *bhikkhu-sangha*'s identity, Venerable Silananda explicitly warned. Venerable Walpola Piyananda, abbot of Dharma Vijaya Buddhist Vihara, Los Angeles, shared his fear that, by cutting up the *Vinaya*, the monks would be "dismembering" the Buddha, since the Buddha had appointed the *Vinaya* as teacher after his physical death. Another conference participant, Samaneri Sunanda, cautioned against a slippery slope effect: better to keep all the rules, even strict and inconvenient ones, since breaking a few so-called minor rules now will lead to breaking more rules later and eventually to having no rules at all.

My conversations with American-convert Theravāda *bhikkhus* have uncovered a clear strain of conservatism on *Vinaya* matters, which may characterize this group.[49] One told me straightforwardly that ethnic Asian monks in America, not American-convert monks, are behind the push to modify the *Vinaya* to suit the American context. Another *bhikkhu* agreed that American-convert monks do not wish to change any *Vinaya* requirements, since the discipline provided by the *Vinaya* remains crucial to a viable monastic expression of Buddhism. "The Vinaya is something that requires a lot of time to appreciate," one of the monks wrote me. He went on: "When I first was ordained, the prospect of memorizing and having to live by a lot of picayune rules was the least appealing part of the training. And yet I came to realize, after living several years in the [monastic] community, that almost all of the issues that created friction within the community came from people breaking the rules." In the wake of scandals involving some leaders within larger American Buddhism in the 1980s,[50] the value of what one respected American-convert monk calls "the protective envelope that the Vinaya provides for monastics" has drawn renewed appreciation.[51]

To get a fix on the present state of Theravāda *Vinaya* adaptation in the United States, let us briefly examine two key, practical issues—monastic attire and relations with women.[52]

The Buddha allowed his monks three robes: an undergarment, a loose-fitting top piece, and a double-layered cloak.[53] Triple-robed Theravāda monks in America face two challenges. First, the climate poses a real health concern. The possibility of hypothermia so troubled the director of security services for one Midwestern Thai temple that he circulated a letter through the Council of Thai Bhikkhus in the USA suggesting adoption of a "proper winter uniform for Monks," with yellow clerical collar and Buddhist lapel pin to identify the wearer as legitimate clergy. Second, beyond the climatic incompatibility of robes and the harsh North American environment lies the more disturbing incompatibility of robes and American cultural prejudices. Often mistaken for "Hare Krishnas," Theravāda monks have endured "cat calls or rude comments, and in rare cases [have been] assaulted by religious bigots" while out in public.[54]

Among Theravāda monks in United States temples to date, adaptation of the three-robes requirement has entailed donning certain items of protective clothing, for instance, saffron-colored T-shirts under the upper robe in southern California, sweaters over the robes in the Midwest, the latter practice receiving approval from the Supreme Patriarch of Thailand according to one of my Thai monastic consultants. Suggestions that monks adopt a "proper winter uniform" or perhaps confine the wearing of robes to ritual occasions have fallen on deaf ears. The "absence of robes," the reasoning goes, creates more problems than it solves: Buddhist laypeople would be deprived of an object of reverence, "for it is the robe which is honored rather than the person," and non-Buddhist Americans would no longer find their interest piqued by a distinctive monastic symbol that might "stimulate thoughtful conversation."[55] When I questioned one Sinhalese monk about wearing civilian clothes in order to avoid confrontations on the streets of Los Angeles, he responded that, although it might spare him some abuse, he might also forget that he was a monk and be tempted to act in unmonastic ways.

Another important area of Theravāda *Vinaya* adaptation in America concerns monks' relations with women. The tradition sees absolute celibacy as essential to the monastic lifestyle. The *pātimokkha* lists sexual intercourse as the first offense, a *pārājika*, literally a "defeat" or "setting aside (from the *bhikkhu-sangha*),"[56] commission of which automatically renders one no longer a *bhikkhu*.[57] Moreover, in a fashion analogous to Judaism's "building a fence around the Torah," the *pātimokkha* prohibits a monk from being alone with or traveling with a woman, while the tradition forbids a monk's physical touching of a woman.

The dilemma in this for Theravāda monks in America runs along two levels. Strict adherence to traditional etiquette can embarrass and even offend American women visiting a temple or seeking individual counseling or instruction from a monk. One monastic consultant predicted that monks in America will slowly adopt the practices of shaking hands with and hugging women as normal, cultural expressions of courtesy and friendship. As to the second level of the dilemma, while Theravāda monks in America may recognize the stumbling block to monastic recruitment presented by the celibacy rule,[58] none would advocate setting aside the rule. Instead, it appears that efforts will be directed toward ways of cultivating a nonmonastic leadership in United States temples, which I discuss in the next section.

In United States temples where *Vinaya* adaptation has occurred, three principles seem to be at work. First, only minor modifications have been implemented, or, to put it differently, only "minor" *Vinaya* rules have been modified. Clearly "major" rules like triple robing and celibacy stand unchallenged, though accessories to the robes have appeared and social relations with women may be more flexible.[59] Second, practicality comes into play: where *Vinaya* restrictions become impractical, adaptation occurs. This principle depends on the first principle, however, for no matter how impractical a "major" *Vinaya* rule seemingly becomes (for example, wearing robes in public or requiring a celibate monastic community), modification of it has not yet occurred. Third, *Vinaya* adaptation relies on a consensual process, among monks certainly, but also between monks and laity in a temple. Without the approval of its lay constituency, a United States temple's *bhikkhu-sangha* finds it difficult if not impossible to enact even "minor" modifications in the most "impractical" rules.[60]

Experimentation with Intermediate Religious Statuses

Traditional Theravāda Buddhism stresses the distinction between lay and monastic lifestyles. Even so, the tradition offers specific opportunities for lay Buddhists to approximate the renunciatory monastic ideal on a limited basis. Lay devotees may take the Eight Precepts (*aṭṭhaṅga sīla*) during *uposatha* (sacred) days, wearing white and living in a disciplined and reflective manner at the temple. In Southeast Asian countries, laymen typically take temporary ordination into the monastic order. In recent times, some individuals have pursued the path of an *anagārika*, which falls somewhere between lay person and monastic.[61]

Various Buddhist groups in the West have implemented novel hierarchies of graduated religious statuses for their members. The Friends of the

Western Buddhist Order, for instance, offers three stages of increasingly serious commitment to the ideal Buddhist lifestyle: (1) Friend, (2) Mitra, or Spiritual Friend, and (3) Ordination, this without distinction as to lay or monastic status. The International Buddhist Meditation Center in Los Angeles advocates a four-stage ordination procedure, which culminates in either the full vows of monasticism or twenty-five vows, excluding celibacy, for married ordinands.

For more than a decade, Dharma Vijaya Buddhist Vihara of Los Angeles has experimented with such categories, in part to provide initiation ceremonies for American converts to Buddhism, but more importantly in an effort to train an indigenous American leadership in lieu of cultivating a native *bhikkhu-sangha*. "Buddhism can hardly occupy a firm place in the mainstream of American society if it constantly has to be replenished with foreign born clergy who themselves may not be integrated into our society," asserts Dharma Vijaya's pamphlet describing its most recent hierarchy of lay statuses. Taken as a whole, Dharma Vijaya's five categories represent intermediate religious statuses between the ordinary layperson and the *bhikkhu*, which create something of a para- or quasi-monastic order reminiscent of the efforts of Theravada Buddhist Ministries described earlier in this essay.

At the first level, Upasaka, a person makes "a commitment to approach life from a Buddhist point of view." The Upasaka receives an ivory-colored sash at an initiation ceremony, promising to live by the Five Precepts and to recite some basic Buddhist verses twice daily. The special nature of the initiation ceremony and the restrictions placed on becoming an Upasaka— at least one year of study and practice, at least eighteen years of age (or parental and temple monks' approval)—set this apart from the traditional status of Buddhist lay devotee (*upāsaka/upāsikā*).

A Dhammacari, the next status, must be an Upasaka of at least two years' practice and deemed "suitable" by the monks of the temple. "A Dhammacari is a committed practicing Buddhist, at least 18 years of age, who has the knowledge and experience in practice to teach Dhamma school, give Dhamma talks, conduct meditation classes, and even organize Buddhist groups." The candidate receives a light yellow sash at an initiation ceremony, pledging to adhere to nine precepts in life—the standard Five Precepts plus abstention from "tale-bearing," "harsh speech," "idle chatter," and "wrong livelihood"—and to practice a twice-daily recitation ritual.[62]

Dharma Vijaya considers the third status in its hierarchy to be on the same level as the Dhammacari, though it reflects one "difference in lifestyle." The Anagarika is a Dhammacari who substitutes the more stringent precept of abstention from all sexual relations (*abrahmacariyā*) for the usual precept of abstention from simple sexual misconduct (*kāmesu micchācārā*).

With the institution of the next status, Bodhicari, Dharma Vijaya has sought to fill the "gap" in the Western transmission of Theravāda Buddhism created by the dearth of monks. "A Bodhicari is a Buddhist lay minister, neither a lay person nor ordained Sangha," whose responsibilities and authority exceed that of the previous level (Dhammacari) by including "the possibility of conducting certain religious services [when monks are unavailable], holding chaplainships, conducting weddings and funerals, [and] initiating upasaka." Nomination requirements are more demanding at this level, including a minimum of four years of college and three years of training with a monk. Significantly, the Bodhicari receives an "ordination" rather than an "initiation" as in the previously mentioned levels, taking a bright yellow sash to symbolize this status. The Bodhicari follows twelve precepts, the twelfth being most important in emphasizing the selfless service exemplified by the Buddha in his previous lives as bodhisattva or Buddha-to-be: "I undertake the precept to practice the ten perfections [or ten virtues, *dasapāramī*] with compassion and skill." The Bodhicari also holds to a detailed daily ritual regimen.

The final special status granted by Dharma Vijaya is Brahmacari, a Bodhicari who abstains from all sexual relations (*abrahmacariyā*).

Dharma Vijaya claims to have initiated too many Upasakas and Dhammacaris over the years to give an accurate count. The temple has ordained a total of four Bodhicaris, including the former *sāmaṇerī* Reverend Dhammamitta mentioned earlier.

Prospects for the Theravāda Monastic *Sangha* in America

Because the *bhikkhu-sangha* comprises the core of traditional Theravāda Buddhism, prospects for the Theravāda *bhikkhu-sangha* in America become prospects for Theravāda itself in this country. Moreover, if we take seriously the view that the Theravāda school of Buddhism has been slowly dying in Asia over the past several centuries,[63] then prospects for Theravāda Buddhism in Western countries like the United States take on great historical significance, since Theravāda's chances for global survival may hang in the balance.

Prospects for the Theravāda *bhikkhu-sangha* in America depend on key dynamics within the two constituencies comprising Theravāda Buddhism in this country—ethnic Asians and non-Asian converts. If immigration trends hold steady or increase, we should see the continued proliferation and consolidation of Theravāda Buddhist temples in coming decades. Barring a tightening of United States visa restrictions, and assuming a constant source of monks in the home countries, these temples can import their monastic staffs from Asia indefinitely. Communal recitation of the *pātimok-kha* will become easier, minimal adaptation of *Vinaya* requirements will continue. However, unless these imported monks can speak to the off-spring of Asian immigrants in culturally and spiritually meaningful ways, a native-born *bhikkhu-sangha* will not likely arise among this group. Theravāda Buddhist monasticism would then remain a perpetually replenished "green-house garden," rather than becoming a deeply rooted, natural outgrowth of the United States Theravāda experience.

Prospects for the Theravāda *bhikkhu-sangha* in America also depend on the attitudes and actions of non-Asian Theravāda converts. To date, efforts at recruiting and supporting non-Asian monks have yielded only minimal success. Although we may be seeing a renewed appreciation for the value of the monastic path among American converts, it seems unlikely that such appreciation alone will overcome the strong cultural sentiments favoring lay-oriented religiosity in this country.[64] As the experience of NAMO TASSA shows, American converts to Theravāda Buddhism easily gravitate to the insight meditation movement and away from traditional Theravāda's em-phasis on the *bhikkhu-sangha*. Even so, experimentation with para- and quasi-monastic religious statuses such as we see in Theravada Buddhist Min-istries and Dharma Vijaya Buddhist Vihara of Los Angeles may foreshadow a viable partnership between American-convert lay leaders and Asian monks that will help to establish a more culturally attuned, albeit still im-ported, *bhikkhu-sangha* in America.

The controversy over reestablishing the Theravāda *bhikkhunī-sangha* in America continues. This issue seems peripheral to most Theravāda temples in the United States today. Traditional Theravāda's generally unsympathet-ic stance on women's ordination has certainly turned many potential Amer-ican converts away from Theravāda and toward other Buddhist schools, but my sense is that most of those who become and remain Theravāda Bud-dhists, both women and men, hold a conservative, even fundamentalist outlook that will not challenge traditional Theravāda on this issue.[65] With so few *sāmaṇerīs* and no *bhikkhunīs* currently in America, the issue may be-come moot as women either seek ordination in Mahāyāna schools or es-tablish an independent order.

It seems fitting to conclude with the emotional appeal of an American-convert novice monastic at the Conference on World Buddhism in North America in 1987, whose words epitomize the precarious prospects for the Theravāda monastic *sangha*, and thereby for Theravāda Buddhism per se in America: "Make Theravada monasticism workable in this country. Please. We need it for the purity of the teachings. If you don't, the teachings will turn into something else. They will turn into Ram Dass. They will turn into therapy. I'm seeing it happen."[66]

*Insight Meditation
in the United States:
Life, Liberty, and the
Pursuit of Happiness*

GIL FRONSDAL

Among the various and varied Buddhist meditative disciplines taught in the United States, Insight Meditation, or *vipassanā*, has been, since the early 1980s, one of the fastest growing in popularity. To a great extent this can be attributed to the practice being offered independent of much of its traditional Theravāda Buddhist religious context. This autonomy has allowed the American *vipassanā* teachers and students to adapt and present the meditation practice in forms and language that are much more thoroughly Westernized than most other forms of Buddhism in America. As the number of people participating in the mindfulness practices of Insight Meditation has increased, a loose-knit lay Buddhist movement, uniquely Western, that is sometimes known as the "*vipassanā* movement," has evolved. With minimal remaining connection to Theravāda Buddhism, the movement speaks of "*vipassanā* students and teachers," "*vipassanā* centers and communities," and even a national "*vipassanā* journal." As a result, many more Americans of European descent refer to themselves as *vipassanā* students than as students of Theravāda Buddhism.

Vipassanā meditation is offered in America in a wide range of contexts. The most traditional is within some of the more than 150 ethnic Theravāda temples where Thai, Lao, Cambodian, Burmese, or Sri Lankan monastics may function as meditation teachers. Here *vipassanā* practice is usually intermixed with Theravāda forms of worship, chanting, teachings, and efforts at cultural preservation.

At the other end of a spectrum, *vipassanā*-derived mindfulness practices are taught in hospitals, clinics, prisons, and schools without any hint of their Buddhist source. Here the practice is primarily offered as an effective method of stress reduction, pain management, and self-understanding. The biggest influence *vipassanā* practice will have on American society may eventually be in such non-Buddhist applications. For example, in the fall of 1995, the book *Emotional Intelligence* by Daniel Goleman was regularly on the *New York Times* best-seller list. The Buddhist and *vipassanā* teachings that were an inspiration for the book are nowhere acknowledged. Of his earlier book, *Vital Lies, Simple Truths*, Goleman states, "The Dharma is so disguised that it could never be proven in court."[1] Similarly, Jon Kabat-Zinn's much-copied work at the Stress Reduction Clinic of the University of Massachusetts Medical Center and his book *Full Catastrophe Living: Using the Wisdom of Your Body and Mind to Face Stress, Pain, and Illness* can be pointed to as "disguised" introductions of *vipassanā* practice into American society.[2]

Between these secular and traditional contexts for *vipassanā* practice, we find the loosely bounded *vipassanā* movement. Primary stimulants for its growth and its most clearly visible organizations are the Insight Meditation Society (IMS) in Barre, Massachusetts; its sister center, Spirit Rock Meditation Center in Marin County, California; and the semi-annual *vipassanā* journal, the *Inquiring Mind*, published by people closely affiliated with these two meditation centers. The teachers associated with IMS (such as founders Joseph Goldstein, Jack Kornfield, and Sharon Salzberg) and Spirit Rock (such as founders Jack Kornfield, James Baraz, Sylvia Boorstein, and Anna Douglas) have been the primary propagators of *vipassanā* practice through their books, cassette tapes,[3] and the retreats they lead across the United States. Because of the influence of IMS, Spirit Rock, their teachers, and the *Inquiring Mind*, and because of the close association among these, this study takes them to represent the mainstream of the American *vipassanā* movement, which is the primary focus of this chapter.

Outside of this "mainstream," many independent *vipassanā* teachers and organizations are active. The lay Indian *vipassanā* teacher S. N. Goenka teaches or oversees intensive meditation courses in various parts of the country, particularly at the Vipassanā Meditation Center in Shelburne Falls, Massachusetts. Several former Theravāda monks, both Asian and American, teach *vipassanā* as autonomous teachers (for example, Dhiravamsa, Sobin, John Orr, Greg Galbraith, Jason Siff). The highly respected and most senior American *vipassanā* teacher, Ruth Denison, is also an unaffiliated, independent teacher. Because of the numerous autonomous teachers and centers and the absence of a guiding national organization that certifies *vipassanā* teachers, the American *vipassanā* movement is inherently open, amorphous, and arbitrarily defined.

Developments in the United States

The mainstream of the American *vipassanā* movement is based on the systemization of *vipassanā* meditation developed and propagated by the

Burmese monk and meditation teacher Mahāsi Sayādaw (1904–82). An important feature of the "Mahāsi approach" is its dispensing with the traditional preliminary practice of fixed concentration or tranquilization (*appanā samādhi, samatha*). Instead, the meditator practices *vipassanā* exclusively during intensive periods of silent retreat that can last several months with a daily schedule of meditation from 3:00 a.m. to 11:00 p.m. Two key elements in Mahāsi's method for developing mindfulness are the careful labeling of one's immediate experience together with the cultivation of a high level of sustained concentration known as "momentary concentration" (*khanika samādhi*).

The primary purpose for which Mahāsi offered his form of *vipassanā* practice is the attainment of the first of the four traditional Theravāda levels of sainthood (that is, stream entry; *sotāpatti*) through the realization of *nibbāna*, or enlightenment. In championing this goal, Mahāsi deemphasized many common elements of Theravāda Buddhism. Rituals, chanting, devotional and merit-making activities, and doctrinal studies were downplayed to the point of being virtually absent from the program of meditation offered at the many meditation centers he founded or inspired.

With the precedence given to meditation and meditative realizations, Mahāsi also deemphasized Theravāda Buddhism's central focus on monasticism. Indeed, in teaching *vipassanā* meditation more to the laity than to monastics, Mahāsi and the meditation teachers he trained greatly contributed to breaking down the almost exclusive monopoly the monastic order had on such practice. While the monastic *sangha* remains central to the Southeast Asian Theravāda tradition, the inclusion of the laity in the ultimate soteriological path made it much easier for the Western teachers to dispense with monasticism.

Mahāsi was part of what is sometimes called a twentieth-century Theravāda modernization movement and sometimes a revival of original and canonical Buddhist ideals.[4] The movement tended to simplify Theravāda religious practice, sometimes to the point of relying primarily on a single practice. In stressing religious practice and experience and in downplaying much of the traditional devotional, doctrinal, and cosmological aspects of Theravāda Buddhism, its emphasis was on "orthopraxy," that is, particular practices and realizations, rather than "orthodoxy," that is, particular doctrines, teachings, and sectarian identification. Teachers such as Mahāsi, U Ba Khin, Goenka, Achaan Buddhadāsa, and Achaan Chā seem to have had little, if any, interest in making "converts" to Buddhism. Rather they offered their teachings and meditation practices freely to anyone interested, regardless of the person's religious affiliation.

The first American *vipassanā* teachers studied with Asian teachers who were part of this twentieth-century modernization movement. Joseph Goldstein (b. 1944) studied with Mahāsi and his students Anagārika Munindra and U Pandita; Sharon Salzberg (b. 1952) with Goenka, Mahāsi, Munindra, and U Pandita; Jack Kornfield (b. 1945) with Achaan Chā and Mahāsi Sayādaw; Ruth Denison with Goenka's teacher, U Ba Khin. Focusing on soteriology and meditation, these Westerners were seldom introduced to the wider Theravāda religious world, including its complex interrelationships with Southeast Asian society. They therefore returned to the United States as importers of *vipassanā* meditation but not of the much wider religious tradition of Southeast Asian Theravāda Buddhism. As Jack Kornfield, one of the senior American *vipassanā* teachers, has said, "We wanted to offer the powerful practices of insight meditation, as many of our teachers did, as simply as possible without the complications of rituals, robes, chanting and the whole religious tradition."[5] The early American *vipassanā* teachers went even further than most of their own Asian teachers in presenting *vipassanā* practice independent of the Theravāda tradition. Teaching as laypeople to an almost exclusively lay audience, they were thus free to package the *vipassanā* practice in American cultural forms and language.

Prior to approximately 1970, very little *vipassanā* meditation was taught in the United States. Occasionally a visiting Theravāda monk would teach meditation on a college campus. Soon after it was founded in 1966, the Buddhist Vihara in Washington, D.C., offered regular instruction in mindfulness practice to a handful of interested Westerners. Around 1971, a few Americans who had studied in Southeast Asia during the 1960s returned to the United States and began offering retreats in *vipassanā* meditation. Best known of these first Western teachers were Sujata, Ruth Denison, and Robert Hover, all of whom had studied in Burma.[6]

Arguably the most significant event for the introduction of *vipassanā* to America occurred when Jack Kornfield and Joseph Goldstein taught summer meditation courses at the Naropa Institute in 1974, at the invitation of the Tibetan teacher Chögyam Trungpa and the Hindu teacher Ram Dass (Richard Alpert). Kornfield and Goldstein's classes proved immensely successful and launched a sixteen-year teaching partnership. For the next two years they traveled around America offering meditation retreats attended predominantly by Americans in their twenties and thirties.[7]

The retreats led by Goldstein and Kornfield were a hybrid of Asian forms. The basic practice taught was the Mahāsi technique. The structure in which it was taught was modeled on the ten- and thirty-day retreats taught by S. N. Goenka. Instead of giving the full meditation instruction all at once, as in the Mahāsi meditation centers, Goldstein and Kornfield offered the instructions progressively over the first days of the retreat, much like Goenka's courses. And, like Goenka's, the first days of the retreats typically focused on mindfulness of breathing. While Mahāsi never taught loving-kindness meditation (*mettā*) together with *vipassanā*, Goldstein and Korn-field ended each retreat with a guided loving-kindness meditation, as is done in Goenka courses.

In 1976, Kornfield and Goldstein, together with fellow teachers Sharon Salzberg and Jacqueline Schwartz, bought a former Catholic seminary and boys' school in Barre, Massachusetts. This became a permanent, year-round meditation retreat center called Insight Meditation Society (IMS). IMS quickly became the most active *vipassanā* center in the West, with students coming from all over the United States and Europe to participate in ten-day to three-month retreats throughout the year.

In 1981, Jack Kornfield moved to California and a few years later co-founded Spirit Rock, a West Coast sister center to IMS. In 1984, Kornfield started his first four-year program to systematically train teachers for the growing number of *vipassanā* students. By 1997, Kornfield and the Spirit Rock teachers' collective plan to start a "community leader" training pro-gram to prepare mature *vipassanā* students to lead community meditation classes and gatherings. In creating these training programs, Kornfield has taken a leadership role in fostering the development of the *vipassanā* move-ment. Other teachers have trained and authorized teachers to teach, but not by the same systematic and planned approach.

Both IMS and Spirit Rock have institutional mechanisms for approving teachers. For the most part, teachers are those who studied in Asia (Joseph Goldstein, Jack Kornfield, Sharon Salzberg, and Christopher Titmuss) and Westerners trained by these four. As the two centers are closely connected, their lists of approved teachers overlap. Commonly, teachers teach retreats together; larger retreats may have as many as five teachers. Such coopera-tion has meant that the teachers associated with Spirit Rock and IMS may be less prone to the difficulties that may befall spiritual teachers who do not have the close support and feedback of peers.

Since the mid-1970s, the "mainstream" *vipassanā* teachers have held yearly meetings of *vipassanā* teachers from the United States and sometimes Europe to discuss teaching and the growth of the *vipassanā* movement. While not always harmonious, these meetings have helped nurture an in-teractive teacher community and created the most coherent representative body for the movement.

American Adaptations

While still in its infancy, the *vipassanā* movement provides an interesting example of one shape Buddhism is taking in its North American setting. With its primary focus on a particular meditation practice, it has been rel-atively unencumbered by the issues of cultural preservation and accommodation that confront those Asian Buddhist traditions transplanted to America in a more intact form. It has been much easier, almost inevitable, for *vipassanā* teachers and students to organize themselves according to Western values, worldviews, and institutional preferences. The *vipassanā* movement has tended to incorporate such values as democracy, equality, feminism, and individualism to a much greater degree and faster than most other Buddhist groups in the United States.[8]

In taking on a North American form, the *vipassanā* movement has aligned itself with, and borrowed elements from, particular aspects of American culture. This becomes clear if we contrast it with the True Pure Land (Jōdo Shinshū) tradition of the Buddhist Churches of America (BCA). In establishing itself in America, the BCA chose to emulate many of the forms, procedures, and terminology of mainstream Christian churches. Its "churches" hold regular Sunday religious services, instituting forms of public and communal worship unfamiliar to the True Pure Land tradition in Japan but quite common among Christian denominations in the United States. The BCA installed pulpits, pews, and organs, used hymns and sermons, started Sunday schools and adopted official titles like "reverend" and "bishop." The underlying assumption of such adaptation is that the BCA is a religion or a community of worship much like mainstream Christianity.

In theologian Ernest Troeltsch's classic typology of religious orientation, the BCA would be either a church or a sect.[9] In contrast, the orientation of the American *vipassanā* movement would be what Troeltsch called "mysticism" or "religious individualism." While Troeltsch's usage of the term *mysticism* is awkward and somewhat idiosyncratic, he uses it to describe a Western religious orientation in which personal and inward experience and belief predominate over collective belief and worship. It typifies the *vipassanā* movement better than the commonly used categories of "cult" or "new religion," which have been contrasted to "church," "sect," or "denomination." Troeltsch claims that the "mystical" orientation arose in the context of the growth of Western individualism and of a prosperous middle class. While too facile correlations between religious typologies and social class are often problematic, it could be fruitful to consider the relationship between the middle-class status of most American *vipassanā* students and the religious orientation of the movement.

Rather than borrowing from the normative American religious landscape, the early American students of *vipassanā*—many of whom were part of the counter-culture youth movement of the sixties and seventies—distanced themselves from mainstream religious values and institutions. These practitioners were much more likely to describe their involvement with Buddhist practice as "spiritual" rather than "religious." More interested in personal transformation and individual meditative experience than building a cohesive religious community, these young people had more in common with Western psychotherapy and the Human Potential Movement—especially with what is now called Transpersonal Psychology—than with Christian churches. Organizationally, individuals participate in the *vipassanā* movement more like therapy clients than members of a church; virtually nothing is required of the student except to pay for retreats or classes. Thus, with no required commitment to an organization, a teacher, or Buddhist teachings, even the most active *vipassanā* students may retain their preexisting lifestyles, religious affiliations, and political, philosophical, and cultural points of view without conflict.

A further connection with psychotherapy appears both in the professional training of many of the teachers and in the content of their teachings. The most dramatic example is at Spirit Rock, where nine of the fourteen regular teachers are trained psychotherapists. The books on mindfulness practice by American teachers frequently address psychological issues. For example, in *Insight Meditation: The Practice of Freedom*, by Joseph Goldstein, we find such section titles as "Unworthiness," "Guilt," "Jealousy," "Emotional Bondage, Emotional Freedom," "Psychotherapy and Meditation," and "Birth of the Ego." In 1988, the *Inquiring Mind* devoted an entire issue to the subject of psychology, psychotherapy, and meditation.[10] This Western concern with the psychology and psychotherapy of emotions contrasts with the lack of such discussion among traditional Theravāda meditation teachers in Southeast Asia.

Historically, Buddhism has assimilated into a new culture by incorporating elements of the indigenous beliefs. Perhaps the "indigenous belief" that the *vipassanā* movement will at least partly assimilate is Western psychology. Jack Kornfield writes, "Of the Western 'inner practices,' the one that is having the most significant impact on Buddhism and on all contemporary spiritual life is the understanding and practice of Western psychology. Many serious students and teachers of the spiritual path in the West have found it necessary or useful to turn to psychotherapy for help in their spiritual life. Many others who have not done so would probably benefit by it."[11] Kornfield's chapter titled "Psychotherapy and Meditation" in *A Path with Heart* is in part a plea for complementing spiritual practice with psychotherapy. He writes that "at least half of our students at our annual three-month retreat find themselves unable to do traditional Insight Meditation because they encounter so much unresolved grief, fear, and wounding and unfinished developmental business from the past that this becomes their meditation."[12]

The connection between psychotherapy and the *vipassanā* movement, however, may not simply be a response to the psychological needs of the American students. Both may be expressions of a strand of Western individualism that focuses on personal experience, inner change, and freedom.

Teachings

The teachings that the Western *vipassanā* teachers are developing in America are noticeably different from those in Southeast Asia. In discussing the Western teachings it must be kept in mind that the *vipassanā* movement, even in its "mainstream" manifestation, is not a coherent movement with an established and collectively agreed-upon teaching. Among American teachers, variations in teachings usually appear in doctrinal formulations and, less often, in the practical instructions given for meditation and mindfulness practice. Since the *vipassanā* movement is so praxis-oriented, this is not surprising. Indeed, we find that many of the Western *vipassanā* teachers give such importance to meditation and mindfulness that they are much more likely to present Buddhism as a meditation-centered religious or spiritual tradition than Theravāda teachers would in Southeast Asia. In the introduction to the book *Living Buddhist Masters*, Jack Kornfield writes, "The essence of Buddhism is its meditation practices."[13] And in an informational brochure distributed by Spirit Rock it is similarly written that "the heart of the Buddhist path is the practice of meditation."

While traditional Theravāda teachings make some references to freedom (*vimutti*), freedom is central to the teachings of the American *vipassanā*. Joseph Goldstein writes, "The essential teachings of the Buddha [are concerned with] the nature of suffering and the realization of freedom."[14] The realization of freedom is so closely tied to *vipassanā* meditation that Goldstein titled his most recent book *Insight Meditation: The Practice of Freedom*.

The American teachers almost exclusively discuss a freedom relevant to one's current life, while the traditional teachings focus more on freedom from the endless rounds of rebirth, or at least from future births in the lower realms of existence (*gati;* the animal, hungry ghost, or hell realms). So, in advocating a "liberation" *from* this world, Mahāsi Sayādaw writes:

> The Wheel of Rebirth (samsara) is very dreadful. Every effort should therefore be made to acquaint oneself with the miserable conditions of Samsara and then to work for an escape from this incessant cycle, and for the attainment of Nirvana. If an escape from Samsara as a whole is not possible for the present, an attempt should be made for an escape at least from the round of rebirth in the realm of hell, or animals, or petas. In this case it is necessary to work for the total removal from oneself of the erroneous view that there is a self, which is the root-cause of rebirth in the miserable states.[15]

In contrast, Jack Kornfield writes:

> For twenty-five hundred years the practices and teachings of Buddhism have offered a systematic way to see clearly and live wisely. They have offered a way to

discover liberation within our own bodies and minds, *in the midst of this very world.*
[emphasis added][16]

When Asian teachers do talk about freedom, it is primarily in reference
to what one is free from—that is, from greed, hate, delusion, grasping,
attachment, wrong view, self, and most significantly, rebirth. For the Asian
teachers the religious path ends with final freedom or *nibbāna*, which has
no purpose beyond itself. Achaan Chā exhorts:

> Come to practise for liberation! It isn't easy to live in accordance with true
> wisdom, but whoever earnestly seeks the Path and Fruit and aspires to Nibbana
> will be able to persevere and endure. Endure being contented and satisfied with
> little; eating little, sleeping little, speaking little and living in moderation. By
> doing this we can put an end to worldliness.[17]

In contrast, the Western teachers often stress the potential found
through freedom. Freedom is a means to living happily, compassionately,
and wisely without drastic changes in lifestyle. So Joseph Goldstein writes:

> We practice the Dharma in order . . . to be free. That is the heart of all the
> effort we make, because from freedom come connectedness, compassion, loving-
> kindness, and peace. . . . The Buddha saw with such clarity how different states
> of mind and courses of action lead to different results. Unwholesome mind states
> have certain consequences. Wholesome mind states have results of their own. As
> we begin to understand the truth of how things are, we see for ourselves what
> brings suffering in our lives, and what brings happiness and freedom.[18]

In defining freedom in terms relevant to anyone's life, the American
teachers make virtually no reference to Buddhist doctrines that would be
foreign and perhaps unacceptable to most Americans. While the practice's
potential for ending one's involvement with the cycles of rebirth underlies
the teachings of Asian teachers, the *vipassanā* teachings in the West are not
predicated on the traditional belief of rebirth. Other traditional teachings
on realms of existence, merit-making, the four stages of enlightenment,
and monastic renunciation are virtually absent as well. Without the traditional Theravāda doctrinal framework and goals motivating practice, American *vipassanā* students are given pragmatic and experiential goals. In this
light the practice is offered as a form of therapy from which practitioners
can benefit in their current lives.

Four spiritual practices are central to American *vipassanā* teachings.
These are mindfulness (*sati*), loving-kindness (*mettā*), ethics (*sīla*), and generosity (*dāna*). While mindfulness receives primary emphasis and is often
taught independent of the other three, most mainstream *vipassanā* teachers
would present all four as important elements in a mindfulness-based spiritual life.

Mindfulness practice involves the cultivation of undistracted attentiveness to what is being experienced in the present. As such it is a practice that can be applied both to formal meditation and to all one's daily activities. American teachers do not always distinguish between these two areas of cultivation. An informational brochure from Spirit Rock states:

> In Insight Meditation we pay clear attention to whatever exists naturally in this present moment. The specific focus of our awareness can vary, from bodily sensations to sights to thoughts and feelings. We often begin by paying attention to the sensations of breathing. We sit still, either cross-legged on the floor or upright in a chair, and allow our eyes to close gently. Then we turn our attention to the breath and simply experience, in as continuous a way as possible, the physical sensations of breathing in and breathing out. . . . Meditation can also be carried on throughout our daily activities. We can be mindful of the movement of our body, the sensations in walking, the sounds around us, or the thoughts and feelings that come into our mind. As our meditation practice develops, we find that the mind becomes calmer and clearer. We start to see the influence of our habitual patterns of moods, expectations, hopes, and fears. In seeing through the mind's conditioning, we can live more fully in the present moment with balance and spaciousness. We are no longer so swayed by the shifting thoughts and feelings of our conditioned responses. This [is] the first taste of freedom.[19]

The formal meditation practice most commonly taught by the "mainstream" teachers is derived from Mahāsi Sayādaw's systemization of traditional *vipassanā* meditation. Instead of having a fixed object of attention, such as the breath, the practitioner is taught to become aware, with clear recognition, of the full range of physical, sensory, emotional, psychological, and cognitive experiences. Mindfulness of these events is not a cognitive analysis however, but rather a careful, sustained, and simple sensory perception of how each experience is registered prior to contemplative reflection or evaluation. Important to the Mahāsi approach, but somewhat less emphasized by most of the American teachers, is supporting the mindfulness practice with a continuous stream of mental labeling of what is experienced.

Intensive periods of meditation practice in residential retreats are emphasized as an important means for deepening one's mindfulness practice. All the mainstream American *vipassanā* teachers offer retreats, which can range from two days to three months in length. Typically these retreats have a daily schedule of sitting and walking meditation from about 5:30 a.m. to 9:30 p.m. and are conducted in silence except for instruction and teachings. As a student's meditation practice deepens, he or she is individually guided through what are known as the "stages of insight," which involve strong sustained degrees of mindfulness.[20]

Loving-kindness meditation is practiced as a complement to mindfulness meditation, both to stabilize the mind and to infuse mindfulness practice with a spirit of friendliness. Much as compassion (*karuṇā*) is the primary spiritual emotion of Mahāyāna Buddhism, so loving-kindness is the fundamental spiritual emotion stressed by the Western *vipassanā* movement. Loving-kindness, one of the four *brahmavihāras*,[21] is the heartfelt intention for the welfare and happiness of oneself and others. The practice of loving-kindness is the cultivation of both that intention and the accompanying feelings of friendliness, warmth, and love.

The American *vipassanā* teachers place more emphasis on the practice of *mettā*, or loving-kindness, than do most Asian *vipassanā* teachers and they often combine loving-kindness meditation with a forgiveness practice that seems to be unknown in the formal *mettā* practice found in Southeast Asia.[22] References to loving-kindness are virtually absent in the many books by Mahāsi Sayādaw except for a book specifically about the *brahmavihāras*. Similarly, except for one reference to formal loving-kindness meditation as a "rather elementary practice" that is "child's play,"[23] Achaan Chā does not mention *mettā* in his books published in English. When it is taught in Asia, *mettā* is seldom mixed with *vipassanā* practice. In contrast, most retreats led by the teachers from IMS and Spirit Rock include at least one guided loving-kindness meditation during each day of the retreat, and individual students may be instructed to practice *mettā* even more frequently. Virtually every book on *vipassanā* practice by an American teacher contains lengthy discussions on *mettā*. It is the primary theme in Sharon Salzberg's book *Lovingkindness: The Revolutionary Art of Happiness*.[24] One may speculate that the American near-obsession with happiness and love has influenced the American teachers to put special emphasis on loving-kindness. The emphasis also arises out of a real need to offer an alternative to practitioners for whom mindfulness practice is unsuitable. As an awareness practice, mindfulness reveals the workings of the practitioner's mental life. If the practitioner has a strong tendency to self-criticism or self-deprecation, what is revealed in mindfulness can sometimes fuel enough self-criticism that it becomes an impediment to meditation. In such circumstances, loving-kindness practice can be an antidote to this tendency. In addition, *mettā* meditation is offered as an effective practice for strengthening a meditator's concentration. This is especially important when a student is too mentally or physically restless to practice mindfulness.

The third practice taught by American *vipassanā* teachers is ethics or precepts. Most commonly, precepts—specifically the five lay precepts—are understood as aids to cultivating a mindful and wise life. So Jack Kornfield writes: "We can use the precepts to train ourselves, to awaken ourselves and make our relationships more open and harmonious. When we are about to break them, the precepts are like warning lights and alarms signaling us to take a careful look at the mind state behind the action in which we are involved. If we look closely, we can usually discover where we became caught or confused and how we can let go and be free. Use the precepts. They are incomparable tools for changing ourselves and the world around us."[25] With such a utilitarian approach, *vipassanā* students are left to decide for themselves the extent to which they use the precepts as guidelines for their ethical behavior. The only time that students are required to abide by the precepts is during intensive residential meditation retreats. The most common time that *vipassanā* students formally and somewhat ritualistically "take" or recite the precepts is during the opening of such retreats.

Until the mid-1980s, *vipassanā* was taught in the West with much less emphasis on ethics than in Southeast Asia. Since then, and particularly in the United States, an increasing stress has been placed on ethics and on the traditional Buddhist precepts for the laity. The change was to a great extent a response to both a wider cultural interest in ethics and to a significant number of ethical transgressions by Asian and Western teachers of Tibetan, Zen, and Theravāda Buddhism. At the instigation of Jack Kornfield, the collective of teachers affiliated with the Insight Meditation Society and Spirit Rock formulated an Insight Meditation Teacher's Code of Ethics.[26]

The Theravāda practice of *dāna*, or generosity, is a key element in the spirituality of the American *vipassanā* movement because it both supports and expresses the openheartedness and happiness that are said to come from mindfulness practice. Kornfield writes: "To cultivate generosity directly is another fundamental part of living a spiritual life. Like the training precepts and like our inner meditations, generosity can actually be practiced. With practice, its spirit forms our actions, and our hearts will grow stronger and lighter. It can lead us to new levels of letting go and great happiness."[27] The centrality of *dāna* to the *vipassanā* movement is at least partly a result of the manner in which the teachings are offered. It is customary for the *vipassanā* teachers associated with IMS and Spirit Rock to offer their teachings freely and without being paid. Furthermore, the Insight Meditation Teacher's Code of Ethics states that teachers "agree to offer teachings without favoritism in regard to students' financial circumstances."[28] While retreat and class fees are charged, these cover the expenses of putting on the event (rent, food, mailings, and so on). The fees are kept as low as possible and scholarships are offered to those who cannot afford to pay. The teachers receive *dāna*, that is, voluntary and usually anonymous donations from students. To a great extent this financial arrangement replicates the lay-monastic exchange system found in traditional Theravāda Buddhism. However, since the American teachers have much greater financial needs than monastics, the long-term success of this *dāna* system is still uncertain.

In the Melting Pot of American Buddhism

One of the salient features of the *vipassanā* movement is its ecumenical interaction with other meditative traditions of Eastern spirituality. Because their pragmatic approach is loosely bound, if at all, to traditional Theravāda metaphysics and soteriological definitions, *vipassanā* teachers and students tend to be religiously eclectic, participating in and borrowing from any religious or psychological tradition that seems to aid in the pursuit of "freedom" and happiness. The articles and interviews in the *Inquiring Mind* reveal that both *vipassanā* students and teachers actively participate not only in other Buddhist traditions, such as in the Tibetan and Zen traditions, but also in non-Buddhist traditions such as Hindu Advaita-vedānta. In their Dharma talks and writings, American *vipassanā* teachers are almost as likely to quote a Sufi, Hindu, Tibetan, Taoist, or Zen teacher as they are to quote the Buddha or a Theravāda teacher.[29]

At the same time, many students of Zen and Tibetan Buddhism have complemented their own practice with some *vipassanā* meditation. Some have done so enough to have become recognized as teachers in two different traditions. For example, teaching *vipassanā* at Spirit Rock is a Zen priest who received Dharma Transmission at the San Francisco Zen Center. In recent years, some of the teachers at Spirit Rock and IMS have been involved in intensive meditation retreats in the Tibetan *dzogchen* tradition. The nondualistic *dzogchen* teachings about awareness have thus influenced the *vipassanā* instructions that they give.

Perhaps the pragmatic interests of Euro-American Buddhists will lessen the sharp divisions that exist in Asia among the various meditative traditions of Buddhism. Certainly, many of the Buddhist traditions in America are losing their traditional metaphysical, mythological, and institutional underpinnings. Instead, one finds an increasing stress on the common foundation of all schools of Buddhism, that is, the Four Noble Truths, the Eightfold Path, and straightforward practices of mindfulness, concentration, loving-kindness, and compassion.

In September 1994, Spirit Rock and the San Francisco Zen Center sponsored what was billed as the first American Buddhist Teacher's Meeting. Invited to the meeting were almost exclusively American-born meditation teachers of the Tibetan, Zen, and *vipassanā* traditions. One attending Zen teacher with an affiliation to the Japanese Jōdo Shinshū tradition complained of the elitism of a meeting called "American Buddhist Teachers' Meeting" that included only representatives of these three traditions. While the title of the meeting may have been a misnomer, the exclusiveness of the meeting highlights the commonality among these traditions as they develop in America. Most American *vipassanā* practitioners have more in common with American Zen students than with Thai or Burmese participants at a local Thai or Burmese temple. Similarly most Zen students will have more in common with American Tibetan Buddhist practitioners than with the Japanese American congregation at the Sōtō Zen temple in San Francisco's Japantown.

In areas without a *vipassanā*, Zen, or Tibetan center, it is common for students from the various traditions to create a single sitting group where they all practice together. With some awkwardness as they decide which meditation hall customs to follow and what text to read together or Dharma tape to listen to, these groups offer mutual support to the participants.

Demographics

It could perhaps be argued that some of the eclectic, nonsectarian and noncommittal tendencies that are found in much of the American *vipassanā* movement are an expression of its focus on freedom. For many American *vipassanā* students freedom has meant, among other things, freedom from religious formalism, dogmatic teachings and teachers, religious identifications, and narrow-mindedness. Indeed, we find some *vipassanā* teachers discouraging students from even identifying themselves as Buddhists:

> It is important to realize that to identify oneself as a meditator or a spiritual person or even a Buddhist can be another way we get caught or lose one's true balance. This is like carrying the raft on your head instead of using it for a vehicle to the other shore. The purpose of meditation is not to create a new spiritual identity, nor to become the most meditative person on the block, who tells other people how they should live. To practice is to let go.[30]

This lack of identification is paralleled by a lack of organizational affiliation. Neither Spirit Rock nor IMS, the largest centers in America, makes a clear distinction between members and nonmembers. This is in large part because they are primarily retreat centers providing classes and retreats where anyone is invited to learn and practice meditation. They are not churchlike community centers where the full range of people's daily spiritual needs and expressions are met. Rather than being based on membership dues, Spirit Rock and IMS are financed by charging fees for retreats and classes offered and by donations.

Since no institutional membership is required, demographic data on the *vipassanā* movement are hard to obtain. Even so, some observations can be made.

In the 1970s and early 1980s, the loose network of *vipassanā* practitioners consisted mostly of young adults attending intensive meditation retreats. Since the mid-1980s the practice has been extended beyond retreats into daily life as *vipassanā* students settled down to family lives and as older, working people with families became attracted to mindfulness practice. As a result, currently at least three hundred weekly *vipassanā* meditation groups meet throughout the United States to sit together in support of each other's ongoing mindfulness practice. This compares to about thirty such groups in 1984.[31] While most groups are small, a few have up to a hundred or more weekly participants. A couple of dozen are led by teachers. The smaller, teacherless groups usually substitute for a teacher's presence by playing Dharma talks on tapes or by reading Dharma books.

The growth in the number of sitting groups is paralleled by the growth in the number of retreats. In 1984, the *Inquiring Mind* listed ten residential retreats around the country. For 1995, the number was one hundred.[32] It is conservatively estimated that between 1970 and 1995 about fifty thousand Americans attended *vipassanā* retreats of one day to three months. Perhaps five thousand attended such retreats in 1995.[33]

Most sitting groups and retreats have more women participants than men. Spirit Rock's mailing list of 24,000 contains twice as many women as men. At a weekly sitting group in Palo Alto, California, typically about 65 percent of the approximately one hundred participants are women. A four-day residential retreat in Kansas City in the spring of 1995 and a seventeen-day residential retreat for experienced practitioners held in San Rafael, California, in the fall of 1995 both had ratios of 65 percent women to 35 percent men.

Of the forty people attending the Kansas City retreat, 80 percent were over forty years of age; 40 percent were over fifty. In the San Rafael retreat, 80 percent of the fifty participants were over forty years old. The average age was forty-nine. In a survey done in April 1995 at the Palo Alto sitting group, the average age was fifty, with 81 percent of the respondents being over forty.

American *vipassanā* students are overwhelmingly Caucasian. While it is difficult to discern the economic class of these students, most seem to be middle class. In the Palo Alto sitting group a majority of the participants are college-educated professionals.

While people are interested in *vipassanā* in every state of the country, the mailing lists for the *Inquiring Mind*, Spirit Rock, and the Dharma Seed Tape Library show that by far the biggest interest seems to be in California, New York, and Massachusetts, in that order.

In 1995 approximately seventy lay *vipassanā* teachers were active in the United States. The fall 1995 edition of the *Inquiring Mind* listed forty-eight teachers leading retreats around the country. Exactly half of the forty-eight were women. All except three or four were Caucasian and the vast majority were college-educated.[34] At least 30 percent of this group have received professional training in psychotherapy. They all appear to be over the age of forty.

These demographics suggest questions concerning the future of the movement. Is the aging population of *vipassanā* students an indication that interest in *vipassanā* is primarily a phenomenon of the Baby-Boomer generation and so will decrease as that generation ages and dies? Or does the average participant age of fifty suggest that interest in *vipassanā* extends beyond the Baby-Boomers but is still age-related? Is there something about what the American *vipassanā* movement offers that is more attractive to people who have already been through twenty or thirty years of work and raising a family? Do the time and money required to attend retreats have a bearing on the age and economic status of retreatants? Furthermore, it would be interesting to discern what, if any, is the relationship between the middle-class and Euro-American identity of many of *vipassanā* students and the doctrinal and institutional preferences of the movement.

Conclusion

The twenty-five-year-old American *vipassanā* movement is a significant player in the development of American forms of Buddhism and in the introduction of Buddhist influences into American culture. Its popularity is growing rapidly as the number of teachers and students increases, and as its mindfulness practice is introduced in such places as hospitals, schools, and prisons independent of its Buddhist doctrines or context.

Most forms of Buddhism arrived in the United States as full religious traditions. The *vipassanā* movement is significantly different since it involved the importation of a few particular spiritual practices and soteriological goals largely independent of the wider Theravāda teachings and its Southeast Asian cultural expressions. Without the conservative force of an established religious tradition, the American *vipassanā* movement has been free to experiment with new religious expressions, teachings, and institutional structures that are perhaps uniquely adapted to contemporary American society. It is thoroughly lay-based. Its orientation is closer to mysticism or religious individualism than to churches or organized religion. Its practitioners do not identify themselves as members of an institution. It has rapidly incorporated Western values and worldviews. And it has been open to influences from outside its Theravāda background, including Mahāyāna Buddhism, Advaita-vedānta, and, perhaps most intriguing and uniquely American, Western psychology.

A fascinating development of Buddhism in the modern world is the meeting in America of Buddhist traditions that existed independent of one another in Asia. It is too early to tell whether these various traditions will merge or how they will affect each other in the long term. Many American *vipassanā* practitioners freely borrow from the different schools, especially those with strong meditation traditions. Perhaps *vipassanā* will become a vessel within which these traditions will come together.

The forms and direction the amorphous *vipassanā* movement will take, and even from where leadership might come, are uncertain. The two biggest *vipassanā* centers, IMS and Spirit Rock, and their associated teachers are significant influences, but they do not provide a particularly cohesive, organized focus for the wider movement.

Many interesting questions can be asked about the future development of the *vipassanā* movement. Having already lost much of its Theravāda identity, how thoroughly will it maintain its Buddhist identity? If it remains pragmatically orthopraxical, will the mindfulness teachings be contextualized in any traditional Buddhist framework, or will a new doctrinal framework be developed in the West? When such central Buddhist tenets as noself (*anattā*) can be reformulated so that at least one American teacher can refer to a "true self," will the movement eventually lack a uniform enough doctrinal foundation to hold it together, even loosely?[35] If the movement has minimal shared doctrinal, ritual, or institutional underpinnings, can shared spiritual practices create a cohesive enough identity for it to remain an identifiable movement? And what do the demographics of its teachers and practitioners say about the movement's long-term viability?

While it is far from clear how it will develop, the *vipassanā* movement promises to be influential in the development of American Buddhism. Perhaps this preliminary study will inspire further research on the movement during this formative time.

Part Two

ISSUES IN AMERICAN BUDDHISM

Who Is a Buddhist? Charting the Landscape of Buddhist America

JAN NATTIER

T he study of Buddhism in North America is still in its infancy. While Christianity and Judaism have long been recognized as basic ele-ments in the American religious tapestry, Buddhism received scant attention—if indeed any at all—in surveys of religion in North America published before 1980.[1] Since then the situation has improved somewhat,[2] but Buddhism still remains very much a "fringe element" in most accounts of religion in this region.[3]

Likewise, North America is a relative newcomer to the field of Buddhist Studies. In a discipline shaped primarily, during its formative period, by the analysis of classical texts, Buddhism in North America—or, for that matter, in Europe and other non-Asian parts of the world—has seemed too new, too immature, and often too unorthodox to warrant serious scholarly attention. Here the turning point came slightly earlier, with North America beginning to receive at least a modicum of attention in surveys of Buddhism published after the mid-1970s.[4] Nonetheless even the most generous of such accounts occupy only a few pages, and the observant reader will find that these treatments of Buddhism in the West are generally more descrip-tive (that is, less analytical) than the corresponding sections on Buddhism in Asia. There have been, of course, several scholarly or semischolarly books dealing with various aspects of Buddhism in North America, but it is the treatment of North American Buddhism in more broadly based works that tells us the most about its standing in the fields of North American Reli-gions and Buddhist Studies, respectively. And here the evidence is une-quivocal: Buddhism in this hemisphere is only now, at the very end of the twentieth century, beginning to be recognized as a legitimate subject of study.

This relative neglect can be attributed to a variety of causes, but one of the most significant is certainly the relatively small number of adherents to Buddhism in North America.[5] While accurate statistics are difficult to come by, it is generally accepted that Buddhists in the United States number somewhere between one and two million, thus comprising well under 1 percent of the population.[6] One could argue, with some justification, that such a small population deserves only a small proportion of scholarly attention. Yet these numbers do not tell the whole story. First, because a number of North American Buddhists are prominent figures in the arts, literature, and media, Buddhism has acquired a visibility and a level of influence far out of proportion to the actual number of its adherents.[7] And second, on a methodological level the study of Buddhism in North America points to the need for refinement in some of our scholarly tools. It is this second issue that will be the focus of this chapter, for—as I hope to show—a study of the Buddhist presence in North America can evoke perspectives that may well reshape how so-called new religions in general are studied.

In an essay of this length it is of course not possible to deal with the whole range of methodological issues involved in the study of Buddhism in North America. I will focus, therefore, on only three topics: first, the problem of defining the subject matter (that is, who is to be considered a "Buddhist"); second, a proposal for a new way of categorizing Buddhist groups in North America; and third, some observations on the issue of cultural assimilation. The following discussion is by no means intended to offer the last word on these topics, but only to provide a stimulus for future research.

Delineating the Data: Who Is a "Buddhist"?

One issue that must be faced at the outset in any study of American Buddhism is precisely who is to be included within the category of "Buddhist." Is it enough merely to call oneself a Buddhist, or are other features—certain beliefs, certain ritual practices (such as meditation or chanting), or perhaps even active membership in a specific organization—required as well? Though these questions may arise in the study of any religious tradition, they are particularly acute in the case of religions that are so new or so small in a given region that very few people have any firsthand familiarity with them. To take a not uncommon example: if a college sophomore buys a book on Zen by Alan Watts, reads it, likes it, and subsequently begins to think of himself as a Buddhist—but without ever having encountered any form of Buddhism beyond the printed page—should he be included within the scope of a study of Buddhism in North America?

Many scholars, and an even larger number of Buddhists, would probably reply in the negative. Yet just as one senses that an all-inclusive stance will net more "Buddhists" than we may have had in mind, there are difficulties with more exclusive approaches as well. Criteria of belief or ritual practice quickly begin to resemble standards of orthodoxy, for one cannot require these elements for inclusion without specifying *which* beliefs and *which* practices are meant. To take another example: if an elderly Kalmyk Mongol from New Jersey—herself perhaps a thirteenth-generation Buddhist—occasionally places offerings of money and food before Buddhist images at her local temple, but does not meditate or chant *sūtras* and knows little of the technicalities of Buddhist doctrine, would such criteria lead to her exclusion from the list? If so, it seems clear that something is wrong not with her, but with our procedures.

Official membership in a specific Buddhist group might seem an obvious solution to this problem, but even this approach yields significant difficulties. For Americans are, on the whole, notorious non-joiners: statistics regularly demonstrate a far higher level of belief (such as in the existence of the Jewish or Christian God) and practice (for example, prayer) than of participation in church or synagogue activities.[8] If one were to count as Christians or Jews only those who are active members of a religious organization, the population of these groups in the United States would suddenly plunge dramatically.

Some compromise between these two extremes of uncritical inclusiveness and arbitrary exclusiveness, therefore, seems clearly necessary, and fortunately one possible solution is readily available. In a study dealing with a broad range of religious groups, but with special attention to the so-called new religions, sociologists Rodney Stark and William Sims Bainbridge have introduced a fruitful typology that can be applied with considerable benefit to Buddhist data.[9] To the traditional Weberian categories of "church" (here defined as a religious organization supported by and supportive of the established powers in a given society) and "sect" (defined as a breakaway reform movement that attempts to restore a degree of religious purity and critical spirit that the "church" has lost), Stark and Bainbridge add a third category, designed specifically to accommodate new religious movements that are *not* derived from existing religious institutions. The term "cult," which they use to designate such genuinely new movements—is perhaps unfortunate, given the negative connotations of that term in common parlance, but the category itself offers a useful lens for analyzing Buddhist materials.

In the case of genuinely new religions, Stark and Bainbridge argue, three subtypes can be distinguished. The first of these, the "audience cult," requires no more of its participants than that they attend an occasional lecture, read an occasional book, or perhaps subscribe to a periodical. There is no community, no ritual, no catechism; the only criterion for inclusion is a vague level of interest. Not surprisingly, participants in these activities are often involved in more than one such "cult," and may maintain membership in their hereditary religious faith as well. Participation in an audience cult does not, in other words, result in the replacement of one's existing religious worldview; it merely adds extra spice to the mix. Readers of Shirley MacLaine's accounts of paranormal experiences, for instance, would be included in this category, as would viewers of the television guru Osho.

A higher degree of personal involvement is found in the second category, the "client cult." Here the participant engages in direct interaction with a member of the group, but this relationship (like that of the psychotherapist and client, on which this category is clearly based) is limited to the client's use of certain techniques received from a teacher, sometimes at considerable expense. As with the audience cult, participation in a client cult does not require the renunciation of one's existing religious affiliation, but merely supplements it with what could be described as coping techniques. Nor does the use of the teacher's services result, in most cases, in the formation of a client "community." Thus while the client cult does involve a face-to-face relationship, it is an individual and hierarchical one, not accompanied by horizontal bonds with other members of the group, and often requiring no ongoing contact. Here a good example would be Transcendental Meditation, which—with the exception of those few who take up leadership positions in the organization—generally involves no regular group activities, but only the individual practice of a meditation technique obtained from an "initiator."

In both audience cults and client cults there is, of course, the possibility that one's worldview will be altered in small or significant ways by contact with these alternative ideas and techniques. But it is only in Stark and Bainbridge's third category, that of the "cult movement," that a wholesale shift of religious identity takes place. Here the new religious practices and ideas are not merely additive, but involve a genuine conversion to a new religious perspective and the renunciation of one's previous commitments. A person who joins the Sōka Gakkai, for example, would not continue to receive the Catholic sacraments, nor would a resident of a Hare Krishna community be likely to take part in a Passover seder. A cult movement, in other words, provides a complete religious identity, comparable to—and in direct competition with—that offered by the more traditional "churches" and "sects."

Applying this typology to Buddhism in North America, we obtain two results simultaneously: on the one hand, the model allows us to draw some distinctions within American Buddhism that were difficult to make before; and on the other, the Buddhist data point to the need for certain modifications in this model. To begin with the first, the Stark and Bainbridge model allows us to substitute a spectrum of degrees of intensity of participation for more specific (and often sectarian) criteria for inclusion. Rather than defining a Buddhist as "anyone who meditates," or "anyone who believes in the doctrine of no-self," or even "anyone whose parents were Buddhist," we can use this model to identify different styles of relating to the Buddhist tradition. Once this has been done, the researcher can decide, on the basis of the parameters of a given line of inquiry, how narrowly or how broadly to draw the lines.

Two limitations of the model become apparent, however, when it is applied to Buddhists in North America. First, the fact that the model is framed in terms of religious (or parareligious) organizations and not of the individual member means that an entire organization must be defined as belonging to one or another of these categories. But in many cases a single group may include a wide range of participants who fall into two or even all three of Stark and Bainbridge's categories. Members in residence at the San Francisco Zen Center, for example, might fit the definition of participants in a cult movement, but the many readers of *Zen Mind, Beginner's Mind* (written by the founder of that center) would bear a stronger resemblance to members of an audience cult.[10] In between we might find Zen practitioners who have learned the basic technique of meditation at the Zen Center, but now practice meditation on their own without any continued contact with the group (thus belonging to Stark and Bainbridge's category of client cult). A reorientation of the model toward the individual practitioner and away from the institutions themselves might therefore allow for a more flexible and nuanced description of the dynamics of such groups.

A second difficulty with this model is of a different order, and can best be dealt with by supplementing rather than emending Stark and Bainbridge's categories. In their threefold model no distinction is made between religions that are genuinely "new"—that is, religions that were only recently founded—and those that have a long heritage elsewhere in the world but have recently been transplanted to a new environment. Such "transplants" (as I will call them) are treated by Stark and Bainbridge simply as part of the category of cult. This may well be accurate insofar as the perceptions of their neighbors are concerned: for those who know nothing of the long history of Hinduism, for example, the presence of a Hindu temple in their city will seem new and strange indeed. Yet it is vital to distinguish between genuinely new religions (for example, the emergence of the Latter-day Saints or "Mormons" in the nineteenth century) and transplanted ones (for example, the migration of Muslims to North America in the twentieth century).[11] This is not merely a matter of historical technicality, for a "transplant" will behave very differently in its new environment than will a genuinely new religion.[12] Moreover, such a transplant may have belonged to any of Stark and Bainbridge's three types—church, sect, or cult—in its home country, and how it functions in its new environment will have much to do with its typological ancestry. To choose only a single example: a transplanted cult or sect is likely to engage in considerable missionary activity, while a transplanted "church" may not attempt to gain any converts at all.

In sum, while the threefold typology proposed by Stark and Bainbridge offers a productive framework within which Buddhism in North America can be investigated, it is clear that some expansion of the model will be required in order to accommodate the Buddhist data. Such an expanded model can then be applied in turn to other recently transplanted traditions (such as Hinduism and Islam) and may yield rich possibilities for the comparative study of older transplants to North America, such as Judaism and Catholicism, and perhaps even to the dominant tradition of Protestantism itself.

Varieties of Buddhism in America: Making Sense of the Data

Despite the relatively small Buddhist population in North America, this hemisphere is host to a bewildering variety of Buddhist forms. Immigrant communities from East Asia, Southeast Asia, Tibet, and the (then) Soviet Union have brought Buddhist traditions from their homelands; proselytizing by the Sōka Gakkai has produced converts from a wide range of ethnic and economic backgrounds; and middle- and upper-class Americans have shown a particular fascination for the meditative aspects of Theravāda Buddhism, Tibetan Buddhism, and Zen. At first glance this colorful assortment of Buddhists seems virtually impossible to characterize in any meaningful way. Yet characterize them we must, for simply to list them all will tell us next to nothing.

One approach that has gained some currency in recent years speaks of "two Buddhisms": the Buddhism of Asian Americans, on the one hand, and that of European Americans (sometimes labeled "White Buddhism") on the other.[13] Admittedly these categories reflect a real distinction of sorts: most Buddhist Americans of Asian ancestry were born into the faith, for instance, while most European American Buddhists are recent converts; at a typical meeting of the latter the vast majority of participants will be in their forties or early fifties, while at an Asian American Buddhist service many generations are usually present. Still, one quickly senses that such a simple opposition cannot provide us with the whole picture. How would one classify, for example, a Chinese American who meditates with a predominantly Caucasian group, or a Latino adherent of the Sōka Gakkai? In addition to such conceptual difficulties there is a practical one as well, for such a polarized scheme (especially one based on race) can easily exacerbate existing tensions among Buddhists themselves.[14]

The notion of "two Buddhisms," then, is clearly inadequate to the task, primarily because it fails to account for the full spectrum of racial and ethnic diversity in Buddhist America. Happily, though, another approach to categorizing the data seems to be readily available. Since I have discussed this typology in detail in another forum,[15] I will only summarize its general contours here.

Religions—not just Buddhism—travel to new places in three ways: as import, export, and baggage. "Import" in this case refers to what might be described as "demand-driven" transmission (to pursue the economic metaphor): here Buddhism is actively sought out by the recipient. The initial familiarity with Buddhism can come about in a variety of ways—through travel, meeting a visitor from Asia, or (most commonly) through reading— but it is the future convert who takes the initiative to pursue this topic further. What is distinctive about this category is that, to import a form of Buddhism from Asia successfully, one must have two items in sufficient quantity: money and leisure time. For many people, even buying a book on Buddhism is an undreamed-of luxury; a trip to Japan for several years of Buddhist practice would be out of the question. Once such a group has been founded, it is not surprising that like attracts like, and most members of Buddhist groups in this category are of middle-class background or above. In addition they are overwhelmingly (though not exclusively) of European ancestry, and their religious interests are focused on meditation. This is, in sum, a Buddhism of the privileged, attracting those who have the time, the inclination, and the economic opportunity to devote themselves to strenuous (and sometimes expensive) meditation training. In North America Buddhist groups of this type have a variety of sectarian connections, but most are affiliated with a form of Tibetan Buddhism, Vipassana, or Zen. Because the primary common feature of this group is not its ethnicity or sectarian affiliation but its class background, this type can be described as *Elite Buddhism*.[16]

"Export" Buddhists, by contrast, have come into contact with Buddhism not through active seeking on their part, but through "selling" by a Buddhist missionary. The group that best fits this profile in North America is the Sōka Gakkai, which through active proselytizing in a wide range of settings has attracted an ethnically and economically diverse membership. Advertising worldly benefits as well as "spiritual" ones as among the results of Buddhist practice, the Sōka Gakkai has appealed to groups for whom the meditative Buddhism of the Elite type has little or no appeal. In every respect, therefore—ethnicity, socioeconomic level, style of practice, and basic concerns—"Export" Buddhism represents a distinct category. Since missionary activity is not only what has brought most Buddhists to this group, but is expected as a part of their ongoing practice as well, this category is aptly labeled *Evangelical Buddhism.*

"Baggage" Buddhism, as the name suggests, is the religion of those who came to North America as immigrants, but who did not (unlike the missionaries of Evangelical Buddhism) travel for religious reasons. Rather, these are the vast majority of Asian immigrants who came to North America in search of jobs, new opportunities, and a better future for their families, simply bringing their religion along. In a new and often hostile environment, religious centers built by recent immigrants serve a number of functions, not only in transmitting specifically religious ideas and practices but in helping to preserve a sense of cultural identity as well. As a result, Buddhist communities of this type are almost always deliberately mono-ethnic at the outset, though outsiders may eventually be brought in through intermarriage or other means. Because Buddhist associations in this category are defined primarily by their ethnicity, I have labeled this group *Ethnic Buddhism.*[17]

Space does not permit a more extended discussion of this typology here, but it is particularly important to note that apparent sectarian identity often masks radical differences of thought and practice, while great affinities can be observed within each of the above categories even across sectarian and national-origin lines. Thus while "dharma exchanges" are not at all uncommon between Zen and Tibetan Buddhist groups (whose members seem to have a great many attitudes and values in common), some Buddhist organizations that would seem to fall within a single category—for example, the Sōtō Zen Mission in Honolulu and the Diamond Sangha (likewise a Zen group of Japanese lineage) in the same city—have virtually no common features, and indeed many of the members of the two groups seem blissfully unaware of one another's existence.

In sum, by studying Buddhist groups in North America in terms of the types of transmission that have led to their formation, we can identify patterns that would be impossible to see by other means.[18] These patterns obtain above all, of course, in the initial period of transmission, and there is much research to be done on the adjustments that take place as each form of Buddhism evolves over subsequent generations.

Culture and Change: A Note on Assimilation

When *Tricycle* editor Helen Tworkov wrote in 1991 that "the spokespeople for Buddhism in America have been, almost exclusively, educated members of the white middle class," and went on to say of Asian Americans that "so far they have not figured prominently in the development of something called American Buddhism," her comments evoked a storm of protest, the results of which have not yet abated.[19] Asian Americans, some of whose ancestors had arrived in the United States over a century ago and had played key roles in transmitting Buddhist traditions to this hemisphere, felt (quite understandably) that their own forms of Buddhism were being slighted. "It is apparent," wrote one Japanese American reader, "that Tworkov has restricted 'American Buddhism' to mean 'white American Buddhism.' "[20] Tworkov, however, held her ground, contending that her statements were not at all racist (as the reader had alleged), but simply made "an accurate distinction between Buddhism in America and American Buddhism."[21]

What is striking about this debate is the vast difference in the issues that the two sides view as central. For Tworkov's critics, what matters is the transmission of Buddhism to North America, a process in which Asian Americans have clearly played a major role. For Tworkov herself, by contrast, mere transmission is not enough: the product must be repackaged to suit the domestic market. From one perspective, the basic issue is continuity; from the other, it is change.

Given that most religions, including Buddhism, make the official claim to be the carriers of a timeless truth, it might seem odd to require that Americans "reinvent the Wheel of Dharma" (as a student of mine once put it) before it can be considered "the real thing." And yet the historical record clearly demonstrates that Buddhism has undergone significant cultural adjustment in each region where it has taken root. Should we conclude, then, that such a process of assimilation is required if Buddhism is to survive in any new environment, including that of North America?

Here we may take a comparative approach and turn for insight to the country whose experience with Buddhism, though vastly different in many ways, most closely resembles that of North America. There are two models, one might say, by which Buddhism has been transmitted from one region to another: at the government-to-government level, on the one hand, and by the "trickle in" approach on the other. In the former case, as for example in the transmission of Buddhism from Korea to Japan, Buddhism is conveyed from one country to another by state officials, often for reasons closely connected to national security. If the recipient country decides to adopt the new religion, it is then imposed by the government on the population, often with considerable resistance at first. This top-down scenario is not at all uncommon in Buddhist history, and has also taken place in such countries as Sri Lanka and Tibet.

In China, by contrast, Buddhism was first accepted not by the government but by the aristocracy. Brought to China by an assortment of immigrants, foreign merchants, and the occasional wandering guru, Buddhism soon gained a certain cachet as an item of cultural exotica, and much of the fascination of the aristocracy eventually centered around the notion of "emptiness." Though few took up the monastic life, many enjoyed debating the nature of ultimate reality, and there soon developed a subculture among the privileged that might best be described as "salon Buddhism." Though a small number of Chinese were attracted to Buddhism prior to this time, it was not until all that China stood for as a culture was suddenly called into question with the fall of the Han dynasty in 220 C.E. that Buddhism experienced a sudden growth in its membership, attracting a following that would eventually make it one of the major players on the Chinese religious scene.

The similarities between the first Buddhist communities in China that are visible to the scholar and what I have described above as Elite Buddhism—including the attraction of Buddhism for members of the socioeconomic elite, the fascination with emptiness and the relative lack of interest in monasticism, and above all the sudden increase in membership that came in the wake of America's own crisis of legitimacy, provoked by the Vietnam War—are evident, and might offer much fruitful material for comparison.[22] There are, of course, a great many significant differences as well. But for the purpose at hand one particular issue will be our focus: the process of cultural assimilation.

It is well known that Buddhism underwent significant changes as it settled into its long tenure in China, a topic to which Kenneth Ch'en devoted an entire book, titled *The Chinese Transformation of Buddhism.*[23] The Chinese did indeed, in a manner of speaking, reinvent the wheel, and succeeded in producing a product that has continued to function for nearly two millennia. Yet such adjustments were not all in one direction. The initial phase of transmission to China clearly did involve a massive incorporation into the Buddhist repertoire of indigenous ideas and values (often labeled, though not with complete accuracy, as "Taoism"). This would seem to resemble, at first glance, a parallel to the "Americanization" that Tworkov has in mind.

A look at the second phase of Chinese Buddhism should give us pause, for here we see a move in the opposite direction: realizing that things had gone too far, Chinese Buddhists from the late fourth century on began to retreat from such extreme accommodation. This second period was characterized, in fact, by an active attempt to *remove* elements of Chinese influence that now seemed incongruous with Buddhist values, and to introduce previously overlooked elements that were now viewed as central to the Buddhist tradition. This involved, among other things, the purging from Buddhist scriptures of vocabulary identified as "Taoist," and the translation, at long last—some three or four centuries after Buddhism first arrived in China!—of the basic texts dealing with monastic rules.[24]

What might we see on the North American scene if we were to peer through the lens of the Chinese experience? First of all, we would note that Buddhism—in all three of its basic types, though in varying degrees—has been adapting to our landscape since its arrival. Already in the nineteenth century the Elite Buddhists described by Thomas Tweed (though he does not use that term) had made sweeping accommodations to such core Victorian values as optimism and activism.[25] Similar adjustments can be seen in the late twentieth century, as interpretations of Buddhism have been modified to fit American preferences for egalitarianism, feminism, and even a positive valuation of sexuality (an idea it seems certain the Buddha himself would have found outrageous). In Ethnic Buddhist circles—at least, in those that have been present in North America for more than one generation—one finds comparable forces at work, as for instance in the Japanese American Buddhist Churches of America, where Protestant elements have found their way into everything from terminology to architecture.[26] (Here we should recall that in making such accommodations Asian Americans were not simply acting on their own preferences, but in many instances were deliberately attempting to present themselves in ways that might be acceptable to the Protestant majority.) Interestingly, the smallest degree of change between the form of Buddhism practiced in the homeland and in North America is observed in Evangelical Buddhism, perhaps because the only real representative of this category, the Sōka Gakkai, has been subject to the tightest control by its missionary-oriented Japanese headquarters. In this group, adjustments seem to be taking place only on the most superficial level, as American songs and images drawn from American history are mobilized to serve quite unaltered religious ends.

Despite these noticeable instances of cultural assimilation, however, moves to reverse them are also becoming visible. Japanese American Shin Buddhists, for example, no longer sing "Onward Buddhist Soldiers" in their Sunday services,[27] and a proposal has even been made to change the clearly acommodationist name "Buddhist Churches of America" to "Jōdo-Shinshū Buddhists of America."[28] Once again the attitudes of the larger society are clearly a factor: as acceptance of Asian Americans has grown in the years since World War II (and especially since the 1960s), we begin to find "Asianness" being viewed as a positive value, not a liability.

Just as relatively few instances of accommodation have taken place within Evangelical Buddhisms (in comparison to Elite and Ethnic Buddhist groups), relatively little evidence of the reverse process is visible here. What changes have taken place have for the most part originated not in North America but in Japan, and have come about in the wake of the recent excommunication of the Sōka Gakkai by its Japanese parent, the Nichiren Shōshū school. Much use has been made by the Sōka Gakkai, in defending its position in this conflict, of anticlerical and antiauthoritarian rhetoric associated with the Protestant Reformation. It will be interesting to see whether the democratic implications of this rhetoric are realized in practice.

It is in Elite Buddhist circles, perhaps, that the greatest accommodation to existing cultural values has taken place, and it is here that some of the most noticeable reversals of direction can be observed today. In Vipassana circles (many of which, incidentally, bear a closer resemblance to Stark and Bainbridge's client cult than to a full-blown religious movement) some practitioners have begun to question the isolation of meditation from other parts of the Theravāda tradition, while in Zen circles recent scandals have led to a new interest in the cultivation of the Buddhist moral precepts. And even in those Tibetan Buddhist groups where antinomian rhetoric—sanctioned by a long tradition in Indian and Tibetan Buddhist tantra—has long held sway, doubts about the adequacy of meditation as the "onefold path" (as students at the Naropa Institute labeled it in the mid-1970s) are now being openly debated. What remains to be seen is whether certain core values of late twentieth-century America will turn out to be "nonnegotiable," however different from Asian Buddhist values they might be. If the Chinese model holds, Buddhism in North America will never completely shake off the influence of the dominant tradition, much of which is derived from Protestantism.

Prospects for Future Study

The sense that Buddhism is unique among world religions—being the only "atheistic" religion, for example, or the only religion that denies the existence of the soul—has deeply colored the study of Buddhism in the West, and one result of this misapprehension has been a failure to take advantage of the possibilities for comparative research. Yet the typology of Elite, Evangelical, and Ethnic Buddhism points to rich opportunities for the comparison of Buddhism with other typologically similar traditions.

Elite Buddhists in North America, for example, could be fruitfully compared with other Elite movements here: Hindu-based Yoga centers, for example, or American Sufi groups might provide illuminating data for comparison. With the Sōka Gakkai one could compare the experiences of other Evangelical groups: how does the success rate of the Sōka Gakkai in recruiting members among minority groups in the United States, for example, compare with that of the Latter-day Saints among the Maori in New Zealand? Finally, an obvious possibility would be to study Ethnic Buddhism in light of the experiences of other Ethnic religious communities—Italian Catholics in New York, for example, or Iranian Muslims in California, or for that matter Korean Methodists in Chicago. The comparative study of a wide range of such groups would allow considerable refinement in our understanding of the relative weight of race, ethnicity, and religion (as well as other factors) in maintaining the separateness, or in fostering the assimilation, of an immigrant community over time.

It is rare that the scholar has the opportunity to be present at the creation of new forms of a religious tradition, but this moment in North American history and in the history of Buddhism is one of those auspicious occasions. There is much to be done in the study of Buddhism in North America, and the time could not be more opportune.

Divided Dharma: White Buddhists, Ethnic Buddhists, and Racism

RICK FIELDS

T wo very different events date the beginnings of the project of American Buddhism: first, the construction of America's first Buddhist temple in San Francisco's Chinatown in 1853 by the Sze Yap Company; and second, the taking of the Three Refuges Vow by a New York businessman, Charles Strauss, from the Sinhalese Anagarika Dharmapala in the aftermath of the World Parliament of Religions held in Chicago in 1893. On the one hand, an Asian ethnic community builds a temple to protect and preserve its values, as well as to minister to the spiritual needs of its members. On the other hand, a mostly white and middle-class group adopts and adapts a Buddhism taught by a charismatic, or at least a compelling, missionary. These two very different beginnings, separated by forty years, symbolize the dual development of American Buddhism.

Today, more than a hundred years after the most recent of these two events, Buddhism in America has proliferated wildly. There are groups of mostly white middle-class students organized around missionary teachers from Japan, China, Korea, Burma, Sri Lanka, Vietnam, and Tibet. At the same time, there are communities of Asian Buddhist immigrants, or their descendants, organized around ethnic temples. The strong presence of both these groups indicates that late twentieth-century America has become not only a refuge for Buddhist immigrant communities but the staging area for an entirely new project in Buddhist history, the creation of something called American Buddhism. With all its diversity, it is not surprising that no one can claim to know with any accuracy the number of Buddhists in America as we approach the millennium, but a telephone survey in 1989–90 found that at least one million Americans identified themselves as Buddhists, while the number of people with no formal Buddhist affiliation who have attended Buddhist teachings or meditation retreats probably runs into the hundreds of thousands.[1]

A few years ago, I attempted to write an essay for an American Buddhist journal as part of a special section titled "Dharma, Diversity and Race."[2] Attempting a view from my own experience as a white middle-class American who had studied with teachers from Japan, Tibet, and Burma, I ran into a classificatory bramble. The term *American Buddhist* was far too broad to address the distinctions I was trying to uncover, and was descriptive only of a still unclear future. The reality, in any case, revealed a landscape of complex and bewildering variety: what might be called American Tibetan Buddhists, American Japanese Zen Buddhists, American Korean Buddhists, American Burmese (or Vipassana) Buddhists on one side; and immigrant Asian Buddhists and their often native-born bicultural children: Japanese American Buddhists, Korean American Buddhists, Vietnamese American Buddhists, Burmese American Buddhists on the other. But even this attempt at a rough classification is problematic: the largely Japanese American Buddhist Churches of America (BCA), for example, includes thoroughly acculturated fourth-generation Japanese Americans, as well as at least a scattering of white Americans. In fact, five out of sixty BCA ministers are white Americans. In what sense, then, can this be considered an "ethnic" or immigrant Buddhism?

Some scholars have suggested the term *missionary Buddhism* to refer to the Buddhism of native-born Americans organized around Asian teachers, but the term has no resonance among the people it attempts to describe (who neither use it nor would recognize themselves in it) and is in any case descriptive only of the founders of these groups.[3] A whole new generation of native-born teachers, complete with its own organization and conferences, is now active. Another possible term, *Euro-American Buddhism*, leaves out African Americans and Asian Americans. And the most inclusive term, *Western Buddhism*, fails to distinguish between the very different national styles of, say, British and French Buddhist groups. This definitional frustration led me to the term *white Buddhist*. This term was not without its problems, of course, but it had the virtue of bringing to light a situation that is so pervasive it is hardly noticed—the fact that the so-called missionary or Euro-American Buddhism, in all its bewildering variety, is largely white and middle-class. The term *white Buddhist* is admittedly somewhat arbitrary, as Americans of all races can be found scattered through some "white Buddhist" communities. The place of African Americans in largely white Buddhist communities has only recently begun to be addressed. In a recent issue of *Inquiring Mind*, a journal serving the Vipassana community, the African American Buddhist Lewis Woods, a founder of the Interracial Buddhist Council, suggests the creation of "a predominantly African American meditative Buddhist community, where Black folks can go to study and practice the dharma without having to deal with racism and Eurocentric assumptions, attitudes and behaviors." Such an alternative, he says, would be "along the lines of Asian American and Asian immigrant communities, or Black Churches," though he goes on to say that he sees this sort of "separatism" as an interim measure, "a form of medicine that one ceases to take once the disease has been cured."[4] The term *white Buddhist* is certainly problematic. Still, I feel the term has a certain provisional and heuristic value at this point in American Buddhist history. After all, what unites the adherents of white Buddhism is not so much their common European cultural background, which not so long ago did not look very common, but their identified color in the new land of America. Historically, European immigrants arriving in America invented whiteness as a classification to upgrade their status and privilege themselves as separate and superior to blacks. So the term seems to illuminate more than it obscures, and gives us at least a provisional if provocative description. It sheds some light on the racism (unconscious though it may be) that makes up one many-braided strand of American society and so of American Buddhism. What's more, those whom I have described as "white Buddhists" immediately recognize themselves in the description.

White Buddhism

As it turns out, the term *white Buddhist* also has a certain historical resonance. The term was first used in connection with Col. Henry Steel Olcott and Madame Blavatsky, the founders of the Theosophical Society. Blavatsky considered the mysterious masters to be "Esoteric Buddhists." In Ceylon, Olcott and Blavatsky (who had taken out American citizenship) became the first Americans to become Buddhists in a traditional sense. On May 25, 1880, both he and Blavatsky knelt before a Buddhist priest at a temple in Galle and performed the ceremony of taking *pansil*—the Five Precepts, a lay vow to undertake to refrain from killing, stealing, sexual misconduct, lying, and intoxicants. They recited the vows in Pāli, as well as the Triple Refuge in Buddha, Dhamma, and Sangha, before a large crowd. "When we had finished the last of the Silas," Olcott noted in his diary, "there came a mighty shout to make one's nerves tingle."[5]

Olcott later campaigned vigorously in the anticolonial struggle of Sinhalese Buddhists, giving speeches and founding Buddhist schools and seven branches of the Buddhist Theosophical Society of Ceylon. Part of this work included mentoring a young Buddhist by the name of Anagarika Dharmapala, the same man who would give the Three Refuges to Strauss at the World Parliament of Religions in 1893.

Olcott's Buddhism has been criticized for contaminating Sri Lankan

Buddhism with Protestant elements, thus giving rise to "Protestant Buddhism," a case in point being the popular (still in print) *Buddhist Catechism* (1871), used in the Buddhist schools he was instrumental in starting. Certainly there were Protestant elements in Olcott's rationalized approach, which encouraged Buddhists to adapt Christian missionary methods against the Christians, but Olcott was also an avid student. Before writing his *Buddhist Catechism*, he read some ten thousand pages on Buddhism in English and French translation, went over the Sinhalese version of the manuscript word by word with Sumangala, principal of the Vidyodaya College, and received Sumangala's imprimatur. In Olcott's introduction, he suggested that *Buddhism* was a Western term; the proper term was *Buddha Dharma*. Nor should it be thought of as a religion. "The Sinhalese Buddhists," he wrote, "have never yet had any conception of what Europeans imply in the etymological construction of the Latin root of this term. In their creed there is no such thing as a 'binding' in the Christian sense, a submission to or merging of self in a Divine Being."[6]

In some ways, these first white Theosophical Buddhists presaged the concerns of white Buddhists a century later. They rationalized Buddhism by trying to remove its "superstitious" folk elements in favor of an original pure teaching. At the same time, they identified Buddhism with an esoteric secret teaching, referring to Lord Buddha as a "master-adept." And finally, they saw themselves as the political saviors of the embattled Sinhalese Buddhists. More than a hundred years later these themes—a rationalized "pure" Buddhism that coexists with a taste for esoteric wisdom, and an activist or "engaged Buddhism"—still sound the bass notes of white Buddhism.

Unlike white Buddhists, ethnic Buddhist communities suffered the racism that has been the nightmare squatting at the heart of the American dream from the very beginning. Judge Charles T. Murray of the California Supreme Court laid bare the underlying pattern in 1854, just one year after the Sze Yap Company built America's first Buddhist temple in San Francisco's Chinatown, when he disallowed the testimony of a Chinese eyewitness to a murder involving two white men. Ever since the time of Columbus, said the judge, "the American Indian and the Mongolian or Asiatic were regarded as the same type of species," which is to say, less than human and without white rights.[7] The same pattern repeated itself in the Chinese Exclusion Act of 1882, "the first departure from our official policy of open *laissez-faire* immigration to be made on ethnocultural grounds," as Stuart Creighton Miller points out in *The Unwelcome Immigrant*.[8] This anti-Asian legacy culminated in Executive Order 9066, which relegated 110,000 Japanese Americans to internment camps in 1942.

It is true that white Buddhists are nearly all students of Asian Buddhist missionaries, and that many of them have adopted the customs of their teachers. However, though white Buddhists may go by Japanese, Chinese, Korean, Tibetan, Sinhalese, or Vietnamese Dharma names, wear robes and shave their heads, affect to speak with a Japanese or Tibetan accent, eat soba, kim-chee, or mo-mos, sip green tea or chai, they remain part of the mainstream white culture. To put it crudely in the lexicon of racism, "they can pass." If it ever became necessary or convenient, in the event, say, of a right-wing fundamentalist Christian coup, white Buddhists could shuck it all and emerge safe and sound. Ethnic Buddhists, in contrast, being people of color, cannot always "pass" Asian Americans, be they recent immigrants or third-generation Sansei, are always in peril of being placed by color and race, no matter that they may be Christian (as perhaps more than half of Asian Americans are) or live an exemplary middle-American suburban life.

Racism at its deepest level is the power to define, which is always the paramount power in a racist society. It is hardly surprising, then, that in the ongoing discussion about the meaning of an emergent "American Buddhism" from the present and confusing plurality of Buddhisms in America, it is mainly white Buddhists who are busy doing the defining. Nor is it surprising that they are defining it in their own image. This image has been in large part formed by the countercultural movement of the sixties, which crested in a great wave of white Buddhist activity. The Beat Buddhism of the fifties had been largely literary, but beginning with the sixties, the dramatic rigors of Zen practice galvanized the most zealous white Buddhists. Psychedelics may have had more to do with this than most would like to admit these days, but I would suggest that the mind-blowing intensity of the psychedelic experience gave practitioners in the sixties a taste—at times a thirst—for extreme experiences. White Buddhists who came of age during the sixties wanted enlightenment, and they wanted it immediately. If white Buddhism grew out of a heady countercultural mix of antiwar activism and psychedelic consciousness, it was also in some ways a response to the extremes of the same counterculture. Meditation came to be seen as a way to "get high" without the dangers or inevitable come-downs of drugs; and cultivating peace through meditation was seen as a more effective way to achieve peace than by taking part in increasingly strident antiwar demonstrations. But countercultural "radicalism" still prevailed. White Buddhists in the seventies continued to see themselves as part of a counterculture tacking against the prevailing winds of American materialism.

Community Life of the White Buddhists

In Asia disciplined and regular meditation had been largely limited to monks. But in America, the monastic emphasis on meditation was practiced in coed Dharma centers and retreats. This has led to a worthy experiment, but one with certain inherent contradictions. As Suzuki Rōshi once said, scratching his head: "You Americans are not quite monks and not quite laypeople." Nevertheless, a bias toward hard-style monastic and yogic practice has remained the central focus of white Buddhists, and has become part of the founding legend of American Buddhism. Suzuki Rōshi, it is said, came to America to minister to the ethnic Sōtō Zen mission in San Francisco. But he found that the Japanese American Buddhist members of the temple were interested largely in social affairs and ritual. Only the young and wild Americans were willing to undergo the rigors of true Zen training. And so Rōshi left the Japanese American Sōtō Zen mission to forge the brave new world of American Zen.

After the death of Suzuki Rōshi, the San Francisco Zen Center continued to serve as a paradigmatic force in American Buddhism. The transmission of the teaching seemed to have been successfully passed to Zentatsu Richard Baker Rōshi, and the *sangha* came to exemplify the successful integration of lay community and authentic Zen practice. Tassajara Zen Mountain Center was the monastic jewel, Page Street was the urban residential center, while Green Gulch Farm in halcyon Marin County served as an easy entryway into the rigors of Zen. Sunday *zazen* began at the relatively leisurely hour of 8:30, followed by a beginner's Dharma talk, then tea and whole-wheat pastries and muffins served outdoors, with a vegetarian lunch, and samu, or work-practice, in the organic garden available for those so inclined. A city bakery, a fashionable gourmet vegetarian restaurant, and an urban grocery selling produce from Green Gulch rounded out this white yuppie version of the Pure Land.

In the late seventies, this idyllic community was shaken by charges that the rōshi had engaged in affairs, abused power, and generally lived an un-Zenlike lifestyle. Other Buddhist communities would soon go through similar tempests. In some ways, the reaction to the scandals of the seventies unleashed a particularly American mythos: the toppling of the rōshi-guru-authority by the aggrieved and abused community of the *sangha*. The upshot of this democratic revisionism, for the Zen Center at least, was to create a two-year rotating abbotship made up of senior teachers.

This shift soon took yet another turn. Distrustful of authority, the representatives of the mostly lay *sangha*, after holding a series of meetings with psychological consultants, turned to two figures deemed especially trustworthy: the Dalai Lama of Tibet and the Vietnamese monk Thich Nhat Hanh. Both men exemplified the virtues of the monastic *sangha*, but with a modern twist: they were also spokesmen for a socially active engaged Buddhism. Just what American Zen or American Buddhism might be is still unclear. Will it be some hybrid of all the Buddhisms now present, or will the various lineages maintain their boundaries (and, some might say, integrity)? Will it be some version of that chimera, a "pure" or "essential" Buddhism, or perhaps a distillation of a meditative practice (*vipassanā* instead of Theravāda Buddhism, Zen instead of Zen Buddhism, or *dzogchen* instead of Tibetan or Vajrayāna Buddhism)?

Though the shape of this incipient white Buddhism in America is necessarily hazy at present, several general trends can be identified.[9] The first is that it is largely a layperson's movement, at least as far as the majority of practitioners are concerned, though monks and nuns have certainly played a central role as teachers and leaders. Second, it is based on a strenuous practice of sitting meditation associated with Zen or *vipassanā*, especially mindfulness of breathing. Third, it welcomes Western psychology as a valid and useful, some argue necessary, adjunct. The classic formulation by psychologist Jack Engler—"You have to be somebody before you can be nobody"—has been expanded by Jack Kornfield, a former Theravādin forest monk, now a psychotherapist and married meditation teacher: "Of the Western 'inner practices' the one that is having the most significant impact on Buddhism," he writes in his popular book *A Path with Heart,* "is the understanding and practice of Western psychology. . . . What American practice has come to acknowledge is that many of the deep issues we uncover in spiritual life cannot be healed by meditation alone."[10] Fourth, American Buddhism is increasingly shaped by feminist insights and critiques. There are women teachers in most traditions, conferences, journals, and the growing literature. Some teachers hold retreats solely for women, arguing that women's spirituality is different from men's. Fifth, it harbors an impetus toward social action. The Buddhist Peace Fellowship, which seeks to bring the teachings of Buddhism to the peace movement, and the peace movement to the attention of Buddhists, is one of the few viable pan-*sangha* organizations in existence. The Vietnamese Zen teacher Thich Nhat Hanh is also a powerful voice for a politically engaged Buddhism. And, sixth, it contains democratic and antiauthoritarian or antihierarchical sentiments: at least one *sangha* has limited the terms of its leaders, and other groups have devised codes of ethics, with special attention being drawn to abuses of sexuality and power.

All these trends, except for the second, are characteristically American components that seem to run counter to Asian norms. Many white Buddhists see these trends as natural adaptations, necessary and salutary correctives to out-of-date Asian hierarchies and patriarchies. Whether they prove helpful or damaging in the long run, only time will tell.

Ethnic Buddhism and Racism

Today there is a whole new wave of Asian immigrants: Vietnamese, Thais, Cambodians, Burmese, Taiwanese, Mainland Chinese, and most recently, even a few thousand Tibetans. Unlike the first Chinese and Japanese, these Asian immigrants are entering a country that has, for the first time in its history, an active if small Buddhist population. No doubt there have been many instances of fellowship and communication and help between Asian and white Buddhists. As early as 1899, for example, five white Californians joined Jōdo Shinshū Japanese missionaries to form an organization called the Dharma Sangha of Buddha, publishing an English-language journal called *The Light of Dharma.* In the thirties and forties Julius Goldwater was an important figure who worked to bring white Americans into the Buddhist Churches of America.

Whatever outreach that had occurred was derailed, however, by the traumatic experience of the internment camps. During the fifties a small number of whites participated in the Buddhist Churches of America. One of the most interesting if unlikely connections between ethnic and white Buddhists developed from the Friday-night Berkeley BCA study group led by the Reverend Kanmo Imamura, which was attended by Gary Snyder, Alan Watts, and Philip Whalen. The group's journal, *Berkeley Bussei,* edited for the year of 1956 by Will Petersen, published poems by Jack Kerouac (haiku and a chorus from *Mexico City Blues*) as well as work by Allen Ginsberg, Whalen, and Snyder. So we have here an unlikely twist of the ethnic-white dialectic: the staid ethnic BCA serving as an early meeting place and literary forum for wild white Beat Buddhism.[11] Another more recent example of contact is the series of Buddhist-Christian dialogues hosted by the BCA at the Graduate Theological Seminary in Berkeley, California.

And yet, such instances remain more the exception than the rule. In general, there was, and still is, far less fellowship and communication between the two groups than one would expect. Much of this split stems no doubt from the natural ethnic fellowship of an immigrant community in which Buddhist temples have functioned as cultural and community centers above all else. Activities are conducted in a particular Asian language. Even when English is used at ethnic Buddhist temples, many white Buddhists are reminded of the empty and yet required religious rituals of their childhood, just what they fled from into Buddhism. "It's just like church" is a common reply when white Buddhists are asked why they don't have more contact with their fellow Asian American Buddhists.

Of course, there are many reasons for this situation. Some of them are obvious: by definition an ethnic Buddhism serves and protects the interests of a particular community within the bubbling cauldron we used to call a melting pot. And it is true, as well, that deep historical and ethnic animosities exist between various Asian immigrant and Asian American communities. Furthermore, there do seem to be very real differences in styles of practice; the division between white and ethnic Buddhists may be less racial and more the continuation of an ongoing sectarian dialectic about how best to realize liberation.

Whatever the tangled, tragic, interdependent chain of cause and effect may be, since racism remains such a powerful force, such a ubiquitous component of national ego, as unconscious on the national level as the notion of solid self is on the personal level, some white Buddhists have begun the task of deconstructing their racism under the hard bright light of meditative awareness. From this vantage point, racism turns out to be nothing less than the terrified apprehension of the other, which in itself is a reflection of the old Buddhist problem of self. But it is not easy to see how this can work in community practice. As the black feminist writer bell hooks asks, "How to separate the need to dismantle racism and white supremacy in Buddhist circles from the desire to construct more diverse hierarchies of domination? That is a challenge only profound spiritual practice can help us meet."[12]

When racism is brought fully into the light of meditative awareness, it may become evident that the "other Buddhism," as exemplified by new Asian immigrants as well as by the long-established Pure Land Buddhist Churches of America, holds an important clue to the creation and survival of American Buddhism. To begin with, the other Buddhism is inseparable from community. It is a Buddhism that is part of a culture and is not self-conscious. This in itself is a lesson well worth considering, especially by Buddhists exerting themselves to see through the delusion of self.

And if the Asian American Buddhists may seem to lack the bent-for-enlightenment zeal of some white Buddhists, they also lack the self-centered arrogance that all too often accompanies it. I remember the teaching offered by a Vietnamese woman when she felt my irritation that the weekend retreat had been delayed by a wedding at the temple. "Hey, take it easy," she said. "You're in the temple now."[13]

Another characteristic of white Buddhism is, or certainly has been, its naïveté. Some of this naïveté may come from a bent for idealistic thinking, endemic to Judeo-Christian theism. Some comes from a simpler cause: this generation of white Buddhists are all first generation, at least as far as their Buddhism is concerned, and every first-generation experience is bound to lack a certain breadth. White Buddhists are just now beginning to have the opportunity to find out what all their talk about impermanence really means. Witnessing old age, sickness, and death in a way the young rarely can in contemporary society is doing much to deepen the practice of the white Buddhist community. A very practical result of this is involvement in hospice work. Indeed, one of the main correctives that Buddhism offers contemporary American society is in its skillful and straightforward teachings about dying and death.

It is useful to remind ourselves that ethnic Buddhism is a relative term; ethnic Buddhism in one country is simply Buddhism in another. Until quite recently my entire experience of Buddhism had taken place right here in the United States. There seemed more than enough—more than I could deal with, in any case. But about five years ago I visited ethnic Tibetan exile communities in Nepal and India for the first time. And I found myself getting up with more enthusiasm than I ever had for meditation to join hundreds of ordinary Tibetans as they circumambulated the great *stūpa* in Bodhnath every morning. I found this form of Buddhism refreshing, to say the least. It was intensely devotional and also intensely intergenerational. There were elderly white-beards, young children, teenagers, mothers and fathers, as well as monks and nuns. It was a great relief after spending so much time around the intensely self-conscious and at times self-important white American Tibetan Buddhist communities.

It was also very moving. On one occasion I was circumambulating with my *mālā* (rosary) reciting a mantra with a New York American accent. One of the monks fell in step alongside me, straining with great concentration and difficulty to make out what exactly I was saying. It took a while but about the third time around he suddenly figured it out: the hundred-syllable Vajrasattva mantra. I was rewarded, or blessed, with a great radiant grin of comprehension as my garbled syllables suddenly arranged themselves in a meaningful sequence for him.

Conclusion

That aspect of Buddhism which is subsumed under the rubric of "faith," and the practices connected with it, are still a kind of a terra incognita for American Buddhists in general. One reason for this is that the practices such as prayer and other forms of devotion are, for many Americans, tarred with the sticky feathers of their Judeo-Christian past.

This suggests another interesting point of intersection, since the two aspects of faith and effort, of other and self-power as it is expressed in the Japanese tradition, are not as far apart as adherents of both traditions suppose. Indeed, anyone who has gone through the boot camp of a Rinzai Zen *sesshin*, for example, knows that at a certain point there is nothing to do but give up. Or to put it another way, at a certain point the seeking mind simply gives up, sometimes through what we might call grace but more often through nothing more miraculous than sheer exhaustion. When the compulsively seeking mind stops seeking, a great relaxation dawns. And along with it comes a tremendous feeling which manifests as compassion and gratitude. This is a great release, and relief, and can be found expressed quite fully in the Jōdo Shin tradition. If you really recognize that we are all already "saved" by virtue of Amida's vow, then you can finally (1) relax and (2) be grateful to everyone around you.

It may well be that certain aspects of Asian American Buddhism will provide the turning word for white American Buddhists caught in the dilemma of a lay practice based on monastic models. Shinran, the founder of Japanese Pure Land, was a revolutionary who insisted that the liberating insights of Dharma were fully available to the ordinary man and woman. And the teachers who continue to insist that this is so are neither monks nor priests nor rinpoches nor rōshis but married "ministers." This model, which has existed right in front of our noses, may be at least worth contemplating, both for its successes and failures. The community aspects of ethnic Buddhism have a great deal to offer a white Buddhism caught in the dilemma of a lay practice based on monastic models. A Zen practitioner writes in a recent issue of *Turning Wheel*, the journal of the Buddhist Peace Fellowship, on family:

> We Buddhist parents often believe we're making history, forging a family based Buddhism. In one sense, we are; most of our Asian teachers are from monastic traditions. But in the widest sense we are not. The Japanese branch of the Pure Land tradition, for instance . . . has family-based communities all over the country, complete with English-language services, dharma schools for children, festivals, rites and rituals and individual practice. . . . In many parts of Asia, lay people of strong spiritual inclination have recourse to formal daily practice, such as [to] mantra practice and to a teacher. And they raise families. Although we live in different cultural circumstances, I believe we still have much to learn from lay Buddhist parents and lay Buddhist traditions from other cultures.[14]

The devotional aspect of gratitude practice, so central to the Pure Land traditions, may also have much to contribute to the creation of American white Buddhism. The chanting heard in Vietnamese and Korean temples, for example, may well contain the seed syllables of our own Buddhist spirituals. And Amida, it turns out, is not a monotheistic Judeo-Christian creator God, nor is the Pure Land a Judeo-Christian Heaven. It is noteworthy that no less a Zen patriarch of American Buddhism than D. T. Suzuki wrote his last book on Pure Land Buddhism, pointing out that if you stop looking for it, the Pure Land is right here and now. I remember asking one minister what the core of the Jōdo Shin teaching was. He thought about it a little, and then said that what he told the kids in Sunday school was that the core of it was gratitude. "Every day," he told them, "we say, 'Thank you. Thank you. Thank you.' "

This attitude of thankfulness or gratitude provides a valuable addition to the enlightenment-seeking tendencies of white Buddhism. The result of this thankful awareness will, perhaps, open the way to a nondualistic wisdom and appreciation of the many varieties of Buddhisms in America. Such a Buddhism would continue to provide a safe haven for ethnic Buddhist communities from a beleaguered Asia, as well as an experimental crucible for creative and effective adaptations, and would give all of us the chance to create a truly liberating, multicultured, many-hued, shifting, shimmering Pure Land of American Buddhism. And that would be something to be thankful for.

Americanizing the Buddha: Paul Carus and the Transformation of Asian Thought

MARTIN J. VERHOEVEN

Just before Christmas 1899, Paul Carus, editor of *The Open Court* and *Monist* periodicals and ardent promoter of Buddhism in the United States, wrote to Daniel C. Beard, an art professor at the New York School of Applied Design for Women, with the following suggestion: "An artist who would succeed in *Americanising the Buddha* ideal, modernising the figure, depriving it of its Asiatic peculiarities, and endowing it with those features which, according to our best knowledge of Oriental lore he ought to possess, would make a great hit." Carus elaborated: "The Chinese, Mongols, Japanese, and the Siamese have given the Buddha ideal their own interpretation and conception." But regretfully, noted Carus, "pictures of Buddha in Occidental taste have not as yet been forthcoming."[1] An Occidental Buddha should exude classical simplicity and graceful composition, be "Greek in taste and most noble and elevating." Carus critically observed that the Buddha has been represented too passively, "almost exclusively in the attitude of meditation." Needed instead for a robust America was "an artistic conception of Buddha in the various phases of his lifework"; in other words, an active, socially engaged Buddha like the figure of Jesus. "Christianity possesses a series of beautiful representations of Christ's life," noted Carus, and therefore Buddhism should have the same: a lively, progressive, handsome Greco-Roman Buddha ideal.[2]

Carus, at the time of his writing to Beard, had been for over a decade seriously exploring Buddhism as an alternative altar, a bridge between the widening chasm of religion and science. Along with Asian collaborators like D. T. Suzuki, he had since the World Parliament of Religions in 1893 turned his intense energy and resources of the Open Court Publishing Company to the popularization of Buddhism in America. Carus had even written a three-act play on the Buddha and composed a collection of

Buddhist hymns set to modern Victorian music. Now he sought an American image—a Westernized embodiment of the Oriental enlightened ideal. And Beard seemed to Carus the perfect man for the task. Daniel Carter Beard (1850–1941) illustrated the first edition of Mark Twain's *Connecticut Yankee in King Arthur's Court*, and had amassed sufficient notoriety to have the mountain adjoining Mount McKinley named for him. He was affectionately known all over the country as "Uncle Dan," for his role as one of the founders of the Boy Scouts (1910) and as a popular illustrator of boy's books such as *Boy Pioneers* and *Sons of Daniel Boone*. Carus called on the quintessential Americana artist to fashion a quintessential American Buddha.

American interest in the Orient, of course, did not begin with Paul Carus (1852–1919). A slow but steadily growing curiosity can be traced from Cotton Mather through the New England Transcendentalists. Interest peaked during the Gilded Age and became something of a vogue in the late nineteenth century. Enthusiasm for the "light of Asia," then as now, engaged some of the most prominent thinkers of Europe and America. Paul Carus had as early as 1894 attempted with his *Gospel of Buddha* and then *Karma* (c. 1894) to "modernize" the "spirit of Buddhism" so as to make it more accessible to Western readers. Carus himself published thirty-eight books on Oriental subjects; his periodicals, *The Monist* and *The Open Court*, gave Eastern religions in the United States more extensive and favorable attention than any other American publications, until perhaps after World War II. An especially articulate American apologist for Asian ideas, Carus proved instrumental in convincing many that the East might well have an answer to much of what ailed the West spiritually, philosophically, and psychologically. There was, as John Dewey noted with concern, a "pathological segregation of facts and values" or "bifurcation of nature" whose integration posed "the deepest problem of modern life."[3] Carus believed Asian religious thought, especially Buddhism, held vital antidotes for this troubling "sickness of soul" afflicting Western civilization in the modern era—the splintering of matter and spirit. He felt Americans could and should learn *from*, not simply *about*, the East. Thomas Tweed points out that "with the possible exception of [Henry Steel] Olcott, Carus probably was more influential in stimulating and sustaining American interest in Buddhism than any other person living in the United States. Through his books and articles about Buddhism, his contacts with Asian and Western Buddhists, and his work as editor of Open Court, Carus made crucial contributions to the public discussion about the nature and value of Buddhism."[4]

In his pioneering quest for an American Buddha, however, Carus was merely reenacting an established pattern in a new setting, the United States. This immensely complex phenomenon has attended Buddhism since its beginnings in India nearly 2,500 years ago, namely, a syncretic tendency to adapt from culture to culture. Throughout the Asian world, the "original" Buddhist teachings and practices were adapted to and by indigenous cultures as they spread out from India. Borrowed elements such as new religions are seldom accepted in toto, completely supplanting the older beliefs. Rather new beliefs get superimposed on the existing template and are made to dovetail with the main currents of the old. Thus, hybrids arose where Buddhism encountered conditions in cultural and geographical settings far removed from the Indian subcontinent.

In most cases, the Indian-born teaching absorbed as much as it impacted. Buddhism did not merely coexist with other religious systems, but radically transformed each country it entered. Simultaneously, each country transformed Buddhism into something of its own image and likeness. In Tibet it became theocratic, blending with lamaism and the *bon-po* cult—a tradition rich in rituals (including animal sacrifices anathema to the Buddhist precept of cherishing all life). In Japan it acquired a distinctly "thisworldly" bent. Gradually it took on a uniquely secularized form, which led to the majority of Japanese clergy abandoning celibacy, marrying, and passing on their temples to their sons while often holding down other jobs. The assimilation of their local deities—in this case the *kami* of Shinto—illustrates how a society tends to adapt Buddhism to its own needs, and how Buddhism allows itself to be adapted.

The innovators of Buddhism in China propagated it by deftly arguing that Buddhism harmonized favorably with preexisting Confucian and Taoist conceptions and practices. Mou-tzu, the famous Buddhist monk, when asked why he quoted Chinese texts instead of Buddhist *sūtras* in support of his arguments, said: "It is because you know the contents (of the classics) that I quote them. If I should speak about the words of the Buddhist sutras and explain the essential meaning of Nirvana (*wu-wei*), it would be like speaking about the five colours to the blind, or playing the five tones to the deaf."[5] New ideas such as karma, nirvana, rebirth, *anātman*, and Dharma, as well as the practice of monastic withdrawal from worldly life, presented a foreign and unfamiliar mental landscape to the literate Chinese public. The early exegetic technique, *ko-i* (literally, matching meanings), however, enabled a student familiar with Chinese concepts to comprehend the less familiar Indian concepts by directly linking Buddhist terms with traditional Chinese terms. The tendency extended so far in some cases as to portray the Buddha as reincarnations of Lao-tzu or Confucius, and conversely to represent Lao-tzu and Confucius as avatar bodhisattvas preparing the way for Buddhism among the Chinese. Interestingly, we see a parallel development in both Europe and America, in the fascination with identifying Jesus Christ and Christian saints with Buddha and the bodhisattvas, as in the Barlaam and Josaphat legend. Even D. T. Suzuki acquired this view: "My conviction is: If the Buddha and the Christ changed their accidental places of birth, Gautama might have been a Christ rising against the Jewish traditionalism, and Jesus a Buddha, perhaps propounding the doctrine of non-ego and Nirvāṇa and Dharmakāya."[6]

The American encounter with East Asian religion and philosophy at the turn of the century (1880–1920) in this and many other ways recapitulates the patterns and problems of acculturation that have characterized the spread of Buddhism elsewhere throughout its long history. In the American version, however, we see Buddhism blend into a uniquely American "soup stock" (to use William James's metaphor). Drawing on a model suggested by the historical pattern in Asia where Buddhism underwent various amalgamations as it was gradually assimilated into the societies of China, Japan, Tibet, and Korea, the question arises: how will Buddhism be reconfigured to accommodate embedded Western cultural patterns; how will it be reworked to attune to modern American life and norms?

Many Americans, then as now, sought the "light of Asia" as a palliative to the corroding "acids of modernity," or as a way of mending the seemingly irreconcilable split between faith and reason. But that *ex orient lux* was also refracted through a distinctly Occidental prism. East Asian thought filtered into late nineteenth-century American culture through long-continuing and distinctive modes of thought, values, and attitudes. Just as Confucianism, Taoism, and the imperial dynastic system profoundly altered the form and substance of Buddhism in China, the powerful and combined influences of Christianity, science, and what I call "liberal-modernism" have shaped the form and substance of Buddhism in America.[7] Interestingly, those interpretive paradigms seem to be holding and continue to define the contemporary encounter. They foreshadow perhaps as well the course that a distinctly American Buddhism is likely to take in North America.

Finally, this "Americanizing of the Buddha," though successful in adapting new and unfamiliar Buddhist conceptions to more comfortable and familiar American thoughtways, may also be working against what many, then and now, hoped would be Buddhism's fresh contribution to the revitalization of an ailing Western civilization. Thus, Paul Carus illustrates in microcosm a larger phenomenon: personal and cultural presuppositions inescapably color even the most sincere effort at understanding. Carus's treatment of Buddhism, a religion and philosophy he held in utmost esteem, reveals how deeply ingrained biases and thoughtways at a particular point in history come to affect and condition one tradition's attempt to understand another.

Paul Carus was born in 1852 in Ilsenburg am Harz, Germany. The young Carus dreamed of following in the clerical footsteps of his father, a respected Protestant Reformed minister. After taking a doctorate in philology in 1873 from the University of Tübingen, he assumed a modest teaching position at the academy of the Royal Saxon Cadet Corps in Dresden. His views on religion and ethics, however, brought him into conflict with school officials, resulting in his resignation in 1881. Carus then emigrated to England, where he polished his English, apparently earning a living by teaching school. In 1884 he arrived in New York, where he landed a job as coeditor of a minor German-language literary magazine. In 1885 Carus published his *Monism and Meliorism* which came to the attention of Edward C. Hegeler, a successful German American zinc manufacturer in Illinois who held a deep interest in problems of philosophy, ethics, religion, and science. Their monistic views meshed and Carus soon moved to LaSalle, married Hegeler's daughter Mary, and at age thirty-five assumed his life-long position as editor of *The Open Court* and *The Monist*. Both magazines (which usually ran in the red) were funded by Hegeler to advance his monistic philosophy: "that science was the key to knowledge and progress" and "that the fundamental unity of all things entailed the reconciliation of science and religion."[8]

The key to unraveling Paul Carus's Buddhism lies in understanding his shattered faith in Christianity, subsequent born-again experience, and timely encounter with Buddhism at the World Parliament of Religions in 1893. Like so many well-educated individuals of the late nineteenth century, Carus saw his traditional Christian faith undermined by a widespread "spiritual crisis" precipitated by the rising prominence of the scientific method and outlook. Carus describes his religious crisis and phoenixlike rebirth: "From my childhood I was devout and pious; my faith was as resolute as that of Simon whom, for his firmness, Christ called the rock of His church. On growing up I decided to devote myself as a missionary to the service of Christianity. But alas! inquiring into the foundations of the fortress which I was going to defend, I found the whole of the building undermined."[9]

Though losing faith in Christianity left Carus distraught, it did not destroy his religious impulse. "I soon aroused myself and gathered the fragments of the wreck which my heart had suffered," he writes, and "began to formulate in strictly scientific terms a religion that should be based, not upon belief, but upon the well-ascertained experiences of the human race alone," by which he meant scientific knowledge. To his pleasure and surprise he found he could construct a new faith without sacrificing "the main truths of the old faith" of his youth. Gone only was the "letter" of dogmatic Christianity, "gone beyond the hope of ever being redeemed, but the spirit remained. . . . I have lost the dross only, the slags and ashes, but my religious ideals have been purified." With a born-again zeal, the young Carus felt called upon to share his religious revelation:

My life was such that I could not help becoming a missionary, but I became a missionary of that religion which knows of no dogmas, which can never come in conflict with science, which is based on simple and demonstrable truth. This religion is not in conflict with Christianity. Nor is it in conflict with Judaism or Mohammedanism, or Buddhism, or any other religion. For it is the goal and aim of all religions.[10]

The "Rock of Ages" Carus now found refuge in was neither biblical scripture nor the Church, but what he termed the Religion of Science.

Thus he reconciled, in his own mind, the painful split between science and the security of his childhood faith—a goal, as Carus points out, of many of his contemporaries. "Nothing of the scientific rigor of criticism which characterizes the period of negation has been surrendered," he pronounced, "and yet all the hopes contained in the religious faith of my childhood have found their fulfillment. How many are the hearts that investigate like me."[11] Science, the destroyer of his orthodox religious belief, in an ironic twist, had become the harbinger not of irreligion, but of an even better religion. Science metaphorically stood for John the Baptist. It represented a radical "threshing" and cleansing of the soul in a "river of fire" in preparation for the coming of the new Way, the Truth, and the Light. Carus extolled in 1899, "There is no peace of soul for him whose religion has not passed through the furnace of scientific criticism, where it is cleansed of all the slag and dross of paganism. If God ever spoke to man, science is the burning bush; and if there is any light by which man can hope to illumine his path so as to make firm steps, it is the light of science . . . for science is holy, and the light of science is the dwelling-place of God."[12] Carus's God was "the rationality of reason . . . the ultimate norm of reason . . . the never failing certainty of natural law," as he explained to Reverend Hayacinthe Loyson in 1895. In short, proclaimed Carus, "he is the possibility of science."[13] From his Religion of Science, Carus would make his next leap of faith into Buddhism. His conversion occurred not in pilgrimage to the Far East, however, but in the American Midwest, at the World Parliament of Religions convened in Chicago.

Chicago, 1893

Carus, like many in attendance at the parliament, was particularly enraptured with the promise that late nineteenth-century science held for attaining absolute truth. If God was the "possibility of science," then science proffered the possibility of God. A "Truth," religious or otherwise, by the mid-nineteenth century was increasingly required to conform to scientific understanding; one could not credibly depend on the existence of a divine being to explain things.[14] Anticipating, and themselves influenced by, this modernist proclivity of the West, the Asian delegates to the parliament presented a "Buddhism" so remarkably resonant with liberal-modern thought as to seem the very heir of the Enlightenment tradition. For example, Anagarika Dharmapala (1864–1933), the young Buddhist missionary from Ceylon, proclaimed, "Buddha inculcated the necessity of self-reliance and independent thought" and "accepted the doctrine of evolution as the only true one, with its corollary, the law of cause and effect, [and] he condemns the idea of a creator." Lest his audience take offense at this suggestion of atheism, Dharmapala was quick to reassure them that Buddhism meshed quite nicely with both scientific and Christian views. There was a "supreme god," Dharmapala affirmed, "who is all love, all merciful, all gentle, and looks upon all beings with equanimity," and who accepts the cosmos "as a continuous process of unfolding itself in regular order in obedience to natural laws." Dharmapala stretched Buddhism to the utmost to provide a messiah—a Buddhist one: "To guide humanity in the right path a Tathagata (Messiah) appears from time to time."[15]

The Ceylonese missionary to America had obviously given a great deal of thought to his speech—a speech crafted to win over the predominantly liberal-Protestant body. Carus must have felt himself included among "the most thoughtful men of the day," who, according to Dharmapala, were conducting the Western inquiry into Buddhism. That Western interest, the young speaker announced, had begun with Eugène Burnouf's "first rational, scientific, and comprehensive account of the Buddha's religion."[16] Carus heard his own ideas validated as the eloquent, white-robed Dharmapala observed that "the tendency of enlightened thought of the day all over the world is not towards theology, but philosophy and psychology. . . . The fundamental principles of evolution and monism are being accepted by the thoughtful."[17]

This ecumenical gathering of world faiths marked a turning point in Paul Carus's life and thought. For him, this historic East-West encounter heralded the Dawning of the New Age of global religious unity and universal human progress that he and other delegates so eagerly anticipated. The discovery that this venerated teaching from the East so closely mirrored his own philosophy, the Religion of Science, came almost as an epiphany to Carus. One year after the parliament, Carus published his *Karma: A Story of Early Buddhism.* In that short time, he had already incorporated his understanding of Buddhism into his own Religion of Science. He writes in the epilogue (c. 1894):

> There is a philosophy . . . which, in its scientific, religious, and ethical aspects . . . may be briefly characterised as Positive Monism, that is to say, a unitary world-conception, which endeavors to become a systematised statement of facts. . . . "The Religion of Science" is in agreement with Buddha's teachings, so lucidly set forth in his farewell address to the disciples, as recorded in the Mahāpari-nibbāna Sutta, where we read that Buddha said: "Hold fast to the truth as your

lamp. Seek salvation in the truth alone." The "Religion of Science" outlines the philosophical basis of religion, and traces all the essential religious needs and aspirations, the comfort man finds in affliction, the guidance of conduct, and the fervor with which man may consecrate the various exertions of his life to the facts of experience, be they of a psychical, physical, or a social nature. Thus, "Religion of Science" is, like Buddhism, a religion which bases man's hopes for a deliverance from evil upon enlightenment.[18]

Prior to the parliament, Carus had mentioned Buddhism only twice in his seven years at the editorial helm of Open Court, and both times in a distinctly bland and disinterested way. In fact, he had warned readers in 1890 about the personally and socially debilitating effects that belief in nirvana could potentially entail: "If conceived as mere pessimism . . . [it] will . . . lead to apathy, to destruction and death."[19] After the parliament, however, Carus proclaimed that Buddhism held out the hope that religious truth could indeed square with scientific fact. In response to a critical article on Buddhism written by the Reverend John Henry Barrows (chairman of the parliament), which appeared in the Chicago *Tribune* in 1896, Carus replied, "Buddha taught the irrefragability of law, but this is a point in which, as in so many others, Buddha's teachings are in exact agreement with the doctrines of modern science."[20] On some main tenets of faith—the soul, the existence of God, and creation—Carus observed that "modern science, represented exclusively by scientists educated in Christian schools and with a Christian tradition of two millenniums, will certainly side with Buddhism."[21] In the five years following the parliament, Carus wrote seven new books: six on Buddhism, one on Chinese philosophy.

Why this dramatic shift from mild indifference to missionary zeal regarding Buddhism? Certainly Carus's educational training and cultural assumptions predisposed him to a worldview that seemed so consistent with Darwinian evolution. The prospect of a cosmos ruled by a natural law and not by a divine hand exerted a strong appeal for educated Victorians like Carus. The Buddhist notions of rebirth governed by the impartial mechanism of karma, which explained how humans could transform into animals and vice versa, how entire galaxies arose and disappeared in endlessly repeating cycles and patterns, the inexorable unfolding of phenomena over vast periods of time (geologically rational)—all of these came much closer than Christianity in explaining "reality" by natural law. The world of Buddhism resembled the world of Darwin, Huxley, and Lyell. Though some disagreement and confusion remained as to whether the Buddhist karma was identical with Darwinian evolution, most enthusiasts East and West were content to point out their compatibility and leave it at that.

Thus when Shaku Sōen, a Buddhist monk from Japan, began his address to the delegates of the World Parliament of Religions in 1893, he caught the ear of Paul Carus and many other Victorians, an ear predisposed to the empirical, the evolutionary, and the natural. Sōen's speech pampered Victorian temperaments and conceptions: he set forth with calm, Aristotelian logic how reason and inference demonstrate that "there is no beginning . . . there is no end to the universe . . . the causal law is in a logical circle changing from cause to effect, effect to cause." Nor did one need the intervention of divine will to explain wealth and poverty, growth and decay, or misery and happiness, because the law of causality is "the law of nature, independent of the will of Buddha, and still more the will of human beings." The law exists for eternity, without beginning, without end; "just as the clock moves by itself without any intervention of external force, so is the progress of the universe."[22]

Hearing of another religion seemingly so compatible with the tenets of science opened a wide port of entry. Like so many Victorians, Paul Carus could thus incline toward those aspects of Buddhism that endorsed current sentiments (that is, the scientific), and downplay or disregard aspects that ruffled conventional thought. He would soon write with excitement and authority, "There are many similar agreements that can be traced between Buddhism and the tenets of science . . . and this is not at all surprising, for Buddhism is a religion which recognizes no other revelation except the truth that can be proved by science."[23] Thus noticeably absent from Carus's "Americanised" Buddhism is any serious treatment of the "fantastic" cosmological insights and "supernatural" descriptions found in the Buddhist teachings. Nor would Carus delve into the meditational practices indispensable to gnosis, the esoteric, psychical, and "miraculous" elements—all integral to Buddhism. Carus's Buddha was "the first positivist, the first humanitarian, the first radical freethinker, the first iconoclast, and the first prophet of the Religion of Science."[24] Carus could believe in this liberal-modern Buddha, and was led to believe in this Buddha by the robed Buddhist priests representing the sacred traditions of the East.

Standing Face-to-Face

Education and predisposition, however, do not explain the almost overnight conversion of this rather staid German American philosopher. Although Carus had read widely the available Western works on Oriental religions, it was the personal, face-to-face encounter of the Asian monks and priests at Chicago that moved him most deeply. Carus seemed to be personally affirming the last two lines of Kipling's oft-quoted verse:

> Oh, East is East, and West is West, and never the twain shall meet,
> Till Earth and Sky stand presently at God's great Judgment Seat;
> But there is neither East nor West, Border, nor Breed, nor Birth,
> When two strong men stand face to face, though they come from the ends of
> the earth!

On the one hand, Carus instinctively placed his trust in the Asian missionaries at the parliament for his understanding of Buddhism. On the other hand, he harbored an aversion for what he called "scholarmania," the purely academic approach to religion. The Asian clerics were "living Buddhists," not just "scholars," explained Carus to Professor Washburn Hopkins of Yale. "I have seen all these men, and was in personal contact with them," Carus vaunted, "I have been in correspondence with a number of high priests of various countries; and I suppose I know more about real, genuine Buddhists than Prof. Oldenberg."[25] The "genuine Buddhists" Carus met during the time of the religious parliament not only guided his understanding of Buddhism, but endorsed his unique interpretation of it. Of these mentors, the most important were Shaku Sōen, Dharmapala, and D. T. Suzuki. Yet "genuine Buddhism" is an elusive trophy; simply because it arrives from Asia, conveyed by Asians, does not guarantee it is authentic.

Shaku Sōen (1859–1919), for example, was a leading figure in "Buddhist modernism." After attending Keio University, where he studied English and Western philosophy, Sōen attempted to reform Japanese Buddhism and make it in tune with its age. In 1893, despite opposition from critics who said an abbot should not leave his temple, Shaku Sōen attended the World Parliament of Religions in Chicago. Here he met Carus. To him, Carus was "a second Columbus who is endeavoring to discover the new world of truth." The Japanese missionary proclaimed the West, and particularly America, as the new birthplace of Buddhism. "Buddha who lived three thousand years ago," Shaku Sōen wrote to Carus in early 1895, "being named Gautama, now lies bodily dead in India; but Buddha in the twentieth century being named Truth, is just to be born at Chicago in the New World."[26]

Shaku Sōen intended to reverse the missionary tide then moving from West to East. Carus seemed an ideal ally. To Shaku Sōen, Carus resembled a "Taoist sage" whose writings came as a veritable gift from heaven. Carus's "outstanding reputation in literary circles" would, Shaku Sōen believed, help in establishing a Buddhist foothold in America. "As both an eminent philosopher and a scholar of comparative religion, Carus is a beachhead here for us," wrote Shaku Sōen in his introduction to the Japanese translation of Carus's *Gospel of Buddha*. "If . . . he could be brought to understand the true meaning of Buddhism, it would be better than converting a hundred thousand ordinary people."[27]

Shaku Sōen and another Japanese Buddhist priest spent a week in tête-à-tête dialogue at the Hegeler-Carus mansion in LaSalle, Illinois, following the parliament. The details of their meeting were not recorded, but according to D. T. Suzuki, they confirmed their mutual belief that religion must stand on a firm scientific foundation purged of all "mythological" elements.[28] In the course of their correspondence over the following years, this relationship and understanding held fast. "I believe," wrote Shaku Sōen to Carus, "that if the present Christianity be reformed it will become the old Buddhism, and if the latter be reformed it will become the future Religion of Science which is still in the womb of Truth, but which is steadily growing up there to be born [into] full power."[29] Thus Shaku Sōen found in Carus an influential partner in his mission to spread reformed Buddhism throughout the world—a Buddhism now called "the future universal religion of sciences." This new Buddhism of Shaku Sōen, "as relating to this life and as real, positive, altruistic and rather optimistic,"[30] resonated squarely with Paul Carus's liberal-modernist inclinations.

After translating Carus's *Gospel of Buddha* into Japanese, Shaku Sōen's disciple Daisetz Teitaro Suzuki (1870–1966) expressed a yearning to reside in the United States, both to further his Western studies and to promote Japanese Buddhism. Again, Paul Carus presented an ideal "beachhead." Shaku Sōen wrote to Carus that Suzuki desired to go abroad and "to study under your personal guidance."[31] This symbiotic arrangement, Shaku Sōen promised Carus, would spread the German philosopher's ideas to the Orient and Shaku Sōen's Buddhism to America. "If that be realized [i.e., Carus's sponsoring Suzuki to America] by your kind agreement, your and other eminent American thinkers' opinions will be introduced to Japan through him more favorably than ever, and I believe your country may have also a good opportunity to know what the Japanese Buddhists would say."[32] Suzuki and Carus worked together from 1897 until 1908 in LaSalle, translating and interpreting Asian religious and philosophical classics.

Shaku Sōen's use of the word *beachhead* raises the question of whether a more aggressive strategy lay behind the Japanese religious mission to America than is commonly assumed. In December 1892 the *Japan Weekly Mail* reported the sentiments of Shaku Sōen and another Japanese Buddhist delegate selected to attend the Chicago parliament. According to the representatives, the parliament presented "a great opportunity for spreading Buddhism in the West." As the article points out,

Already the Smaller Vehicle has found many adherents in Europe and America. It has been taken there not by priests of the faith, but by foreigners themselves. The Westerns, proud of their own civilization, are thus becoming enlightened. Religion is the only force in which the Western people know that they are inferior to the nations of the East. . . . Let us wed the Great Vehicle [Mahāyāna Buddhism] to Western thought. Heaven has now given us the opportunity to do this. At Chicago next year the fitting time will come.[33]

The spiritual crisis of the West exposed its Achilles' heel to the vanquished. Though economically and technologically bested by the Western powers, Japan saw a chance to reassert its sense of cultural superiority via religion. Buddhism could drive a wedge in the crack of the Western hegemonic dam and open the way for restoring Japan's greatness. The parliament presented a rare opportunity to launch a religious counteroffensive as dramatic as Comm. Matthew Perry's sailing four black ships into the Bay of Tokyo only forty years earlier in 1853. There is "a distress among Christians conscious of the destruction of the basis of their faith by the forces at work in civilization," the Japanese delegates noted. "Here is hope for Buddhism."[34]

The parliament marked a pivotal moment in the history of Buddhism in the United States. In its aftermath, Carus served as a father-figure, financial backer, and mentor to a number of Asian Buddhist missionaries to America. With Anagarika Dharmapala, Carus formed a remarkably close relationship that lasted many years. The young Buddhist preacher from Ceylon urged Carus to start a branch of the Maha Bodhi Society in Chicago, which Carus did and faithfully supported until his death.

After his apprenticeship with Carus, Suzuki went on to become a major interpreter of Asian thought in the West. In 1911 he married an American, Beatrice Erskine Lane, a Radcliffe graduate and Theosophist. Together they published the English-language journal *The Eastern Buddhist*. Under the auspices of the Rockefeller Foundation, Suzuki returned at the age of eighty to the United States, where he lectured on Zen and Buddhism at various universities, especially Columbia. He influenced many Westerners, including Carl Jung, Karen Horney, Erich Fromm, Martin Heidegger, Thomas Merton, Alan Watts, and the "Beat Buddhists" Jack Kerouac, Allen Ginsberg, and Gary Synder. The historian Lynn White, Jr., praised Suzuki as someone who broke through the "shell of the Occident" and made the West's thinking global.[35]

Did these Asian missionaries influence the "American Buddhism" of Carus, or did he sway them, making their modern Buddhism more an Americanized version of Carus's own philosophy? Most likely an ongoing dialogue evolved over the years that gradually syncretized the diverse strands into a more or less cohesive view. In any event, the mutual influence is undeniable. Their writings, especially in the area of religion, are so closely parallel as to seem indistinguishable at times. Like Carus, or perhaps *because* of Carus, Suzuki presents a Buddhism to Americans that recapitulates the German doctor's. In his English work *Outlines of Mahayana Buddhism* (1907), Suzuki's nirvana resembles the Christian heaven gained by following God's commandments. His notions of karma and Dharma both cleave to the authority of science, not enlightenment, as arbiter of truth. "This doctrine of karma," he states, "may be regarded as an application in our ethical realm of the theory of the conservation of energy. . . . We need not further state the conception of dharma in its general aspect is scientifically verified." Suzuki dismisses "pious religious enthusiasts who see a natural enemy in science" as well as "those men of science who think that science alone must claim the whole field of soul-activities as well as those of nature."[36]

Suzuki served as translator for his teacher, Shaku Sōen, on his tour of America in 1905 and 1906. Carus promoted Shaku Sōen's vision of Buddhism to an American audience by publishing these lectures in *Sermons of a Buddhist Abbot* (1906), later entitled *Zen for Americans*.[37] In San Francisco, Los Angeles, Sacramento, Fresno, San Jose, Oakland, Washington, New York, Philadelphia, and Boston, Americans learned of Buddhism in terms they found most familiar and agreeable. Shaku Sōen tells an audience at National Geographic Society in Washington, D.C. (April 1906), that "Buddhism is always ready to stand before the tribunal of science and let her pass judgment upon its merits or demerits . . . due to this intellectual tenor."[38] But to appear credible before that tribunal, Suzuki made accommodations to Western audiences that often entailed taking considerable license with central Buddhist concepts, such as when he states, "the doctrine of Dharmakāya . . . may be considered to correspond to the Christian conception of God," or that "the practical ethics of Buddhism is to manifest the glory of God in all our conduct, in all our thoughts, and in all our wishes and desires." In fact, Buddhist ethics are strictly based on the impersonal working of cause and effect and have nothing to do with a divine mediation. The Kantian "indwelling reason of the universe . . . the universal reason" which Carus posits as the philosophical God-surrogate behind creation, is borrowed by Shaku Sōen to convey the meaning of the "Buddha-nature."[39] When Shaku Sōen (or Suzuki) writes that we must be in harmony with the "will of the Dharmakāya" which is *"the norm of existence and the reason of being,"* he is using expressions that come directly from Paul Carus's monist writings, not from any Buddhist text.[40] His notion of "absolute surrender of the self to the will of the Dharmakāya" is far more Christian than Buddhist, which would be more likely to state that fundamentally there is no self and no divine being to surrender it to.

Paul Carus must have been aware of his influence on Suzuki. When K. Nukariya was studying at Harvard, he wrote to Carus seeking advice on publishing his own book on Buddhism. Carus responded, "I wish some one familiar with western philosophy could revise your book . . . and the best person I know for this purpose would be our mutual friend, Teitaro Suzuki." Carus, however, expresses to Nukariya a significant apprehension about his possible sway over Suzuki: "I have gone over some of the translations of Mr. Suzuki and my only fear is that I impressed him too much with my own philosophical conception, but after all when I consider that many passages become positively unintelligible to the western world, it seems to me better to have such done."[41]

Yet the retranslation of passages that Carus feared would seem otherwise "positively unintelligible to the western world" had in a sense already been done—not in America, but in Asia. For long before the East came West, the West went East. Thus, the "Buddhism" filtering into America in the late nineteenth and early twentieth century was itself already partially Western-ized prior to its arrival. This prefiguring resulted primarily from the impact of Western imperialism and colonial rule throughout Asia. Both the "Prot-estant Buddhism" of Ceylon and the "new Buddhism" of Japan represented syncretic blends of traditional Asian and modern Western forms. The Dharma that early Asian missionaries brought to the West, one which proved so accessible to American enthusiasts like Paul Carus, was a Dharma considerably acculturated to Western ways. Suzuki's and Shaku Sōen's Bud-dhism in particular represented a unique hybrid of East Asian and Euro-American influences that grew out of the Meiji persecution and subsequent "modernist" revival of Buddhism in Japan.[42] Ironically, then, the immense popularity that Oriental religions and philosophy enjoyed in the West can be attributed somewhat to the strange fact that the hybrid forms of Asian thought exported to the Occident were already customized for Western consumption. The Buddhism that Americans such as Paul Carus encoun-tered early on was something of a "mirror in the shrine"—a looking glass that reflected back the image of the beholder.[43]

When the mirror reflected images seemingly at odds with the beholder's self-image, Carus proved adept at adjusting the focus. He took great pains, for example, to counter popular misconceptions surrounding key Buddhist concepts such as _nirvāṇa_ (extinguished, or cessation) and _śūnyatā_ (empti-ness). He wrote that far from teaching negativism, "the Buddha's sermons, parables, and sentences abound in exhortations to indefatigable and en-ergetic activity."[44] Carus also astutely observed that although the Buddha denied the existence of a "self," this in no way implied total nihilism. Carus saw in Buddhism the affirmation of an abiding spiritual nature, a "soul" as he put it. He vaguely understood this soul to "remain untouched by death and continue to live," in the form of karma or one's deeds.[45] Even though he often failed to grasp the letter of the teaching, he did appreciate and convey the spirit. He sensed that "Buddha actually opens the door of im-mortality to mankind," and "any one who does not see the positive aspect of Buddhism, will be unable to understand how it could exercise such a powerful influence upon millions and millions of people."[46]

Sensing the complexity that available Buddhist writings presented to a Western audience, Carus wrote his own text, _The Gospel of Buddha_ (1894). Here he sought to convey the "spirit of Buddhism" stripped of its "apoc-ryphal adornments" and brought in tune with modern scientific and phil-osophical thought. As illustrated by Miss Olga Kopetzkey of Munich, the Buddha and his followers, although situated in Asian landscapes, are clearly Greco-Roman in face, body poses, and ethnicity. Along with these Western faces, Carus included a table reference pointing out "parallelisms with Western thought, especially in the Christian gospels."[47]

In keeping with this idealistic bent, Carus titled his version of the *Tao Te Ching* as *The Canon of Reason and Virtue*. Just as the Chinese had rendered *Dharma* as *Tao*, to make the foreign concept more understandable to the Chinese mind, now Carus rendered *Tao* as *Reason*, to make *Tao* more comprehensible to a Western philosophical mind. Although D. T. Suzuki went along with the dubious translation at the time of his collaboration with Carus on it in 1898, later he would write, "What is important in the Chinese language is the feeling quality. . . . Thus in order to translate passages from Lao-tzu, I had to explain to Dr. Carus the feeling behind each Chinese term. But being himself a German writing in English, he translated these Chinese ideas into abstract conceptual terms." Suzuki nonetheless felt their translation remained "one of the best" and that Carus "very often succeeded in entering into the spirit of Lao-tzu's philosophy."[48]

Part of the appeal that Carus's Buddhism held for Americans was his ability to render a "difficult subject" simply and clearly—most important, making it appear eminently compatible with approved values. Thus, Carus was particularly impressed with what he called the "Shinshu" sect of Japan, "which has been justly called the 'Buddhistic Protestantism.' " This sect Carus felt was the "most progressive" (read "Western"). Like the Protestants, "their priests eat fish and meat, and are allowed to marry, because they claim that Buddha had refused to make any difference between priest and layman, that austerities are of no avail." They stand in "opposition to a monkish morality" and believe that "faith in Amita [Amitābha] alone . . . can set us in that state of mind which ensures eternal salvation."[49]

Yet even more problematical for Carus than the "apocryphal adornments" were the "religious enthusiasm" and "exuberance of wonder which delights in relating the most incredible things." Since these phenomena, symbols, and beliefs "come in conflict with science, the educated classes are estranged from religion."[50] Belief in Amitābha Buddha approached the "incredible." Carus preemptively dismissed phenomena beyond the ken of natural laws. He thus interpreted Buddhism as a "religion which knows no supernatural revelation, and proclaims doctrines that require no other argument than the 'come and see.' " Unlike other religions, argued Carus, Buddhism is based "solely upon man's knowledge of the nature of things, upon provable truth."[51]

So how did Carus handle the belief in salvation through devotion to Amitābha? He simply reconstructed the Buddha of Limitless Life into an idealized abstraction, in keeping with his German philosophical training. For Carus, Amitābha, like God, was a transcendent regulating power that provided continuity and order in the universe—a Kantian "form of forms." Thus Amitābha, according to Carus, was not real in a bodily way, "but in a higher sense . . . an eternal ubiquitous presence." Carus asks, "What is Amitabha?" Amitābha is a "world order, the ultimate norm of truth and right" which "determines the law of evolution, making it possible that in the course of cosmic processes, life originates, sentient beings develop reason and rational beings learn by experience the folly of egotism and so develop universal goodwill."[52] *This* Amitābha, Carus points out, every scientist could recognize the existence of—but perhaps not every Buddhist could do so.

In 1897, Carus even published an entire book devoted to a sympathetic comparison of Buddhism and Christianity titled *Buddhism and Its Christian Critics.* He hailed "both Buddha and Christ . . . as saviours of the world."[53] The dovetailing of Buddhism with the culturally preferred beliefs of Christianity was clearly intended to make Buddhism more acceptable to Americans. A Christlike Buddha also filled an urgent longing of turn-of-the-century Victorians: the yearning for a personal God, an intimate flesh and blood personification of the divine. As Dharmapala proclaimed in 1894, "Christ is the Buddha of a latter time."[54] The fact that *The Gospel of Buddha* went through thirteen editions, sold more than three million copies, and was translated into Chinese, Japanese, Spanish, German, Dutch, French, Russian, Czech, Italian, Thai, and other languages attests to its universal appeal, though not necessarily its accuracy.

Conclusion

Confucianism, Taoism, and the imperial dynastic system profoundly influenced the course of Buddhism in China. In a similar way, Christianity, science, and liberal-modernism are shaping Buddhism in America. Ironically, the success in adapting unfamiliar Buddhist conceptions to more ingrained American thought-ways may conceal a loss. The American encounter with Buddhism presents a unique historical situation. Buddhism is entering a civilization exerting unprecedented dominance and hegemonic influence worldwide. The tendency of America to co-opt and absorb all that it touches, or that touches it, is overwhelming. Thus Buddhism will no doubt continue to be assimilated through our basic "sense-making" categories: Christianity, science, and liberal-modernism. Such assimilation is inevitable and in some ways healthy. Yet a facile, uncritical "Americanizing" of the Buddha diminishes both America and Buddhism.

Buddhist philosophy and practice offers fundamental and countervailing challenges to our prevailing worldview, especially in the areas of humanity's basic relationships: (1) humans with Nature, (2) individual with individual, and (3) a person with him or herself—that is, the natural, social, and psychological dimensions of existence. The Buddhist perspective could initiate a provocative dialogue leading to a reexamination of some of the most entrenched paradigms governing our culture. The rapid and whole-sale Americanizing of Buddhism, however, greatly attenuates that potential to challenge and thereby enhance American society.

One must also ask and wonder in what ways Buddhism may be trans-forming America, short of outright conversion. Just as "Protestant Bud-dhism" evolved in Ceylon in response to the Western missionary and co-lonial presence, might not America be undergoing a parallel development, "Buddhist Protestantism"? Could changes in areas of Christian thought and practice reflect an assimilation of certain Asian influences? The interest in meditation, comparative religion, Buddhist-Christian dialogues, as well as the "immanentist" and psychological orientation of modern liberal Chris-tianity, and even the "New Age" phenomenon—all could be read as Chris-tian attempts to accommodate Eastern religion, or in some cases, to un-dercut its appeal. This would not be unprecedented. In medieval China, neo-Confucianism sprang back into cultural center stage by incorporating key elements of the "foreign import," Buddhism. Neo-Confucianists rein-terpreted their tradition in a more "mystical" light as a counter-response to the growing popularity of Buddhism. Is Christianity in the West subtly reworking its tradition, either consciously or unconsciously, in order to win back or hold onto its own believers?

Moreover, we need to examine more closely to what extent these Amer-ican cultural paradigms actually convey the meaning of Dharma. Perhaps a remarkable resonance exists between Buddhism and Western science, its Judeo-Christian heritage, and liberal-modernist ideology; perhaps not as significantly as we think. D. T. Suzuki's initial enthusiasm for identifying Buddhism with modern science waned toward the end of his life. He came to doubt the sufficiency of a religion based on science, and even saw the need for religion to critique science. In 1959, Suzuki wrote of how his and Shaku Sōen's early agreement with Hegeler and Carus that "religion must stand on scientific grounds . . . that Christianity was based too much on mythology" was ill-founded. "If it were possible for me to talk with them now," he continued, "I would tell them that my ideas have changed from theirs somewhat. I now think that a religion based solely on science is not enough. There are certain 'mythological' elements in every one of us, which cannot be altogether lost in favor of science. This is a conviction I have come to."[55]

Suzuki, of course, was enjoying the wisdom of hindsight; his new convic-tion was formed from witnessing the relationship between science and reli-gion dramatically shift in the twentieth century. The triumphalist nine-teenth-century image of science held by Carus had given way by the twentieth century to a less deterministic and reductionist view. For Carus, natural science provided a norm of truth. As used in the nineteenth century, *science* meant "knowledge" that was acquired objectively, with the implication of certainty. Paul Carus, like many Victorians, believed that science provided truth eternal and universal, that the laws of the universe are fixed and everywhere the same. This science further assumed that these governing principles were objective and discoverable through "natural" versus "supernatural" means or explanations. Such positivistic certainties were eclipsed even within Carus's own lifetime as he struggled in vain to make sense of Bertrand Russell's math, William James's pragmatism, and Einstein's relativity—all irrational fads by Carus's absolutist notion of scientific truth.

As Suzuki's turnabout shows, by the 1960s it was becoming more difficult for informed people to regard scientific theories as sacrosanct or as the ultimate arbiter of truth. With the groundbreaking work of Niels Bohr (1885–1962), Werner Heisenberg (1901–76), and Arthur Eddington (1882–1944), the naive "scientism" of an earlier period began to dissolve. Rock-solid presuppositions once central to classical scientific thought crumbled before the iconoclasm of the "new science." The possibility of achieving a description of the world that was independent of the means by which it was investigated could no longer be taken for granted. Gone too was the neat subject-object distinction. It now seemed entirely possible, as Heisenberg pointed out, that the very act of measurement interferes with what one is attempting to measure. If the scientist in search of truth alters the very truth he or she seeks, then the very existence of a world external to the observer could be doubted. The "new physics" of quantum theory thus no longer claims to describe "reality," but probable and possible *realities*—realities so elusive that no one model could exhaustively account for everything. The indeterminacy of models replaced the certainty of laws. Even Einstein felt the challenge, maintaining and defending with increasing difficulty his belief in the reality of an external world governed by mechanisms that science could disclose. Freud's positivistic assertion that it would be "an illusion . . . to suppose that what science cannot give us we can get elsewhere" (*elsewhere*, of course, meaning religion) has, like his own psychoanalytic theory, become a matter of intense debate. Heisenberg observed, "Even in science the object of research is no longer nature itself, but man's investigation of nature."[56]

As Thomas S. Kuhn pointed out in his *Structure of Scientific Revolutions* (1962), "man's investigation of nature," like religion, comes encumbered with its own baggage of presuppositions, nonrational procedures, doctrines, and heresies. Kuhn demolished the logical empiricist view of science as the impartial progression toward universal truth. Far from being free of theoretical constructs, Kuhn found that science is often ensconced in a cultural matrix and a core of received wisdom. It tends to conserve and perpetuate these entrenched ideas and beliefs (paradigms) until an intellectual revolution (paradigm shift) forces acceptance of a new conceptual worldview. Thus modern science presents less of a unified front. Certainly, many still see themselves as living in a black-and-white world, describing an external reality, defending Truth against Error. Other scientists, however, have come to define their discipline in a more humble and tentative way—as a method or a form of inquiry into natural phenomena, a consensus of information held at any one time and all of which may be modified by new discoveries and new interpretations at any moment. In contemporary science, uncertainty seems to rule. Paul Carus would no longer recognize the infallible prophet of his dawning new age—science.

Carus's prediction of a "dawning of a new age" based on a Religion of Science already began to evaporate during his lifetime with World War I. Another world war and the atomic bomb further strained what to many seemed an ill-fated marriage of scientific technology and human ignorance. Doubts that would never have troubled Paul Carus's infatuation with science became commonplace: Do scientific advances necessarily mean progress? Is science sufficient for describing reality? Is science capable of meeting human needs? The unfortunate separation of matter and spirit, reason and faith, that so troubled Paul Carus, however, remains a central issue of our times. Alfred North Whitehead (1861–1947) suggested the future course of history would center on his generation's resolving the issue of the proper relations between religion and science. Buddhism, then as now, seemed to offer a resolution.

In ways reminiscent of the late nineteenth century, contemporary interest in the relationship between Buddhism and science has become a serious pursuit, even something of a fad in the West. Fritjof Capra, in *The Tao of Physics* (1975), argues not only that modern science and Eastern mysticism offer parallel insights into the ultimate nature of reality, but "that the profound harmony between these concepts, as expressed in systems language, and the corresponding ideas in Eastern mysticism, is impressive evidence for my claim that the philosophy of mystical traditions, also known as the 'perennial philosophy,' provides the most consistent philosophical background to our modern scientific theories."[57] This current excitement echoes the earlier hope of Carus: that Buddhism can reconcile religious belief and scientific fact. But how close and profound really is the relationship between Buddhism and science? By the 1950s Suzuki had come to believe that a religion tied to science ignored essential "mythological" elements in the human condition. Other Buddhist missionaries to the West pointed out more fundamental discrepancies.

For example, Ch'an Master Hsüan Hua (1918–95), another pioneer in introducing Buddhism to America, felt that science fell within the limited world of "relative, not absolute dharmas." Thus, "science absolutely cannot bring true or ultimate happiness to people—neither spiritually or materially." He specifically took issue with the "progressive" presumptions of modern science. To him, the novelty and modernization in weapons represented only "progressive cruelty," and bespoke moral flaw. At root science lacked a moral compass and thus could regard "human life as an experiment, as child's play," and "fulfill its selfish desires through force and oppression."[58]

In a 1989 convocation address at the University of Kelaniya, the Venerable Dr. Walpola Rahula noted that our daily life is permeated by science and observed that we have almost become slaves of science and technology. "Soon we shall be worshipping it," he warned. The Theravādin monk found early symptoms of this malaise in the growing trend to "seek support from changing scientific concepts to prove the validity of our perennial religious truths, to justify them and to make them modern, up-to-date, respectable and acceptable." While he found some intellectually exciting parallels and interesting similarities between Buddhism and modern science, they were, he stressed, "peripheral and do not touch the essential part, the center, the core, the heart of Buddhism."

The Venerable Rahula first pointed out that the "instrument" used in Buddhism to discover these parallel truths (such as the nature of the atom, the relativity of time and space, or the quantum view of an interdependent and interrelated whole which includes the observer) was "insight developed and purified by meditation (bhavanā)"; they were discovered "without the help of any external instrument." Moreover, the scientific quest for a precise analysis of the material world lacked heart and did not appreciate the inner world of humankind. "It knows nothing about love or compassion, righteousness, or purity of mind," observed Rahula. In contrast, Buddhism "aims at the discovery and study of man's inner world: ethical, spiritual, psychological and intellectual world." Buddhism, unlike science, deals with humanity in toto. "It is a way of life," he insisted, "a path to follow and practice. It teaches man how to develop his moral and ethical character (śīla), and cultivate his mind (samādhi), and how to realize the ultimate truth, nirvana."[59]

Aspects of the above epistemologic formula—ethical character, mind-cultivation, and wisdom (Sanskrit: śīla, samādhi, prajñā)—appear throughout the Buddhist tradition. The Visuddhimagga (Path of Purification), an early Buddhist manual compiled in the fourth century by Buddhaghosa, lists the Buddha's "science" of inquiry as an interrelated three-step exercise of virtue, meditation, and insight. The Eightfold Path of the Four Noble Truths that leads to nirvana, in fact, comes down to these three basic elements: morality, concentration, and wisdom.

It would seem then, that fundamental and qualitatively different views of what constitutes knowledge and the acquisition of knowledge separate Buddhism and science. Their aims and methods, though tantalizingly parallel, on closer analysis diverge. Correspondences do exist, but important differences inhere as well. To gloss over them runs the risk of repeating Paul Carus's error. The science Carus relied on for interpreting Buddhism to an American audience turned out to be constitutive of his reality, not simply descriptive. His received beliefs provided a ready idiom through which he could construct an "Americanized" Buddhism which then confirmed those same beliefs, in this case Carus's own Religion of Science. This tendency, as one recent scholar has pointed out, represents arrogance or "imperialism of the idea."[60]

The continuing effort to link science and Buddhism may conceal a similar cultural hubris, as it embraces those elements of Buddhism that seem consonant with the modern Western way of life and gives short shrift to the rest. It is now generally acknowledged that the early Orientalist scholars in Europe and America presented a Buddhism that was conditioned in its selection and treatment by their particular cultural presuppositions. Is it possible that our current treatment might be subject to similar blindness and constraints? Henry Clarke Warren, the late-nineteenth-century Harvard Indologist and translator, inadvertently may have hit on an alternative approach: let Buddhism imperfectly fit. Unlike Carus, the pleasure and stimulation Warren discovered in Buddhism came not from its familiarity, but from its strangeness. He wrote:

A large part of the pleasure that I have experienced in the study of Buddhism has arisen from what I may call the strangeness of the intellectual landscape. All the ideas, the modes of argument, even the postulates assumed and not argued about, have always seemed so strange, so different from anything to which I have been accustomed, that I felt all the time as though walking in Fairyland. Much of the charm that the Oriental thoughts and ideas have for me appears to be because they so seldom fit into Western categories.[61]

Buddhist and Western Psychotherapies:
An Asian American Perspective

RYO IMAMURA

S ince the foreword by Carl Jung in D. T. Suzuki's *Introduction to Zen* in 1949, followed in 1960 by the classic *Zen Buddhism and Psychoanalysis* by Erich Fromm, D. T. Suzuki, and Richard De Martino, interest in Buddhist thought and practice by Western psychologists has grown steadily and dramatically. At the same time, the growing popularity of Buddhism with middle-class educated Euro-Americans, many of whom are consumers and providers in the mental health field, has led to much inquiry into the possible connections between Western psychotherapy and Buddhism on both the personal and the professional levels. In stark contrast, interest in Western psychotherapy by Asian American Buddhists has been so minimal and sporadic that it can safely be said to be virtually nonexistent.

Clearly there are distinct differences between how Euro-American and Asian American Buddhists understand and practice Buddhism, which are confirmed in my experiences with both populations.[1] As a Buddhist priest of the Jōdo Shin (True Pure Land) sect, I speak almost exclusively to Japanese American Buddhists. The usual themes of my talks are gratitude, oneness, death and dying, compassion, and humility; I tie in the traditional rituals, special observances, and symbols, and always speak in terms of the family, temple, and community. These topics comprise pretty much what Japanese American Buddhists want and expect to hear. It would be very strange and uncomfortable for everyone if I were to talk about Buddhism and psychotherapy.

In contrast, the Euro-American Buddhist audiences that I address are very excited to learn that I am a professor of psychology and a psychotherapist as well as a Buddhist priest. They seem to share a burning interest in how the Buddhist teachings and meditation can be utilized to cure the disease and dysfunction that appear to them to be legacies of modern Western life. They show little interest in and patience for the traditional topics that the Japanese American Jōdo Shin Buddhists want to hear from me as a priest. Instead it is clear that they regard the temple to be a kind of therapy center and the Buddhist priest to be a type of psychotherapist. Anyway, I must always be prepared to make major adjustments in the topic, vocabulary, examples, and even humor to fit the particular audience.

From my previous comments, my ambivalence in addressing the topic of Buddhism and Western psychotherapy should be understandable. It is a source of some personal discomfort and disinterest because of my Asian American Buddhist heritage and, at the same time, strokes my intellectual curiosity from a professional standpoint.

Buddhism and psychotherapy. Do they go together like chips and salsa? Or are they less related like chips and salamanders? Educated white middle-class Americans are certainly psychologically minded. They tend to see a relationship between psychotherapy and just about anything: psychotherapy and work, relationships, sports, children, adults, aging, families, marriage, learning, computers, religion, eating, sleeping, cooking, sex, and art. This was the topic of Zilbergeld's popular book titled *The Shrinking of America*.[2] So why not psychotherapy and Buddhism?

It seems that Euro-American Buddhists who have a shallow understanding of Buddhism would tend to see Buddhism as being just another form of psychotherapy. It is such a comforting though very simplistic thought, like smugly saying that all religions are different paths up the same mountain. Many others who have a stronger understanding of Buddhism would state that there are both similarities and differences but would still feel more comfortable focusing on the similarities. We mostly see what we want to see. Psychotherapists in particular have a great personal and professional need to see a strong relationship between Buddhism and psychotherapy. After all, it gives them another exciting, new approach and technique to add to their arsenals in their war against unhappiness, dis-ease, abnormality, and the unexplainable.

Just as white middle-class Americans tend to psychologize everything, I, like many Asian American Buddhists, tend to relate Buddhism to just about anything. I see Buddhism as being like tofu, in that it coexists unobtrusively in any setting and any population without needing to dominate. I see Buddhism as being like fertilizer, in that it enriches and nourishes all beliefs and practices without trying to replace them. So Buddhism and psychotherapy should coexist and interpenetrate quite easily.

Clearly Buddhism, which has brought understanding and peace to countless individuals over a period of over 2,600 years, is not to be confused with still youthful Western psychotherapy, which seems to be a confusing mishmash of literally hundreds of conflicting theories and divergent techniques. We have psychoanalysis, behavioral techniques, cognitive approaches, existential-humanistic therapies, dream interpretation, psychodrama, hypnosis, bodywork, sandplay, art therapy, group work, self-help groups, and so on. R. J. Corsini has stated that, as of 1994, there were probably over four hundred different systems of psychotherapy.[3] To make things worse, there is still no clear proof that psychotherapy is anything more than a hit-or-miss placebo, and there is no sure way of distinguishing its "cures" from spontaneous remission, except in the case of psychotic symptoms that can be controlled (not cured) by certain drugs. And some of its techniques, including shock treatment and psychosurgery, are little more than desperate experiments on human guinea pigs. Even experienced leaders in the field have seriously questioned the effectiveness and ethics of psychotherapy. For instance, Robyn Dawes, a noted psychological researcher and former member of the national ethics committee of the American Psychological Association, wrote the following: "Mental health practitioners base their practice on what they believe to be an 'intuitive understanding' of their client's problems, an understanding they have supposedly gained 'from experience.' But when they practice on this intuitive basis, they perform at best as well as minimally trained people who lack their credentials and at worst as licensed, expensive (if inadvertent) frauds."[4] It follows that many psychotherapists in the West are attracted to Buddhism because they see Buddhism as not only complementing Western theory and practice, but also expanding Western therapeutic assumptions and practices in a wiser and more compassionate direction.

Western versus Buddhist Psychotherapy

Can I rightfully speak of a "Buddhist psychotherapy," since it is not a term commonly sanctioned or recognized by the mental health profession? In recent years, several books[5] have attempted to explore the possible interface between Buddhist theory and practice and Western psychotherapy. And a few identifiable Buddhist-based psychotherapies, such as the Morita and Naikan therapies of Japan, have been introduced to the West.[6] So it is clear that Buddhist thought and practice have already made significant inroads into the psychological consciousness of the West. For the purposes of this still early discussion, I will refer to the teachings and practice of Buddhism, in terms of its therapeutic benefits, as "Buddhist psychotherapy."

And while there are hundreds of different Western psychological theories and modalities, there are some root qualities that they seem to share. For the sake of discussion, I will conveniently group these diverse approaches under the title "Western psychotherapy." At the same time, it must be acknowledged that, within the transpersonal psychology camp, some theorist-practitioners have already begun to integrate Buddhist thought and practice into their pioneering efforts to develop a more holistic integration of Western and Eastern perspectives on the psyche. Transpersonal psychotherapists are still relatively few in number, however, and have only a marginal presence in the mental health field at this time.

Western psychotherapy and Buddhist psychotherapy appear to have very different characteristics, assumptions, goals, and practices. In fact, it may initially be difficult to see a relationship other than the fact that both are attempts to address human suffering. By pointing out some of the differences between Western psychotherapy and Buddhist psychotherapy, I want to make clear that Buddhist psychotherapy is less a repudiation of Western psychotherapy and more an expansion of Western psychotherapy. It appends dimensions of compassion and nonduality to the rational clarity and precision of Western psychotherapy.

Western psychotherapy has an obsession with happiness and the need to eradicate suffering and pain, which are seen as unwelcome intruders. Happiness and contentment in relationships and work are the signs of normalcy and mental health. Simply put, to be happy is to be normal; to be unhappy is abnormal. Some of the signs of normalcy are being clear and rational, enjoying physical health, having material comfort, following the laws of our society, being productive in one's work, feeling fulfilled and meeting one's life goals, having good relationships, and living for a long time. Buddhist psychotherapy does not reject the Western therapeutic objective of happiness in love and work. Rather Buddhist psychotherapy goes further than the simple goal of relative happiness by recognizing that life is *duḥkha* (like riding on a cart with badly made wheels). Life's imperfections and pain are not eradicated but are instead embraced as familiar friends and transformed into valuable lessons that show us again and again our blind self-centeredness, the result of clinging to a very limited and impoverished view of life. Suffering or unhappiness is the outcome of a failure to see that life is in constant flux and that nothing is permanent in this world, a failure to see the interconnectedness and interpenetration of things in the world, and a failure to see the illusory nature of the conceptual self or ego. Happiness requires a complete transformation of the individual's paradigms or worldviews, that is, a cessation of erroneous worldviews.

Western psychotherapy tends to be highly judgmental. The strong need and desire to determine which behaviors and attitudes are normal or abnormal have resulted in the detailed and widely used practices in the helping professions of diagnosis and labeling. In our society, abnormal behavior and attitudes that receive attention and treatment are codified in the *Diagnostic and Statistical Manual of Mental Disorders (DSM)*,[7] the bible of the mental health profession used by therapists, the courts, and the insurance companies to define normal and abnormal thought and behavior. It comes as a shock to most people to learn that, if one were to walk into a mental health clinic today and mention that one is unhappy, one would receive at least one diagnosis in the *DSM*, which will become part of one's permanent database record. In other words, one can never be "normal" again. And, despite all the relatively recent interest in Jungian psychology and various transpersonal approaches, the *DSM* has grown in its influence in the mental health field. It is interesting to note that the third revised edition of the *DSM*, published in 1987, had 567 pages whereas the current fourth edition, published in 1994, has 883 pages, representing an increase in size of 56 percent. Buddhist psychotherapy does not deny the convenience and helpfulness of having terminologies that summarize specific constellations of characteristics and symptoms. At the same time, Buddhist psychotherapy points out the inherent dangers of reducing wonderfully complex and constantly changing human beings to static labels, where often the diagnoses take on more significance than the persons they attempt to describe. Instead of making a rational analytical attack on our problems that depends on diagnosis and labeling, Buddhist psychotherapy would remind us to simply observe the life that flows through us and notice when the needs of our ego cause temporary blockages in the flow of mindfulness. Appreciation of mystery, of the enigmatic, and of depth of feeling is encouraged. Out of this emptiness emerges wonder and humility rather than the professional detachment and hubris that are often encountered in mental health settings. Buddhist psychotherapy also encourages troubled people to perform constructive and productive work rather than attaching themselves to their disturbed thoughts and feelings. For example, Morita Therapy, a Japanese therapy with Zen Buddhist roots, emphasizes doing what is necessary regardless of one's emotional state.[8] Although most of us may not look forward to doing mundane household chores, the work must be completed regularly, simply because it needs to get done. It is pointless to wait until one "feels" like doing it or to spend hours in therapy examining childhood experiences that may have caused us to dislike washing dishes.

In Western psychotherapy, the process of therapy is analytical on the part of the therapist alone or both the therapist and client, depending on the approach. Intellect and reason are primary. And therapy is carried out almost completely through talking: being able to talk clearly and rationally about problems is crucial to the success of therapy. The purpose of all the talking is to change the client from "abnormal" attitudes and behavior to "normal" ones, with or without the client's knowledge and cooperation. Instead of hours and hours of talking about problems, Buddhist psychotherapy stresses mindfulness or meditation. Excessive talk is seen as an escape from and disguise for reality. Instead of talking endlessly about a problem until it virtually takes over one's consciousness, we reflect on the problem and its ever-present and immediate cause—that is, our old friend, blind self-centeredness. Just as important, we also reflect on that which is good and wonderful in our lives, including the gift of just being alive. It is not to say that Buddhist psychotherapy does not use talking, but rather that talking is used skillfully to lead the client back to mindfulness. The Buddhist therapist encourages and assists the client to see the illusion of her persona, the limited and impoverished view of her identity. Instead she is helped to understand and accept her self, her identity that is interrelated with all other existences. In doing so, she is no longer isolated and focused on her own ego needs, which can only make her unhappy in the long run.

Because professionalism is important in Western psychotherapy, the dichotomous relationship between helper and helpee must be maintained. There is to be no confusion of roles. The "greed of giving" is ever present. In other words, the therapist has everything of value to give, while the client has nothing to give back except money and cooperation. Wouldn't it be wonderful if the therapist could say to the client at the end of the hour, "I gained so much from this hour that I insist that I pay you instead"? Of course, if the client feels better, then the credit for the cure goes to the therapy and the therapist. The efforts and experiences of the clients and their families and friends during the other 167 hours and 10 minutes of the week receive little credit. In contrast, the relationship between Buddhist therapist and client is nondichotomous. Instead they are in oneness as fellow travelers on the path from confusion and self-centeredness to wisdom and compassion. The Buddhist therapist encourages the therapist to come alive in the client and the client to come alive in the therapist. The Buddhist therapist respects and encourages the healing skills of the client and those in his environment, and sees herself as just another participant, a catalyst at best. It is essential that the Buddhist therapist herself be actively involved in the process of transforming her inner garbage into beauty and joy. An unhappy and spiritually lazy therapist is of no use to her clients.

Western psychotherapy is a highly politicized and coercive process.[9] The therapist is supposed to steer the troubled client into becoming a good and productive member of society. The client must value and strive to adopt "normal" goals as determined by the powerful segments of our society. For instance, the *DSM* for 1994 is devised by, with little exception, committees of successful Euro-American psychiatrists and psychologists, and imbued with their homogenous class- and culture-specific values. In contrast, Buddhist psychotherapy is not a tool or agent of culture but rather a constant and nonviolent criticism of the culture with which it is involved. For example, the Gautama Buddha was quite clear in his disapproval of the Indian caste system and his desire to expand the role of women in religious life. It is the task of the Buddhist therapist to bring about a reconciliation between the client's values and views and social norms without sacrificing the integrity of the client. He tries to help the individual to awaken to her true nature, even if it means living outside of social convention. In other words, the Buddhist therapist must himself be actively engaged in social criticism by helping the clients to liberate themselves from the societal standards of ethics, law, language, aesthetics, gender roles, identity, philosophy, and religion. This is where many Western psychotherapists fail; they are so intent on promoting their own professionalism and their particular systems of assumptions and definitions that they become blinded to reality. They can become truly helpful to their clients only if they can see through their own paradigms and institutions. But their standardized training and their own economic interests usually do not encourage them to do so.

In Western psychotherapy, therapy is successful if the clients feel better about themselves, that is, if they are functioning fairly normally in society and have mental stability. More therapy is prescribed if the client still feels unhappy or confused, or is not functioning acceptably at work or in relationships. The goal of Buddhist psychotherapy is enlightenment—seeing things-as-they-are, the perfection of emotions into compassion and of cognition into wisdom. In other words, what tends to develop is a seeing and deep acceptance of life-as-it-is, including one's own karmic limitations, and a more compassionate way of relating to all "others" because the interconnectedness and interdependence of life are the very heart of the enlightenment experience. Feeling better about oneself is, at best, a secondary benefit, a by-product, of Buddhist therapy. At the same time, it is vitally important for the client to be aware that feeling good about himself may indicate increased self-centeredness or narcissism and a lack of wisdom and compassion. After all, how can one be happy and content with all the suffering and despair in the world?

The following analogy aptly points out a basic difference between Western psychotherapy and Buddhist psychotherapy. Let's imagine Western psychotherapy to be like watering and pruning a plant so that it has a nice shape and colorful flowers. Buddhist psychotherapy goes further by treating the root of the plant. The goal of Western psychotherapy is "normal" functioning and relative happiness, whereas the goal of Buddhist psychotherapy is enlightenment. Buddhist psychotherapy works on the six universal neuroses, those that exist beyond our personal neuroses, called the *kleśas*, or defilements: greed, anger, ignorance, pride, doubt, and false views. Without enlightenment, these *kleśas* still exist no matter how much psychotherapeutic work is completed on our personal neuroses.

Lastly, unlike Western psychotherapy, Buddhist psychotherapy is not just something one turns to whenever one is in trouble; rather, it is in effect the essence of one's reason for being. Thus there is an unending examination and reevaluation of a person's assumptions in all areas of life—one's means of livelihood, one's relationships with loved ones and with the world at large, and the depth and quality of one's inner life. Buddhist psychotherapy addresses itself to the totality of the person's being. It is, put quite simply, a way of life.

Conclusion

In further contemplation of my topic, I had several observations that did not fit into the main body of the chapter. Let me conclude this chapter by discussing these points in no particular order in the hopes that they will provide more illumination on the topic.

It is evident that normalcy and mental stability have little to do with enlightenment or liberation. Bill Clinton, Colin Powell, Lee Iacoca, Oprah Winfrey, and Michael Jordan are considered widely to be normal and successful. But few would claim that they are spiritually awakened. And it seems that spiritual persons are not necessarily normal or successful. In fact many do not have successful careers and close family relationships. We have only to consider Jesus, the Gautama Buddha, and Shinran Shōnin (the founder of the Jōdo Shin sect) to see spiritually awakened people who were rather unproductive in normal terms and seemed not to have close relationships with family and friends.

A common misunderstanding of Westerners is that liberation is "depersonalization" in the sense of regression to a primitive or infantile type of awareness. For example, Freud designated the longing for return to the oceanic consciousness of the womb as the nirvana-principle, and his followers have persistently confused all ideas of transcending the ego with mere loss of "ego strength." This gross misunderstanding continues to this day and appears in popular psychology books quite regularly.[10] This is another example where a little knowledge can be most misleading and dangerous. Liberation in Buddhism means seeing through or transcending the illusion of ego. The direction of Buddhist practice is to expand the illusion of the individual isolated ego to the greater matrix of Self, which is interrelated and interdependent with all other existences. The blind and insensitive applications of Western psychological assumptions and practices to non-Euro-American populations have led to countless questionable and even laughable findings. For example, the administration of the Rorschach inkblot test by American researchers to Burmese Buddhist monks "revealed definite psychopathology among the monks" who "showed marked regression in the manifestations of aggressive and oral needs, hypochondriasis, 'erotic self-cathexis,' great fear of female or mother figures, great defensiveness, and apparently latent homosexuality."[11]

I cannot help but notice the difference in age and life stage between the Euro-American and Asian American Buddhist groups that I address. The

Euro-American Buddhists tend to be quite young, single, highly educated, and generally discontented with their lot in life. In contrast, the Asian Americans tend to be middle-aged or older, married with children and grandchildren, with a practical rather than formal education, and generally quite stable and contented with their outer circumstances. Most Asian Americans seem to be following a traditional Indian model of life stages: student, householder, forest dweller, and renunciant. They begin looking within in a spiritual sense when they reach the forest dweller stage in their fifties, that is, after completing their student and householder stages. One completes basic developmental tasks before one earnestly begins the search for truth in the latter life stages. For example, the Gautama Buddha embarked on his spiritual quest at the advanced (at that time) age of twenty-nine only after fulfilling his student and householder responsibilities. In contrast, it appears many Euro-American spiritual seekers are trying to avoid or prematurely transcend basic developmental tasks. Everyone is in such a hurry to become enlightened that therapy and *sesshin* "addicts" are not uncommon. It certainly smacks of narcissism. One can become overly enchanted with and immersed in one's own personal growth until nothing seems to matter except lying on the therapist's couch or sitting on one's meditation cushion and spending countless hours delving into one's emotions, dreams, archetypes, and relationships. It is important that a stable ego-structure be established before liberation from attachment to the illusion of individual isolated ego can occur. But with the breakdown of extended families and tightly knit communities and the ungrounded life in an increasingly urban-technological culture, a stable ego-structure is difficult to develop.

Most of us Asian American Buddhists know from our experience that disengaging from our emotional blockages and practicing the living Dharma (teaching) happens naturally when one is an integral part of a large supportive intergenerational community, or *sangha*, where one interacts regularly with other community members in receiving and giving help and support. The venerable Vietnamese teacher Thich Nhat Hanh wrote, "A good Sangha is crucial for the practice."[12] There simply isn't time in an active *sangha* to fixate on one's own needs and problems. Of course the isolation and frantic mobility of Western society is not conducive to community building and instead requires us to seek out or create artificial communities. This task seems to be especially challenging for Euro-American Buddhists, because most seem to convert to Buddhism as isolated individuals in the midst of existential pain and confusion, which makes it difficult to form close and trusting communities similar to those that Asian American Buddhists enjoy.

Clearly, the fundamental differences between the tenets and practices of mainstream Western psychotherapy and Buddhist psychotherapy are enormous and far-reaching. Western therapists who were hopeful of conveniently adding Buddhist psychotherapy to their eclectic collections of theories and techniques must instead undergo fundamental transformations of their self-identities and the purposes of their work. This thought concludes my initial contribution as an Asian American Buddhist priest-therapist to the stimulating dialogue heretofore participated in mainly by Euro-American Buddhists and their acknowledged Buddhist teachers.

Helping the Iron Bird Fly: Western Buddhist Women and Issues of Authority in the Late 1990s

RITA M. GROSS

Among several issues critical to the successful transmission of Buddhism to the West and to women's involvement in that transmission, I have chosen for this context to limit my comments to issues surrounding authority.[1] I will start by discussing alleged misuse of authority by currently empowered spiritual teachers, mainly men. This analysis of alleged abuse of power will be balanced in the second half of this presentation by suggestions regarding models and concepts of spiritual authority appropriate for Western Buddhism, including especially the relationship between women and authority.

These comments on authority rest within a larger context. I do not regard the issue of teachers' sexuality to be as central an issue as do some other Western Buddhists. Rather, in my view, the development of postpatriarchal feminist patterns of community and postpatriarchal modes of authority are the concerns that cry out for our attention. Since I have already devoted considerable attention to the complex issue of community in other contexts,[2] in this presentation I will discuss only one of those two issues—authority in spiritual communities. It must always be remembered, however, that these two concerns really belong together and are somewhat artificially split due to limits of space and time in this context.

In these comments, I will be drawing on my experience and knowledge as a feminist Buddhist "theologian" and directing myself primarily toward Western Buddhists, toward both explicitly feminist Buddhists and those who do not use feminist resources as directly as I do in thinking about troublesome issues, such as spiritual authority. Non-Buddhist scholars of Buddhism, who are not directly affected by or involved in these controversies, should take my comments primarily as part of the ongoing debate within contemporary Western Buddhism, rather than as a report on that debate.

Sexual Behaviors of Male Buddhist Teachers and Sexual Misconduct

I take up the issue of alleged "sexual misconduct" on the part of male Buddhist teachers—a topic that I had thus far successfully avoided discussing publicly—with extreme reluctance. Though the misconduct issue involves a host of behaviors, including use of drugs and alcohol, misappropriation of funds, and general abuse of power, I will focus on the sexual misconduct charge because it is the most volatile and the most central to women, and also because no other alleged abuse has touched the exposed nerves of American Buddhists so sharply or caused so much anguish for so long in the American Buddhist community. The fact that I did not even mention this topic in my book *Buddhism after Patriarchy*, which I expect to live longer than I will, indicates that I do not consider this to be a central issue in the long-term goal of developing postpatriarchal Buddhism. In fact, I would argue that excessive attention devoted to the foreground of teachers' alleged misconduct is diverting much-needed energy from more basic issues which must be adequately attended to if Buddhism is to be transmitted to the West and if genuine Western Buddhism, rather than Asian Buddhism hothoused in the West, is ever to emerge.

While those more attuned to academic Buddhist studies might be relatively unaware of, or at least emotionally distant from, the turmoil swirling around many major Buddhist teachers in the West, no Buddhist practitioner involved in any major Western Buddhist community can be unaware of this phenomenon. Nor are most Western Buddhists unopinionated on this topic; indeed, some show more dogmatism on this topic than on any other issue facing Western Buddhists. Since the early eighties it has torn apart many prospering North American Buddhist organizations, including, among others, the Zen Center of San Francisco, by then headed by Richard Baker Rōshi; Vajradhatu, the international association of meditation centers founded by Vajracharya the Venerable Chōgyam Trungpa Rinpoche, and headed by the Vajra Regent Ösel Tendzin during its most difficult phase; the Los Angeles Zen Center, headed by Maezumi Rōshi; and the New York Zen Center, headed by Eido Rōshi. Though most of these communities are now picking up the pieces and regrouping, controversy and bad feelings have not abated and many students have abandoned long-term association with a Dharma center, apparently for good.

In March 1993, a meeting between selected Western Dharma teachers and the Dalai Lama resulted in a statement that gives the impression that there is only one correct opinion regarding the issue. The behaviors alleged to be misconduct, including sexual misconduct, were declared misconduct indeed and should be exposed and criticized as such. Western Buddhist teachers then met at Spirit Rock near San Francisco in September 1993 to continue the discussion. At this meeting, which was largely facilitated by non-Buddhist therapists, some Western Dharma teachers engaged in highly emotional expressions of disapproval of their own Asian Dharma teachers. Some found the whole event cathartic and others found it appalling. A few months later, in March 1994, another conference with the Dalai Lama was held. According to some reports, he distanced himself from the whole issue at that time. Then, later in 1994, a large suit for damages for alleged sexual misconduct was brought against Sogyal Rinpoche, the author of the popular *Tibetan Book of Living and Dying.* Undoubtedly, this is not the last event in the story, but only the most recent at the time of this writing. As an indication of how much emotional force the issue still packs, one can note that almost half of the issues of the new Buddhist journal of opinion *Tricycle* have carried some content devoted to the sexual behaviors of teachers, if only in the form of letters to the editor.[3]

If it is not already clear, it will quickly become obvious that I do *not* share the horror felt by some people about these Buddhist teachers' alleged sexual misconduct. My central concern, however, is not to condone, justify, or explain the sexual behaviors of some male teachers, either. My central point is that, while I do not have a strong opinion regarding the sexual behaviors of male Buddhist teachers, most especially my own teacher, Chögyam Trungpa, I do feel, very strongly, that other issues need our attention far more. This view runs counter to that of many articulate female and feminist Buddhists; therefore, I will try to explain why I take the stand that I do.

It is important to defuse the view that I am not appalled by the sexual activities of male teachers out of blind loyalty to my own teacher. On the contrary, I am known within Vajradhatu as something of a rebel and a troublemaker, someone who has a mind of her own, because of my consistent advocacy of a feminist agenda within Buddhism. If I were convinced that the sexual behavior of teachers was an overriding concern for the transmission of postpatriarchal Buddhism to the West, I doubt that loyalty to my teacher would keep me from speaking out, since my loyalties, which are very deep, have not deterred me on other issues.

Probably my stance is in part dependent on my being the student of Chögyam Trungpa, rather than some other teacher. I say this because in my view, the crisis-precipitating conduct has not been the sexual behaviors themselves, but *secrecy surrounding sexual behaviors.* Certainly when Vajradhatu fell apart, in 1988–90, it was not over Trungpa's womanizing and drinking, which had been totally common knowledge for years, but over secrecy surrounding sexual activities of his Dharma heir, the Vajra Regent Ösel Tendzin. Perhaps I would have been more stung and hurt by the sexual conduct of my teacher if I had been the student of a teacher who gave one appearance in public but acted oppositely in private. When I was deciding whether to become Trungpa's student, I knew about his behaviors, though I was never in the inner circle of students who witnessed or participated in them. Quite frankly, initially I was more distressed by his ostentatious and pretentious lifestyle and its cost to his students who, as a group, are not wealthy. I literally had to make a decision as to whether my discomfort with his expensive lifestyle was worth keeping me from his brilliance as a Dharma teacher and his ability to illumine mind to me. I think everyone who accepts a spiritual teacher has to make such a decision, though the specifics are different for each teacher-student relationship.

My reasons for not pouncing on teachers' alleged misconduct as the central problem for Buddhist women circle around two issues. The first question is what a guru or spiritual teacher is or is not, which is closely connected with the question of what a guru could be expected to provide for students. The second question is whether one can suggest that women should not or cannot consent to certain kinds of sexual activities if they also want to function as self-determining adults.

What a Guru Isn't

Being a feminist before I became a Buddhist has perhaps stood me in good stead in not expecting too much from a guru, in not expecting someone I can completely model myself after, someone who will never disappoint me, or someone who is always all wise. Since I have not yet met a guru who thoroughly understands, manifests, or has assimilated feminism into his or her being, it has always been obvious to me that the guru is not the perfect, infallible authority on all issues. (This is not to say no gurus are sympathetic to feminism, for some, including Trungpa, clearly are.) On this point we have the most complete example from Buddhist tradition and history that we could possibly have or want. Even the Buddha was not all wise on every social issue, as is clear from his handling of the founding of the nuns' *sangha* and his insistence on the eight special rules.[4]

If even the Buddha is not a perfect role model, why should we expect it of the men and women who have enough spiritual insight to function as gurus today? This principle that the guru is not an authority on all issues needs to be much more thoroughly assimilated, for in my view much of the disappointment many people express about their teachers' conduct results from theistic expectations of the guru, from confusing the guru with God, or from longing for him or her to be the perfect mummy or daddy one never had. It is also my view that the demand for a perfect guru is, in practice language, an aspect of resistance, one of the tricks of habitual mind or "ego," in the Buddhist sense, to protect itself from deconstruction and freedom, a phenomenon well known to every meditator and meditation instructor. The demand for a perfect guru is resistance, in the form of the statement, "Unless I find a guru and a spiritual scene that I totally approve of, I won't practice meditation with them." I do not think there is a spiritual teacher out there who is also a perfect, flawless role model in every regard, whatever that might be. I would suggest that the quest and the demand for such a teacher are quite immature and that the student's rejection of a teacher who is not "perfect" says more about the student than about the teacher.

If teachers are not authorities on all issues and cannot be expected to be perfect role models, in what areas are they authorities and role models? A teacher understands the nature of mind and can point that out to the student. If one doubts the teacher's insight into that sharp nameless quality, one should abandon the teacher forthwith. Every teacher with whom I have worked would say the same thing in his or her own words. A teacher also understands the skillful means—the meditation practices—to bring a student to penetrating insight into his or her own unsullied mind, can transmit those practices, and can instruct the student regarding them. I sought and seek these skillful means from my teachers, for my feminist view and practices did not give me sufficient access to them. In fact, I first met my teachers as a skeptic who doubted that so-called spiritual teachers knew any more than I did. But in a penetrating nonverbal interchange, it became immediately obvious to me that Trungpa Rinpoche was the only person I had ever met who knew something that I wanted to know and that I wouldn't learn easily, if at all, by myself. His Mercedes became small potatoes in that context. I do not have to approve of every nuance of a teacher's behavior to respect and learn from him or her, because I do not expect a teacher to be all-wise and I do not expect my teacher to model for me all aspects of my life.

This middle path of revering the spiritual teacher as an authority on mind-to-mind transmission but not necessarily an all-wise or all-perfect role model guards against excessive attention to a teacher's everyday actions at the same time as it protects the heart of the teacher-student bond. My questioning, or even my disapproval of certain actions taken by a teacher, does not harden and solidify into ideology or fixed mind. To me, the ideological fixation and conventional moralism of those who insist that teachers' sexual misconduct is an overriding concern send up red flags. More than anything else, their self-righteousness and moral rigidity make me suspicious and wary. My experience of Buddhist meditation practice is precisely that it enhances a quality of flexibility, humor, and nonjudgment that has nothing to do with being passive and manipulable. When I encounter ideological moralism instead, I am not inclined to take the complaints too seriously. And I fear that the energy exhausted by grief and ideology over teachers' disapproved behaviors is seriously depleting Western Buddhism at a critical time.

Likewise, my assertion that the guru is not the authority on all issues does not conflict with the devotion to the guru that is so important in Vajrayāna Buddhism and some other forms of Buddhism. One is required to appreciate and follow the guru's meditation instructions, but one is not required to worship or imitate his or her lifestyle. Devotion is not blind hero worship but intelligent application of the teacher's methods and messages, which is why I am completely confident when confronted by some Buddhists, usually men, who object to my feminist Buddhist teaching as disloyalty to my guru. Some discrimination regarding devotion is especially important. If one confuses devotion to the guru with imitation of the guru, rather unfortunate behaviors result, as was the case with many of Trungpa's students, who imitated his lifestyle in rather unhealthy ways. The ridiculous results of confusing devotion and imitation are aptly summed up by the reprimands some self-righteous imitators of Trungpa directed at me, suggesting that I was being disloyal to my guru, since I like cats very much and he, reportedly, hated cats, in keeping with widespread Asian prejudice. Even now, students sometimes ask me why he disliked cats so much, and I reply, "Because he was wrong on that point, which has nothing to do with his reliability as a teacher." To be unable to differ from the teacher, to imitate the teacher's every behavior is the flip side of requiring the teacher to fulfill one's own expectations of morality. Both are serious misunderstandings of devotion and the absolute bond that holds a student to a teacher in Vajrayāna Buddhism.[5]

For these reasons, I reject the frequent comparison of sexual encounters between spiritual teachers and their students to sexual contacts between bosses and secretaries or between professors and students. Secretaries and academic students rarely choose their bosses or professors in the way that Dharma students choose a spiritual mentor, and they usually cannot exercise the degree of discrimination that is required of a Dharma student vis-à-vis his or her guru. Most especially, I reject the comparison of the guru-student relationship to the therapist-client relationship, which is so inegalitarian that sexual relationships would almost always be exploitative. I reject both elements in this comparison. The guru is not a therapist and the meditation student is not a therapy client. While I am sure others have had more positive experiences of therapy, in my experience, therapists see themselves as experts and their clients as incompetent and in need of fixing. If the client questions a therapist's conclusions or advice, the client is said to be in denial, which puts the client in a double-bind situation in which she is encouraged to mistrust her own intelligence. Gurus, at least the ones I have worked with, do not treat their students in such a fashion but encourage students to test a guru before committing to the relationship and then encourage them to discover their own basic goodness and intelligence. Furthermore, I do not see a meditation student as a needy client in a dependent therapeutic relationship but as someone capable of rejecting sexual propositions from teachers if the terms are not acceptable. Certainly in the community in which I participate, such rejections occurred.

Because the guru is not an all-wise absolute authority and the student is not a needy, immature person in need of fixing up by such an authority, it cannot be claimed that a sexual relationship between a spiritual teacher and a student *must* be inappropriate and exploitative, though under certain conditions such a relationship *might* be exploitative and inappropriate. Such a relationship could also be mutual and mutually enriching, and in some cases surely is, as has been attested by some women I know. (I have the same reservation about absolute rules prohibiting sexual relationships between most other "unequal" partners, such as professors and students, or deans and professors, as well.) Finally, as difficult as it may be to understand the sexual behavior of someone like Trungpa, who had numerous partners, I have never thought his behaviors were motivated by the obvious egotism and personal neediness that motivates some well-known womanizers in politics or entertainment. I cannot make the same claim about other teachers, with whom I have had no connection; their own students would have to make that judgment.

Sexual Partners as Moral Agents, Not Victims

Many women for whom teachers' sexual activity is a serious problem experienced extreme pain as a result of their own or friends' experiences of sexual relationships with teachers. Others were not personally affected by such a relationship but have a strong ideological position regarding sex between supposed unequals. They concur in labeling the teachers' behavior as "sexual misconduct" or "sexual abuse."

But I have observed, from my own experience if nothing else, that sexual relationships often eventually produce pain, even if they also, at other times, involve deep communication and spiritual growth. Sometimes I think that if it were not for breakthroughs that can occur through sexual communication, no one would risk relating sexually with anyone because of the pain that so often eventually comes. Things rarely work out as well as one can envision in an encounter between two people. Therefore, disappointment is almost endemic. The leap from experiencing disappointment to labeling it abuse is troubling to me. Why it should be different with teachers, if we recognize that teachers are not always all wise, is incomprehensible to me. Some women may have had sexual relationships with their teachers that turned out in the long run to have been unwise and unhealthy. That does not necessarily mean they were exploited, but only that they made decisions they later regretted.

I am extremely troubled by the development in recent feminist discourse to proclaim women as victims in such sexual encounters and to seek to make rules that would protect women from such "victimization." I am troubled because this move is directly counter to the basic feminist drive to define women as adult human beings who have a right to make their own choices. I see no way in which we can affirm both that women are self-determining adults and that adult women cannot be trusted to make their own decisions regarding relationships with "powerful" men, but must be protected from sexual advances from such men. Formerly, women were often coercively paired with powerful men; now some would forbid such pairings under any circumstances. But either rule equally denies the agency of women; there is not much difference between telling a woman that she must become the sexual partner of a certain man and telling her that she should not or cannot become his partner. Rather than making it almost impossible for men to make sexual advances without facing the possibility of sexual harassment charges, we need to encourage women's self-esteem so that they do not feel pressured by offers that are unattractive to them. And, of course, women must be protected unconditionally from the negative consequences that can come with refusing a sexual proposition in a patriarchal context.

But if a spiritual teacher and his or her student accept each other's invitation to sexual activity, it is quite unfair for the student later to claim that he or she was a victim of sexual abuse. Nor could such students claim that they expected the relationship to proceed like a conventional romance. Only the most naive person could have begun a sexual liaison with someone like Trungpa expecting that he was entering into a permanent romantic relationship with her.

For these reasons, I am reluctant to make blanket condemnations of teachers who have sex with their students, but would suggest that only under certain circumstances are such encounters abusive and inappropriate. If teachers are bound by vows of celibacy, obviously they should not be engaging in sex with their students. If a teacher were to withhold Dharma instruction or transmissions unless the student engaged in sex or if the teacher were to insist that a sexual relationship is necessary to the student's spiritual practice, these would be serious problems and should be dealt with as such. They would indeed constitute sexual abuse. If the teacher has a track record of brief relationships with troubled, immature, distraught students, especially those new to Dharma practice, one should become suspicious. In addition, I am skeptical when the teacher practices what I call "the patriarchal politics of mate selection," which is to say that the female partner is most often young and conventionally attractive, whatever the age of the male partner.

In my view, the current Buddhist furor over teachers' sexual behaviors is in large part our own version of the moralistic backlash now sweeping our society in general, a phenomenon whose long-term effects will probably not be positive. I want to suggest that those who adamantly condemn sexual relationships between spiritual teachers and their students are overly reliant on conventional morality, especially conventional sexual ethics, which are often erotophobic and repressive. On the one hand, there simply are too many examples of outstanding people, including religious teachers, who engage in unconventional behavior to assume that adherence to conventional sexual morality is any safe guide to judging people's worth. On the other hand, the repressiveness of conventional sexual ethics produces a great deal of pain. Since I have never been particularly impressed by conventional standards of sexual morality, I am not quick to judge or condemn the sexual activities of others. I would suggest that it is unfair and inappropriate to deny to spiritual teachers an active sex life simply because they are spiritual teachers. I do not expect my teachers to be less interested in an active, enjoyable, meaningful sex life than I am.

What troubles me most about the topic of teachers and their sexual activities is the hold it has on Buddhist practitioners and communities. Many people seem to have a great deal of trouble practicing the Buddhist virtues of equanimity and detachment when discussing their teachers' sex lives. The way in which people nurse wounds and hold grudges is not at all a Buddhist way of working the issues. Nor am I impressed by the dogmatism and absolutism that flares up in conjunction with the issue of sexual relationships between teachers and students. The emotionalism that swirls around teachers and sexual ethics is quite detrimental to the founding and flourishing of Buddhism in the West. While I do not feel a personal need to initiate comment on teachers' sexual behavior, I do feel, quite strongly, that too much energy is going into this issue, and that this energy needs to be spent on much wiser causes and issues. I appeal to the feminist principle of choosing our battles wisely because we cannot fight them all. I consider the interdependent issues of community and authority to be much more basic to the well-being of Buddhism in the West.

Natural Hierarchy, Buddhism, and Feminism

One of the reactions to the scandals surrounding Buddhist teachers has been to question whether hierarchy in spiritual communities should exist and whether gurus should have spiritual authority. Many attempts to decentralize Buddhist communities and disperse authority among more people have occurred. Therefore, this is a very provocative time at which to suggest that I think the most important issue for Buddhist women is the transmission of spiritual authority to female gurus. Indeed, on some occasions when I have introduced the issue, women have adamantly insisted that guruship is an inherently corrupt phenomenon and should have no place in postpatriarchal Buddhism. And feminism is a notoriously anti-hierarchical movement. Since I have already written extensively about why *female* gurus are so important,[6] I will not repeat those arguments in this context, but will confine myself to some comments about natural hierarchy, feminism, and Buddhism.

Natural Hierarchy as the Middle Way

I would not give my life energy to a community, spiritual or secular, that was either completely authoritarian or completely democratic in its organization. My reasons for withholding support and commitment from organizations that are too authoritarian or too egalitarian are the same. Learning, discipline, accomplishment, and wisdom, qualities that I believe are essential to human well-being and should therefore be honored, are irrelevant in both authoritarian and ultra-egalitarian institutions. In fact, some ultra-democratic groups strive for leaderless communities, which strikes me as an oxymoron. In particular, I cannot imagine a spiritual community without hierarchy and leadership being very successful at effecting spiritual transformation among its members.

Among the many things I have learned as student of Chögyam Trungpa, none has been more helpful to me than the principle of "natural hierarchy" that he taught, but not too publicly.[7] At first hearing, this concept would be construed by most people to mean that hierarchy is inevitable or inherent in human life and so we had just better kowtow to the powers that be. The first part of that conjecture is correct, but the second part is not. Hierarchy is natural in the sense that, for example, a tree grows best when its roots are in the ground, its branches in the sky, and its trunk joins them. Thinking that all the parts of the tree should be equal and, therefore, equally exposed to the earth or sky is not too helpful. But nothing in the concept of natural hierarchy assumes that whatever hierarchies we may currently experience exemplify natural hierarchy. In fact, since most conventional hierarchies that we experience are based on irrelevant and arbitrary criteria, such as gender, race, class, sexual orientation, and so on, rather than on learning, discipline, accomplishment, and wisdom, they are most certainly *unnatural* hierarchies.

The term *hierarchy* seems to imply a vertical structure, a pyramid. In any specific moment, a natural hierarchy may indeed look like a pyramid, because one person or a small group of people are the focal point of activity, for now. But at heart, the basic geometric form that describes natural hierarchy is the circle rather than the pyramid. The more accurate picture of "natural hierarchy" is the *maṇḍala* structure of center and fringe, in which the parts are organically connected, mutually interdependent, and in constant communication. It is difficult to talk about authority in such a circular and interdependent manner.

Natural hierarchy has much to do with recognizing that not everyone is equally good at everything and, therefore, communities flourish when people can find the niche in which they are most comfortable, most productive, and most able to contribute to society. Natural hierarchies are also fluid hierarchies, in the sense that no one is always in the center and most people will be in the center at some point. In some situations I will be in a middle position, in other situations in a bottom position, and in others at the top of the current hierarchy. Sometimes I serve, and sometimes I direct, depending on what needs to be done and on my abilities, achievement, and training. All roles are valuable as learning experiences.

In living out natural hierarchy, I am grateful to have learned many things that I am sure I would otherwise have missed, such as how to serve a table properly and how to receive such service. But more important, I have learned that serving is not inherently degrading but is extremely pleasurable and dignified. Two things make service difficult in our egalitarian setting. One is the standard interpretation of the concept of equality to mean that serving is demeaning because not everyone does the same thing. The other is the fact that there is little fluidity in our supposedly egalitarian society, which means that servers stay in their positions, which builds resentment. But for myself, I would not trade for anything the hours spent running the institutional-size dishwasher or slicing endless vegetables during the work period assignment at meditation programs. They are the perfect counterpoint and antidote for the weekends I spend as top dog directing programs, teaching, and being served. Without my experience of filling all positions in a fluid natural hierarchy, I suspect I could be an arrogant and humorless director.

Natural hierarchy degenerates into unnatural hierarchy when the issue of who may fill any niche is predetermined by irrelevant criteria, such as gender, which is what has happened since the creation of patriarchy. Natural hierarchies also degenerate into unnatural hierarchies when their fluidity is lost and a permanent, rigid, static pyramid emerges. If, because of harsh experiences with unnatural hierarchy, we try to insist that everyone is equally good at everything and there should be no hierarchies at all, the only result is that we lose the gifts of the gifted, whatever their gifts may be. As a society, we seem now to be in a phase in which our belief in equality has resulted in the practice of pretending, to quote the slogan of mythical Lake Wobegon, that "all the children are above average." Obviously, if *all* of the children are above average, the needs of the truly above-average children are not met, which was my experience forever in childhood. It did not do the slow students any good to pretend that all have the same achievements, and my own achievement was sabotaged—particularly since, as a girl, I was supposed to defer and pretend that boys who achieved little were more worthy nevertheless. This is why I see natural hierarchy as the middle way between absolutism and the kind of democracy that ignores merit. Natural hierarchy honors the experience and achievements relevant for authority in any particular situation, but does not limit who might have that relevant experience and achievement. To say that in natural hierarchy, anyone might have the relevant experience and achievement for authority at any particular task is also to say that the training and apprenticeship required to be able to assume authority must be available to everyone.

Needless to say, in situations of genuine natural hierarchy, women would flourish. We would not be shunted into roles based on anatomy, but could find our niches in the tree of life. Some of us would become spiritual leaders, among other things. The fact that this is such a rare occurrence demonstrates quite clearly that most of the hierarchies we live are at least partially unnatural hierarchies and therefore deserve to be challenged. I suspect that the allergic reaction most feminists have to the word *hierarchy* is due to the fact that women have fared so badly under unnatural hierarchies, which have so arbitrarily, meaninglessly, and cruelly limited our flourishing. But I find the opposite, which is sometimes touted in feminist circles, equally appalling. The elevation of process over accomplishment is enervating, and the claim that all opinions are equally valid is ludicrous. Having been trashed on a number of occasions by feminists for my allegiance to excellence, I have some understanding of the cliché that men seek to destroy the weakest among them and women seek to destroy the strongest among us. There has to be a middle way between these extremes, and I believe it is in a natural hierarchy that honors, respects, and gives authority based on experience and accomplishment, but does not limit who might have the relevant experience and the accomplishments in any way.

Women and Authority in Buddhism

Two issues predominate in a discussion of women and authority in Buddhism. One is the issue of why spiritual authority is so central in Buddhism. The other issue is why it is so crucial that women attain and exercise spiritual authority in Buddhism.

For a spiritual community to be without authorities selected by natural hierarchy is unimaginable to me. It cannot be the case that the beginning meditator should not regard the guru as an authority on meditation or that her opinions about spiritual discipline are as valid as those of the guru. But she may know more about finances and building codes, which are also relevant concerns for the exercise of authority in a Dharma center. Such is the interplay of natural hierarchies as the middle way between complete authoritarianism and total lack of hierarchy.

Particularly in the case of spiritual discipline, experience and authority seem to me to be crucial, because, in Buddhist shorthand, ego is so slick and self-deception is so easy. Without guidance, most self-medicated spiritual disciplines become some version of "doing what feels good," which brings short-term satisfaction, but little long-term growth and development. I have long argued with my colleagues in post-Christian feminist spirituality that it is dangerous to make up spiritual disciplines and to become one's own meditation instructor unless there are utterly no alternatives, especially during the beginning stages of a meditative discipline.

Furthermore, the long-standing Buddhist practice of progressing along a path, following the established curriculum of learning and development, and being authorized to take on different levels of authority progressively cannot be eliminated. There is nothing that could replace it, though the process needs to be constantly on guard against ossification, or rigidities, such as those that limit the teaching authority women could assume. Nevertheless, except in extreme circumstances, such as women authorizing each other as spiritual teachers if all else fails, such authorizations must come from the top down, not from the bottom up. Transmission is much more trustworthy than election as a way of choosing spiritual authorities. In this regard the two worlds that I inhabit, the world of Buddhist practice and the world of academia, are remarkably similar. Students do not confer doctorate degrees on each other. People who already have a Ph.D. and teach at a Ph.D.-granting institution confer the degree on those who have successfully completed the course of training. Those of us in academia know there are cases of inhumane injustice in which people are denied the terminal degree or tenure because those in authority are wrong. The same thing happens in Dharma lineages. But no system is foolproof and the alternative of self-conferred titles is even more nightmarish.

Therefore, I would argue that it is counterproductive to talk about abolishing spiritual authority or guruship because of the recent problems Western Buddhists have encountered with gurus. I would argue instead to carefully do away with the excesses to which the phenomenon is subject—namely, theistic excesses of regarding the guru as always all wise and the near-monopoly men have on the position. As for theistic excesses, in at least some cases, they have as much to do with what students project onto the spiritual teacher as what the guru expects or demands.

In patriarchal systems, by definition, women are forbidden to hold authority, though feminist research shows that they often wield considerable power, nevertheless.[8] Since the defining trait of patriarchy is formal male control of the society, clearly women who held formal authority would fundamentally contradict the system. With some exceptions, Buddhism has followed this patriarchal norm throughout its history. There is no question that Buddhism cannot become postpatriarchal until women wield authority in Buddhism—however that comes to be defined and structured eventually in Western Buddhism. That is one of the reasons why I claim that the presence of female gurus is so crucial as the central issue for Western Buddhist women.

Even if we understand gurus realistically rather than theistically, they are powerful and compelling presences. As I argued extensively in *Buddhism after Patriarchy*, given what we know about sex, gender, and role models, it will be transformative and powerful, for both women and men, to relate routinely to women whose presence exudes confident, compassionate *authority*. That is why one of the things I would most like to see within my lifetime is a female and feminist lineage holder in my lineage. I am not too optimistic about that possibility. In general, Vajrayāna Buddhism in the West seems to be well behind Zen Buddhism in the West in giving Dharma transmission to women. I am not sure of the reasons for this, but I suspect there are two major ones. First, it seems that fewer people receive Dharma transmission in Vajrayāna Buddhism than in Zen Buddhism, and second, in Vajrayāna Buddhism, most of those who do are chosen in infancy as *tulkus*. As we know, the *tulku* system is controlled by Asian males, who despite the film *Little Buddha*, have not, thus far, been very serious about seeking female *tulkus*, or Western *tulkus*, for that matter.

Within Vajradhatu, the situation is perhaps unique. There is only one person with the status of guru or lineage holder, Sakyong Mipham Rinpoche.[9] I do not expect that to change anytime soon. Nevertheless, some natural hierarchy is evident within Vajradhatu. Much of the Dharma teaching is done by people like myself—senior students with various levels of teaching authority. I certainly have never been muzzled, despite my outspoken feminism, and I am starting to give seminars *within* Vajradhatu on Buddhism and feminism. Natural hierarchy as center and fringe is in operation as I am listened to even by people in the hierarchy whose first reaction is dismissive. Nevertheless, if someone with formal authority as a lineage holder were saying what I am saying, the same words would have much more impact. Changes necessary to end sexist practices, such as the lack of female imagery in the meditation halls and generic masculine chants and texts, would quickly happen. That is the nature of authority and that is why it is so crucial to have female and feminist lineage holders.

Eventually that will happen, as Venerable Jetsun Kusho-la Rinpoche assured me when I discussed the issue with her. The transition point when women finally achieve authority in Western Vajrayāna Buddhism is, however, fraught with another grave danger. Earlier I expressed my longing to see a female *feminist* lineage holder in my lineage within my lifetime. That second word is crucial. Unfortunately, in many systems, the first women to achieve authority are clones of the men who have always held authority, which solves almost nothing. As many in academia have learned, many a nonfeminist female dean or chancellor is worse than many a male dean or chancellor. Why this is so is quite clear. A system that has functioned under unnatural hierarchy for millennia cannot be basically healthy. Therefore, merely putting a woman in charge does almost nothing. Using the analogy of the tree house with the sign "No Girls Allowed," I often suggest to my students that just getting into a messy dilapidated tree house is not enough. It needs to be cleaned up and restructured, which is why it is so critical to have not only female but also feminist gurus involved in the transmission of Buddhism to the West and the transition to postpatriarchal Buddhism.

We have now come full circle. When noncelibate women become gurus, in a sense, the shoe will be on the other foot. I would predict that some of the same behaviors that are so troubling when done by men will also occur with female gurus because the teacher-student relationship, in my view, always includes passion that can become erotic. How will we handle the inevitable yearnings that develop between teacher and student when the teacher is female and the student lover is male or, perhaps, female? Conventional morality and prurience are not the answer, nor are the excesses or the secrecies of some male gurus.

Coming Out in the Sangha: Queer Community in American Buddhism

ROGER CORLESS

A feature of American society that is receiving increasing attention is the open and vocal presence of persons who identify themselves as "queer."[1] In modern America, it is quipped, homosexuality has gone from "the love that dared not speak its name" to "the love that will not shut up."[2] As Buddhism becomes a familiar part of America it interacts with the queer community, and both Buddhism and the queer community are changed.

This phenomenon is new, and has been little studied. This essay will address some of the issues involved in the interaction between Buddhism and the queer community and attempt to characterize the main changes that are occurring.

Buddhism and Homosexuality

The concern of Buddhism in sexual matters is with the danger of sexual desire in general, with only subsidiary attention being paid to the gender or orientation of the sexual partners.[3]

The basis of moral conduct in all lineages of Buddhism are the Five Precepts (*pañca-śīla*): to abstain from harming life, stealing, sexual misconduct, lying, and drinking alcohol. Since the precepts are couched in general terms, their precise meaning and application are matters of extensive commentary and, in the living situation, of discussion with the practitioner's principal Dharma teacher. It is not possible to use the precepts as a way of proclaiming that "all Buddhists must act in such a way," especially as there is no worldwide Buddhist legislative organization or universally recognized person who speaks for all, or even most, Buddhists.

We are left, therefore, somewhat on our own in trying to interpret the words of the third precept (Pāli: *kāmesu micchāchārā*; Sanskrit: *kāmamithy-ācarā*), "false conduct in regard to sensuality." Broadly, it is taken to mean any conduct that violates the established mores of a given society, so that it usually precludes adultery although it may allow concubinage. Since there were no self-identified queer communities in the cultures where traditional Buddhism developed, the precepts assume heterosexism, and homosexuality or homoeroticism is largely ignored. The commentary on the third precept by Gampopa (1079–1153), however, explicitly includes homosexuality in the list of prohibitions, albeit almost as an afterthought. His remarks are short enough and curious enough to deserve quoting in full:

> Sexual misdemeanour . . . has three subdivisions: against those who are guarded (i) by the family, (ii) by a master and (iii) by religion and custom. The first is sexual misdemeanour with our mother, sister or other female relative; the second is with a woman who has been married by the ruler or any one else; while the third is of five varieties: even if she be our own wife, sexual relation with her is considered to be improper if it is practised (a) at an improper part of the body, (b) in a place or (c) at a time that is improper, (d) too often and (e) in general. Of these the first (a) is to have sexual intercourse by way of the mouth or the anus. (b) Improper place is near the retinue of a Guru, a monastery, a funeral monument (*stūpa*), or where many people have gathered. (c) Improper time means to have sexual intercourse with a woman who has taken a vow, is pregnant or nursing a child, or in daylight. (d) Improper frequency is more than five successive times. (e) General improperness means to coerce a woman to sexual intercourse by beating. *It also means to have intercourse with a male or in a eunuch's mouth or anus.*
>
> Of the three results of such actions, maturation means that the culprit is reborn among spirits [i.e., *pretas*]; natural outflow of the existing conditions means that even if the evil-doer is born as a human being, he will be one who gets a hostile wife; while the general result is that he will be born in a place with much dust.[4]

Gampopa gives no reason why any of these activities are on the prohibited list.[5] We might speculate that they concern themselves with three areas: (1) sexual activity that is similar to stealing (for example, of another's wife); (2) sexual activity that causes scandal according to the expected cultural presuppositions; (3) sexual conduct that manifests addictive behavior. Because the karmic consequences include rebirth as a *preta* or in a dusty place, Gampopa appears to regard wrongful sexual activity as the expression of unbridled lust or as somehow "dirty." The lack of further explanation may indicate cultural axia: in Gampopa's time and place, such actions were "obviously" wrong.[6]

There is one lone, and rather bizarre, *sūtra* description of a special hell in which males who engage in homosexual activity are reborn:[7] it is embedded, like a fly in amber, in Śāntideva's *Śikṣāsamuccaya*, an anthology that has preserved other oddities, such as the prediction that one who wipes snot on a scared text will be reborn as a book, or a man who urinates against a monastery wall will be reborn as a wall. Such statements are hardly mainstream Dharma.

The Five Precepts are primarily for observant laypeople, most of whom are assumed to be heterosexual married couples. This may partly account for their vagueness—it is impossible to specify detailed conduct for many different households. Monasteries, however, are a different matter: they are controlled environments, and the legislation of the *Vinaya* is precise to, one might feel, a fault. Because the monk or nun is expected to be celibate, any sexual activity at all is condemned, and this includes, in the case of monks, intentional emission of the semen (that is, masturbation) and any form of penile penetration of a mouth (even, in the case of an especially supple monk, his own mouth) or anus as well as a vagina, "even to the extent of a sesame seed," so that any form of homosexual interaction would be regarded as illegitimate. The rules for the nun are not quite as clear, but the prohibition against sleeping in the same bed with another nun is probably intended to exclude lesbian activity.[8]

It is notable that these prohibitions against homosexuality in the *Vinaya* are not given any special (homophobic) metaphysical, philosophical, or doctrinal support. They are merely expressions of uncontrolled desire (*tṛṣṇā, upādāna*) on the part of persons who have vowed to control their desires. The only time we find homosexuality treated as a phenomenon in its own right is in the treatise (*śāstra*) discussions of the *paṇḍaka*, a word of uncertain meaning that Leonard Zwilling has suggested translating by using the English colloquialism "without balls," that is, a male who lacks, or is perceived to lack, the strength, courage or insemination ability which a male is supposed to possess. Some *paṇḍakas* might be recognized today as gay or homosexual, while others would not, but in any case the condition is not condemned in the *śāstra* but, rather, reported as a medical disorder.[9]

The few instances of homophobia that I have encountered among living Buddhist teachers in America may likewise be based on medical rather than moral considerations. S. N. Goenka, a teacher of a special form of Insight Meditation (*vipassanā*), feels that homosexuality is dangerous because it mixes what he regards as male and female energies: he is also opposed to the practice of more than one form of meditation in the same room for a similar reason—it mixes energies.[10] When a gay man approached the Korean Master Sŭngsan for a way to "cure" his homosexuality, he was led to believe that his condition was the fruiting of karma—an explanation used in Tibetan Buddhist medical texts for certain preexisting conditions.[11] The explanation of the third precept authorized by the late Venerable Master Hsüan Hua says, "homosexuality . . . plants the seeds which lead to rebirth in the lower realms of existence."[12]

There was a curious phase in the history of SGI-USA (Soka Gakkai International, USA). During the days when it was called Nichiren Shōshū of America, before the split in the parent body in Japan between the clerical and lay wings,[13] it recommended that its gay male followers participate in "human revolution" (*ningen kakumei*) by marrying a woman so as, it was hoped, to become heterosexual.[14] The experiment failed: not only has it been abandoned, but SGI has announced that it will conduct same-sex marriages.[15]

The conclusion seems warranted that traditional Buddhism has been largely neutral on matters of sexual preference. In America, because of the prominence of a queer community, Buddhism has been asked to take a stance, and the stance has largely been positive. The stimulus for taking a position other than neutrality is usually attributed to Robert Aitken Rōshi,[16] who asked Richard Baker Rōshi, in the course of a queer caucus at San Francisco Zen Center, what was being done to make Zen practice available to the gay community. Aitken Rōshi is supposed to have said, "If you are not in touch with your sexuality, you are not practicing Zen," and "You can't do zazen in the closet."[17] His remarks lent encouragement to the fledgling Maitri (first called the Gay Buddhist Club and now known as the Hartford Street Zen Center) in the Castro district of San Francisco.[18]

Two prominent Buddhists, H. H. Dalai Lama XIV and the Thai activist Sulak Sivaraksa, have come out in favor of, or at least not opposed to, homosexuality. Sulak claims that the Buddha never mentioned homosexuality and only said that we should not use sex harmfully.[19] In a similar vein, the Dalai Lama, speaking on his own authority, has stated that homosexual conduct is not a fault as long as both partners agree to it, neither is under vows of celibacy, and the activity does not harm others.[20]

Professor Taitetsu Unno of Smith College, a scholar of Buddhism and a Jōdo Shinshū Honpa-Honganjiha minister, has performed two ceremonies of commitment between gay couples who self-identified as Buddhists, "based upon [his] understanding of the Buddhist teaching of interconnectedness, brought about by deep karmic conditions beyond rational comprehension, which should be cherished, celebrated and strengthened with the passage of time."[21]

Two gay men, one Buddhist and one Catholic, were married in a ceremony in Boulder, Colorado, solemnized by a PLWA (person living with AIDS) Catholic priest (who acted, however, without the knowledge of his ordinary) and a Buddhist minister, and supervised by the minister of the Unitarian Church in which the wedding was held. The Buddhist minister was Dr. Judith Simmer-Brown, a well-known teacher at the Naropa Institute. The Buddhist partner had gone for premarital counseling to Dzigar Kongtrul, Rinpoche, who, on discovering that the partners were both men, "skillfully addressed some issues specific to gay couples."[22]

Buddhist groups in the San Francisco Bay area that I have interviewed on the question of queer practitioners were either neutral or openly accepting. Homophobia seemed to be unusual and needed a special search to be uncovered. As Michael Ferri of the Seattle Gay Buddhist Fellowship has written, "this [is] definitely not the Church of Rome."[23]

Oppression and Coming Out

There is some evidence that, in certain cultures at certain times, homosexual conduct was ignored, permitted, or even encouraged,[24] and it has been argued that outright oppression of homosexuals in the West began only around the eleventh and twelfth centuries.[25]

Nevertheless, whenever or wherever homophobia began, modern America is predominantly so. Homophobia can be explicit, as in the laws of those states that prohibit homosexual conduct between consenting adults, or it can be implicit in the "heterosexual assumption" of most of society. In various ways, the authority structure tells us that we are monstrosities: the Christian Church tells us we are sinful,[26] the law threatens to punish us, our parents may disinherit us, our friends may desert us, and society at large does its best to ignore our existence.[27]

Faced with this opposition we may, on the one hand, try to stuff our feelings or deny them, and we will almost certainly develop self-hatred by internalizing society's homophobia. On the other hand, we may decide to "come out," especially when we realize there are others of us out there, more especially when it begins to seem that there are so many of us that America as we know it could not function if all queers disappeared.

Coming out is a bit like growing up. There is a birth which is followed by a process. One sequence has been suggested by Rob Eichberg,[28] another by Craig O'Neill and Kathleen Ritter.[29] The models are complementary, in that Eichberg focuses on coming out as a public (or, as he calls it, a political) act of benefit to the entire queer community, while O'Neill and Ritter concentrate on a more private form of coming out, a process of realizing what we have lost by growing up queer and how we can integrate that sense of loss into our adult lives.

Eichberg proposes that there are nine stages, or levels of consciousness, to coming out, each level building on, and being built into, the other, beginning with "Powerless/Depressed" and ending with "Power/Empower."[30] O'Neill and Ritter suggest an eightfold scheme, beginning with "Initial Awareness" and ending with "Transforming Loss." Despite their ideological differences—Eichberg was a Reform Jew with Buddhist leanings and adopted a religion-neutral, psychotherapeutic stance, while O'Neill and Ritter are explicitly Roman Catholic and therefore assume monotheism as the norm—the models describe broadly similar movements from an initial state of fear, imprisonment, and reliance on others for self-validation toward a goal of love, freedom, and reliance on an inner spring of spiritual strength.

The resonance of this movement with the Buddhist path is apparent.

Oppression, AIDS, and Spirituality

When many people come out, as Calvin Coolidge might have said, queers become visible. Although homosexual activity is as old as humanity, gayness (or queerness) as a personal and public phenomenon appears to be new. Gay, says Boswell, "refers to persons who are conscious of erotic inclination towards their own gender as a distinguishing characteristic [and] 'gay sexuality' refers only to eroticism associated with a conscious preference."[31] Persons who today self-identify as queer often live in, or at least identify with, self-identified queer communities, and they live, or more or less consciously reject, so-called gay (or queer) lifestyles. Queers have developed a sense of belonging to each other just by reason of being queers—words such as *family* and *tribe* are commonplace—despite differences in age, race, class, intelligence, and lifestyle.[32]

The queer community, having formed as a reaction to explicit and implicit homophobic oppression—just as, and just where (the San Francisco Bay area) it was smelling some sort of freedom—was hit by the AIDS crisis. At first, it seemed to affect only gay males, but it soon became clear that it was an illness that could strike anybody. Lesbians, although statistically less prone to AIDS, have been shown to be, for some reason, more liable to develop breast cancer. What this amounts to is a perception, both by itself and by outsiders, that the queer community is a diseased community in some way that the larger community of Americans is not, and this has led, in turn, to an intensification of the feeling of a queer family or tribe.

The AIDS crisis has also been, quite literally, sobering. For many years, the only way queers could meet was to pick each other up in a gay or lesbian bar. There was consequently a lot of drunkenness and, for those with the still mysterious predisposition for it, alcoholism. The hyper-genitalized environment favored the making of money by barkeeps and hustlers, but it did not encourage the establishment of meaningful relationships, and it certainly did not promote spirituality. In fact, because of the strident opposition of mainline Christianity to homosexuality, many queers regarded any form of spirituality as totally beyond the pale: being queer and spiritual was an oxymoron.[33]

The possibility that a single sexual encounter could lead not merely to an annoying but curable sexually transmitted disease, but to a painful and protracted death at some time in the uncertain future, was a wake-up call. One of the traditionally listed stimulations to earnest Buddhist practice is the realization, not only intellectually but existentially, of the reality of death. Every human knows that he or she will die sometime, but most of us, especially in the United States, deny it.[34] When old people die invisibly in nursing homes, we can pretend that death will not happen to us. But when our young and healthy friends suddenly get sick and die, and when, after some years, we find that all our friends have friends or lovers who have died of "an early frost,"[35] we can no longer escape the conviction that we ourselves will surely die, and maybe die quite soon. Faced with oppression, "It is no wonder that Gay men are in touch with the spiritual in this world."[36] Faced in addition with AIDS, the mind is further concentrated: "I believe that if I had not been gay and had not had to face this epidemic [of AIDS] that I would not have heard the dharma. The contrast between the decay and fear caused by the illness on the one hand and the vitality of the response of gay people on the other provides a powerful illustration of the Buddha's teachings. The dharma has come to me through the medium of gay life and the AIDS epidemic."[37]

It was precisely because of the AIDS crisis in the queer community in San Francisco that Eric Kolvig, a student of *vipassanā* under Joseph Goldstein, came to California from the Insight Meditation Society in Barre, Massachusetts, in 1993. He felt that the entire queer community in San Francisco was going through post-traumatic stress syndrome, dealing with fear, grief, rage, and isolation, and he hoped that the Dharma could help to heal this syndrome.[38]

The direct relationship between the realization of death and a Buddhist spirituality of detachment from selfishness leading to compassion is clearly stated by Gregg Cassin, the founder of The Healing Circle,[39] a support group he established in San Francisco as a response to the HIV-AIDS challenge:

> In meditation I had reflected on the many deaths of friends and lovers . . . and on the power of death—not only these deaths, but the many small deaths we face in our daily lives. The message I received [from my spiritual teacher] was this: It is the dying that is bringing you new life. Die, Gregg, die daily. Die to everything you think you are or need to be—your body, your fear, your disease, all—die to it all. Let your ego be smashed.
>
> Our suffering is the womb of compassion. . . . Like a woman giving birth, I am changed with each death. I'm never the same. I am new. I am a mother.[40]

In both Theravāda and Mahāyāna texts, the Buddhas and Bodhisattvas are compared to mothers. As a mother automatically thinks first of her only child rather than herself, so the Buddhas and Bodhisattvas spontaneously put the welfare of other beings first. HIV and AIDS calls out to, and arouses, our Buddha-nature.

Even apart from the HIV-AIDS issue, Buddhism is helping queers to recognize, and dissipate, self-hatred stemming from internalized homophobia.[41] Eric Kolvig claims that *vipassanā* meditation allows us to see how much we hate ourselves, and to allow that hate to dissipate in the light of wisdom (*prajñā*). "By watching our minds vigilantly, minutely, subtly, instant by instant, we can train ourselves to catch the unworthiness and shame that were lodged in us when we were too young to refute them. Like mildew or mold, these things depend on staying in darkness; they cannot survive the clear light of knowing."[42]

At the same time as "wisdom obliterates the self-hatred of internalized homophobia by revealing what is real,"[43] love (*karuṇā*) liberates us from isolation, both from other queers and from the heterosexual majority. "Non-separation is love."[44] Because society marginalizes and oppresses queers, we isolate from each other, and we need a supportive community to heal our wounds. Kolvig referred to an incident in the *suttas* in which a monk with dysentery lies in his own excrement because the other monks will not take care of him. The Buddha, helped by Ānanda, bathes him and says, "Monks, you have not a mother, you have not a father who might tend you. If you, monks, do not tend one another, then who is there who will tend you? Whoever, monks, would tend me, he should tend the sick."[45] Queers are often estranged from their families, and it is in the queer community that we can find a family of choice to replace our family of origin. Many find that a spiritual community is more nurturing than a club or a bar and, having been deeply wounded by their contact with Christian homophobia, feel they have found a home in the Buddhist *sangha.*[46]

Some Examples of Coming Out

In August 1994 I conducted interviews with various persons who self-identified as being to a greater or lesser extent "out" in the *sangha,* and they referred me to other persons, groups, and informational material. The resulting data is evocative rather than scientific, since the sample was restricted in quantity and geographical extent to those persons I was able to contact during my brief fieldwork in the San Francisco area.[47]

Undoubtedly the most colorful figure to surface was Issan Dorsey, whose life is something of a modern, and Buddhist, version of Augustine of Hippo's journey from hedonist to spiritual teacher. Issan died in 1990, but I met many people who remembered him, and there is a biography of him.[48] Beginning his life as Tommy Dorsey in a hard-working family in Santa Barbara, he early began to feel that he was different. Growing up at just the right (or wrong!) time, he threw himself into the life of a drag queen in New York, Chicago, and San Francisco, with its attendant drugs, alcohol abuse, and promiscuity. Through the hippie scene in San Francisco, and especially his friendship with a man named Grant Dailey, whom

Issan called "my psychedelic guru,"[49] he came in contact with spirituality, and his life began to change course: " 'Grant was one of the main people in my life. He introduced me to everything that even resembled Zen practice. Before that, I just had been a crazy drag-queen junkie, but there was this complete metamorphosis that happened to me when I lived with Grant.' "[50]

The somewhat free-floating monism of Grant became more recognizably Buddhist for Issan on his visits to the *zazen* sessions held by Shunryū Suzuki Rōshi, founder of the San Francisco Zen Center. His conversion was not immediate, in fact he seemed to give Suzuki Rōshi quite a rocky ride, but eventually Issan found himself living and working at Tassajara, the retreat house of Zen Center whose bucolic isolation is legendary, and he became more and more identified with Zen as a lifestyle. Back in San Francisco, he joined the Gay Buddhist Club (unofficially renaming it the Posture Queens), which had formed in the predominantly queer Castro district. The Gay Buddhist Club became the Hartford Street Zen Center, and Issan was its abbot from 1989 until a few months before his death. Today, the center functions as a quiet, spiritual, and healing place in the cruisy, boozy Castro, without even a sign on its door to proclaim its presence to casual passersby.[51]

Philip Whalen (Zenshin Ryūfu), the resident teacher at Hartford Street Zen Center (HSZC), said that the attraction of Buddhism is that it frees us, in William Blake's terms, from "mind-forged manacles," especially the "poisonous Puritanism" of ordinary American religion which asks, "How can we be pure?" and answers, "No smoking, no drinking, no fucking." Queers come to Hartford Street rather than the San Francisco Zen Center on Page Street, he said, because the HSZC charter says it is for gays and lesbians, and so they feel more comfortable there. At other places, he felt, it was "don't ask, don't tell," just like the military.[52]

Do queers at the Page Street Zen Center feel subtly oppressed? John Grimes, a long-time resident of Zen Center and former guest master, doesn't think so.[53] He came to Zen Center from Tassajara in 1986 as, quite openly, the spouse of another man. As it turned out, his spouse lost interest in Zen and moved away, while John gained interest in Zen, and stayed. He has never experienced any homophobia at Zen Center, even though Mrs. Suzuki (the wife of the founder) was bothered by homosexuality when she first found out about it. She had never heard of it in Japan and, thinking it to be an American phenomenon, wanted to return to Japan to escape it.[54] She came to accept it, however, calling gays "soft men" and seeming to like them.[55] In all, John said he had no interest in, or need for, the Hartford Street Zen Center or the Gay Buddhist Fellowship (see later) and has even felt uncomfortable at them.

Some established American Buddhist centers go beyond accepting queers and actively address queer issues in special retreats. Most notable is Spirit Rock Meditation Center in Woodacre, California (near San Rafael), the western branch of the Insight Meditation Society. Spirit Rock hosts three queer Vipassana retreats a year: one for gays, led by Eric Kolvig and Robert Hall, one for lesbians, led by Arinna Weissman, and one for gays and lesbians, led by Eric and Arinna. In March 1994, Zen Mountain Center, a branch of Zen Center of Los Angeles, held a retreat for gays and lesbians led by Koren Baker and Pat Enkyo O'Hara.[56] Although Zen Mountain Monastery in Mount Tremper, New York (not to be confused with Zen Mountain Center), "has a very strong gay/lesbian presence," the status of queer practitioners there is ambiguous.[57] Nevertheless, in the fall 1991 issue of its newsletter, *Mountain Record, sangha* members published a section called "Practicing Out of the Closet—Sexual Minorities Appreciating the *Sangha.*" The San Francisco center of the Friends of the Western Buddhist Order (FWBO), an ecumenical and innovative *sangha* begun by Venerable Sangharakshita, a British teacher with multiple lineage affiliations, held, apparently for the first time, "an introductory meditation course by and for Gay, Lesbian, Bisexual, and Transgender people" on five Sunday evenings beginning on April 8, 1995.[58]

Two Buddhist groups in San Francisco—the Gay Buddhist Fellowship (known as the Gay Buddhist Fraternity between its founding in 1991 until June 1, 1994) and the Dharma Sisters[59]—have formed on the basis of members being queer first and practitioners of a specific lineage, or disciples of a certain teacher, second. GBF has an exclusively gay male membership,[60] while the Dharma Sisters, as would be expected, are composed of lesbian and bisexual women. Estimating the size of GBF and the Dharma Sisters is difficult since neither has a formal membership but, judging by the number of names on their respective mailing lists, GBF was, in 1995, more than double the size of the Dharma Sisters. In the summer of 1996, the Dharma Sisters ceased to function as an active group, but they revived in early 1997.

The groups are similar in that both are explicitly cross-traditional (although a sort of hybrid *vipassanā*-Zen sitting is favored, as the "lowest common denominator" of Buddhist practice) and both provide a safe place in which to be queer and spiritual-Buddhist. Members of the GBF weekly sitting group told me that they formed the group in order to combine sexuality and spirituality, to heal the wounds of a gay childhood, and to have a safe place to come and sit—where, because there was no need to fight the heterosexual assumption of straight society, the false ego (*ātman*) could be let go. The notion of "tribal intimacy" surfaced as important.[61]

The Dharma Sisters said that many of them are not out to their home *sanghas*, and they come to the Sisters for socializing and to experience intimacy; they can be themselves, getting on with being Buddhist without raising the lesbian issue as a big deal. There is a joyous, multicultural feel.

"Here," said Jackie Weltman, "a Jewish girl does not have to marry a nice Jewish boy."[62] Commenting on the Dharma Sisters' retreat of June 1994, Perri Franskoviak wrote:

> To create a period of time and space in which we can come together as lesbians and bisexual women practicing the dharma can be a powerful and healing force in our lives. Not only does it give us an opportunity to see the noise of our daily lives for what it is, but we support each other as we look deeply into our own true nature, discovering who we are as we open to the full range of our experiences. As sisters in the dharma we are all teachers to each other. ["We have no teacher or rōshi," commented Jackie.] This weekend gave us an opportunity to cultivate this sense of sangha, or community, more fully with each other. May this retreat be a continuing tradition for our sangha.[63]

There were only two significant differences between the Gay Buddhist Fellowship and the Dharma Sisters that I noticed. First, GBF members were directly confronting HIV and AIDS, whereas the Sisters stated that they were only informally involved, and that feminine diseases associated with the queer community, such as breast cancer, had not become a real issue.[64] Second, the Dharma Sisters strongly identified with feminist issues and admitted to a Wiccan influence—as, for example, arranging one-day *sesshin* on the solstices and equinoxes—while, on the other hand, when I asked GBF members about "masculinist" issues, Robert Bly–style, they got a cool reception.

A gay Buddhist teacher who is striking off somewhat on his own is Tundra Wind, who has a center in Monte Rio, California. He received Sōtō transmission through Jiyu Kennett Rōshi via Zen no Etsu, practiced Chogye in Korea, was abbot of Sŭngsan's group in New York City, and has studied Fukeshū. He regards his triple transmission as a strength that gives him permission to innovate,[65] and he is moving away from Zenlike practice to tantra. Learning that, according to Tibetan tradition, Tārā has made a vow always, until her enlightenment, to be reborn in the body of a woman so as to relate to the oppression of women, Tundra composed twenty-four vows beginning with "I will always take rebirth in the body of a gay man," so as to be available to oppressed gays.[66] Extending the tantric imagery into gay sexuality, he has "often wondered if Avalokiteshvara and Manjushri[67] in sexual embrace would make an effective tantric representation of the union of wisdom and compassion for gay males."[68] Tundra and his students discuss their novel ideas in the irregularly published *Zen Wind* magazine which "uses e-prime, a form of english [sic] that does not use the verb 'to be' . . . because it consistently reflects the meaning of dependent origination[69] [and] uses capital letters only at the beginnings of sentences, after a colon if what follows the colon constitutes a full sentence, in titles, and for names of individuals."[70]

Conclusions

The motives and characteristics of queer Buddhist groups are summed up well in the mission statement of the Seattle Gay Buddhist Fellowship:

> The Seattle Gay Buddhist Fellowship exists to provide support for Gay [note the initial capital] men in the Dharma.
>
> We aim to create:
>
> - a safe environment in which we can be ourselves as Gay men.
> - a fellowship in which members of various Buddhist paths can meet, meditate together, exchange ideas, discover similarities and differences of belief, and mutually support each other's practices.
> - a community in which to meet social and psychological needs.
> - a practice of compassion through social action.
> - a place of exploration for Gay men who wish to investigate whether or not a Buddhist practice meets their spiritual needs.
>
> In the Fellowship, a diversity of approaches to the practice of Buddhism are [sic] recognized, respected and welcomed. We do not exist to proselytize, convert one another or establish one particular Buddhist path.
>
> All Gay men with an interest in Buddhist practice are invited to join us.[71]

In general, we see that American Buddhism is producing groups of practitioners who are mostly laypeople and who typically belong to other lineages and groups with recognized monastic teachers, but who gather to practice as self-identified gay, lesbian, bisexual, and transgendered persons. The queer community takes on the role traditionally filled by cultural bonding (for example, as Cambodian or Thai Buddhists), lineage bonding (for example, as Gelugpa or Shin), or common devotion to a specific Dharma teacher (for example, Ajahn Chah or Venerable Master Hsüan Hua). The motivation is to heal, by mutual support and by the generation of wisdom and compassion, the childhood wounds of internalized homophobia and the adult wounds of the AIDS pandemic. This is a Buddhism that meets us, as queer Americans, where we live, and where we die, and leads us to liberation. As such, it is an authentic expression of the Dharma.

Resources

The resource list on page 39 of the fall 1992 issue of *Turning Wheel* (c/o Buddhist Peace Fellowship, P.O. Box 4650, Berkeley, CA 94704: telephone 510/525-8596) is useful, but many of the addresses are by now out of date. Of more enduring value is the special section on gay, lesbian, and bisexual Buddhism (pages 16–39).

For the San Francisco Bay area, an updated list appears in the Spirituality section of the classified ads of the *San Francisco Bay Times.*

The Gay Buddhist Fellowship can be contacted by mail at 2261 Market Street, #422, San Francisco, CA 94114; and by phone (24-hour information line) at 415/974-9878; Web page: http://www.planetaria.net/home/abaki/directory %20 pages/directory/html

Jackie Weltman, formerly of the Dharma Sisters, is now at Harvard and can be contacted via E-mail at <jaxers@well.com>

Spirit Rock Meditation Center can be contacted by mail at P.O. Box 909, Woodacre, CA 94973; by phone at 415/488-0164; and by fax at 415/488-0170.

Hartford Street Zen Center can be contacted by mail at 57 Hartford Street, San Francisco, CA 94114; and by phone at 415/863-2507; Web page: http://members.aol.com/HSCZ/

The San Francisco Buddhist Center (FWBO) can be contacted by mail at 37 Bartlett Street, San Francisco, CA 94110; and by phone at 415/282-2018; Web page: http://www.bluelotus.com/sfbc/sfbc/html

The Buddhist AIDS Project can be contacted by mail at 555 John Muir Drive, #803, San Francisco, CA 94132; and by phone at 415/522-7473; Web page: http://www.wenet.net/~bap/

Maitri can be contacted by mail at 401 DuBoce Avenue, San Francisco, CA 94117; by phone at 415/863-8508; and by fax at 415/863-0227; Web page: http://www.wenet.net/~maitri/

Tundra Wind can be contacted at P.O. Box 429, Monte Rio, CA 95462.

Responding to the Cries of the World: Socially Engaged Buddhism in North America

DONALD ROTHBERG

*And in these worlds there are . . . Bodhisattvas walking,
sitting, engaged in all kinds of work, doing charitable
deeds out of a great compassionate heart, writing various
treatises whereby to benefit the world.*

THE *GANDAVYŪHA SŪTRA*

I t is January 1991, in San Francisco, California. Three days earlier, the
United States, under the United Nations' aegis, has begun massive
bombing of the cities of Iraq. For two days, some seventy persons—
most Buddhists, and most activists, many of whom are involved in the days
before and after in demonstrations, civil disobedience, educational work,
and public forums—are guided by Buddhist teacher Joanna Macy through
a "Despair and Empowerment" workshop. In this training, they begin with
individual and group exercises and rituals exploring the pain and suffering that they feel in relation to "the world." The onset of war brings up
rage, despair, fear, and loneliness, as well as love and hope. The war also
stimulates awareness of related pains—of ecological degradation, racism,
and the more individual suffering of abuse, loneliness, or isolation. In one
ritual, wailing, cries of anger and despair, affirmations of concern and
compassion, and attempts to understand are received by the group in silent mindfulness. The participants are then guided to see how their very
ability to feel the "pain of the world" suggests a caring and wider perspective beyond that of the separate and isolated self. Cultivating this wider

perspective, in part through modifications of traditional Buddhist practices, they find resources to help themselves not to be so easily overwhelmed or paralyzed by such powerful events, and to more readily act,
however they choose, out of wisdom and compassion, rather than out of
reactivity.[1]

It is July 1993, in New York City. A retreat has been organized by Bernard
Tetsugen Glassman Sensei (now Rōshi), a Dharma heir of the late Maezumi
Rōshi. Glassman, the abbot of the Zen Community of New York, has had a
particular interest in responding to the needs of homeless persons. He has
founded the Greyston Mandala in Yonkers, New York, a complex of activities, including: a bakery, which has trained more than two hundred chronically homeless persons and provides over forty persons with jobs; Greyston
Family Inn, which has built permanent housing and provides support services for homeless families; and several other projects related to providing
AIDS care, employment for chronically unemployed women, and the development of interfaith alliances. The ten persons participating in this
"street retreat" with Glassman Sensei are "practicing" for five days while
living on the streets of Manhattan without places to sleep or changes of
clothes. In preparation, participants have been asked to raise $1,000 for
each day of the retreat, with the funds to be given to organizations helping
the homeless. They then have walked together into the streets, with only
their clothes and minimal possessions, social security cards in case they are
arrested, and a few dollars. They eat at soup kitchens, walk continually, visit
shantytowns under bridges, share the life of the street with the homeless,
learn survival skills, are asked for money and themselves panhandle, and
get sick and dehydrated. They also practice *zazen* twice a day, conduct a
service for hungry ghosts, and closely investigate desire, fear, self-image,
and some of the root causes of homelessness. To some extent, they then
know from the "inside" what it is to be homeless and have transformed
their relationship to the homeless.[2]

These two vignettes offer glimpses of the growing phenomenon (some
would even say "movement") of socially engaged Buddhism in North America. With often close links to recent Asian developments (as well as to like-
minded persons in Europe), socially engaged Buddhists in North America,
many with roots in the activism of the 1960s, have attempted to explore
what it would mean to bring together social, political, economic, and ecological concerns with traditional Buddhist practice. Out of such explorations have come several innovative (yet usually traditionally based) practices, activities, and ideas, sometimes about the very meaning of what it is
to be Buddhist in North America. The influence of socially engaged Buddhist perspectives and projects is evident both generally in many North
American Buddhist centers and communities (especially those that are
primarily Euro-American), and in the work of organizations such as the

Buddhist Peace Fellowship (BPF) and the Bangkok-based International Network of Engaged Buddhists (INEB).

In this essay, I would like to offer an analysis of the nature of socially engaged Buddhism, with particular emphasis on its North American versions. I first speak about the very idea of "engaged Buddhism," identifying two basic meanings of the idea, one a more specific sense having to do with *social action,* and one a more general sense having to do with bringing Buddhism into *everyday life.* I then interpret socially engaged Buddhism in this first sense as an innovative extension of traditional Buddhist training and practice in ethics, meditation, and wisdom. I also attempt to place socially engaged Buddhism in the contemporary North American historical and cultural setting, identifying what I believe to be its great contemporary promise as a visionary yet practical response to the suffering and potential enlightenment of our times. Finally, I point out what I take to be some of the main contemporary challenges and possible directions of development for socially engaged Buddhism, if it is to meet such promise.

The Idea of an Engaged Buddhism

Two Aspects of the Term

Socially Engaged Buddhism. A first sense of the term, often identified when one speaks of "*socially* engaged Buddhism," has come to cover a broad range of approaches, unified by the notion that Buddhist teachings and practices can be directly applied to participation in the social, political, economic, and ecological affairs of the nonmonastic world. (It is this sense of the term that is the main focus of this essay.) Speaking of his experiences in Vietnam, Thich Nhat Hanh, the contemporary Vietnamese teacher and poet, identifies this first, more activist sense of engaged Buddhism:

> When I was in Vietnam, so many of our villages were being bombed. Along with my monastic brothers and sisters, I had to decide what to do. Should we continue to practice in our monasteries, or should we leave the meditation halls in order to help the people who were suffering under the bombs? After careful reflection, we decided to do both—to go out and help people and to do so in mindfulness. We called it engaged Buddhism. Mindfulness must be engaged. Once there is seeing, there must be acting. . . . We must be aware of the real problems of the world. Then, with mindfulness, we will know what to do and what not to do to be of help.[3]

Used in this way, the term implies a critique of some Buddhists as "disengaged" from involvement with these concerns. Such a critique points to the dangers that Buddhists may, contrary to the deeper intentions of the tradition, become self-absorbed, complacent about others' suffering, and cut off in terms of both inner response and often physical proximity from the "cries of the world." (This is not to say that disengagement in terms of proximity and apparent action necessarily falls prey to these dangers.) It also suggests a willingness in many cases to enter into types of social service and social action that traditionally have not been understood as part of Buddhist practice.

In Asia, for example, socially engaged Buddhists have responded to violence in Sri Lanka and Cambodia with peace walks, dialogue, and nonviolence trainings.[4] They have formed resistance and reconciliation movements in the midst of war and/or oppression in Vietnam, Tibet, Burma, and the Chittagong Hill Tracts of Bangladesh.[5] In Sri Lanka, the Sarvodaya Shramadana Movement, a massive network of village-based community development activists led by Dr. A. T. Ariyaratne, has for nearly forty years linked personal and social liberation.[6] In Thailand, the so-called development monks have emphasized grassroots activism, community development, and alternative economic forms, such as local "buffalo banks."[7] Thai monks have also led local movements against ecological devastation, with some monks ordaining trees to protect them from logging.[8] In India, a movement for a "Dhamma Revolution" among the "ex-Untouchables" has brought together education and social welfare projects in many urban areas.[9] Activists and writers such as Sulak Sivaraksa of Thailand and the Swedish-born Helena Norberg-Hodge, based in Ladakh and England, have articulated penetrating critiques of the prevailing Western models of "development" and globalization offering alternative Buddhist-based models.[10] Chatsumarn Kabilsingh of Thailand, along with the Sakyadhita international organization of Buddhist women, has brought up issues concerning the status of women in Theravāda Buddhism, particularly working for the reinstitution of full ordination for women as nuns (*bhikkhuṇī*).[11]

In the West, to give some further examples, socially engaged Buddhists have worked on human rights issues, especially concerning Asian countries such as Tibet, Burma, and Cambodia, but also have safeguarded the lives of human rights activists in Central America.[12] They have brought a Buddhist presence to the movement seeking the control and eventual abolition of nuclear weapons, regularly joining protests at the Nevada Test Site. They have also participated in various other movements, protests, and activities—antiwar, antiviolence, and environmental, among others. Joanna Macy and many of her colleagues have developed the Nuclear Guardianship Project for the responsible care of radioactive waste.[13] Several socially engaged Buddhists have formed an Interracial Buddhist Council, with discussion groups, days of meditation, and workshops. Some, such as the English *vipassanā* teacher Christopher Titmuss, who has twice run as Green Party candidate for Parliament, have entered the political process.[14] There have been numerous meetings and conferences of Buddhist women, concerned especially with the patriarchal strands of Buddhist teachings and organizations, the revisioning of Buddhist practices, and sensitivity to gender issues in Buddhist communities.[15] Socially engaged Buddhists have also, in organized ways, brought Buddhist teachings to prisons, and worked as tutors with children in poor communities.[16] The Zen Center of San Francisco has for many years run a hospice and trained numerous volunteers. The Reverend Suhita Dharma in Richmond, California, has developed a center for people with AIDS, complementing a Zen AIDS Hospice in San Francisco.[17] Glassman Rōshi, as we have seen, has founded a bakery and other enterprises employing homeless persons, as well as several projects providing services for persons with AIDS, and for the homeless and chronically unemployed, that collectively represent a significant response to social problems in the Yonkers, New York, area.[18]

The main socially engaged Buddhist organization in North America, the Buddhist Peace Fellowship, was founded in 1978 in Hawaii by Robert Aitken and Anne Aitken, Nelson Foster, and several others.[19] Their intention, reflected in the mission statement, was "to bring a Buddhist perspective to the peace movement, and to bring the peace movement to the Buddhist community." The current mission emphasizes as well Buddhist nonviolence and the protection of all beings; the importance of environmental, feminist, and social justice, as well as peace concerns; and the need for dialogue and exchange between varied Buddhist *sanghas* in America and globally.

The BPF at the moment is guided by a fifteen-person board of directors and by an international advisory board, which includes as members many of the most prominent socially engaged Buddhists, such as Robert Aitken Rōshi; A. T. Ariyaratne, the founder of the Sarvodaya movement in Sri Lanka; Pema Chödrön, an American-born Tibetan Buddhist nun and abbess of Gampo Abbey in Canada; Christina Feldman, writer, meditation teacher, and cofounder of Gaia House in England; Mahā Ghosananda, currently serving as the main Buddhist leader of Cambodia; Lodi Gyari, an activist on issues concerned with Tibet; Mamoru Kato, who works with the Japanese section of the INEB; Joanna Macy; Thich Nhat Hanh; Sulak Sivaraksa; the poet and activist Gary Snyder; and Christopher Titmuss. Ghosananda, Nhat Hanh, and Sivaraksa have all been nominated for the Nobel Peace Prize. The national office is in Berkeley, California, with a full-time national coordinator, Alan Senauke, and several part-time staff members, including Susan Moon, the editor of the quarterly journal *Turning Wheel*. There are some four thousand members, many of them organized in seventeen decentralized chapters across the United States. The chapters, generally meeting semiregularly, may be involved in particular local, national, and international projects, and may serve as discussion and support groups.

Out of this office have come several varied international and domestic projects. In the last few years, for example, there has been ongoing work on human rights issues, particularly in Asia (Tibet, Burma, Sri Lanka, the Chittagong Hill Tracts, Cambodia, and so on). Financial support has been generated for several service projects in Asia, for example, funding medical teams for displaced Burmese, making loans for projects in Tibetan exile communities, and aiding Tibetan children in refugee camps. Starting in 1995, the BPF has organized six-month training programs for people working in social service or social action (the Buddhist Alliance for Social Engagement, or BASE). There has been cooperation with other like-minded groups on events and programs to control nuclear weapons, land mines, and community violence. Workshops and town meetings have been organized on Buddhist approaches to such themes as nonviolence, conflict resolution, education, group dynamics, Buddhist economics, and the abuse of power in spiritual communities. Three four-to-six-day summer intensives in socially engaged Buddhism have occurred since 1991, each attended by between 100 and 150 people. The BPF has also coordinated, as an ecumenical Buddhist organization, a network of teachers and support materials having to do with issues of ethics and the abuse of power for Buddhist individuals and communities raising these concerns. The national office also has close connections with groups of socially engaged Buddhists in Asia and Europe, especially through participation in the yearly INEB meetings in Thailand, and affiliations with American Buddhist groups that are working on questions such as those of race, sexual orientation, and aging.[20]

It should be said, however, that the term *engaged Buddhism*, as used both in Asia and in North America (and Europe), usually implicitly refers to movements and activities guided by "liberal" or "progressive" values (such as justice, democracy, human rights, ecological balance or sustainability, and so on). The common (and certainly provocative) assumption seems to be that these latter values somehow fit better than more "right-wing" values with Buddhism as such. Some, such as Ken Jones in *The Social Face of Buddhism*, have attempted to make such assumptions explicit and to justify them. At this point in the evolution of North American Buddhism, however, there are no prominent politically "conservative" Buddhist public voices and movements, and no clear criticisms of "left-wing" socially engaged Buddhism, that is, nothing like the controversies that exist within the Christian and Jewish worlds. Nonetheless, assumptions that Buddhist values easily or naturally align with current "progressive" values need to be critically examined; there are many dangers of an uncritical acceptance of such assumptions. In the Asian context, for example, some of the apparent

examples of Buddhist social "engagement" in the last two thousand years
have been linked to military aggression and nationalism.[21] Arguably, one
of the most prominent twentieth-century examples of Buddhist social and
political engagement has been the more right-wing involvement of Japanese Buddhism in Japanese militarism and aggression.[22]

Engagement in Everyday Life. While the predominant use of the term *engaged
Buddhism* (and the main focus of this essay) has to do with this first, more
activist sense of the term, there is also a *second*, more general sense of
engaged Buddhism. In this second, related usage, Buddhism is to be brought
into life "in the world" in *all* its aspects, including the everyday contexts of
families, interpersonal relationships, communities, and work. From this
perspective, everything we do is potentially an act of engaged Buddhism.
Thich Nhat Hanh stresses the continuity of this sense of engaged Buddhism
with traditional Buddhism:

> How can we practice at the airport and in the market? That is engaged Buddhism.
> Engaged Buddhism does not only mean to use Buddhism to solve social and
> political problems, protesting against the bombs, and protesting against social
> injustice. First of all we have to bring Buddhism into our daily lives. . . . Do you
> practice breathing between phone calls? Do you practice smiling while cutting
> carrots?[23]

Elsewhere, Thich Nhat Hanh says, "Engaged Buddhism is just Buddhism.
If you practice Buddhism in your family, in society, it is engaged Buddhism."[24]

For many, this second sense of engaged Buddhism is particularly appropriate for Buddhists living and practicing "in the world" in North America.
As Buddhism has evolved in the West, for example, few Buddhist practitioners have become monks or nuns, or lived at retreat centers. Yet for
many, there has been an interest in bringing aspects of Buddhist practice
into their daily lives with something of the intensity found in monastic or
retreat experiences. Questions are often raised about the appropriateness
of importing the sometimes strict distinction between monastic and lay
practitioners (and often the higher valuation of the former) often found
in Asia. Likewise, there is frequently an awareness of the common danger
that formal spiritual practice may be disconnected from the rest of life, that
spiritual intentions and intensity may be confined to the meditation cushion or retreat experience.

Using the term *engaged Buddhism* in this second sense, however, does not
necessarily imply an interest in or involvement in social service or social
action. Using the phrase in this way, while clearly pointing to important
needs, thus arguably runs the risk of conflating important distinctions between different aspects of engaged Buddhism, as well as being so general

as to be of dubious value (if authentic Buddhism is already "engaged"). Indeed, many Buddhists who wholeheartedly practice "in the world" do not call themselves "engaged" Buddhists.

The Genealogy of "Engaged Buddhism"

In this context, an understanding of the genealogy of the term *engaged Buddhism* can shed some light on these two basic meanings of the term. As far as I know, the actual term *engaged Buddhism* surfaced in the West primarily through the work of Thich Nhat Hanh and as a translation from French words like *engagé* and *l'engagement* (even if the general phenomenon identified by the term occurred in many other Asian countries).[25] These were central terms in French intellectual and political discourse of the postwar period, and especially linked to core existentialist concepts, particularly those of Jean-Paul Sartre. For the Sartre of *Being and Nothingness* (published in 1943), to be "engaged" is to actualize one's freedom by both acknowledging one's inescapable involvement in the world and deliberately and explicitly making commitments.

Presumably Nhat Hanh was choosing an appropriate French (and later English) term to convey what was actually a more complex and differentiated set of at least three Vietnamese terms and Buddhist social movements that emphasized, respectively, awareness in daily life, social service, and social activism. Identifying these different emphases helps us to conceptualize the different aspects of engaged Buddhism and to ask about their interrelationships.

Initially, starting in the early 1950s in Vietnam, there was an effort among some in the Buddhist community to make Buddhism more accessible and practical in the daily lives of those outside of the monasteries. The word used for this movement was *Nhân Gian* (Buddhism for everybody) and the focus was in cultivating awareness in daily life. In the late 1950s and early 1960s, however, a term with a more social tone, *Nhâp Thê'* (going into the world), was used, often with an emphasis on social service, education, and charity work. A third movement, *Dâ'n Thân* (getting involved), dated from 1963 and the closing of the Buddhist churches by the government, and was connected with more explicit activism. Some of the adherents of this movement even ran for political office, although the main focus was on issues of freedom, social justice, repression, and an end to the war. This activism was combined with the emphases of the first two movements; that is, it was based in applying Buddhism to daily life and often connected with social service, particularly the setting up of schools.[26]

The Vietnamese history thus makes clearer a way of relating the two emphases in engaged Buddhism. Here, the more activist approach rests on the foundation of daily practices and community (or *sangha*), and in large part depends upon them for its efficacy. Likewise, efforts to bring awareness and wisdom into relationships, families, communities, and work, while not always issuing in explicit efforts at social change or social service, nonetheless may provide much of the foundation for institutional change and larger-scale responses to suffering.

A Revisioning of Traditional Buddhist Practice

Both the social action and daily life emphases in engaged Buddhism, in Asia and in the West, arguably reflect both continuity with Buddhist traditions and significant innovation. One way to highlight such continuity and innovation is to interpret socially engaged Buddhism as a revisioning of the traditional Buddhist model of a threefold training in ethics (*śīla*), meditation (*samādhi*), and wisdom (*prajñā*).[27]

Ethics

While grounding themselves explicitly in traditional models of *śīla*, many socially engaged Buddhists have also attempted to develop a social ethics. They have extended the meaning of Buddhist precepts beyond their usual sense of being limited to personal and face-to-face relationships; this traditional interpretation, to be sure, may have been more suitable in much simpler, agrarian societies. For example, the precept concerning killing (expressed in its Theravādin form as "I undertake the precept to abstain from the taking of life") has become in Thich Nhat Hanh's version: "Do not kill. Do not let others kill. Find whatever means possible to protect life and prevent war."[28] Robert Aitken interprets the first precept by noting the collective harming and killing committed by governments as well as the ways in which we are harming or killing the beings of the natural world through soil depletion, clear-cutting, laboratory testing, and pollution. He writes that "politics in our day of nuclear overkill is a matter of ignoring the First Precept or acting upon it."[29]

Sulak Sivaraksa comments on the second Theravādin precept, concerning refraining from stealing, by noting our participation in social, economic, and political systems that often condition more complex forms of stealing: "We may not literally steal in our face-to-face interactions, but do we allow the rich countries to exploit the poor countries through the workings of the international banking system and the international economic order? Do we allow industrial societies to exploit agrarian societies? The First World to exploit the Third World? The rich to exploit the poor generally?"[30] Sivaraksa links the third precept concerning improper sexuality with broader consideration of conditioning about gender and sexuality,

male domination, and the exploitation of women, particularly through images, as in advertising and the media, that promote sexism, lust, and greed.
In like manner, Ken Jones speaks about some of the complexities of "right
speech" in the context of power issues and communication difficulties in
organizations and public discourse, massive amounts of information (and
sometimes disinformation), propaganda, advertising, and censorship.[31]

Interpreting the precepts in these ways helps ground in traditional teachings various kinds of social interventions, whether responding to tyrannical
regimes; to conditions of war, violence, and extreme suffering; or to some
of the systemic roots of suffering in contemporary societies. It also guides
attempts to develop more spiritually based institutions and communities.
What is innovative is thus both the wider perspective on what is ethically
meaningful, in the context of contemporary social realities, and the imperative to act in a series of contexts that are, at least from the point of
view of traditional Buddhist practice, relatively new and unexplored.

Historically, of course, Buddhists have been ambivalent about such interventions. The Buddha was clearly concerned about the conditions that
lead to social peace, justice, and harmony. He counseled kings, and apparently intervened several times to prevent wars. Yet he also prohibited his
monks and nuns from any contact with "political" affairs having to do with
kings and power. Indeed, most scholars maintain that the Buddha took no
systematic interest in the transformation of the "political" realm as such.[32]
Later Buddhists often moderated this separation of "spiritual" and "political" spheres, as in the case of the great Buddhist ruler Aśoka and, sometimes less happily, in the case of many alliances between Buddhists and
rulers over the centuries. Nonetheless, there has remained up to the present, both in Asia and in the West, considerable ambiguity about whether
social and political involvements represent appropriate Buddhist activities.
In this context, socially engaged Buddhists are taking the clear stand that
certain kinds of interventions are not only acceptable but also often the
wisest and most compassionate responses possible. To be sure, the wider
institutional interventions and applications of social ethics to public policy
issues of North American engaged Buddhists remain largely preliminary,
especially in comparison to some of the work both of Asian engaged Buddhists and North American Christian and Jewish groups.

Meditative Practice

The traditional practice of meditation has also been foundational and
yet further extended by socially engaged Buddhists (and by many other
Buddhists who have not called themselves "engaged"). While finding
traditional formal daily practice, weekly or monthly days of practice, and
periodic retreats an essential basis for practice in the world, many have also

brought a sense of meditative practice into the varied aspects of contemporary Western life. Indeed, there are often poetic passages in texts by authors such as Aitken Rōshi, Joko Beck, Jon Kabat-Zinn, and Thich Nhat Hanh, among others, invoking a meditative spirit in such activities as driving, going to meetings, taking a bath, cleaning the stove, answering the telephone, and changing diapers.[33]

Others have also extended a sense of meditative practice into interpersonal relations, families, communities, and work. Such writers as Stephen and Ondrea Levine and John Welwood have focused on intimate personal relationships as a path of practice and suggested numerous concrete practices, in part derived from traditional Buddhist practices.[34] Exploring and developing new practices for life in contemporary Western families, communities, and work has also been central to many socially engaged Buddhists.[35] The Marin County, California, chapter of the BPF, for example, has for many years organized family practice days.

Socially engaged Buddhists have also explored bringing meditative awareness into the arenas of social service and social change, both in traditional and more innovative ways. Through the cultivation of mindfulness in work, the development of special practices in particular areas of service (such as working with the dying and aging), the organization of small support groups (as in the Zen Hospice program and the BPF BASE program), or retreats such as the "Street Retreat" organized by Glassman Rōshi, service work can more readily become a field of meditative practice.[36] Joanna Macy and many of her colleagues have developed innovative exercises and workshops, mentioned at the beginning of this essay, in which mindfulness is brought into what she calls the "pain for the world" (anger, rage, despair, sadness, fear, and so on). Given attention and public space, such pain may be transformed by the traditional tools of awareness, compassion, and wisdom, often articulated in more contemporary ways.

Some Buddhists have developed exercises and practices in relation to the environment. Stephanie Kaza, an environmental studies teacher and writer at the University of Vermont and past president of the BPF, found, in her sustained practice of "conversations with trees," a progression in her relationship with trees. From a beginning mindfulness and awareness of trees, there was then a movement through to a greater sense of the complex histories and webs of human-tree interactions, leading to openings of heart and mind to suffering and a sense of interconnection, and, finally, an impetus to social action born of insight into mutual causality.[37] The Ring of Bone Zendo in California, following a conception of Gary Snyder, has over the last fifteen years organized "Mountain and Rivers Sesshin," combining backpacking, a sense of pilgrimage, and formal intensive meditation practice.[38]

What is distinctive about these approaches is not only the extension of traditional practices into new contexts and, further, the development of new types of meditative practices within these contexts. There is also often the exploration of more *relational* modes of practice. For example, many of the exercises and practices mentioned earlier are carried out in dyads and small groups, rather than by the individual, as in the work of the Levines and Joanna Macy's "Despair and Empowerment" workshops. A relational model can be seen as more "feminine" and contrasted with a more "masculine" model of the spiritual practice of the heroic individual, who begins in separation, and comes to know the relationality of things only on reaching spiritual maturity.[39]

In the BPF BASE program, to give another example, there has been a special emphasis on group process, on the relationships within the group and the development of the group in intimacy, trust, intensity, and balance.[40] Although the usual Buddhist model of the cultivation of individual awareness remains foundational, there is a somewhat different model of practice, in which interaction with others in the group is also a fundamental aspect of practice. Such group work may uncover aspects of greed, hatred, and ignorance (as well as generosity, love, and wisdom) that may not be accessible through individual formal practice, even within a community. This reflects the insight, often noted by contemporary Western meditation teachers, that some Buddhists may find individual practice a way to flee from fears and confusion that become very evident in relational settings. Long-term practice and even high levels of spiritual insight can coexist with unresolved issues on a relational or social level.[41]

Wisdom

Socially engaged Buddhists have also begun to expand traditional notions of wisdom, particularly in articulating principles and analyses that might guide activity in the social spheres. I want to identify briefly four principles, which can be reconstructed from socially engaged Buddhist writings and practices, as well as some of the beginning attempts at Buddhist social analyses.

A first principle is that the "inner" (the more personal, private, and subjective) and the "outer" (the more social, public, and systemic) are very closely linked. For example, we cannot easily separate our supposedly personal pain from the more "social" or even "global" pain related to social issues and problems. As Christopher Titmuss observes: "Some people experience inside of themselves what they conceive of as being the pain of the world, but in a way it's the pain of themselves. There are others who experience inside of themselves what they conceive of as being purely personal pain. In a way, it's the pain of the world."[42] Santikaro Bhikkhu, a North American–born senior student of the late Buddhadāsa Bhikkhu of

Thailand, roots a concern with *both* personal suffering and others' suffering in traditional teachings. He claims that it is a misinterpretation of the Buddha's teaching about *duḥkha* (suffering) to focus primarily on "my" *duḥkha* or "your" *duḥkha*. The Buddha's injunction was to see, understand, and respond to *duḥkha* as such; the First Noble Truth is simply that there is *duḥkha*. For Santikaro, this teaching is misunderstood if I focus on "my" *duḥkha* and remain oblivious to or unconcerned with the massive suffering all around me, or if I see only "your" or "their" suffering, and do not recognize the deep-seated *duḥkha* within.[43]

In the work of socially engaged Buddhists such as Joanna Macy and Thich Nhat Hanh, among others, connections are explicitly made between the personal and social dimensions of suffering, as well as between more "inner" and more "outer" transformative practices. The development of a social ethics, as we have seen, also helps bring out this sense of a more dialectical relation between individual experience and the workings of larger systems. Tendencies to greed, hatred, and ignorance (or generosity, loving-kindness, and wisdom) might be more easily seen as closely linked to the systemic manifestations of these tendencies in the world, both as cause and effect. Santikaro, for example, has attempted to show how greed, anger, hatred, lust, and delusion are expressed through (and in turn condition) particular institutions (such as in capitalist economics, the armed forces, the entertainment industry, and schools) and ideologies (such as racism, sexism, consumerism, militarism, and nationalism).[44]

A second, related principle is that of "coresponsibility" with others for the state of affairs. Problems cannot easily be attributed only to others, to those who are "evil" or "bad," whether they be a ruling class, politicians, or members of different ethnic groups. We cannot so easily, if we look deeply and openly, separate ourselves from others (who are suffering or who are causing suffering). All beings share the roots of greed, hatred, and delusion. Through accessing one's "shadow" in a variety of ways, particularly through meditation, study, and inquiry in group work, there may be a taking back of the tendency to project evil and the roots of violence outwardly, while simultaneously not simplistically equating all persons as identically responsible.

Many socially engaged Buddhists in North America have developed practices and projects that mitigate such tendencies to polarize "*our* good" and "*their* evil." The writer and poet Deena Metzger, based in the Los Angeles area, has developed imaginative techniques to help uncover the ways that the structure of our psyches, even among those who call themselves democratic or antiauthoritarian, commonly mirrors often oppressive social structures; in one exercise, for example, she asks participants to describe their inner experience as if it were a society, replete with political philosophies, police, and class stratification.[45] Gene Knudsen-Hoffman, a long-time activist and writer from Santa Barbara, and David Grant, a former BPF board member and former organizer of the "Listening Project" in North Carolina, have stressed the importance of compassionate and impartial listening for depolarizing a situation. They and others have brought such an approach into the international arena through visits to Libya, Central America, the former Yugoslavia, and Africa, arguably with relatively small but significant impact in many cases.[46]

A third principle, shared with other nonviolent traditions, is that of linking means and ends. The means *are* in a deep sense the ends. As Thich Nhat Hanh says, "Peace is every step," or as A. J. Muste said once, "There is no way to peace. Peace is the way." Here, the key is to be nonviolent or peaceful at the same time as one is working for these ends, and to avoid the very common tendency among social activists to separate means and ends. Nhat Hanh, for example, has questioned the efficacy of movements for change rooted in anger and hatred, even if they are nonviolent in terms of overt tactics.

A final principle is that the long-term vision of social action and transformation is that of reaching reconciliation rather than defeating an opponent. Violence, for example, is not so much to be addressed by banishing those who are most outwardly violent from the society, but rather in healing and transforming the roots of violence, helping to bring those who are violent back into the society. Several socially engaged Buddhists have attempted to develop Buddhist-based approaches to "conflict resolution" and reconciliation, and trainings have been organized by INEB in many countries of South and Southeast Asia.[47] Thich Nhat Hanh, inspired by traditional monastic practices of resolving conflicts, has developed what he calls a "Peace Treaty" for Buddhist communities, similar in many ways to a grievance policy enacted at the San Francisco Zen Center.[48] Paula Green, a long-time BPF board member, psychotherapist, activist, and nonviolence trainer based in Massachusetts, has focused on reconciliation by guiding a convocation at Auschwitz in 1995, with participation including Jews and non-Jewish Germans, and leading nonviolence workshops in the former Yugoslavia, Israel, and Rwanda.[49]

In workshops, retreats, and writings, some socially engaged Buddhists have also used basic Buddhist teachings as analytic tools with which to understand social problems. Santikaro Bhikkhu, following the lead of his teacher, Buddhadāsa Bhikkhu, has given many workshops with varied groups in Asia and North America, applying the Buddha's basic teachings to various social issues and experiences. He has particularly emphasized the value of applying as analytic tools the teachings of the Four Noble Truths and dependent arising (*pratītya-samutpāda*); the latter is reportedly the fruit of the Buddha's enlightenment and helps to clarify the ways in which ignorance, coupled with the basic structure of human experience, leads to grasping and the perpetuation of suffering and continual rebirth, in both individual and social contexts. Stephanie Kaza has explored using the teachings of emptiness (*śūnyatā*) and dependent arising as the basis for environmental ethics.[50] Others have attempted to use Buddhist teachings as a basis for developing analyses of the "good" (or "Dharmic") society. Buddhadāsa Bhikkhu for many years taught and wrote of "dhammic" socialism.[51] Other writers have attempted to develop analyses of the nature of the just ruler, Buddhist economics, and Buddhist education.[52]

The Contemporary Promise of Socially Engaged Buddhism

These expansions of Buddhist practices and teachings, many of which have been initially developed in Asian settings, have found an enthusiastic reception in North America among many "Euro-American" and some "ethnic" (particularly Vietnamese) Buddhists, as well as attracting many non-Buddhists concerned with social issues. For a significant number of Buddhists who had earlier been politicized through the various social movements of the 1960s and 1970s (civil rights, antiwar, ecological, women's, gay and lesbian), socially engaged Buddhism offers a potentially powerful integration of the different aspects of life in contemporary America. It makes available to many activists an approach in which spirituality is not set off in a polarized way against social action and involvement. This kind of integration, although presently touching relatively few persons, may well be of tremendous importance to our society.

Indeed, the visions and practices of socially engaged Buddhism may play a very significant role in helping to develop spiritual responses to some of the main suffering and healing potentials of our times. As the Christian activist and editor of *Sojourners* Jim Wallis suggests:

> Our intuition tells us the depth of the crisis we face demands more than politics as usual. An illness of the spirit has spread across the land, and our greatest need is for what our religious traditions call "the healing of the nations." . . . Most of the social, economic, and political issues we now face have a spiritual core. . . . *We can find common ground only by moving to higher ground.* . . . Spiritual values must enter the public sphere.[53]

In this context, socially engaged Buddhism is one of the main vehicles of nonregressive spiritual response to the crises of our times.[54] Other nonregressive contemporary resources for socially engaged spirituality can be drawn from many interpretations of the following approaches: the nonviolence of Gandhi, King, Merton, and other Hindu, Christian, and Islamic traditions; liberation theology and other biblical prophetic traditions;

feminist reworkings of traditional religions and "paganism"; ecologically grounded spirituality, often related to indigenous traditions; and attempts to link humanistic and transpersonal psychology to social action.[55] What socially engaged Buddhists can contribute both to the wider resources of socially engaged spirituality in general and as a response to the suffering of our times is, I would argue, especially a sense of *socially engaged spiritual practice*. In the last section, I will explore this further.

One way to clarify the potential contributions of these forms of socially engaged spirituality, including socially engaged Buddhism, is by showing how they can be analyzed as offering part of a powerful response to the core structural problems of modernity. Here, I want to interpret modernity as the movement, emerging in the sixteenth and seventeenth centuries in Western Europe and North America, associated with the development of the empirical sciences, capitalism and industrialism, political democracies and individualism, and secularization. Modernity can be understood, following Weber and Habermas, as a process by which the relatively integrated medieval religious framework gave way to a differentiation of separate spheres, notably the separation of the empirical sciences and technological applications from values and subjectivity. With modernity and secularization, religion and spirituality have increasingly been generally either eliminated (as suitable for the dustbin of history, for example, as dogmatic theology and metaphysics) or marginalized (as private and subjective, separate from the public worlds where truth, justice, and public policies are decided).[56]

In our late modern (some say postmodern) context, there have been strong tendencies, in the Western reception of Buddhism, to interpret it within such a modern framework. Buddhist practice has commonly been interpreted as primarily inner, private, and subjective, organized around the individual quest for realization. Community life is often fit into the model of churches and congregations, meeting on weekends and at holidays. In terms of the three aspects of Buddhist training, there has been (outside of Asian American Buddhist communities) often a de-emphasis on *śīla* and *prajñā*, and a central focus on *samādhi* and meditative training.[57]

Yet to interpret Buddhism in these ways, within the modern framework, does more than truncate Buddhism. It also fits Buddhism within a modern way of life at a time when the limits of the modern framework, as well as the limits of the particular ways that modernity has developed, have become more and more apparent. At the present time, there sounds a loud and well-known chorus of complaints about modernity from both the left and right. Great technical achievements and material abundance for many coexist with a growing fragmentation, lack of coherence, nihilism, and meaninglessness in people's lives. Much of the modern potential for democracy and heightened subjectivity has been eclipsed for the majority of the population by the control of resources by the wealthy, limited forms of instrumental thinking, routinized work, and the breakdown of families and communities. For some, modernity and many of its core concepts are all too closely linked with the domination of the earth, women, and indigenous peoples.

A socially engaged Buddhism (and other contemporary forms of socially engaged spirituality) can be understood as resisting (while learning from) the very modern structures into which much of Western Buddhism has often been fit. It offers potentially nonregressive ways to integrate spheres typically split off in a fragmented way from each other: private and public, personal and political, spiritual and social, inner and outer. In this way, forms of socially engaged spirituality may provide major alternatives, as they are further developed, to the increasingly attractive and potentially dangerous forms of regressive fundamentalism.

Socially engaged Buddhists usually do not have all of these issues and analyses in mind, but I think that the kind of vision that I have suggested is indeed the intuitive horizon of many socially engaged Buddhists. In other words, a new kind of world, another kind of "new world order," is implicitly being invoked when there are attempts to link inner and outer work, the private and public spheres, means and ends, meditation and social action, or compassion and social systems.

The Challenges of Socially Engaged Buddhism

Whatever the power of such a long-term vision for socially engaged Buddhists, developing the appropriate forms and practices and living this vision is clearly a great challenge. I want in this last section to indicate three important horizons for the continued development of socially engaged Buddhism. In brief, I would say that the further blossoming of socially engaged Buddhism is particularly dependent on cultivating a more sophisticated Buddhist social analysis, clearer and more grounded practical action strategies, and a fuller sense of socially engaged Buddhist spiritual practices.

Buddhist Social Analysis

Among socially engaged Buddhists, both in America and worldwide, there is considerable consensus about the need for spiritually based analyses of contemporary institutions and systems (social, political, economic, ecological, and so on). Such analyses would integrate the best of contemporary social theories and practices, developing something like a Buddhist "liberation theology." These analyses are important in order to clarify contemporary trends so as to act strategically on a large scale and in alliance with others. They are also crucial in terms of understanding how various systems influence consciousness and action; how, for example, systems of race, class, and gender operate; or how North Americans are affected by their participation in an international economic system in which many are privileged, but many are also impoverished.

Generally, the focus among many socially engaged Buddhists, such as Thich Nhat Hanh and Joanna Macy, has often been more on the "inner responses" to social and ecological events and states of affairs, on developing wider understandings of Buddhist ethical precepts, and on forming a host of contemporarily applicable individual and group transformative practices. There has been little collective transformation at the levels of institutions. Not surprisingly, there have also been only some very preliminary and general social analyses articulated, for instance, in the works of writers such as Ken Jones, Sulak Sivaraksa, Rita Gross, Stephanie Kaza, Kenneth Kraft, and Santikaro Bhikkhu.

Such Buddhist social analyses might be further developed in two main ways. First, basic Buddhist teachings can be extended to economic, social, political, educational, and ecological domains. What do the Four Noble Truths mean in looking at some of the roots of suffering in our society? How, for example, might Buddhist psychology be used to understand the roots of the increasing contemporary violence in our society? How might the teaching of dependent arising be broadened to make sense of the various social systems that support compulsive desire, grasping, and the sense of a separate self? How might the model of the "perfections" (*pāramitās*) such as ethics, wisdom, meditative concentration, effort, and generosity help guide contemporary revisionings of educational systems? Second, we might integrate the best of contemporary social analyses within a largely Buddhist framework, while recognizing the limits of these theories. This use of social theory and practice might be analogous to the integration of spiritual and social perspectives in the work of many liberation theologians and political theologians, or in the writings of such religiously based American Christian and Jewish analysts as Cornel West, Rosemary Ruether, Jim Wallis, and Michael Lerner.[58] We might imagine a series of continuing "dialogues" between socially engaged Buddhists and progressive environmentalists, feminists, social and political theorists, and economists.

There promises to be considerably more energy devoted to such analyses. The International Network of Engaged Buddhists held a week-long conference titled "The Dhammic Society" in Thailand in February 1995, with some of the major representatives of socially engaged Buddhism worldwide present. Some of the main themes discussed in depth included the relation of socially engaged Buddhism to Buddhist tradition, the oppression of women, the breakdown of families and communities and the role of community as a locus for personal and social transformation, understanding exploitation and the development of a Buddhist economics, the nature of "structural violence," and Buddhist education.[59] A second conference in Japan in May 1997 initiated the "Think Sangha," dedicated to Buddhist social analysis and initially focused on consumerism.[60]

Practical Strategies

Part of the growing maturity of socially engaged Buddhism will necessarily involve greater sophistication not only about social systems, but also about strategy and social and political practice. How can socially engaged Buddhists respond to the major structural problems of North American society: to the growing violence and anomie; to racism, sexism, and other forms of discrimination and oppression; to the deterioration of many democratic institutions and the growing apathy of the population; to the increasing polarization of rich and poor both domestically and internationally; to the problems linked with the growing globalization and coordination of capitalist systems?

While many of the activities of socially engaged Buddhists mentioned in this essay represent responses to these issues, there is also a need for larger-scale strategies of transformation. Socially engaged Buddhists are presently far less organized and strategic than some of their Christian and Jewish counterparts—whether in terms of general social and political strategies, concrete interventions in particular institutions, or participation in public policy discussions. The work of Glassman Rōshi and his colleagues in addressing issues of homelessness marks a particularly instructive move in this direction, and resembles some of the larger scale work of Asian engaged Buddhists, such as the Sarvodaya movement in Sri Lanka, the Trailokya Bauddha Mahasangha Sahayaka Gana (TBMSG) movement in India, the School of Youth for Social Service founded by Thich Nhat Hanh and active in Vietnam in the 1960s and 1970s, and the various projects initiated by Sulak Sivaraksa in Thailand. Nonetheless, coalitions and much greater sharing with others with similar concerns and similar visions of a socially engaged spirituality seem important for the maturation and significant impact of socially engaged Buddhism in North America. The formation of various kinds of coalitions, communities, and practices seems imperative to provide a base for this rather immense work of addressing and transforming the suffering of America. Such a work is no doubt as demanding as that which is required of the traditional bodhisattva, who would save all sentient beings and fathom the unfathomable wisdom.

Socially Engaged Buddhist Spiritual Practices

Socially engaged Buddhists may profitably learn from and with followers of other traditions or approaches in developing spiritually based social analyses and strategies. However, it may be in making more available to the larger society a sense of socially engaged spiritual *practice* that socially engaged Buddhists will make their greatest contribution. In developing further and making more accessible the practices of ethics, meditation, and wisdom, socially engaged Buddhists can help respond to immediate suffering as well as to deeper structural problems, and complement the resources of other traditions and approaches.

There are two main but not necessarily competing models of the role of spiritual practice for socially engaged Buddhists. The first model is that of socially engaged Buddhism as an *application* of traditional practice to the social field, bringing what one has learned especially in formal practice, retreats, and periods in monasteries out "into the world." A second model is that of socially engaged Buddhism itself as a *path* of spiritual development. While traditional practices clearly play an important role in this second model, it is significantly through activity *in the world* that spiritual (and other) learning occurs. The differences between the models may be more a matter of emphasis. Most socially engaged Buddhists believe that some degree of inner peace and understanding is necessary before social action is meaningful and beneficial.

As we saw in the discussion of the socially engaged Buddhist revisioning of traditional practice, there is considerable interest in this second model. The question is whether the second model of socially engaged practice in the world can approximate the depth and focus of traditional training. What therefore needs particular attention, in my view, are the practices, teachings, and learning communities of socially engaged Buddhists, in order that they might develop sufficient transformative power. This is relevant both for those emphasizing daily-life practice and for those active socially. Few Westerners, after all, have the opportunity (or the inclination) for sustained traditional practice to an advanced level prior to social involvement. Given the lives that most Westerners (and most Buddhists) live, they will have to find their spiritual learning and maturation through their engagement in the world.

Of particular importance to making possible such socially engaged Buddhist practice is the development of communities of different kinds, especially given some of the difficult present conditions of North American societies. Socially engaged practice in the world, after all, occurs in the midst of the breakdown of traditional communities, little support for Buddhist practice, widespread isolation at work and at home, and a declining economic status for most. Such tendencies occur against the background of a culture of "hyperindividualism," materialism, consumerism, and selfishness. Without significant community support, it is very difficult to live daily life as spiritual practice, and harder still to respond to social suffering. Without a spiritual context, it is often much harder to avoid the "burnout" and "shutting down" typical of those in social service and social change work. In this context, the development of small groups, as in the BPF BASE program, may be a crucial foundation, resonating with many other historical exemplars such as the Christian "base communities," the European and American traditions of councils, collectives, and affinity groups, and women's "consciousness-raising" groups. Such groups may be at the heart of a socially engaged Buddhist revisioning of *sangha*, and a necessary container for transformative energies.

Epilogue: The Colors and Contours of American Buddhism

KENNETH K. TANAKA

T he study of Buddhism in America is still in its infancy. The essays in
this volume, however, have contributed to the drawing of an increasingly clear picture of the many faces of Buddhism in America at the
end of the twentieth century. While this picture is far from being fully clear
or reflective of all the Buddhist traditions, the colors and contours of these
faces are now coming into sharper focus. This epilogue describes some of
the main outlines of this emerging picture as reflected through five issues:
ethnicity, democratization, practice, engagement, and adaptation.[1]

Ethnicity

The issue of ethnicity refers to the recognition of two distinct and mutually
isolated brands of Buddhism practiced by groups composed largely of Asian
Americans, on one hand, and Euro-Americans, on the other (see the chapters by Fields and Imamura). The two groups are referred to by several
appellations, for example, ethnic, immigrant, Asian, and Asian American
for the former, and white, Caucasian, Western, Anglo, and Euro-American
or European American for the latter.

Ethnicity determines not only the composition of members but also the
activities of the groups. Ethnic temples serve not only the spiritual but also
the cultural and social needs of their members, particularly among the most
recent of the immigrant population. In contrast, most observers note that
the Euro-American groups focus primarily on the spiritual. We should, however, remain cautious about the underlying implication in these observations that regards ethnic groups as less spiritual. The cultural activities have
always played a vital part in Buddhist temples in Asia and were integrated
into the spiritual life of the communities. Perhaps, therefore, what is

required is a deeper analysis and a more nuanced understanding of these cultural and social activities for their connection to Buddhist spiritual meaning. Realizing the "hidden" treasure of these cultural expressions, some writers (see the chapters by Nattier and Fields) have suggested that Euro-American Buddhists reevaluate and even learn from the rich complex of cultural-religious heritage practiced in the ethnic temples.

This division has also contributed to the simmering debate concerning the question, Who represents true American Buddhism? Some Asian American Buddhists are offended at the suggestion that white Buddhists are the sole contributors to the creation of American Buddhism, while ethnic Buddhists are seen as having played virtually no role in it.[2] Such perception, in their view, ignores the contributions made by the Asian American Buddhists with much longer history, some entering their second century on American soil. What is often implied, according to Asian American critics, is that Buddhism becomes truly American only when white Americans become seriously involved. This form, then, is called "American Buddhism," distinguished from simply "Buddhism in America," as practiced by Asian American Buddhists.[3] Such a distinction was probably considered in the recent flurry of media mentioned in the Introduction, for virtually all of the coverage has focused on white American Buddhists.

While this division cannot be denied completely, perhaps, the reality is not as serious as reported. Certainly, no pervasive animosity is driving apart the two camps. The separation that we do witness is not due to any conscious effort to exclude the other but is more a natural tendency to gravitate to those with shared background and interests. Many groups, in both camps, find themselves preoccupied with concerns of their own, and still struggling economically and socially to be established. The recent immigrant groups are particularly vulnerable to economic and social pressures. The division may, thus, be practical and not ideological. When circumstances allow for greater interaction, there have been active regional Buddhist councils that include members of both groups in New York, Chicago, southern California, northern California, Seattle, and Hawaii.

Further, we may need to question the accuracy of the sharp dichotomy drawn between the two camps, for the membership patterns along racial lines are much more ambiguous and fluid within some of the Buddhist communities. The Soka Gakkai International in America (SGI-USA), for example, boasts an extremely diverse group that includes a high percentage of African Americans and Hispanics (see chapters by Hurst and Nattier). Within the Dharma Realm Buddhist Association, we witness an ironic situation in which Euro-American monks and nuns routinely give instructions to a largely Chinese American laity (see chapter by Chandler). Changes are evident also in the venerable Buddhist Churches of America, an institution long considered the bastion of ethnic Buddhism. In 1997, five of the sixty priests were European Americans, and at least one-fourth of the Dharma School students on Sundays were not of full Japanese American parentage, with even higher percentages in regions outside California.[4]

Democratization

Democratization refers to the more inclusive and egalitarian developments in Buddhist groups, which manifest in two forms. The first is the shift away from hierarchical to more egalitarian structures within the Buddhist tradition itself. The second form refers to the involvement of Buddhism in the promotion of the inclusive and egalitarian ideals in American society as evidenced, for example, in the feminist and gay-lesbian communities. As the ancient Buddhist institution is democratized, Buddhism concurrently engages in the democratization of American society.

The nonhierarchical trend is evident in the lay emphasis. The Buddhist groups in America are generally exhibiting a nonmonastic tendency that is tearing down the traditional divide between the monastic and the laity. This is due partly to the small number of practitioners aspiring to become monks or nuns. As a case in point, the ethnic Theravāda communities in America have produced very few monks from their membership (see Numrich). Among the Euro-American Mahāyāna traditions, most of the ordained teachers are married or are not required by their tradition to be celibate. This trend in America is no doubt influenced to some degree by the modern American religious climate in which celibacy is devalued as anachronistic or an unnecessary pious requirement. The privileged status and role of traditional monks meet growing resistance from the more democratically oriented laity who, for example, find it unacceptable that monks do not reciprocate their bows or that the hierarchical relationships automatically place all monks in spiritually superior status. These lay members are often no longer satisfied being simply material providers and passive beneficiaries of monks' transferred merits. Many are eager to practice the teachings themselves and are not satisfied being relegated to secondary status within the Buddhist community. Some, however, find this trend disconcerting and believe that it poses real dangers for the tradition (see Numrich).

Another manifestation of the democratization trend in America is the prominence of women. Not only do women make up a sizable percentage of membership but many of the teachers are women, particularly within the Euro-American groups. Half of the Vipassana teachers, for example, are women (see Frondsal). Even in the more structured institution of the Sōka Gakkai International, American women are taking vital leadership roles (see Hurst). This trend is further manifested in the San Francisco Zen

Center, one of the largest organizations in the country, which in February 1996 installed Blanche Hartman as abbess, to join the ranks of two other abbots.

The strong presence of women is in keeping with the feminist groups that have embraced Buddhism as their spiritual rallying point. Some observers of this development are intrigued by the feminist attraction to Buddhism, given its share of antifeminist rhetoric within the long tradition. Others, however, note the explicitly gender-free teachings of the Buddha that help feminists to overlook the misogynist rhetoric of patriarchal institutions. Perhaps a primary attraction for feminists lies not in doctrinal points but in practices, especially in the meditational insights that empower them in their dealings with the many forces that obstruct and challenge their progress.

The democratization trend was hastened, ironically, by a series of incidences and accusations of sexual misconduct that wracked some of the prominent teachers and groups, particularly during the 1980s and 1990s (see Gross). One outcome has been the questioning of the hierarchical and authoritarian nature of student-teacher relationships. Many groups have taken measures to redefine the protocols for student-teacher interactions as well as to institute democratic procedures such as the length and terms of office for teachers and other leadership personnel. Rita Gross's discussion of "natural hierarchy," for example, aspires to an institution that is neither authoritarian nor egalitarian. The calls for these institutional adjustments are matched increasingly by women's voices calling for women to take greater individual responsibilities in their dealings with their male teachers (see Gross).

Further, the inclusive message of American Buddhism has attracted a growing number of gay and lesbian practitioners. While Buddhist scriptures are not completely exempt from discriminatory messages toward homosexuality, they have not carried the same negative moral tone as espoused among some Christian groups. What is more important is that modern Buddhist groups have generally not generated the hateful and exclusive rhetoric that drove many of the gays and lesbians from these churches. As we will see later, beliefs in doctrine are less vital to these new converts to Buddhism, who find a greater measure of meaning in the practices and the power of mental cultivation in dealing with the struggles of social acceptance and individual identity (see Corless).

Practice

Practice in the form of meditation or chanting is, undoubtedly, the primary attraction for a large number of American converts who find these disciplines accessible, therapeutic, and empowering.[5] Chanting, for example, is the central practice among the Sōka Gakkai members, while meditation, particularly in its sitting form,[6] occupies the central role in the practices of Zen, Theravāda, and Tibetan traditions. It is not surprising, therefore, that these four branches of Buddhism are those that have attracted the bulk of the converts.

By their own admission, many of these converts see their Buddhist practices as providing a more concrete path than what was available in the religions of their childhood. Christianity and Judaism, for example, offered ample doctrine, but some people experienced a lack of clear, concrete discipline for realizing the espoused ideals. This sentiment is, perhaps, not unrelated to a growing number of people seeking personal experience over doctrinal belief. Buddhist practices, for many of the converts, are seen as highly accessible "spiritual technology" by which they are able to realize spirituality that had previously eluded them.

The centrality of practice is nowhere more evident than in the insight meditation movement, where *vipassanā* meditation practices overshadow other religious concerns such as rituals, devotion, and doctrine. The majority of its practitioners are drawn first and foremost to *vipassanā* meditation, but not necessarily to the teachings. In fact, for many, their self-identification as Buddhists may be faint or even absent (see Frondsal).

The interest in meditation is intimately connected to the affinity that Buddhist teachings have shown to Western psychotherapy. "With our minds, we make the world," begins a famous verse from the *Dhammapada*, attesting to the primacy of the mind. Buddhist meditators and scholastics, such as the Abhidharmists, delved deeply into the functions of the mind and described them in intricate detail, including the states of unhappiness, their roots, and the means to transcend them. These reasons, therefore, account for the disproportionately high percentage of Buddhist practitioners who are either therapists or in other mental health professions.

The parallels and affinities shared by Buddhist tradition and Western psychotherapy are drawn even closer together by the emerging social issues and themes in contemporary America. The growing interest in the issue of death and dying, abetted by media coverage of euthanasia and the right-to-die movements, has turned increasingly to Buddhist teachings and practices as vital resource. The popularity of Buddhist literature such as *The Tibetan Book of Living and Dying*[7] stems, in part, from its direct and skillful treatment of a subject that in America had been a social taboo of sorts or had received scant attention. Here, we see the case of a new religious tradition that is, perhaps, doctrinally less restricted and more willing to deal with the subject than is the dominant Christian tradition.

In the economic arena, employers are increasingly unable or unwilling to protect their workers, and lifetime employment is quickly becoming an anachronism. As company pensions are whittled away, individuals are increasingly expected to fend for themselves in their retirement. In the rapidly changing global economy, the individuals are pressed to be self-directed and self-reliant. In this environment, chanting and meditation help individuals to realize inner centering through mental clarity, enhanced energy, and spiritual well-being. When the surroundings become less reliable and hospitable, mental discipline helps individuals turn to their inner strength.

These salutary effects of spiritual cultivation have attracted especially those with a "wounded" personal past, stemming from child abuse, dysfunctional families, or discrimination of any sort. We learn of gay Buddhists, for example, whose meditation practice allows them to expose their self-hatred and to dissipate that hatred in the light of wisdom. At the same time, compassion emerges to liberate them from the isolation, both from other gays and from the heterosexual community (see Corless).

Engagement

It has become somewhat of a cliché in Buddhist-Christian dialogue circles to speak of inner practice and social action as the strengths of Buddhism and Christianity, respectively. In the spirit of mutual transformation, Christians are exhorted to learn from Buddhists about meditation, while Buddhists are encouraged to be inspired by Christians about social action. While this perceived Buddhist weakness may apply to situations in Asia—though even that assessment needs to be qualified[8]—social engagement is a more prominent feature among American Buddhists.

As discussed in the Rothberg essay, the largest socially visible Buddhist organization in the United States is the Buddhist Peace Fellowship with its current membership of approximately four thousand nationally. Its numerous projects and the recent dramatic increase in membership[9] reflect a keen interest in peace and social action among Buddhists. This is notably true among many Euro-Americans, who bring to their new faith their extensive prior experience in social and political activism. Equally significant is that the members derive from a broad range of Buddhist centers as well as those without any institutional affiliation. The ecumenical support of this organization further attests to the activist feature of a rather broad section of American Buddhists. In this regard, we see numerous projects such as the Zen AIDS Hospice affiliated with the San Francisco Zen Center and the well-known "Street Zen" of Glassman Rōshi in New York. The Naropa Institute in Boulder, Colorado (the only accredited Buddhist post-secondary institution in the nation), inaugurated in 1994 a master's degree program in Buddhist social action.

This activism has often been galvanized under the rubric of "engaged Buddhism," a term that Thich Nhat Hanh, a Vietnamese monk and activist, made famous in the West through his works. As Rothberg points out, "engaged Buddhism" refers not only to social activism (as alluded earlier) but also to activities that encompass all aspects of one's life. This general sense of the term encompasses the everyday contexts of families, work, and personal relationships. Buddhist practice is, thus, brought out from the monastic confines "into the world," where it is expected to make a discernible difference in the quality of people's daily lives. It is in this framework that Buddhist Peace Fellowship workshops have addressed the issues of conflict resolution, education, group dynamics, and Buddhist economics. Similar themes, such as "meditation in action," encourage the cultivation of a meditative spirit in such activities as driving, going to meetings, taking a bath, cleaning the stove, answering the telephone, and changing diapers (see Rothberg).

Similar activities have also sprung forth within Buddhist groups comprised largely of Asian American members. For example, the Buddhist Churches of America established the Buddhist Life Program in the 1950s to bring Buddhist teachings to daily life, and created the Relevant American Buddhists in the 1970s specifically to address many of the social concerns of the young adults. The highly visible Dāna Project sponsored by the Jōdo Shin community in Hawaii continues to provide social services to the broader Honolulu public. These were the direct expressions of the drive rooted in the assumption that the Dharma can and should demonstrate its relevance beyond the spiritual realm.

This development is generated, in part, by social justice concerns of Christianity and Judaism as well as an American religious penchant for a concrete demonstration of religious ideals in the world. The American tendency is to regard religious claims as invalid or, at best, less trustworthy if they do not provide explicit public evidence. Of course, altruism and service to others are found in traditional Buddhist doctrine, for example, in the bodhisattva ideal where spiritual adepts postpone their own liberation in order to remain in the world to help liberate others. This bodhisattva doctrine forms one of the bases of the call for social engagement by the global Buddhist exemplars such as Dalai Lama, Thich Nhat Hanh, and Sulak Sivaraksa. And in America, perhaps, these traditional Buddhist ideals have joined forces with Western notions of social justice and public demonstration to create Buddhist organizations, such as the Buddhist Peace Fellowship, thereby invalidating the Buddhist stereotype of inwardness alluded to earlier, at least in America.

Not only are many Buddhist groups demonstrating a higher level of social engagement, but they are doing so with a brand of spiritual insight and worldview not explicitly expressed in the Western-based social activist groups. The teaching of "interconnectedness" and "nonduality"—ideas that best capture the distinctive Buddhist contribution—has offered an alternative approach in dealing with many pressing issues such as the environment, gender relationship, and death and dying. Rather than dichotomizing issues into dualities of nature versus human, men versus women, and death versus life, the Buddhist message of nonduality advocates nonattachment to such rigid categories in favor of wholeness and interdependence. For many, this Buddhist vision, which fosters detachment from the rigid notions of right and wrong and "us" and "them," has helped to produce greater clarity, healing, and cooperation in the search for solutions.

Adaptation

Adaptation, as it is being used in this context, refers specifically to those features that many people, including the contributors to this volume, fear are the excesses of "bending" the tradition to meet the needs of the American Buddhists (see Hori, Fronsdal, Verhoeven, and Nattier). This perennial tension between the tradition and its adaptation was certainly evident among the countries in Asia that adopted Buddhism, but perhaps the pace and the fervor of emphasis on adaptation in modern America are unprecedented. Herein lies the potential danger of excessive interpretation, where the tradition is noticeably altered or selectively chosen to meet the needs of the new host culture. While the Buddhists in Asia also experienced this perennial tension between tradition and its interpretation, the strong emphasis on interpretation found among American Buddhists may be unprecedented. Its danger lies in the high demand for the teachings to serve the individual rather than the individual being transformed by the teachings.

The cross-national transmissions of Buddhism in the past have flowed typically from a highly developed to a less developed society, as, for example, in its transmission from China to Korea, Japan, and Vietnam, and from India to Tibet and Central Asia. Even its entrance to China took place during a period of Chinese cultural and political decline after the fall of the Han dynasty. During the next four hundred years, Buddhism appealed to emperors—often those of non-Chinese ethnic origin—who embraced the new religion as an instrument of political unity, national protection, and cultural advancement. The rulers of Korea, Japan, Vietnam, and Tibet were no different.

The United States in the 1990s, however, is the dominant country on earth from the standpoint of its economic, popular cultural, military, and technological influences. The cultural impact of America on the rest of the world is evident from McDonald's restaurants in Russia to major league baseball in Japan. The superior educational and research programs attract intellectuals from all corners of the world to American colleges and graduate schools. The artistic, intellectual, and research achievements are equally impressive and continue to set standards for the rest of the world.

Buddhist groups in America find themselves in an immensely pluralistic religious environment. Virtually every religion found in the rest of the world has a presence in the United States, all with some intention of propagating themselves on the American soil. While the Christian tradition in the country suffers from its share of critics and lingering apathy, its dominant position in American society remains unchallenged. The increasing clout of the so-called Christian Right in politics, education, and moral discussion provides us with a glimpse into the scope of Christian influence. The plurality of religions also characterizes the Buddhist groups as well, for virtually every school of Buddhism has now found a foothold on American soil. These schools now exist side by side, often in the same community—a situation unthinkable in Asia, where they often had no knowledge of each other. Within this new and competitive environment, the Buddhist groups are often forced to adapt to the needs of religious consumers and at times find their messages compromised and relativized in the process.

Further, the attraction of Buddhism in America is on the level of individuals eager to find resolution to their spiritual and emotional concerns, not as the vehicle for acquiring advanced technology or facilitating political unity. The individuals place greater demands on the tradition to serve their spiritual needs with immediate and palpable results. The strength of the individual is accentuated by the peculiar brand of American individualism and secularism, wherein the needs of the self are far more important than those of any group to which one belongs and where the status of the profane and the ordinary is greatly enhanced. These qualities can, in many individuals, foster impatience and even arrogance toward an ancient tradition that is essentially designed to transform the individual and not the other way around.

Does this type of individualized interpretation always denote excessive adaptation and must it necessarily be construed negatively? Perhaps it need not be. In fact, it may be a sign of an active and serious engagement to make sense of a foreign religion in a new culture. Perhaps American Buddhists are not accepting the teachings blindly until they are rendered personally more meaningful, in the spirit of Buddha's famous words, "Make yourself the light, and make the Dharma the light." This active adaptation of the tradition has fostered diffuse affiliation and eclectic tendencies, developments also found in Buddhist Asia but perhaps not to the same degree.

Buddhists with "diffuse" affiliation include those who have had affiliation with more than one form of Buddhism as part of their spiritual journey. Their affiliation with a specific school is the culmination of experiences with other schools, and there is no guarantee that the present affiliation is the final one. Diffuse affiliation also takes the form of concurrent multiple affiliation, whereby an individual maintains active ties with more than one temple or center. In a similar vein, it is not uncommon for Dharma teachers to have trained and even hold teaching certifications from more than one tradition.

Another expression of diffuse affiliation is found among Jewish converts to Buddhism who continue to maintain some ties to their original religious heritage. This phenomenon has been facilitated by the inherent Buddhist tolerance toward other religions, combined with the Jewish community's liberal view toward the flight of their sons and daughters to Buddhism. Books such as Rodger Kamenetz's *Jew in the Lotus* have illuminated the issues of Jewish-Buddhist dual affiliation. Awareness of this connection has triggered the formation of groups of the so-called JUBUs in several U.S. locations to address their interests and concerns.[10]

Eclectic tendencies also characterize the nature of practice *within* many groups, especially those with successes in attracting a large following. For example, Seung Sahn Sunim's Korean Zen is said to be a blending of Korean folk Buddhism and Japanese Zen forms (see Mu Soeng), and Thich Nhat Hanh's approach is described as "a 'New Age' style of Zen and rituals created by him" (see Nguyen and Barber). And in the Gay Buddhist Fellowship and Dharma Sisters, both located in San Francisco, "a hybrid 'Vipassana-Zen' sitting" is favored to appeal to a broad segment of their membership (see Corless).

Similar eclectic developments are evident at Insight Meditation West, centered at Spirit Rock in northern California. Comprised predominately of highly educated Euro-Americans, this group has been extremely successful in gaining a large following. Just as the name of the organization exhibits no explicit identification with Buddhism (Insight Meditation), its adherents are not required to claim Buddhist identity. In fact, the majority of their teachers elected not to be identified with the ancient Theravāda lineage. Many are attracted by the psychological insights and benefits of *vipassanā* meditation. Their eclectic character becomes more apparent when compared to the ethnic Theravāda organizations in America that continue to retain the full range of the Theravādin spiritual tradition including the rituals, the precepts, and the festivals. Voices from within the group have been raised regarding the dangers of excessive selection that may result in spiritual impoverishment.[11]

This trend toward breaking away from the Asian lineage also expresses itself in nonsectarian sentiments. In some of the Chinese traditions, for example, many in the leadership see their presence in America as an opportunity to rid themselves of the cultural accretions and baggage in order for the pristine form of Buddhism to emerge. A radical manifestation of this idea is evident in the Buddhist Association of Wisdom and Compassion, which has no temple and does not support monastic *sangha* members, deeming them unnecessary and a deviation from the original message of the Buddha. Instead, their focus is placed on the compassionate service activities within the larger society (see Chandler).

A fear of premature separation from the spiritual heritage has also led to an intriguing turn of events within another major organization, the federation of Sōtō Zen groups in America. Despite their largely Euro-American membership, they have most recently succeeded in getting their senior American teachers certified and acknowledged by the Sōtō Zen hierarchy in Japan. It appears highly unlikely that a similar move will be made by the Insight Meditation Society with its Theravāda institution in Southeast Asia. These are but two examples of the wide range found in the manner of adaptation, or more specifically with regard to sectarian affiliation with their respective Asian root traditions. Despite the difference on this point, both institutions have been similarly successful and show every sign of continuing to thrive into the twenty-first century.

Optimism and Activism

According to Thomas Tweed, Buddhism failed to become a more abiding presence in America following its initial entrance during the Victorian period, largely due to the absence in Buddhism of two qualities: optimism and activism.[12] While other features of Buddhism appealed to certain elements of Victorian ethos, such as its amenability to scientific worldview and the spirit of individualism, the pessimistic and passive Buddhist image dampened further growth.

A century later, Buddhism in America looks significantly different. It has grown in size, diversity, and stature. These developments took place within a broader set of social, religious, and demographic changes in American society since the 1960s. The sixties marked the demise of the Protestant epoch in American history and the loss of cultural consensus,[13] fostering increased tolerance for plurality of religious outlook. The Vatican II (1962–65) contributed to the spirit of ecumenism and progressive measures that had, among other results, far-reaching impact on the general openness toward other, particularly Eastern, religions. The civil rights movement helped to usher in an era of new consciousness about racial minorities, women, the disabled, and homosexuals. Abetted by the 1965 immigration reform, numerous charismatic Asian teachers and Buddhist immigrants found new homes in the fertile American soil. These newcomers, then, joined existing Buddhist traditions in a new mix to create the faces of Buddhism as reported in this volume.

Within this period of social and religious changes, the earlier labels of pessimism and passivity have weakened and given way to optimism and activism, the very qualities that many found lacking a century earlier. Activism, as defined by Tweed,[14] reveals itself most notably in "engaged Buddhism," which seeks to take Buddhist ideals beyond the inner spiritual concerns and into the social arena and the home. Optimism, as understood by Tweed,[15] saw humans, the world, and history as fundamentally good or capable of becoming good. Nowhere is this sense of optimism expressed more poignantly than in the manner in which American Buddhists regard practice. They practice, largely in the form of meditation and chanting, in the belief that through self-discipline they can transform themselves and the world. Even some of their overzealous adaptations to "Americanize" are reflections of their hopeful intentions. Optimism further reveals itself in the active inclusion of women leaders and the gay and lesbian communities, and in the fostering of more egalitarian organizations designed to harness the potentialities of more of their members.

It is worth noting that as Buddhist groups exhibit these qualities, they do not simply emulate other religious traditions but bring to the mix a distinctive Buddhist flavor. In the call for social action, for example, the Buddhist approach emphasizes the necessity of continual inner cultivation that helps to foster sustained commitment and clear thinking. Activism that is not spiritually centered would be prone to frequent burnout and unskillful decisions. Similarly, Buddhist optimism emerges within the process of personal transformation, not as a result of simply adhering to a hopeful worldview that regards human nature, the world, and history as good. And out of these transformative and empowering experiences, the Buddhist insights of nonduality and interdependence contribute a distinctive dimension to the face of optimism and activism in American religiosity.

Notes

Introduction

1. Peter Berger, *Sacred Canopy: Elements of a Sociological Theory of Religion* (Garden City, N.Y.: Doubleday, 1966), pp. 134, 137.

2. Robert N. Bellah, "The New Consciousness and the Crisis in Modernity," in Charles Y. Glock and Robert N. Bellah, eds., *The New Religious Consciousness* (Berkeley: University of California Press, 1976), p. 341.

3. See the discussion of so-called JUBUs in Rodger Kamenetz, *The Jew in the Lotus* (San Francisco: HarperSanFrancisco, 1994), pp. 7–15.

4. See bell hooks's interesting short article on racism, "Waking Up to Racism," *Tricycle: The Buddhist Review* 4, no. 1 (fall 1994): 42–45.

5. See, for example, Jon Kabat-Zinn, *Wherever You Go, There You Are: Mindfulness Meditation in Everyday Life* (New York: Hyperion, 1995).

6. See, for example, Mark Epstein, *Thoughts without a Thinker: Psychotherapy from a Buddhist Point of View* (New York: Basic Books, 1995).

7. For an introduction to the historical development of Buddhism in America, see Charles S. Prebish, *American Buddhism* (North Scituate, Mass.: Duxbury Press, 1979); chapter 1 discusses the entry of the Japanese, Chinese, Tibetan, and South Asian Buddhist traditions; the following three chapters discuss problems of growth and acculturation.

8. Rick Fields, *How the Swans Came to the Lake: A Narrative History of Buddhism in America*, 3d ed. (Boston: Shambhala, 1992), pp. 70–71.

9. See especially chapter 6, "Optimism and Activism," in Thomas A. Tweed, *The American Encounter with Buddhism 1844–1912: Victorian Culture and the Limits of Dissent* (Bloomington: Indiana University Press, 1992), pp. 133–56.

10. Ibid., pp. 157–62.

11. For an account of the conference, see Eleanor Rosch, "World Buddhism in North America Today," *Vajradhatu Sun* 9, no. 1 (October–November 1987): esp. p. 28.

12. See Peter Berger, *Sacred Canopy: Elements of a Sociological Theory of Religion*

(Garden City, N.Y.: Doubleday, 1966); Harvey Cox, *The Secular City* (New York: Macmillan, 1966); and Theodore Roszak, *The Making of a Counter Culture* (Garden City, N.Y.: Anchor Books, 1969).

13. Roszak, *The Making of a Counter Culture*, p. 156.

14. See Ken Jones, *The Social Face of Buddhism: An Approach to Political and Social Activism* (London: Wisdom Publications, 1989); and Kenneth Kraft, ed., *Inner Peace, World Peace: Essays on Buddhism and Nonviolence* (Albany: State University of New York Press, 1992).

Chapter 1: Chinese Buddhism in America

The research for this article was originally conducted as part of the Pluralism Project at Harvard University. I would like to thank the Lily Foundation for providing financial support for the Pluralism Project. I would also like to thank Diana Eck for her guidance, and Ellie Pierce, Wen-Jie Qin, and my wife, Stephanie Chandler, for reading early drafts of the paper.

1. Joseph de Guignes, *"Recherches sur les Navigations des Chinois du Côté de l'Amerique, et sur quelques Peuples situés a l'Extremité Orientale de l'Asie,"* *Memoires de Litterature, Tires des Registres de l'Academie Royale des Inscriptions et Belles-Lettres,* vol. 28 (Paris, 1761). This book is summarized in Edward P. Vining, *An Inglorious Columbus; or, Evidence that Hwui Shan and a Party of Buddhist Monks from Afghanistan Discovered America in the Fifth Century, A.D.* (New York: D. Appleton and Company, 1885), chap. 2. The memorial quoted by de Guignes is the "Nan-sze" or "History of the South," written in the opening years of the seventh century by Li-yan-cheu and included in the *Nan-eul-sze* or "Twenty-two Historians." See Vining, *An Inglorious Columbus,* 19, 40. I first became aware of this debate within the European scholarly community through reading Rick Fields's "Sailing to Fusang: Did a Chinese Buddhist Monk 'Discover' the New World?" *Tricycle: The Buddhist Review* 1, no. 3 (spring 1992): 9–11.

2. J. Klaproth, "Recherches sur le Pays de Fou Sang, mentionné dans les Livres Chinois, et, pris, mal a-propos, pour une Partie de l'Amerique," *Nouvelles Annales des Voyages,* vol. 51 (Paris, 1831); summarized in Vining, *An Inglorious Columbus,* pp. 39–48.

3. Chevalier de Paravey, *L'Amerique sous le nom de pays de Fou-Sang* (Paris: Treuttel et Wurtz, 1844), p. 18. De Paravey's argument is summarized in Vining, *An Inglorious Columbus,* pp. 49–77.

4. Charles G. Leland, *The Discovery of America by Chinese Buddhist Priests in the Fifth Century* (London: Trübner and Co., 1875), pp. 110–24.

5. Vining, *An Inglorious Columbus,* pp. 403–9, 541, 588.

6. Henriette Mertz asserts that "Fu-sang is no 'geographical myth, figment of Buddhist imagination'—that the plant 'Fu-sang' was 'corn,' and the country 'Fu-sang' was Mexico." See Mertz's *Pale Ink* (Chicago: Swallow Press, 1953), p. 158. Mertz translates both the Hui Shan memorial and stories from the *Shan Hai Ching,* which in her view preserves accounts dating from the crossing of the Bering Strait thousands of years ago.

7. Wei Chu-hsien, *Chung-kuo-jen Fa-hsien Mei-chou* (Taipei: Shuo-wen Chu-tian, 1982), p. ii. This three-volume work covers the following topics: Chinese inscrip-

tions, art motifs, and ceremonial relics found in America; American botanical species, zoological species, mineral items, customs, and geography known early to the Chinese; Native Americans who might have come from China; and ancient Chinese who knew and had been to America.

8. *Historical Statistics of the United States Colonial Times to 1970*, pt. I (Washington, D.C.: U.S. Department of Commerce, Bureau of the Census, 1976), p. 108.

9. Statistics on numbers of Chinese in the United States are derived from ibid., p. 14.

10. Mariann Kaye Wells, "Chinese Temples in California," thesis, University of California, 1962, pp. 19–28. Tin Hou Temple, devoted to the Taoist Goddess of Heaven, closed down in the 1950s but reopened in 1975. Today, it serves a small community of Cantonese-speaking Chinese.

11. *Statistical Abstract of the United States* (Washington, D.C.: U.S. Department of Commerce, Bureau of the Census, 1994), Table 55.

12. This figure may be slightly low, since it is based on those Chinese Buddhist organizations that I have been able to track down. State-by-state figures for organizations run as follows: California, 68 (San Francisco, 21; Los Angeles, 12); New York, 25; Hawaii, 9; Texas, 7; Washington, 6; Illinois, 4; Pennsylvania, 4; Florida, 3; Maryland, 3; Alabama, 2; Colorado, 2; Iowa, 2; Louisiana, 2; Massachusetts, 2; Minnesota, 2; New Jersey, 2; Ohio, 2; Connecticut, 1; Georgia, 1; Indiana, 1; Nevada, 1; Wisconsin, 1.

13. *Statistical Abstract of the United States* (1994), Table 55.

14. Ronald Takaki, *Strangers from a Different Shore* (New York: Penguin Books, 1989), p. 425.

15. The following section on the Chinese Buddhist expressions of compassion is a revised version of my essay "Creating a Pure Land on Earth," in Diana Eck, *On Common Ground* (CD-ROM, Columbia Press, 1997).

16. Will Herberg, *Protestant—Catholic—Jew: An Essay in American Religious Sociology*, new ed. (Garden City, N.Y.: Doubleday and Co., 1960), p. 16.

17. Ibid., p. 19.

18. Ibid., p. 23.

19. Ibid., p. 44, n. 26.

20. The "first Sinic world" refers to those societies in which ethnic Chinese constitute a majority: China, Taiwan, Hong Kong, and Singapore.

21. Charles Prebish, *American Buddhism* (North Scituate, Mass.: Duxbury Press, 1979), p. 51.

22. See Jan Nattier, "Who Is a Buddhist? Charting the Landscape of Buddhist America," in this volume.

23. Tu Wei-ming, "The Living Tree: The Changing Meaning of Being Chinese Today," *Daedalus* 120, no. 2 (spring 1991): 13.

24. The classic work on religions as cultural systems is Clifford Geertz, *An Interpretation of Cultures* (New York: Basic Books, 1973).

25. Han Yu, *Ch'ang-li Hsien-sheng Chi [Collected Works of Han Yu]*, ed. Ssu-pu Ts'ung-k'an (Shanghai: Commercial Press, 1929–36), p. 39:2b–4b. Translated as "Memorial on the Bone of Buddha," in Wm. Theodore De Bary, Wing-tsit Chen, and Burton Watson, eds., *Sources of Chinese Tradition* (New York: Columbia University Press, 1960), vol. 1, pp. 372–74.

26. Hu Shih, "The Indianization of China: A Case Study in Cultural Borrowing," in *Independence, Convergence and Borrowing* (Cambridge, Mass.: Harvard Tercentenary Publications, 1937), p. 247.

27. Buddhism has maintained a close alliance with the ruling elite in Sri Lanka since the third century B.C.E., Burma since the eleventh century C.E., Thailand since the thirteenth century, Laos and Cambodia since the fourteenth century. In Japan, Buddhism dominated cultural, intellectual, and political life from the late Heian (794–1191) to the Muromachi periods (1334–1573).

28. I have come across two explicitly Confucian organizations in the United States: the Confucius Church in Stockton, California, and the Confucius Center in Chicago. Taoist organizations are more numerous, especially if one includes the various centers specializing in wu-chi or t'ai-chi-ch'üan, some of which expressly identify themselves as Taoist, others which do not. Unlike Chinese Buddhist organizations, however, the vast majority of Taoist centers primarily serve a Euro-American clientele.

29. Robert Michaelson observes that the long-term survival of a religious organization depends on its ability to negotiate the tension between such opposites as spontaneity and control, spirituality and practicality, ecstasy and action, grace and morality, virtue and power, individuality and community. Robert Michaelson, *The American Search for Soul* (Baton Rouge: Louisiana State University Press, 1975), pp. 27–28; quoted in Prebish, *American Buddhism*, p. 52.

Chapter 2: Shin Buddhism in America

1. The Jōdo Shinshū sect is structurally divided into ten branches: the Honpa [Main Branch] Honganji, Otani-ha Honganji, Takada-ha, Kibe-ha, Bukkōji-ha, Kōshō-ha, and the four branches in Echizen (Sammonto-ha, Yamamoto-ha, Jōshōji-ha, and Izumoji-ha). The Mother Temples (Honzan) of the Honganji branches are located adjacent to each other in Kyoto and are commonly called Nishi (West) Honganji (with respect to the Honpa Honganji), and Higashi (East) Honganji (with respect to the Otani Honganji).

2. Robert A. Wilson and Bill Hosokawa, *East to America: A History of the Japanese in the United States* (New York: Morrow, 1980), pp. 28–36.

3. Ibid., pp. 56–57.

4. Ruth Tabrah, *A Grateful Past, A Promising Future* (Honolulu: Honpa Honganji Mission of Hawaii, 1989), p. 54.

5. Ibid., p. 76.

6. Roger Daniels, *Asian America* (Seattle: University of Washington Press, 1988), p. 170.

7. Buddhist Churches of America, *Buddhist Churches of America*, vol. I, *75-Year History 1899 to 1974*, p. 83.

8. Ryo M. Imamura, "A Comparative Study of Temple and Non-temple Buddhist Ministers of the Jōdo Shin Sect Using Jungian Psychological Types," Ph.D. dissertation, University of San Francisco, 1986, pp. 77–79, 102–3.

9. Membership statistics are very difficult to ascertain and interpret. The numbers given in the annual report indicate decline. There are a variety of reasons why the numbers have been pared down, however, such as removing the elderly from

the count because they may not be able to pay the dues, or removing nonpartici-
pants and retaining only those who contribute. Since the assessment to the denomination is based on the number of members, such pruning of the rolls reduces the
amount the temple owes. Nevertheless, the decline in the number of ministers
certainly reflects a real decrease in the number of members whom they would serve.

10. Donald Tuck, *Buddhist Churches of America: Jōdo Shinshū* (Lewiston, N.Y.: Edwin Mellen Press, 1987), pp. 79, 96.

11. *Buddhist Churches of America, 1995 Annual Report*, p. 45.

12. Tetsuden Kashima, *Buddhism in America* (Westport, Conn.: Greenwood Press,
1977), p. 157.

13. These numbers were secured from the Department of Buddhist Education.
Detailed statistics first appear in annual reports in 1985, when it is noted there were
2,339 students and 559 teachers. A survey of students for the period from 1934 to
1959 appears to have been made, but is not presently available, according to the
BCA Archives.

14. From a lecture by Professor Yuji Ichioka at UCLA.

15. Kimi Hisatsune, *Wheel of Dharma* 20, no. 2 (February 1993): 4.

16. Charles Prebish, *American Buddhism* (North Scituate, Mass.: Duxbury Press,
1979), p. 67.

17. Christmas Humphreys, *Buddhism*, rev. ed. (London: Penguin Books, 1962),
pp. 164, 165.

18. Paul Williams, *Mahāyāna Buddhism: The Doctrinal Foundations* (London: Routledge, 1989), p. 275. Williams does not address the question, "But is it Buddhism?"
to such teachers as Nichiren, who expressed very distinctive views concerning Buddhism and his position in it. It leads the reader to wonder why this question is
directed specifically to Shin Buddhism.

19. Humphreys, *Buddhism*, p. 163.

Chapter 3: Japanese Zen in America

1. For historical background on the establishment of Buddhism in general in
North America, see Robert S. Ellwood, "Buddhism in the West," in Mircea Eliade,
ed., *The Encyclopedia of Religion* (New York: Macmillan, 1987), 2:436–39; Rick Fields,
How the Swans Came to the Lake: A Narrative History of Buddhism in America (Boulder:
Shambhala, 1981); Joseph T. Kitagawa, "Appendix: Buddhism in America," in Ki-
tagawa, ed., *On Understanding Japanese Religion* (Princeton: Princeton University
Press, 1987), pp. 311–28; Charles S. Prebish, *American Buddhism* (North Scituate,
Mass.: Duxbury Press, 1979); Joseph B. Tamney, *American Society in the Buddhist Mir-
ror* (New York: Garland, 1992); and Thomas A. Tweed, *The American Encounter with
Buddhism 1884–1912: Victorian Culture and the Limits of Dissent* (Bloomington: Indi-
ana University Press, 1992). For the development of Zen in particular, see Helen
Tworkov, *Zen in America: Profiles of Five Teachers* (San Francisco: North Point Press,
1989).

2. Tworkov, *Zen in America*, p. 149.

3. For discussion of this issue, see Sandy Boucher, *Turning the Wheel: American
Women Creating the New Buddhism* (San Francisco: Harper and Row, 1988); Katy
Butler, "Events Are the Teacher," *CoEvolution Quarterly* 40 (winter 1983): 112–23;

Lenore Friedman, *Meetings with Remarkable Women: Buddhist Teachers in America* (Boston: Shambhala, 1987); Stuart Lachs, "A Slice of Zen in America," *New Ch'an Forum* 10 (1994): 12–20; Ellen S. Sidor, ed., *A Gathering of Spirit: Women Teaching in American Buddhism* (Cumberland, R.I.: Primary Point Press, 1987); Tworkov, *Zen in America*; and the *Buddhist Peace Fellowship Newsletter*, "Buddhist Teachers and Sexual Misconduct" (spring 1991), as well as letters in the summer and fall 1991 issues of the same newsletter.

4. For a survey of the Rinzai Zen temple system in Japan, see T. Griffith Foulk, "The Zen Institution in Modern Japan," in Kenneth Kraft, ed., *Zen: Tradition and Transition* (New York: Grove Press, 1988), pp. 157–77. For a detailed picture of Japanese Zen monastic life, see D. T. Suzuki, "The Meditation Hall and the Ideals of the Monkish Discipline," in D. T. Suzuki, ed., *Essays in Zen Buddhism*, First Series (London: Rider, 1961), pp. 229–67; the cartoon book by Giei Satō, *Unsui: A Diary of Zen Monastic Life* (Honolulu: University of Hawaii Press, 1973); and also the first half of the video *Principles and Practices of Zen* (Princeton, N.J.: Films for the Humanities).

5. Personal communication from Jane Doe (January 1995): "The arrangement of participants is with the monks/priests grouped at each end, the rest bunched up in the middle where the officers can keep an eye or two on where the feet are. The frequent admonitions 'eyes down,' 'feet flat on the floor,' 'no coughing,' 'sūtra books on the table,' etc., are far more annoying to the harmonious movement through meals than they are worth."

6. G. Victor Sōgen Hori, "Teaching and Learning in the Rinzai Zen Monastery," *Journal of Japanese Studies* 20, no. 1 (1994): 5–35.

7. Mary Farkas writes, "Sokei-an had no interest in reproducing the features of Japanese Zen monasticism, the strict and regimented training that aims at making people 'forget self.' In these establishments, individuality is stamped out, novices move together like a school of fish, their cross-legged position corrected with an ever-ready stick." See Mary Farkas, ed., *The Zen Eye: A Collection of Talks by Sokei-an* (Tokyo: Weatherhill, 1993), 1.

8. It has been pointed out that this term is found in texts earlier than the *Analects*, in the *Shih Ching* (Classic of Poetry) and the *Ta-Hsueh* (Great Learning).

9. These insights came from Douglas Durham, who is currently researching the effectiveness of the teaching methods now used in Buddhist retreats. I wish to thank him for allowing me to read a manuscript in preparation and for much good advice and counsel otherwise.

10. Rosabeth Moss Kanter, *Commitment and Community: Communes and Utopias in Sociological Perspective* (Cambridge, Mass.: Harvard University Press, 1972), pp. 120–22.

11. Ibid., pp. 87–89.

12. See especially the chapter "The Democratic Nature of the Sangha," in Sunanda Putuwar, *The Buddhist Sangha: Paradigm of the Ideal Human Society* (Lanham, Md.: University Press of America, 1991), pp. 91–96.

13. Trevor Ling, *The Buddha: Buddhist Civilization in India and Ceylon* (New York: Charles Scribner's Sons, 1973), pp. 130–31.

14. See Sukumar Dutt, *Buddhist Monks and Monasteries of India* (London: George Allen and Unwin, 1962), pp. 86–87, and Ling, *The Buddha*, pp. 50–53.

15. Paul S. Adler, "Time and Motion Regained," *Harvard Business Review* 1993 (January–February): 97–108 (reprint 93101).

16. See, for example, the *Buddhist Peace Fellowship Newsletter* articles on Buddhist teachers and sexual misconduct, in the spring 1991 issue, as well as the letters in the following two issues, particularly the book review by Yvonne Rand in the spring 1991 issue, and Diana N. Rowan, "An Open Letter to the American Buddhist Community," in the summer 1991 issue.

17. Zenkei Shibayama, *Zen Comments on the Mumonkan*, trans. Sumiko Kudo (New York: Mentor, 1974), pp. 123–24; also "A good teacher ought to leave the last quarter unspoken, so that each student may work hard with it himself and be personally awakened to it" (p. 245).

18. Tworkov, *Zen in America*, pp. 232–33.

19. The book *Sex in the Forbidden Zone* (New York: St. Martin's Press, 1989), by Peter Rutter, makes this assumption amply explicit.

20. Psychotherapy is itself culturally shaped. For a comment that relates Japanese psychotherapy to its cultural background, see T. S. Lebra, *Japanese Patterns of Behavior* (Honolulu: University of Hawaii Press, 1982), pp. 201–14, 215–31. For a provocative analysis claiming that the American ideal of the psychotherapist is an extension of the American ideal of the competent businessman, see Robert Bellah, Richard Madsen, William S. Sullivan, Ann Swidler, and Steven M. Tipton, *Habits of the Heart* (New York: Harper and Row, 1985), pp. 121–41.

21. Verse X, 578, from *Zenrin Kushū* (Zen Phrase Collection), compiled by Tōyō Eichō Zenji (Kyoto: Baiyō Shoin, 1894).

22. The hold of this nonintellectual image of Zen is so strong that Robert Buswell considers one of the benefits of his study of Korean Zen monasticism to be its challenge of that image. See Robert Buswell, *The Zen Monastic Experience: Buddhist Practice in Contemporary Korea* (Princeton: Princeton University Press, 1992).

23. In English, the only substantial discussion of *jakugo* is in Kenneth Kraft, *Eloquent Zen: Daitō and Early Japanese Zen* (Honolulu: University of Hawaii Press, 1992), pp. 130–50.

24. See n. 21.

25. For a criticism of the notion of transcendence in Zen with an account of its importance in American culture, see Dale S. Wright, "Rethinking Transcendence: The Role of Language in Zen Experience," *Philosophy East and West* 42, no. 1 (January 1992): 113–38.

26. Dharmachari Vessantara, *The Friends of the Western Buddhist Order* (Glasgow: Windhorse Publications, 1988), p. 9.

27. D. T. Suzuki, *Essays in Zen Buddhism*, pp. 106–12.

Chapter 4: Nichiren Shōshū and Soka Gakkai in America

1. Rick Fields, *How the Swans Came to the Lake*, 3d ed. (Boston: Shambhala, 1992), p. 127.

2. *Newsletter* 1, no. 1 (spring 1994) (Cambridge, Mass.: Boston Research Center for the 21st Century, 1994): 1.

3. Daisaku Ikeda, *Buddhism: The Living Philosophy* (Tokyo: East Publications, 1974), p. 53. An early Soka Gakkai publication says Nichiren's father was a demoted

samurai, which would give Nichiren noble ancestry (*The Sōkagakkai,* 2d ed. [Tokyo: Seikyo Press, 1962], p. 43). This statement has been omitted in all subsequent publications in English.

4. Masaharu Anesaki, *Nichiren, The Buddhist Prophet* (Gloucester, Mass.: Peter Smith, 1916, 1966), pp. 33–34.

5. Kiyoaki Murata, *Japan's New Buddhism* (New York: John Weatherhill, 1969), p. 30.

6. Information in the chart is from *NSA Study Booklet* (photocopy: [World Tribune Press?] 1976), p. 17. Note that these are the Nichiren Shōshū priesthood's point of view and are studied by believers as such. For a nonbeliever's account of Nichiren Daishōnin's life and writings, see Laurel Rasplica Rodd, *Nichiren: Selected Writings* (Honolulu: University of Hawaii Press, 1980).

7. Richard Causton, *Nichiren Shōshū Buddhism* (New York: Harper and Row, 1989), p. 97. Causton's work is an excellent overview of Nichiren Daishōnin's teachings as they have been understood by those who practice Nichiren Buddhism in the Western world. A new edition, titled *The Buddha in Daily Life: An Introduction to the Buddhism of Nichiren Daishōnin* (London: Rider Press, 1995), has now appeared.

8. *NSA Handbook No. 4* (Santa Monica, Calif.: World Tribune Press, 1972), pp. 18, 21, 22, 25.

9. *A Dictionary of Buddhist Terms and Concepts* (Tokyo: Nichiren Shōshū International Center, 1983).

10. American practitioners of Nichiren's Buddhism chanted the *Lotus Sūtra* in a Japanese transliteration of the Chinese translation of the original Sanskrit *sūtra.* They did not understand the content of what they chanted, but had faith that it was effective. Soka Gakkai in 1993 commissioned a translation of the *sūtra,* which is now widely available. See Burton Watson, trans., *The Lotus Sūtra* (New York: Columbia University Press, 1993).

11. Daniel B. Montgomery, *Fire in the Lotus* (London: Mandala/HarperCollins, 1991), p. 281.

12. Murata, *Japan's New Buddhism,* p. 69.

13. *Peace, Culture, Education* (Tokyo: Soka Gakkai International, 1995), p. 11.

14. *NSA Handbook No. 1* (Santa Monica, Calif.: World Tribune Press, 1972), p. 8.

15. For further explanation of the concept of ethos and its development in relation to NSA, see Jane Hurst, *Nichiren Shoshu Buddhism and the Soka Gakkai in America: The Ethos of a New Religious Movement* (New York: Garland Press, 1992).

16. See an unpublished paper presented at the Association for Asian Studies Conference (1995), "The Changing Role of the Sōka Gakkai in Japanese Politics," by Daniel A. Metraux (Mary Baldwin College), for more detailed information on Kōmeitō.

17. Conversation with Hokkeko member, November 1994. Nichiren Shōshū Buddhism interprets the Three Treasures thus: Nichiren Daishōnin (the Buddha), *Daimoku* and the *Lotus Sūtra* (the Dharma), and Nikkō and the subsequent high priests (the *sangha*).

18. No author, "Guidance of Daisaku Ikeda" and "SGI 'Gohonzon': Source of Misfortune," sent to the author in 1995 by a current Hokkeko member (no publication data available).

19. *Peace, Culture, Education*, p. 2.

Chapter 5: Tibetan Buddhism in America

I am indebted to Judith Simmer-Brown for her advice and guidance in the construction of this article, and to Liz Locke for invaluable editorial suggestions and support.

1. I am using this term, *lama*, in its most general sense to refer to a class of Tibetan religious teachers. See Geoffrey Samuel, *Civilized Shamans: Buddhism in Tibetan Societies* (Washington, D.C.: Smithsonian Institute Press, 1993), pp. 180–81.

2. Following Geoffrey Samuel, I use the term *order* to refer to the five distinctive traditions of Tibetan Buddhism: Nyingma, Kagyu, Sakya, Gelug, and Bön. The Bön order is not considered here. The term *lineage* refers to the continuity from teacher to student of a particular order's teachings and practices. See Samuel, *Civilized Shamans*, p. 601, n. 2.

3. The term *tulku* refers to a lama who has been recognized as the reincarnation of a previous lama whose office and status he or she has inherited. The reincarnate lama may be recognized as an "emanation" of one or more specific Tibetan deities (Samuel, *Civilized Shamans*, p. 281).

4. From the Sanskrit *kalyāṇamitra*, or spiritual friend, the *geshe* is the product of a lengthy philosophical and scholastic training system, usually at a Gelugpa monastic center (Samuel, *Civilized Shamans*, p. 337).

5. This historical material is culled from Rick Fields's excellent introduction to Buddhism in America, *How the Swans Came to the Lake: A Narrative History of Buddhism in America*, 2d ed. (Boston: Shambhala, 1986), pp. 273–339.

6. This phrase refers to the teaching of Tibetan Buddhist doctrine and ritual practice conducted by Tibetan lamas as well as their Western senior students.

7. Fields, *How the Swans Came to the Lake*, p. 305.

8. There are very few female Tibetan lamas teaching in the West. Judith Simmer-Brown has noted in a personal communication that one woman lama, Jetsun Kusho, has been teaching in Vancouver and elsewhere for more than fifteen years.

9. Samuel, *Civilized Shamans*, p. 513.

10. Again, no female *geshes* are known to me.

11. Personal communication with Sharon Hurley, April 4, 1997.

12. An excellent description of one such process of recognition can be found in Chögyam Trungpa Rinpoche's autobiography, *Born in Tibet* (Boston: Shambhala, 1985).

13. This information is taken from the nonacademic and colorful book by Vicki Mackenzie, *Reborn in the West: The Reincarnation Masters* (New York: Marlowe and Co., 1995).

14. Ibid., p. 75.

15. Rebecca Redwood French, *The Golden Yoke: The Legal Cosmology of Buddhist Tibet* (Ithaca, N.Y.: Cornell University Press, 1995), p. 30.

16. This information was found on the web page for Namgyal Monastery.

17. KTD Sangha Newsletter, February 1996.

18. KTD Sangha Newsletter, August 1995.

Chapter 6: Korean Buddhism in America

1. For an overview of Korean Buddhist history, see Mu Soeng, *Thousand Peaks: Korean Zen—Tradition and Teachers* (Cumberland, R.I.: Primary Point Press, 1987, 1991).

2. Robert Buswell, *The Korean Approach to Zen: The Collected Works of Chinul* (Honolulu: University of Hawaii Press, 1983), pp. 6–7, 37–38.

3. Mu Soeng, *Thousand Peaks*, p. 174.

4. Ibid., pp. 174–75.

5. Ibid., p. 177.

6. Seung Sahn's biography may be found in *Thousand Peaks*, as well as in Stephen Mitchell, ed., *Dropping Ashes on the Buddha: The Teaching of Zen Master Seung Sahn* (New York: Grove Press, 1976), and Diana Clark, ed., *Only Doing It for Sixty Years* (Cumberland, R.I.: Kwan Um Zen School, 1987).

7. *Primary Point*, newsletter of Kwan Um Zen School, Cumberland, Rhode Island, various issues.

8. Clark, *Only Doing It for Sixty Years*, pp. 12–13.

9. Mu Soeng, *Thousand Peaks*, pp. 84–85.

10. Ibid., pp. 179–200.

11. *Primary Point* 10, no. 12 (fall–winter 1993).

12. Richard Hayes in *Zen Lotus Society Handbook* (Toronto: Zen Lotus Society, 1986).

13. Samu Sunim's autobiography may be found in ibid.

14. Ibid., p. 36.

15. *Spring Wind: Buddhist Cultural Forum* 5, no. 3 (fall 1985), issue titled "Buddhism in the Performing Arts," Zen Lotus Society, Toronto, Canada, October 1985.

Chapter 7: Vietnamese Buddhism in North America

1. Theravāda has been present in Vietnam for several centuries. Although its practitioners represent a minority group, they do not seem to have been the object of discrimination. Ordination through Theravāda *Vinaya* was recognized by the Buddhist community and the government; this provided easy access to information and Pāli sources. As far as can be determined, the largest influence that the Theravāda monks had on the Vietnamese Buddhist community was by popularizing *vipaśyanā* and *śamatha* forms of meditation among the monastics.

2. A. W. Barber is approaching his contribution to this study in the traditional participant-observer mode. Cuong T. Nguyen is approaching his contribution as a practicing Vietnamese Buddhist with the self-conscious observation and speculation of an insider.

3. Southern Alberta has had a strong Buddhist presence since before World War II. Historically this was due to the many Buddhist Church of Canada's temples located from Calgary south. This region has produced Professor Richard Robinson,

founder of the University of Wisconsin–Madison Buddhist Studies program, Professor Masatoshi Nagatomi of Harvard University, and Professor Leslie Kawamura of the University of Calgary. Calgary is the largest and most important city in southern Alberta. In recent years it has seen the establishment of three Chinese Buddhist temples, the Vietnamese pagoda, and twelve other Buddhist groups. These include ethnic groups serving the Sri Lankans, Cambodians, and Tibetans, as well as groups not serving any ethnic communities but having affiliations with Zen, Theravāda, and Tibetan lamas. Calgary's population is about 750,000, with a reasonable estimate of the Buddhist population being about 6 percent.

4. Regular membership is counted at three thousand, which does not include a large number of irregular members. Because of the size of this congregation, it is the largest Buddhist group in southern Alberta.

5. See the *Lịch Âm Dương Đối Chiếu* (Lunar and Solar Calendars) published by the Tịnh Xá [*vihāra*] Minh Đăng Quang in Westminster, California, 1995. Approximately twenty of these temples are headed by nuns. This number also includes Canada.

6. Rick Fields, *How the Swans Came to the Lake: A Narrative History of Buddhism in America*, 3d ed. (Boston: Shambhala, 1992), pp. 353–58.

7. Ibid., p. 353. Thích Thiên Ân's book on Vietnamese Buddhism reads like fiction since it does not coincide at all with any Vietnamese Buddhist reality. See Thích Thiên Ân, *Buddhism and Zen in Vietnam* (Rutland, Vt.: Charles E. Tuttle, 1975).

8. Fields, *How the Swans Came to the Lake*, p. 376.

9. Most of Thích Nhất Hạnh's (Vietnamese) disciples read only his books and would not want to have anything to do with any other Vietnamese monks or temples. Recently, Thích Nhất Hạnh has begun to "transmit the Dharma-lamp," as part of his effort to align his teaching with orthodox Chinese Ch'an. See Chân Không, *Learning True Love* (Berkeley: Parallax Press, 1993), p. 248. The question is, if Thích Nhất Hạnh emphasizes this "direct transmission" as the essence of Ch'an (following the view of Shen-hui [684–758] of medieval Chinese Southern Ch'an), then from whom did he himself receive this direct transmission? After all, Thích Nhất Hạnh was not a Ch'an master in Vietnam.

10. We are avoiding using the term *religion* to classify Buddhism due to the considerable problems that develop when placing Buddhism under this label.

11. Léopold Cadière, *Croyances et pratiques religieuses des Vietnamiens*, vol. 1, reprint (Paris: École Française d'Extrême-Orient, 1992), pp. 29–32. There is some truth in Cadière's observation, yet most of the time he was looking through the eyes of a French colonialist at a time when Vietnamese values were under grave duress.

12. The use of the word *church* showed the extent to which Western imperialistic views have been imposed on the system.

13. In the late 1970s Vietnamese immigrants started to settle in Calgary, but the largest influx seemed to come in the early 1980s. In 1985, Venerable Tiên Quang was invited, and in 1986 he helped establish the Vietnamese Buddhist Congregation, temporarily housed in the apartment provided for him in the Vietnamese neighborhood. From its beginning, one of the goals of the Vietnamese Buddhist Congregation was the establishment of a temple to act as a center for Buddhist activities and community relations. Money for building the temple was constantly

collected from the community, with the sum necessary amounting to millions of dollars. The collection of funds was no small task, as the community was made up of recent arrivals with little command of English and even fewer job skills that could be utilized in the Canadian environment. However, the people were willing to make serious personal sacrifices and in only eight years collected sufficient funds. In 1994 Chùa Bát Nhã opened.

14. See Charles S. Prebish, *A Survey of Vinaya Literature* (Taipei: Jin Luen Publishing House, 1994), pp. 70–76.

15. The combination of *Vinaya* and bodhisattva precepts was already a mainstay in China by the time of Saichō's visit. See Y. Kashiwahara and K. Sonoda, eds., *Shapers of Japanese Buddhism* (Tokyo: Kosei Publishing, 1994), p. 32.

16. See Tso Sze-bong, "The Transformation of Buddhist Vinaya in China," unpublished dissertation, Australian National University, 1982. There are serious questions regarding the actual connections Vietnamese Buddhism has with Ch'an. This will require further investigation. In this chapter we have only presented material according to our informants' statements and do not take sides on this issue.

17. Venerable Trí Tuệ informed Dr. Nguyen that after 1964 all monks were required to attend monastic college, although Dr. Nguyen has met many monks who never attended any such college and preferred to remain at their temples. This does not necessarily mean that Venerable Tri Tuệ was misinformed but that the ideals and the realities were often different in Vietnam. It might have been a policy of the Unified Buddhist Church, but how seriously this policy was carried out, or whether it was carried out at all, is another story.

18. Zen gained wide popularity in Vietnam in the mid-sixties due to the translation of books by D. T. Suzuki, Alan Watts, and others. Some Buddhists, however, used this popularity as an excuse for rejecting traditional rituals.

19. This position is supported by Venerable Thích Thiền Tâm. See Thích Thiền Tâm, *Niệm Phật Thập Yếu* [Ten Keys to the Practice of Buddha-Contemplation], reprint (San Jose, Calif.: Huong Nghiem, 1990).

20. There also seems to have been a shift in the understanding of the Pure Land in Vietnam over the centuries. At first it was understood that the pure mind is the Pure Land; however, it seems now that it is understood as an external place where one is reborn. Both elements may have always been present. As noted by Bruno Révertégat (*Le Bouddhisme traditionel du Sud-Viêtnam* [Vichy: Imprimerie Wallon, 1974], pp. 16–17), even though Pure Land Buddhism is the most popular, it seems based on popular ideas. The works of the patriarchs of Chinese Pure Land tradition such as T'an-luan, Shan-tao, and so on, have been unstudied in the Vietnamese tradition.

21. In modern Vietnamese Buddhism the *Lotus Sūtra* is used in a devotional context.

22. The practice of repentance has been emphasized since medieval times in Vietnamese Buddhism.

23. On the worship of Kuan Kung (Quan Vũ, Quan Công in Vietnamese) in Vietnamese Buddhism see Révertégat, *Bouddhisme traditionel*, pp. 157–58. On the cult of Kuan Yu in Chinese Buddhism, see Valerie Hansen, "Gods on Walls: A Case of Indian Influence on Chinese Lay Religion?" in Patricia Buckley Ebrey and Peter

N. Gregory, eds., *Religion and Society in T'ang and Sung China* (Honolulu: University of Hawaii Press, 1993), pp. 75–113, especially 88–90.

24. On Ullambana, see Kenneth K. S. Ch'en, *The Chinese Transformation of Buddhism* (Princeton: Princeton University Press, 1973), pp. 61–64.

25. Unlike some Cambodian Buddhists who struggle to find an answer for the holocaust that befell their country and hold Buddhism responsible for it, Vietnamese Buddhists never question their commitment to Buddhism because they suffered an atrocious war that lasted for almost two decades. For the study of Cambodian Buddhists regarding this issue, see Carol A. Mortland, "Khmer Buddhists in the United States: Ultimate Questions," in May M. Ebihara, Carol A. Mortland, and Judy Ledgerwood, eds., *Cambodian Culture since 1975: Homeland and Exile* (Ithaca, N.Y.: Cornell University Press, 1984), pp. 72–90.

26. Milada Kalab, "Cambodian Buddhist Monasteries in Paris: Continuing Tradition and Changing Patterns," in Ebihara et al., *Cambodian Culture since 1975*, pp. 50–60.

27. Chloe Anne Breyer has touched on this issue in her study of the Vietnamese Buddhist temples in Orange County, California. See Chloe Anne Breyer, "Religious Liberty in Law and Practice: Vietnamese Home Temples in California and the First Amendment," senior thesis, Radcliffe College, March 1992; particularly chaps. 1 and 3.

28. Milada Kalab shows that Cambodian Buddhists also hold the same belief. See Kalab, "Cambodian Buddhist Monasteries in Paris," p. 69.

29. He is alluding to an episode in the chapter on "expedient means" in the *Lotus Sūtra*. See Burton Watson, trans., *The Lotus Sūtra* (New York: Columbia University Press, 1993), p. 30.

30. The attitude of placing the future of Buddhism in the West is widespread among Asian Buddhists. This is also expressed by the Bhutanese monk Ngawang Tenzing Zangbo. See Barbara Crossette, *So Close to Heaven: The Vanishing Buddhist Kingdoms of the Himalayas* (New York: Alfred K. Knopf, 1995), p. 277.

31. For a study of one such prophecy see, for instance, Jan Nattier, *Once Upon a Future Time: Studies in a Buddhist Prophecy of Decline* (Berkeley: Asian Humanities Press, 1991).

32. See Arthur F. Wright, "Buddhism in Modern and Contemporary China," in Robert F. Spenser, ed., *Religion and Change in Contemporary Asia* (Minneapolis: University of Minnesota Press, 1972), pp. 19–20.

33. V. S. Naipaul, *India: A Wounded Civilization* (New York: Vintage Books, 1978), p. 17.

Chapter 8: *Theravāda Buddhism in America*

I presented the contents of this chapter in full at the Buddhism Section and North American Religions Section, American Academy of Religion (AAR) Annual Meeting, Chicago, November 20, 1994. Some content and wording from this essay appear in Paul Numrich, "*Vinaya* in Theravāda Temples in the United States," *Journal of Buddhist Ethics* 1 (1994): 23–32; and Paul Numrich, *Old Wisdom in the New*

World: Americanization in Two Immigrant Theravada Buddhist Temples (Knoxville: University of Tennessee Press, 1996).

1. See Numrich, *Old Wisdom in the New World.*

2. Walpola Rahula, *Zen and the Taming of the Bull: Towards the Definition of Buddhist Thought* (London: Gordon Fraser, 1978), pp. 55–67.

3. I generally rely on the PTS *Pali-English Dictionary* (T. W. Rhys Davids and William Stede, eds., 1986 reprint) for definitions of Pali terms.

4. In order of increasing perfection: *sotāpatti* (stream-enterer), *sakadāgāmi* (once-returner), *anāgāmi* (never-returner), and *arahatta* (holy one or saint).

5. For these terms, see, respectively, W. Rahula, *Zen and the Taming of the Bull*, p. 59; Richard F. Gombrich, *Theravāda Buddhism: A Social History from Ancient Benares to Modern Colombo* (New York: Routledge, 1988), p. 2; Edmund F. Perry and Shanta Ratnayaka, "The Sangha as Refuge in the Theravāda Buddhist Tradition," in John Ross Carter, ed., *The Threefold Refuge in the Theravāda Buddhist Tradition* (Chambersburg, Pa.: Anima, 1982), p. 45; and Bardwell L. Smith, ed., *The Two Wheels of Dhamma: Essays on the Theravāda Tradition in India and Ceylon* (Chambersburg, Pa.: American Academy of Religion, "Studies in Religion" 3, 1972), p. 3.

6. See George D. Bond, *The Buddhist Revival in Sri Lanka: Religious Tradition, Reinterpretation and Response* (Columbia: University of South Carolina Press, 1988), pp. 22–33.

7. W. Rahula, in *Zen and the Taming of the Bull*, gives examples of places where Buddhaghosa's commentaries (fifth century C.E.), which played a crucial role in synthesizing traditional Theravāda, simply assume that the Pali canon has in mind *bhikkhu-sangha* rather than *sāvaka-* or *ariya-sangha*. The order of nuns eventually died out in Theravāda lands.

8. Gombrich, *Theravāda Buddhism*, p. 87.

9. See ibid., p. 2, and Perry and Ratnayaka, "The Sangha as Refuge," p. 43.

10. *Samantapāsādikā* I, 102; cf. *Mahāvaṃsa*, 126; *Dīpavaṃsa*, chap. 14, verses 20–24; *Vinaya-nidāna*, 103.

11. See W. Rahula, *History of Buddhism in Ceylon*, 2d ed. (Colombo: M. D. Gunasena, 1966), p. 56, and Gombrich, *Theravāda Buddhism*, pp. 150–51.

12. Michael Carrithers, " 'They Will Be Lords upon the Island': Buddhism in Sri Lanka," in Heinz Bechert and Richard Gombrich, eds., *The World of Buddhism: Buddhist Monks and Nuns in Society and Culture* (New York: Facts on File, 1984), p. 133.

13. I use the term *American Buddhism* to distinguish this convert expression of Buddhism from immigrant Buddhism in the United States. On a democratized usage of *sangha*, see, for example, Rick Fields, *How the Swans Came to the Lake: A Narrative History of Buddhism in America*, 3d ed. (Boston: Shambhala, 1992); also, consider this advertisement from the summer 1990 Newsletter of Insight Meditation West, Spirit Rock: "Are you looking for a service and would you prefer to hire a Sangha Member? The Sangha Service Directory includes a wide range of services from carpenters to travel agents, accountants to piano tuners."

14. That is, *upāsaka-* and *upāsikā-sangha* do not occur, though, of course, laypeople are theoretically included in the terms *sāvaka-* or *ariya-sangha*. Rather, the texts prefer the term *parisā* (surrounding people), particularly in the phrase *cattāro parisā*, the "fourfold company" of *bhikkhus, bhikkhunīs, upāsakas* (male lay followers), and

upāsikās (female lay followers). Thus, we do read of *upāsaka-* and *upāsikā-parisā*. See W. Rahula, *Zen and the Taming of the Bull*, p. 59; Perry and Ratnayaka, "The Sangha as Refuge," p. 49; and Mohan Wijayaratna, *Buddhist Monastic Life, According to the Texts of the Theravāda Tradition*, trans. Claude Grangier and Steven Collins (New York: Cambridge University Press, 1990), p. 1.

15. I use the term *immigrant* without limiting its meaning to the technical definition given by the Immigration and Naturalization Service. Thus, immigrants include refugees, asylees, illegals—all ethnic Asians who have come to this country.

16. These estimates are extrapolated from data in my 1992 dissertation at Northwestern University, "Americanization in Immigrant Theravada Buddhist Temples," pp. 572–75.

17. I do not include the Southeast Asian custom of temporary ordination of monks in this consideration.

18. Jack Kornfield, "Sex Lives of the Gurus," *Yoga Journal* 63 (July–August 1985): 26.

19. Wijayaratna, *Buddhist Monastic Life*, p. 3. A report on a survey of American Theravāda Buddhists (Reverend Anagarika Martha Dharmapali, "Will North America Have a Traditional Monastic Sangha?" presented to the International Monastic Seminar in Taiwan, October 1993) includes this revealing data, pointing up the tendency to put off monastic renunciation until some future time: "20% felt that they would be ready to enter the monastic life in 5–10 years. About 12% in 20 years; another 20% not at all. Others wanted to enter in 12 months, other variations."

20. Dharmapali, "Will North America Have a Traditional Monastic Sangha?"

21. Rita M. Gross, *Buddhism after Patriarchy: A Feminist History, Analysis, and Reconstruction of Buddhism* (Albany: State University of New York Press, 1993), p. 142.

22. Ibid., p. 40. Commenting on the situation today, Elizabeth J. Harris says, "It reinforces *Theravāda* Buddhism, in the eyes of those women seeking new patterns of relationships between women and men, as male chauvinist and sexist." See "The Female in Buddhism," *Dialogue*, n.s. 19–20 (1992–93): 54.

23. *Vinaya* II, 253–56.

24. The quotation is from Wijayaratna, *Buddhist Monastic Life*, p. 160, though he limits his discussion there to the Buddha's concerns for the *bhikkhunī-sangha* only. Of course, the Buddha's "social and practical concerns" extended to the impact the *bhikkhunī-sangha* would have on the *bhikkhu-sangha*, as evidenced, for instance, by the rules regulating interaction between a monk and a nun (e.g., the *Ovādavagga* section of the *pātimokkha sikkhāpada*).

25. *Vinaya* II, 255; IV, 51; *Aṅguttara-Nikāya* IV, 276; also, Wijayaratna, *Buddhist Monastic Life*, pp. 159–60.

26. This phrase is from Reverend Martha Dharmapali, in an unpublished 1992 document titled "Preliminary Statement on Bhikshuni Order in the West."

27. Gross, *Buddhism after Patriarchy*, p. 37.

28. Ibid., p. 38.

29. See Tessa J. Bartholomeusz, *Women under the Bō Tree: Buddhist Nuns in Sri Lanka* (Cambridge: Cambridge University Press, 1994); Chatsumarn Kabilsingh, *Thai Women in Buddhism* (Berkeley: Parallax Press, 1991); Karma Lekshe Tsomo, ed., *Sakyadhita: Daughters of the Buddha* (Ithaca, N.Y.: Snow Lion, 1988); and *Spring Wind–Buddhist Cultural Forum*, special issue: "Women and Buddhism," 6, no. 1–3

(1986). The *Spring Wind* special issue reports over 2,000 "nuns" in Sri Lanka, 70,000 in Thailand (p. 73).

30. Wijayaratna, *Buddhist Monastic Life*, p. 162: "such a legal act (*saṅgha-kamma*) is no longer possible." According to Senarath Wijayasundara, "Revival of the Order of Buddhist Nuns: Yes or No!!!" *Newsletter on Inter-National Buddhist Women's Activities* 11, no. 1 (1994): 5, the same issue arose in the Mahāyāna tradition in China centuries ago, and was resolved by a *Vinaya* expert in the following way: "monks would be deemed to be at fault only if they had given full ordination without nuns when the latter were available." Nothing prohibited full ordination by the *bhikkhu-sangha* alone when no *bhikkhunī-sangha* could be found.

31. Gombrich, *Theravāda Buddhism*, p. 16, notes: "It seems likely that the Order of nuns will soon be revived in Theravāda by *western* Theravādins, who do not have to bother about public opinion in their own societies, since that opinion is perfectly indifferent to this question" (emphasis in original).

32. *Dharma Voice* (June–September 1989): 19. I have not come across documentation of *sāmaṇerī* ordinations in the United States prior to 1987.

33. *Dharma Voice* (April–July 1988): 17–18.

34. John Dart, "Buddhism Reaches Out in America," *Los Angeles Times*, November 20, 1988, p. 5.

35. *Dharma Voice* (June–September 1989): 19.

36. Kabilsingh, *Thai Women in Buddhism*, p. 106, notes: "This process will lead slowly to the ordination of bhikkhunis in the Theravadin tradition and eventually bring about the revival of the Bhikkhuni Sangha in the Theravadin lineage."

37. Dharmapali, "Preliminary Statement on Bhikshuni Order in the West." Reverend Dharmapali, it will be remembered, was the only "monastic" supported by NAMO TASSA.

38. On the 227 *pātimokkha sikkhāpada*, see Ñāṇamoli Thera, trans., *The Pātimokkha: 227 Fundamental Rules of a Bhikkhu* (Bangkok: King Mahā Makuta's Academy, 1969); and Vajirañāṇavarorasa, Navakovāda: Instructions for Newly-Ordained Bhikkhus and Sāmaṇeras (Bangkok: Mahā Makuta Buddhist University, 1971), pp. 5–31.

39. Kenneth E. Wells, *Thai Buddhism: Its Rites and Activities* (Bangkok: Suriyabun Publishers, 1975), p. 179.

40. More informal procedures (*pārisuddhi*, or purity) are followed with less than four monks; see *Vinaya* I, 124–25.

41. Gombrich, *Theravāda Buddhism*, p. 109.

42. Ibid., p. 108.

43. Wijayaratna, *Buddhist Monastic Life*, p. 124.

44. Ibid., p. 53.

45. The Theravāda texts tell us that Ānanda neglected to query the Buddha about the "minor" rules and that the First Buddhist Council could not make a determination thereupon (*Dīgha Nikāya* II, 154; *Vinaya* II, 287–88).

46. W. Rahula, *Zen and the Taming of the Bull*, p. 63.

47. Quotations from *World Buddhism in North America: A Documentary on the Conference on World Buddhism in North America*, videocassette (Ann Arbor: Zen Lotus Society, 1989).

48. Venerable Dr. Ratanasara immediately modified his statement, perhaps with

the notion of *pālimuttaka-vinicchaya* in mind: "If certain practices are to be altered, if you don't like to use 'alteration' or 'change,' we may call it 'to add.' "

49. I suggest in *Old Wisdom in the New World* that Theravāda Buddhism may hold a particular attraction for American converts from fundamentalist religious backgrounds.

50. See Fields, *How the Swans Came to the Lake*, and Katy Butler, "Encountering the Shadow in Buddhist America," *Common Boundary* (May–June 1990): 14–22.

51. Bhikkhu Bodhi contributed an "open letter" titled "What's Wrong with American Buddhism?" to a forum discussion in the now-defunct newspaper *Dharma Gate* 1, no. 3 (February 1992): 10–11. Two other American-convert monks whom I interviewed stressed the need for a monastic presence in American Buddhism. One spoke of a group in the Boston area that may soon take concrete steps in this direction. Another source told me of similar sentiments among a San Francisco area group. Several consultants pointed to the Bhavana Society's efforts as well.

52. A more detailed examination of these and other issues may be found in my dissertation.

53. *Vinaya* I, 289. The three-robes requirement is assumed in the *pātimokkha sikkhāpada*, the 227 precepts recited bimonthly by Theravāda monks. Specific precepts in the *pātimokkha* prescribe proper reception, possession, and wearing of the three robes.

54. Yogavacara Rahula, "Buddhism in the West: A View by a Western Buddhist Monk," *Dharma Voice* (April 1987): 16.

55. *Dharma Vijaya Newsletter* (February 1982): 3.

56. Gombrich, *Theravāda Buddhism*, p. 104.

57. *Vinaya* III, 109. The other *pārājika* offenses are taking something (above a certain value) not given, murder, and false claims of attaining superhuman states.

58. As mentioned earlier, monasticism goes against the grain of American culture. The perpetual, spiritually motivated chastity of the monastic calling must appear odd to the average American who, as a Sinhalese monk put it to me, seems to consider sex as much a human necessity as food and water.

59. I received slightly different opinions from two monks on the question of where to draw the line between the "major" (that is, unmodifiable) and the "minor" (that is, modifiable) rules in the 227 *pātimokkha sikkhāpada*. One monk, an ethnic Asian, considers the first 19 rules "major"—the 4 *pārājika*, the 13 *sanghādisesa*, and the 2 *aniyata* (these last forbidding a monk to be alone with a woman). The other monk, an American convert, draws the line at the first 17 rules only. An example of a "minor," modifiable rule in both of these interpretations would be the prohibition of traveling alone with a woman, one of the 92 *pācittiya*.

60. Summing up the frustrations sometimes felt by progressive Asian monks in immigrant temples, Venerable Dr. Ratanasara of Dharma Vijaya, Los Angeles, observed that "they often are trapped by their congregation members who wish them to remain 'old country' in order to preserve a nostalgia for their old home life, while they themselves pursue the new American dream." See John Dart, "Los Angeles Monk Advocates an Americanized Form of Buddhism," *Los Angeles Times*, July 8, 1989, sect. II, p. 7.

61. The term *anagārika*, literally "nonhouseholder," originally referred to a Buddhist monastic. Anagarika Dharmapala, the well-known Theravāda Buddhist re-

former who attended the World Parliament of Religions in Chicago in 1893, re-defined the term in significant ways. For Dharmapala, the *anagārika* "was neither a monk nor a layman. . . . [The new role] allowed him to pursue the religious life while being active in the world" (Bond, *Buddhist Revival in Sri Lanka*, p. 54). Bond profiles two modern *anagārikas*, one of whom considers himself a "higher layman," the other "really a monk" though not a member of the official monastic order (pp. 198–202).

62. These nine precepts should not be confused with the traditional Eight Pre-cepts (*aṭṭhaṅga sīla*).

63. Edward Conze notes in *Buddhism: Its Essence and Development* (New York: Har-per, 1959), p. 117: "During the last 1,500 years, the Old Wisdom School has been dying slowly, like a magnificent old tree, one branch breaking off after the other, until the trunk alone remains."

64. Charles Prebish, "Buddhism," in Charles H. Lippy and Peter W. Williams, eds., *Encyclopedia of the American Religious Experience: Studies of Traditions and Movements* (New York: Scribner's, 1988), 2:677, predicts: "It appears that, for the immediate future, Buddhism will remain an almost exclusively lay community in America."

65. The fundamentalist reasoning goes like this: the ancient texts call for women to be ordained by a prescribed procedure; since that procedure can no longer be implemented legally, women cannot be ordained today.

66. Reported in Eleanor Rosch, "World Buddhism in North America Today," *Vajradhatu Sun* 9, no. 1 (October–November 1987): 8. I take the reference to Ram Dass (formerly Richard Alpert) to reflect chagrin at the eclectic popularizing of Eastern religious traditions.

Chapter 9: Insight Meditation in the United States

I would like to thank Nancy Van House for patient and careful help in preparing this essay for publication.

1. *Inquiring Mind* 2, no. 1 (summer 1985): 7.

2. Jon Kabat-Zinn, *Full Catastrophe Living: Using the Wisdom of Your Body and Mind to Face Stress, Pain and Illness* (New York: Delta, 1991). In his subsequent best-selling book, *Wherever You Go, There You Are: Mindfulness Meditation in Everyday Life* (New York: Hyperion, 1994), Kabat-Zinn explicitly acknowledges the Buddhist origin of mindfulness practice.

3. The Dharma Seed Tape Library, a nonprofit business, sells, throughout the country, a large volume of taped Dharma talks by these teachers. Listening to such tapes is a popular activity among many American *vipassanā* students.

4. A discussion of this modernization movement can be found in Donald K. Swearer, *The Buddhist World of Southeast Asia* (Albany: State University of New York Press, 1995), pp. 107–61.

5. Personal communication, June 1995.

6. Sujata wrote a short but popular book on mindfulness practice called *Begin-ning to See* (Berkeley: Celestial Arts, 1987). Ruth Denison teaches at Dhamma Dena, her retreat center outside of Joshua Tree, California.

7. In private communication (November 1995), Jack Kornfield mentioned that

around 1975 the average age of *vipassanā* retreatants was thirty, with most being in their twenties and thirties.

8. For further discussion on these developments, see Jack Kornfield, "Is Buddhism Changing in North America?" in Don Morreale, ed., *Buddhist America: Centers, Retreats, Practices* (Santa Fe, N.M.: John Muir Publications, 1988), pp. xi–xxviii.

9. Ernest Troeltsch, *The Social Teachings of the Christian Churches* (London: Allen and Unwin, 1931).

10. *Inquiring Mind* 5, no. 1 (summer 1988).

11. Jack Kornfield, *A Path with Heart* (Boston: Bantam Books, 1993), p. 244. The influence between Western psychotherapy and the *vipassanā* movement has often been mutual. Mark Epstein, in his popular and influential book *Thoughts without a Thinker: Psychotherapy from a Buddhist Perspective* (New York: Basic Books/HarperCollins, 1995), discusses how Western psychotherapy can be enhanced by Buddhist spirituality, particularly that of the *vipassanā* movement.

12. Kornfield, *A Path with Heart*, p. 246. In 1988, Kornfield published an article in the *Inquiring Mind* 5, no. 1 (summer 1988) titled "Meditation and Psychotherapy: A Plea for Integration."

13. Jack Kornfield, *Living Buddhist Masters* (Boulder: Prajna Press, 1983).

14. Joseph Goldstein, *Insight Meditation: The Practice of Freedom* (Boston: Shambhala, 1993), p. 8.

15. Mahāsi Sayādaw, *The Satipatthāna Vipassanā Meditation: A Basic Buddhist Mindfulness Exercise* (Rangoon, Burma: Department of Religious Affairs, 1979), p. 7.

16. Jack Kornfield, ed., *Teachings of the Buddha* (Boston: Shambhala, 1993), p. x.

17. Ajahn Chah, *Bodhinyāna: A Collection of Dhamma Talks* (Ubon Rajathani, Thailand: Wat Pah Pong, 1980), p. 45.

18. Goldstein, *Insight Meditation*, p. 3.

19. From a brochure titled "The Path of the Buddha," written by *vipassanā* teacher Guy Armstrong.

20. The classic discussion of these stages is in the *Visuddhimagga* by Buddhaghosa (translated into English under the title *The Path of Purification* [Kandy, Sri Lanka: Buddhist Publication Society, 1987]). It is also discussed in Mahāsi Sayādaw, *Practical Insight Meditation: Basic and Progressive Stages* (Kandy, Sri Lanka: Buddhist Publication Society, 1971). These "stages of insight" are seldom referred to in the writings and public talks of the American *vipassanā* teachers. Like most Asian *vipassanā* teachers, they prefer that students not learn about these stages prior to experiencing them for themselves. In part this is to avoid the meditation hindrance of anticipation and in part it is to avoid conditioning students' experience. The absence of public discussion of these teachings should be noted by anyone studying the *vipassanā* movement. The published books and public talks do not provide the researcher with the full range of the movement's teachings.

21. That is, loving-kindness, sympathetic joy, compassion, and equanimity.

22. The first reference in print to the forgiveness meditation that American teachers sometimes use to precede loving-kindness meditation is found in Stephen Levine, *A Gradual Awakening* (New York: Doubleday, 1979), pp. 86–87.

23. Jack Kornfield and Paul Breiter, ed., *A Still Forest Pool: The Insight Meditation of Achaan Chah* (Wheaton, Ill.: The Theosophical Publishing House, 1986), p. 155.

24. Sharon Salzberg, *Lovingkindness: The Revolutionary Art of Happiness* (Boston: Shambhala, 1995).

25. Joseph Goldstein and Jack Kornfield, *Seeking the Heart of Wisdom: The Path of Insight Meditation* (Boston: Shambhala, 1987), p. 183.

26. The *vipassanā* teacher's code of ethics is found in the appendix of Jack Kornfield's *Path with Heart*, pp. 340–43.

27. Goldstein and Kornfield, *Seeking the Heart of Wisdom*, p. 8.

28. Kornfield, *A Path with Heart*, p. 341.

29. A good example of the eclectic and ecumenical utilization of material from the world's spiritual traditions is found in *vipassanā* teachers Christina Feldman and Jack Kornfield's book, *Stories of the Spirit, Stories of the Heart: Parables of the Spiritual Path from around the World* (San Francisco: HarperCollins, 1991).

30. Goldstein and Kornfield, *Seeking the Heart of Wisdom*, p. 173.

31. These figures are conservatively obtained by doubling the number of sitting groups listed in the spring 1984 and the fall 1995 issues of the *Inquiring Mind* (1, no. 1 and 12, no. 1). Probably a majority of the *vipassanā* sitting groups in the United States are not listed in this journal (*Inquiring Mind*, P.O. Box 9999, North Berkeley Station, Berkeley, California 94709).

32. Ibid., 12, no. 1.

33. These figures are calculated based on the number of well-advertised or listed retreats offered each year in the United States and Europe. Estimating that half of the retreatants have attended previous retreats, only half of the participants were counted in these calculations.

34. Of the eleven primary teachers at Spirit Rock, all but one have attended not only college but also graduate or professional school.

35. Jack Kornfield, in the chapter discussing self and no-self in his book, *A Path with Heart*, has a section titled "From No Self to True Self."

Chapter 10: Who Is a Buddhist?

I would like to acknowledge the valuable comments on an earlier draft of this essay provided by Stephen R. Bokenkamp, Gil Fronsdal, George Tanabe, Kenneth Tanaka, and Thomas Tweed. Any errors of fact or interpretation that remain are my responsibility.

1. In the first edition of Edwin Gaustad's *A Religious History of America* (New York: Harper and Row, 1974), for example, there is no entry for Buddhism in the index; in the revised 1990 edition Buddhism receives five brief mentions. Winthrop S. Hudson's *Religion in America* contained four sentences on Buddhism in its first edition (New York: Charles Scribner's Sons, 1965); interestingly, a paragraph devoted to Zen in the second edition (1973, p. 427) had shrunk to two sentences in the third edition (1981, p. 425), a situation that has remained in effect through the fifth edition (1992) coauthored with John Corrigan. There is no mention of Buddhism (at least, none betrayed by the index) in *Religion in America* (New York: Macmillan, 1975) by George C. Bedell, Leo Sandon, Jr., and Charles T. Wellborn. Finally, in Sydney E. Ahlstrom's monumental *A Religious History of the American People* (New Haven: Yale University Press, 1972), Buddhism is accorded a total of only two pages (pp. 1050–51).

2. By far the best treatment of Buddhism in a survey of American religions is Catherine L. Albanese's *America: Religions and Religion*, 2d ed. (Belmont, Calif.: Wadsworth, 1992), where a well-balanced overview of Buddhism in America (including Asian American Buddhism) appears on pp. 310–18. A comparable discussion appeared in the first edition, published in 1981.

3. It is probably not a cause for rejoicing that two Buddhist groups, the Sōka Gakkai (under its old name of Nichiren Shōshū Academy) and Vajradhatu (founded by Chögyam Trungpa), were accorded a place in J. Gordon Melton's *Encyclopedic Handbook of Cults in America* (New York: Garland, 1986).

4. In Richard H. Robinson's *The Buddhist Religion* (Belmont, Calif.: Dickenson, 1970), for example—long the standard textbook in this field—Buddhism in North America is not included in his narrative survey, receiving only a cameo appearance in the introduction (pp. 8–9). Sections on Western Buddhism were added to the second and third editions of the book (1977 and 1982, respectively), which were published after Robinson's death under the coauthorship of Willard Johnson. Though no other textbook ever approached the popularity of Robinson's work, it is worth pointing out the absence of any discussion of North American Buddhism in Sangharakshita's *A Survey of Buddhism* even through its fifth edition (Boulder: Shambhala, 1980) and in Edward Conze's *Buddhism: Its Essence and Development* (Oxford: Bruno Cassirer, 1951), though the latter does add a brief (and quite pessimistic) note on Buddhism in Europe (pp. 210–12). The first textbook I am aware of in which a separate discussion is devoted to Buddhism in the West is Charles S. Prebish, ed., *Buddhism: A Modern Perspective* (University Park: Pennsylvania State University Press, 1975), pp. 248–54; the portion devoted to Buddhism in the United States, however, occupies less than a page (p. 252). More recent surveys and anthologies—e.g., Peter Harvey's *An Introduction to Buddhism* (Cambridge: Cambridge University Press, 1990) and John Strong's *Experience of Buddhism* (Belmont, Calif.: Wadsworth, 1995), though not Donald Lopez's *Buddhism in Practice* (Princeton: Princeton University Press, 1995)—generally devote a separate section to this topic.

5. While the field of North American Religions includes both the United States and Canada, most of the information available to me deals exclusively with Buddhism in the United States. A forthcoming book on Buddhism in America by Canadian resident Richard Hayes, titled *Land of No Buddha* (to be published by Windhorse Press), may help to remedy this situation.

6. Buddhists totaled 0.4 percent of the population of the United States according to a survey conducted in 1990 by the City University of New York; see Barry A. Kosmin and Seymour P. Lachman, *One Nation under God: Religion in Contemporary American Society* (New York: Harmony Books, 1993), p. 3.

7. A comparable situation obtains in Japan, where a similarly small percentage of Christians (likewise comprising less than 1 percent of the population) have exerted a significant influence through literature and other media. In Japan an additional factor has been the status of the United States as a "prestige culture" in the years since Japan's defeat in World War II and the ensuing American occupation. An inquiry into some of the very different ways in which Japan, Tibet, and to a lesser degree other Asian countries are viewed as "prestige cultures" by some sectors of the American population would no doubt yield rewarding results.

8. Rodney Stark and William Sims Bainbridge (*The Future of Religion* [Berkeley:

University of California Press, 1985]) cite statistics that 96 percent of Americans (numbers are drawn exclusively from the United States) "pray sometimes" (p. 83) and 94 percent (or 86 percent, depending on how the question is phrased) believe in the existence of God (p. 79), but that only 54 percent attend church more often than once a month (p. 77). Though separate figures are not given for Jewish participation in formal services, Stark and Bainbridge suggest in passing that these percentages would be even lower (p. 76).

9. Stark and Bainbridge, *The Future of Religion*; the typology discussed here is developed in chap. 2.

10. Or, in the felicitous phrase of Thomas Tweed, "night-stand Buddhists" (in "Asian Religions in America: Reflections on an Emerging Subfield," in Walter H. Conser, Jr., and Sumner B. Twiss, eds., *Religious Diversity and American Religious History: Case Studies in Traditions and Cultures* [Athens: University of Georgia Press, 1997], p. 205).

11. In using the term "new religion" I do not mean to imply that any religion is ever *entirely* new. Religious founders, even while introducing what appear to be radically new ideas and practices, always make use of the raw materials that are available in their own religious environment. There may also be significant differences of opinion between insiders (that is, group members) and outsiders as to whether a given religion is genuinely new (in Stark and Bainbridge's terms, a cult) or a reform and restatement of an existing religion (that is, a sect).

12. Space does not allow an adequate development of this topic here, but one especially striking difference may be pointed out: while a common feature of all genuinely new religions (and I make this sweeping statement advisedly) is rapid change, as their founders and immediate successors try out, reject, and improve various methods of presenting their message, a common feature of transplants (here less universal, for reasons to be discussed below) is their conservatism. Change may well take place (and in fact always does) when a religion is transplanted to a new environment, but such change often comes about slowly and with considerable resistance.

13. The phrase "two Buddhisms" was introduced by Charles Prebish in 1979, though at that time his distinction was based not on ethnicity but on the contrast between a form of Buddhism that "places primary emphasis on sound, basic doctrines, shared by all Buddhists, and on solid religious practice" versus the "other line of development [which] includes those groups that seem to emerge shortly after radical social movements" (*American Buddhism*, p. 51). In a more recent article he redefined the first of these categories as "Buddhism practised by essentially Asian American communities" ("Two Buddhisms Reconsidered," *Buddhist Studies Review* 10, no. 2 [1993]: 187). The term "White Buddhism" was introduced by Rick Fields in the first edition of *How the Swans Came to the Lake* (1981, p. 83), and was used more recently by the same author in an article published in *Tricycle* ("Confessions of a White Buddhist," 4 [fall 1994]: 54–56) and elaborated in this volume.

14. It is probably worth pointing out that the boundary between the arena of Buddhist practice and the scholarly community of Buddhist Studies is quite permeable, and that there is considerable feedback in both directions. This is particularly true with what I will describe later as "Elite" Buddhist communities, though it is increasingly the case with Ethnic and Evangelical Buddhists as well.

15. "Visible and Invisible: The Politics of Representation in Buddhist America," *Tricycle* 5, no. 1 (fall 1995): 42–49.

16. Note that I have used the term "elite," and not "elitist," to describe this category. Being a member of an elite is an objective socioeconomic condition; "elitism" is an attitude.

17. This is not to suggest, of course, that members of Buddhist groups of the other two types do not have their own ethnic identities. In choosing the name "Ethnic Buddhism" for this category I intend only to draw attention to the fact that a shared ethnicity is the *primary* defining feature of these groups, in contrast to Buddhist organizations of the Elite and Evangelical types which—though a given ethnic group (European American, African American, Latino, and so on) may well predominate in a particular community—are defined primarily by another feature.

18. Or perhaps not, if the observer is especially astute. In the course of adapting the typology published in *Tricycle* ("Visible and Invisible") for inclusion in this chapter I had occasion to look at the discussion of American Buddhism in the work of Catherine Albanese (*America: Religions and Religion*). She, too, identifies a threefold pattern in American Buddhist communities, though her analysis does not appear to be based on patterns of transmission as such. Her categories of "meditative," "evangelical," and "church" Buddhism are remarkably similar in their overall contours to the three types presented here.

19. See *Tricycle* 1, no. 2 (winter 1991): 4. Tworkov's editorial was reprinted together with a response by Ryo Imamura, a reply by Tworkov, and an introduction to the controversy by Diane Ames, in *The Sangha Newsletter* (Newsletter of the Wider Shin Buddhist Fellowship), no. 7 (summer 1994): 2–10. This newsletter has a limited circulation and can be difficult to locate in libraries; individual copies can be obtained by writing to the editor at 420 Kearney St., #5, El Cerrito, California 94530.

20. Letter of April 25, 1992, reprinted in *The Sangha Newsletter*, p. 7.

21. Letter of May 14, 1992, reprinted in *The Sangha Newsletter*, p. 9.

22. Just as in our own time the vast majority of published material on Buddhism in North America is written by, for, and/or about Elite Buddhists, so in the Chinese case the vast majority of surviving literature, especially from this early period, deals with the activities and concerns of the elite. We know virtually nothing, for example, about temples founded by and for Buddhist immigrants from Central Asia, and we know little (until much later in Chinese history) about the impact of Buddhist proselytizing on the masses. While analogues to our categories of Ethnic and Evangelical Buddhism almost certainly existed in China, they are not visible in the sources available to us today.

23. Kenneth Ch'en, *The Chinese Transformation of Buddhism* (Princeton: Princeton University Press, 1973).

24. The search for an original copy of the *Vinaya* (then unavailable in China) was the main motive for the trip to India undertaken by the famous Chinese monk Fa-hsien in 399. He succeeded in his task, and several *Vinaya* texts were translated into Chinese in succeeding decades.

25. These two items emerge in Tweed's study as "nonnegotiable cultural demands" (not his term), to which all the participants in this early phase of interest in Buddhism had to accommodate themselves. Two other core values identified by Tweed—individualism and theism—appear to have been more negotiable. See

Thomas A. Tweed, *The American Encounter with Buddhism 1844–1912: Victorian Culture and the Limits of Dissent* (Bloomington: Indiana University Press, 1992), p. 133.

26. The decision by Japanese American Shin Buddhists to refer to their temples as "churches" and their priests as "ministers," for example, seems clearly to reflect Protestant usage. Even more striking are such non-Japanese features as the use of pews for seating and the singing of hymns as part of Buddhist services.

27. For this and other instances of Shin Buddhist recasting of Christian hymns (e.g., "Buddha, Savior, Pilot Me" and "Joy to the World, the Buddha Has Come") see Louise H. Hunter, *Buddhism in Hawaii: Its Impact on a Yankee Community* (Honolulu: University of Hawaii Press, 1971), p. 131. The widely circulated rumor of the existence of a similar hymn titled "Buddha Loves Me, This I Know" appears, as best as I have been able to determine, to be without any basis in fact.

28. Cited in an unpublished paper by Ken Tanaka, "A Prospectus of the Buddhist Churches of America: The Role of Ethnicity," p. 10. A final decision on this proposal, first submitted by the Ministers' Association in February 1994, is to be made following the celebration of the centennial of the Buddhist Churches of America in 1999 (Ken Tanaka, personal communication, 1995).

Chapter 11: Divided Dharma

1. The National Survey of Religious Identification, City College of New York Graduate Center, 1989–90.

2. Rick Fields, "Confessions of a White Buddhist," *Tricycle: The Buddhist Review* 4, no. 1 (fall 1994): 54–56.

3. Jan Nattier, "Visible and Invisible," *Tricycle: The Buddhist Review* 5, no. 1 (fall 1995): 42–49. See also Charles S. Prebish, "Two Buddhisms Reconsidered," *Buddhist Studies Review* 10, no. 2 (1993): 187–206.

4. Lewis Woods, *Inquiring Mind* 13, no. 1 (fall 1996): 47.

5. Rick Fields, *How the Swans Came to the Lake: A Narrative History of Buddhism in America*, 3d ed. (Boston: Shambhala, 1992), p. 102.

6. Henry Steel Olcott, *The Buddhist Catechism* (Wheaton, Ill.: Theosophical Publishing House, 1970), p. 1. See also Stephan Prothero, *The White Buddhist: The Asian Odyssey of Henry Steel Olcott* (Bloomington: Indiana University Press, 1996).

7. Guenther Barth, *Bitter Strength* (Cambridge, Mass.: Harvard University Press, 1964), pp. 123–24.

8. Stuart Creighton Miller, *The Unwelcome Immigrant: The American Image of the Chinese, 1785–1882* (Berkeley: University of California Press, 1969), p. 3.

9. Much of the following discussion has been suggested by Jack Kornfield in "Is Buddhism Changing in North America?" in Don Morreale, ed., *Buddhist America: Centers, Retreats, Practices* (Santa Fe, N.M.: John Muir Publications, 1988), pp. xi–xxviii.

10. Jack Kornfield, *A Path with Heart* (New York: Bantam Books, 1993), pp. 244–45.

11. Carole Tonkinson, ed., *Big Sky Mind: Buddhism and the Beat Generation* (New York: Riverhead Books, 1995), p. 73.

12. bell hooks, "Waking Up to Racism," *Tricycle: The Buddhist Review* 4, no. 1 (fall 1994): 45.

13. Don Farber and Rick Fields, *Taking Refuge in L.A.: Life in a Vietnamese Buddhist Temple* (New York: Aperture Foundation, 1987), p. 14.

14. Pamela Gang Sherman, "Parenting as Path," *Turning Wheel, Journal of the Buddhist Peace Fellowship* (winter 1996): 29.

Chapter 12: Americanizing the Buddha

1. Carus to Beard, December 13, 1899, Open Court Papers, Special Collections/ Morris Library, Southern Illinois University at Carbondale (hereinafter referred to as Open Court Papers).

2. Carus to Sōen, June 29, 1895, Open Court Papers.

3. Milton R. Konvitz and Gail Kennedy, eds., *The American Pragmatists* (Cleveland: World Publishing, 1960), p. 174.

4. Thomas A. Tweed, *The American Encounter with Buddhism 1844–1912: Victorian Culture and the Limits of Dissent* (Bloomington: Indiana University Press, 1992), p. 65.

5. Erik Zürcher, *The Buddhist Conquest of China: The Spread and Adaptation of Buddhism in Early Medieval China* (Leiden: E. J. Brill, 1972), p. 12.

6. Daisetz Teitaro Suzuki, *Outlines of Mahayana Buddhism* (New York: Schocken Books, 1907), p. 29. For the story of Barlaam and Josaphat, see St. John Demascene, *Barlaam and Iosaph*, with an English translation by the Reverend G. R. Woodward and H. Mattingly (Cambridge, Mass.: Harvard University Press, 1953); Joseph Jacobs, *Barlaam and Josaphat*, English Lives of Buddha (London: D. Nutt, 1896); and Rick Fields, *How the Swans Came to the Lake: A Narrative History of Buddhism in America* (Boulder: Shambhala, 1981), pp. 17–19.

7. *Christian/Christianity* I use here to mean Protestantism, but inclusive of the broader Judeo-Christian background from which it emerges. In the American context it gradually assumed a more secular dimension: a "civic religion" and ideology supplying American society with its overarching sense of unity and a structure of values and beliefs. *Christian* thus came to mean not only one who believed in the teachings of the Bible, a divine creator, and redemption through Christ, but also one who equally believed in democracy, free enterprise economics, individualism, and egalitarianism.

Science, as used in the nineteenth century, meant "knowledge" acquired objectively with the implication of certainty. In the twentieth century, modern science has come to mean more a method or a form of inquiry into natural phenomena, a consensus of information held at any one time and all of which may be modified by new discoveries and new interpretations at any moment. For Victorians, however, natural science provided a norm of truth. They believed that science provided truth eternal and universal; that the laws of the universe are fixed and everywhere the same. This science assumes that these governing principles are objective and discoverable exclusively through "natural" versus "supernatural" means or explanations.

Liberal-modernism describes an ideology that matured in the late nineteenth and early twentieth centuries that combined tendencies growing out of classical liberalism and religious modernism. In its American form, it might be expressed as "the progress, prosperity, unity, peace, and happiness of the world," with America cast as the vanguard of world progress, duty-bound to uplift those lower on the evolutionary scale. It implied faith in the ability of humankind to perfect and apply laws of progressive betterment until reaching the earthly millennium. It exhibited a strong internationalist spirit, yet favored Protestant Christianity, Anglo-Saxonism, and professionalism as key ingredients in an American-led global social and economic development.

Modernism refers to a late nineteenth- and early twentieth-century movement that tried to reconcile historical Christianity with the findings of modern science and philosophy. It placed greater stress on the humanistic aspects of religion, and on the immanent rather than the transcendent nature of God. *Buddhist modernism* reflects a reinterpretation of Buddhism as a "system of thought"—a reinterpretation that grew out of a close interrelation between Buddhist resurgence in the East and the modern spread of Buddhism in the West. Traditional cosmology, the belief in miracles, and other elements that were unacceptable to a modern thinker were identified as inessential accretions Buddhism accumulated during its long historical development. Buddhist modernists interpret early Buddhism as a philosophy in relation to contemporary philosophical thought, and tend to downplay the mystical, "mythological," and psychical aspects of religion in favor of the "rational" and psychological.

See Heinz Bechert and Richard Gombrich, eds., *The World of Buddhism: Buddhist Monks and Nuns in Society and Culture* (London: Thames and Hudson, 1984); and Emily S. Rosenberg, *Spreading the American Dream: American Economic and Cultural Expansion, 1890–1945*, American Century Series (New York: Hill and Wang, 1982).

8. Special Collections, Southern Illinois University at Carbondale, "Inventory of the Open Court Publishing Co. Records 1886–1930" (August 1972), p. 4.

9. Taken from Paul Carus, *Homilies of Science* (Chicago: Open Court Publishing, 1897), pp. vi–vii.

10. Ibid.

11. Paul Carus, *Godward: A Record of Religious Progress* (Chicago: Open Court Publishing, 1898), pp. 3–5.

12. Paul Carus, *The Dawn of a New Religious Era, and Other Essays* (Chicago: Open Court Publishing, 1916), p. 72.

13. Carus, "Science, a Religious Revelation," in *Dawn*, pp. 24–26.

14. William James described the scientific zeitgeist: "Never were as many men of a decidedly empiricist proclivity in existence as there are at the present day. Our children, one may say, are almost born scientific. But our esteem for facts has not neutralized in us all religiousness. It is itself almost religious. Our scientific temper is devout . . . the conflict between science and religion [is] in full blast. . . . The romantic spontaneity and courage are gone, the vision is materialistic and depressing." William James, "The Present Dilemma in Philosophy," in *Pragmatism* (New York: Literary Classics of the United States, 1992), pp. 492–93.

15. Reverend John Henry Barrows, *The World's Parliament of Religions: An Illustrated and Popular Story of the World's First Parliament of Religions, Held in Chicago in Connection with the Columbian Exposition of 1893* (Chicago: Parliament Publishing, 1893), 2:829–31.

16. Ibid., pp. 862–73. There is little doubt that Dharmapala, like Sōen, saw himself as Buddhist missionary to the West. So did his audience. The St. Louis *Observer*

reported, "With his black curly locks thrown back from his broad brow, his keen, clear eye fixed upon the audience, his long brown fingers emphasizing the utterances of his vibrant voice, [Dharmapala] looked the very image of a propagandist, and one trembled to know that such a figure stood at the head of the movement to consolidate all the disciples of Buddha and to spread 'the light of Asia' throughout the world." Cited in ibid., p. 95.

17. Ibid.

18. Paul Carus, *Karma: A Story of Early Buddhism* (Chicago: Open Court Publishing, c. 1894), p. 21.

19. Carus, "The Religion of a Forerunner of Christ," *Open Court* 4 (43): 2635–36.

20. Sōen Shaku, *Zen for Americans*, trans. Daisetz Teitaro Suzuki (LaSalle, Ill.: Open Court, 1906), p. 122. Note: Sōen Shaku was credited with the letter of response, "Reply to a Christian Critic," but correspondence between the two strongly suggests that Carus initiated the exchange and penned the letter himself. Sōen merely signed his name to Carus's work.

21. Paul Carus, *Buddhism and Its Christian Critics* (Chicago: Open Court Publishing, 1897), p. 131.

22. Barrows, *The World's Parliament*, pp. 829–31.

23. Carus, *Buddhism and Its Christian Critics*, p. 114.

24. Ibid., p. 309.

25. Carus to Washburn, November 24, 1899, Open Court Papers.

26. Sōen to Carus, March 9, May 17, 1895 (2554), Open Court Papers.

27. Konen Tsunemitsu, "Soen Shaku," *Dharma World* 18 (November–December 1991): 32–36. On their first meeting, Carus impressed Sōen as exuding an almost saintly demeanor: "He held a black straw hat in his hand, and wore a suit. His hair and beard were unkempt and seemed for a long time to have been strangers to the barber's scissors. Since Carus came to America . . . he seems very unusual, like a Taoist sage. Though he wore no diamond on his finger, his eyes were piercingly bright" (ibid., 34).

28. D. T. Suzuki, "A Glimpse of Paul Carus," in Joseph Kitagawa, ed., *Introduction to Modern Trends in World Religions* (LaSalle, Ill.: Open Court Publishing, 1959), p. x.

29. Sōen to Carus, May 17, 1895 (2554), Open Court Papers.

30. Konen Tsunemitsu, "Soen Shaku."

31. Sōen to Carus, December 17, 1895, Open Court Papers.

32. Ibid.

33. As quoted in the *Journal of the Maha-Bodhi Society* 1, no. 11 (March 1893): 5.

34. Ibid.

35. See Eliade, *Encyclopedia of Religion*, pp. 184–86.

36. D. T. Suzuki, *Outlines of Mahayana Buddhism*, pp. 34–35, 26, 29.

37. Sōen Shaku, *Zen for Americans*.

38. Ibid., p. 81.

39. Ibid., pp. 37, 50, 73.

40. D. T. Suzuki, *Outlines of Mahayana Buddhism*, pp. 46–49; a fuller discussion follows in his chap. 9, "The Dharmakaya," pp. 217–41.

41. Carus to K. Nukariya, 1913?, Open Court Papers 32A/3/3.

42. See James Edward Ketelaar, *Of Heretics and Martyrs in Meiji Japan: Buddhism and Its Persecution* (Princeton: Princeton University Press, 1990).

43. Westerners, of course, have long projected their fears and ambitions, dreams, and desires onto Asia. From the earliest contacts to the present, the East has been repeatedly reconstructed from generation to generation—sometimes to explore fantasies and throw off Western restraints; at other times, to discover a mystic spirituality or quest for paradise regained. For example, the very idea of a "spiritual" East in contrast to the "material" West was largely an intellectual chimera of Western thinkers in collaboration with their Western-educated Oriental counterparts. The idea never gained widespread popularity in an Asia eager to modernize, develop, and excel the West. See Stephen N. Hay, *Asian Ideas of East and West: Tagore and His Critics in Japan, China, and India* (Cambridge, Mass.: Harvard University Press, 1970); John M. Steadman, *The Myth of Asia* (New York: Simon and Schuster, 1969). Moreover, the projection onto each other of this East-West spiritual-material fiction encouraged a mystified notion that a new age was dawning—a mythical, golden era of an East-West synthesis. The notion persists that we can harmoniously weld two civilizations and thereby restore humanity's fragmented psyche. See also Henri Baudet, *Paradise on Earth: Some Thoughts on European Images of Non-European Man*, trans. Elizabeth Wentholt (Middletown, Conn.: Wesleyan University Press, 1959, 1965, 1988).

44. Carus, *Buddhism and Its Christian Critics*, p. 159.

45. Paul Carus, *The Gospel of Buddha* (LaSalle, Ill.: Open Court Publishing, 1894), pp. viii–x.

46. Ibid., p. x.

47. Ibid., p. vii.

48. D. T. Suzuki, "A Glimpse of Paul Carus," pp. xii–xiii.

49. Carus, *Buddhism and Its Christian Critics*, p. 159. The Protestant bias of early interpreters of Buddhism led them to commend it as the "Protestantism of Asia." Its suitability to the West could be seen in its seemingly anticlerical, antipriestly bent, its sweeping away of corrupt rituals and superstitions, its reliance on self-culture, and its return to the simple and original spirit of religion. In fact, Buddhism is anything but anticlerical, antiritual, or primarily a lay movement. Richard Gombrich notes, "The position of the monastic Order in Buddhism is even more dominant than that of the church in Christianity. Buddhists believed that where the Order dies out, Buddhism itself is dead." See Bechert and Gombrich, *The World of Buddhism*, p. 9. Moreover, it is generally held that Buddhism is not established in a country until the order of monks and nuns takes root there. And the Buddhist world throughout is rich in elaborate devotions, rituals, and ceremonies.

50. Carus, *Gospel of Buddha*, p. xii.

51. Ibid.

52. Carus, *The Dharma, or the Religion of Enlightenment* (Chicago: Open Court Publishing, 1918), p. 82.

53. Carus, *Buddhism and Its Christian Critics*, p. 174.

54. *Journal of the Maha-Bodhi Society* 8 (December 1894): 59.

55. D. T. Suzuki, "A Glimpse of Paul Carus," p. x.

56. Quotations from John Hedley Brooke, *Science and Religion: Some Historical Perspectives* (Cambridge: Cambridge University Press, 1991), pp. 326, 334.

57. Fritjof Capra, *The Tao of Physics: An Exploration of the Parallels between Modern Physics and Eastern Mysticism*, 3d ed. (Boston: Shambhala, 1975, 1991); p. 10.

58. Hsüan Hua, *Water Mirror Reflecting Heaven: Collected Writings of Triptaka Master Hsuan Hua*, trans. Dharma Realm Buddhist University (Talmage, Calif.: Buddhist Text Translation Society, 1982), p. 4.

59. All quotations are from Walpola Rahula, "Religion and Science," *Dharma Vijaya* 2 (1: 1989): 10–14.

60. James Legge, *Confucius: Confucian Analects, The Great Learning, and The Doctrine of the Mean*, trans. James Legge (New York: Dover, 1893, 1971), pp. 4–7.

61. Henry Clarke Warren, *Buddhism in Translations* (Cambridge, Mass.: Harvard University Press, 1896), pp. 283–84.

Chapter 13: Buddhist and Western Psychotherapies

1. I apologize to American Buddhists who are neither Euro-American nor Asian American for not mentioning them specifically. At this time, they are quite few in number and have not formed distinct Buddhist ethnically or racially based communities to the best of my knowledge. So, for the sake of convenience, I have limited my comments and comparisons to the two large racial groupings of American Buddhists. I should add that there are a handful of Asian Americans who participate in the Euro-American Buddhist groups and a few Euro-Americans who participate in the Asian American Buddhist groups.

2. B. Zilbergeld, *The Shrinking of America: Myths of Psychological Change* (Boston: Little, Brown, 1983).

3. See the introduction to R. J. Corsini and D. Wedding, *Current Psychotherapies*, 5th ed. (Itasca, Ill.: F. E. Peacock, 1995).

4. Robyn Dawes, *House of Cards: Psychology and Psychotherapy Built on Myth* (New York: Free Press, 1994), p. 7.

5. See K. Wilber, J. Engler, and D. P. Brown, *Transformation of Consciousness: Conventional and Contemplative Perspectives on Development* (Boston: Shambhala, 1986); and M. Epstein, *Thoughts without a Thinker* (New York: Basic Books, 1995).

6. See D. K. Reynolds, *The Quiet Therapies: Japanese Pathways to Personal Growth* (Honolulu: University of Hawaii Press, 1980).

7. See the *Diagnostic and Statistical Manual of Mental Disorders*, 4th ed. (Washington, D.C.: American Psychiatric Association, 1994).

8. See Reynolds, *The Quiet Therapies*.

9. See Thomas Szasz, *Cruel Compassion: Psychiatric Control of Society's Unwanted* (New York: John Wiley, 1994).

10. See, for example, A. Guggenbuhl-Craig, *Power in the Helping Professions*, 9th ed. (Dallas: Spring Publications, 1989), p. 34.

11. T. M. Abel, R. Metroux, and S. Roll, *Psychotherapy and Culture*, 2d ed. (Albuquerque: University of New Mexico Press, 1987), p. 63.

12. Thich Nhat Hanh, *Cultivating the Mind of Love: The Practice of Looking Deeply in the Mahayana Buddhist Tradition* (Berkeley: Parallax Press, 1996), p. 71.

Chapter 14: Helping the Iron Bird Fly

1. The title for this chapter derives from a statement widely circulated among Western Buddhists as a Tibetan prophecy: "When the iron bird flies . . . the Dharma will come to the land of the red people."

2. Rita M. Gross, *Buddhism after Patriarchy: A Feminist History, Analysis, and Reconstruction of Buddhism* (Albany: State University of New York Press, 1993), pp. 225–69.

3. For an overview of the major events, see Sandy Boucher, *Turning the Wheel: American Women Creating the New Buddhism* (Boston: Beacon Press, 1993). For a report on the conference with the Dalai Lama, see Surya Das, "Toward a Western Buddhism: A Conference with His Holiness the Dalai Lama," *Shambhala Sun* 2, no. 1 (June 1993): 42–43. For a report on the Spirit Rock conference, see "No Picnic at Spirit Rock: Power, Sex and Pain in American Buddhism," *Shambhala Sun* 2, no. 5 (May 1994): 40–45, 52–53. My source for the most recent conference with the Dalai Lama is personal communication from Dr. Judith Simmer-Brown. For two thought-provoking articles on the complexities of the issue, see Stephen Butterfield, "Accusing the Tiger: Sexual Ethics and Buddhist Teachers," *Tricycle: The Buddhist Review* 1, no. 4 (fall 1992): 46–51, and "No Right, Nor Wrong: An Interview with Pema Chödrön," *Tricycle: The Buddhist Review* 3, no. 1 (fall 1993): 16–24. The next few issues of *Tricycle* after each article also contain revealing letters to the editor.

4. For full discussion of this point see Gross, *Buddhism after Patriarchy*, pp. 32–40.

5. Forms of Buddhism that do not have the same understanding of the teacher-student relationship do not face the same problems in differentiating devotion from imitation and hero worship. For further discussion of the teacher-student relationship in Vajrayāna Buddhism, see Chögyam Trungpa, *Journey without Goal: The Tantric Wisdom of the Buddha* (Boulder: Prajna Press, 1981, reprint Boston: Shambhala, 1985), pp. 55–63.

6. Gross, *Buddhism after Patriarchy*, pp. 249–55.

7. Chögyam Trungpa, *Shambhala: The Sacred Path of the Warrior* (Boston: Shambhala, 1984), pp. 134–48.

8. This distinction between authority and power, which is used by anthropologists, is quite useful. Authority is the formal, publicly recognized right to make decisions and be obeyed. Power involves the informal, unacknowledged processes by which decisions are often, in fact, made.

9. The person behind this title is the eldest son of Chögyam Trungpa, Rinpoche, the founder of Vajradhatu. The title was conferred in May 1995 in Halifax, Nova Scotia, in a formal enthronement ceremony; before that time, he was known for many years as the Sawang Ösel Rangdrol Mukpo. He became the head of Vajradhatu in 1990 immediately after the death of the Vajra Regent Ösel Tendzin.

Chapter 15: Coming Out in the Sangha

1. The term *gay* has been expanded in step with our growing awareness of the existence of sexual minorities. The current politically correct expression is "gay,

lesbian, bisexual, and transgendered (and/or transsexual)" (GLBT). An alternative designation, which I use in this essay because it is less cumbersome, is *queer*—a formerly abusive word that is being reappropriated and empowered by GLBT persons.

2. The first part of this quotation, often assigned (even in such prestigious reference sources as *Encyclopedia Britannica*) to Oscar Wilde, is, according to Joline Ezzell (Reference Librarian, Duke University) the conclusion of "Two Lovers," a poem by Wilde's lover Lord Alfred Douglas, published in the undergraduate magazine *The Chameleon*. The second part of the quotation is uncertainly attributed to Gore Vidal.

3. José Ignacio Cabezón, "Homosexuality and Buddhism," in Arlene Swidler, ed., *Homosexuality and World Religions* (Valley Forge, Pa.: Trinity Press International, 1993), pp. 81–101; see esp. pp. 82–83.

4. *The Jewel Ornament of Liberation by sGam.po.pa*, trans. and annotated by Herbert V. Guenther (Berkeley: Shambhala, 1971), p. 76 (italics added). "Eunuch" is Guenther's rendering of *ma.niṅ* (Sanskrit: *paṇḍaka*, on which see later). Ken and Katia Holmes, in their translation of Gampopa "according to the detailed explanations traditional to the Karma Kagyü Lineage" (*Gems of Dharma, Jewels of Freedom* [Forres, Scotland: Altea Publishing, 1995]), render it as "hermaphrodite" (p. 77).

5. I am indebted to William Ames for referring me to *Abhidharmakośa* 4, on which Gampopa seems to be dependent, but this by no means explains all of the items on his list, and the *Abhidharmakośa* is apparently silent on the subject of homosexuality. See Louis de La Vallée Poussin, trans., *L'Abhidharmakośa de Vasubandhu*, ed. Étienne Lamotte, reprint (Brussels: Institut Belge des Hautes Étude Chinoises, 1971–80), 3:147–89.

6. Incest, for example, is wrong because it is something the barbarians (i.e., the Persians) do. La Vallée Poussin, *Abhidharmakośa*, p. 147.

7. Leonard Zwilling, "Homosexuality as Seen in Indian Buddhist Texts," in José Cabezón, ed., *Buddhism, Sexuality, and Gender* (Albany: State University of New York Press, 1992), p. 209. There is also a single paragraph in Genshin's *Ōjōyōshū* against homosexuality (Philipp Karl Eidmann, personal communication).

8. Zwilling, "Homosexuality," p. 207.

9. Ibid., pp. 204–6.

10. Information from Eric Kolvig, personal communication, August 18, 1994. Goenka is also reported to have said, in the 1970s, "If you sit long and seriously enough, the homosexuality will go away" (Steve Peskind, letter dated May 11, 1995).

11. "It's just a karmic thing. But if you do enough mantras you can become heterosexual." Quoted in "Relationships Aren't a This or a That: An Interview with Bobby Rhodes," *Turning Wheel* (fall 1992): 19. "In response to a personal letter . . . in 1983 regarding AIDS, [Sŭngsan wrote that] AIDS is a 'special' result of 'special' karma, in other words, that AIDS is a fruition of gay karma" (Steve Peskind, letter dated May 11, 1995).

12. *Buddhism: Essential Teachings*, comp. Bhikshu Heng Shure (Talmage, Calif.: City of 10,000 Buddhas, privately circulated, n.d.), p. 65.

13. This split has been under-reported in the American news media. For an

account based on its coverage in the Japanese media, see Jan Van Bragt, "An Uneven Battle: Sōka Gakkai vs. Nichiren Shōshū," *Bulletin of the Nanzan Institute for Religion and Culture* 17 (1993): 15–31.

14. Personal communication, Hugh Hallman (a former member of what was then NSA), September 16, 1994. His memory is that many, or even most, leading members of NSA were, at one time, such "reformed" married gay men.

15. According to the report in *Island Lifestyle* (a free "alternative" newspaper published in Hawaii) for August 1995 (p. 8), quoting *Outlook*, the newsletter of the Honolulu Gay and Lesbian Community Center, Fred Zaitsu, general director of SGI-USA, says that this decision reflects the Buddhist "spirit of nondiscrimination and equality."

16. The first publication to acknowledge that there are queer Buddhist groups in America, and to assess their strengths and weaknesses, appears to have been in the newsletter of Aitken Rōshi's center. Scott Whitney, "The Vast Sky and White Clouds: Gay Buddhists and American Zen Groups," *Blind Donkey* 8, no. 4 (December 1984): 25–32.

17. See the report of the interview between Issan Dorsey (see below) and Michelle Hart in *Kahawai* for fall 1984, reprinted in *Mountain Record* (the newsletter of the Mount Tremper Zen Community) for fall 1991, p. 41, for a version of this conversation. Aitken Rōshi is unsure of the precise form of his remarks, but agrees that the quotations as I have given them are "reasonably close" (letter dated October 29, 1994).

18. "We always felt that Hartford St. started through Aitken Roshi talking with Baker Roshi and then encouraging us." Issan Dorsey, quoted in *Mountain Record* (fall 1991): 41 (see previous note). Note that Maitri is now the name of the AIDS residential care center which, formerly operated by the Hartford Street Zen Center and located in what was effectively the same building (next door, but the intervening walls were knocked down), has become an independent project and has moved to 401 DuBoce Avenue. Maitri is unconnected with the Zen Hospice at 223 Page Street.

19. Reported by Eric Kolvig, personal communication, August 18, 1994. The claimed silence of the Buddha on this matter depends on regarding the treatise statements, quoted earlier, as not the authentic word of the Buddha (*buddhavacana*).

20. Scott Hunt, "Hello, Dalai," *Out* (February–March 1994): 102. At first, His Holiness seemed to answer in accordance with the traditional prohibition, mentioned earlier, about the improper orifice: " 'Blow, here,' he said in broken English, pointing first to his mouth and then to his groin, 'is wrong.' " But then he reconsidered his response. Subsequent remarks on homosexuality by the Dalai Lama have been more ambiguous. It appears that he is still considering the issue.

21. E-mail, September 9, 1994.

22. Jeff Logan-Olivas, "Story of a Gay Wedding," *Turning Wheel* (fall 1992): 20.

23. *Newsletter of the Seattle Gay Buddhist Fellowship*, no. 1, July 30, 1994.

24. The most extensive recent treatment of this is Randy P. Conner, *Blossom of Bone: Reclaiming the Connections between Homoeroticism and the Sacred* (New York: HarperSanFrancisco, 1993).

25. The best study is John Boswell, *Christianity, Social Tolerance, and Homosexuality: Gay People in Western Europe from the Beginning of the Christian Era to the Fourteenth Century* (Chicago: University of Chicago Press, 1980). For an overview, see Denise Carmody and John Carmody, "Homosexuality and Roman Catholicism," in Swidler, *Homosexuality and World Religions*, pp. 135–48. Although Boswell's pioneering work has largely survived critical response, it has been thought a little too optimistic in its assessment of, for example, pre-Christian Greco-Roman tolerance toward homosexual activity. See, for example, Paul Harvey, "After Boswell, Before Theodosius: Assessing Homosexuality in Ancient Rome," paper read at the 29th International Congress on Medieval Studies, Western Michigan University, May 1994.

26. The latest version of the Roman Catholic Catechism not only calls homosexual *activity* a "grave depravity" but extends its condemnation to homosexual *orientation* by calling it "intrinsically disordered." *Catechism of the Catholic Church*, English translation authorized by the United States Catholic Conference (Mahwah, N.J.: Paulist Press, 1994), sections 2357–59 (p. 566).

27. At this and various other places in this essay I speak as a participant-observer and therefore use first- and second-person language. The appropriateness of this as a way of deconstructing the pseudo-objectivity of academic method, especially in discussions about sexuality, is now generally accepted. See, for example, Carter Heyward, *Touching Our Strength: The Erotic as Power and the Love of God* (San Francisco: Harper and Row, 1989).

28. Rob Eichberg, *Coming Out: An Act of Love* (New York: Plume, 1991).

29. Craig O'Neill and Kathleen Ritter, *Coming Out Within: Stages of Spiritual Awakening for Lesbians and Gay Men* (New York: HarperSanFrancisco, 1992).

30. Eichberg, *Coming Out*, p. 119 (diagram), chaps. 10 and 11 (discussion). The levels are derived from Eichberg's experience with est (Scientology), but he changed their original hierarchical approach, which he found disturbing, to a model that sees all the levels happening within each other. He accepted my suggestion that he had moved from a hierarchical to a holarchical structure. Interview, Santa Fe, New Mexico, August 24, 1994.

31. Boswell, *Christianity*, p. 44.

32. Mark Thompson, ed., *Gay Spirit: Myth and Meaning* (New York: St. Martin's Press, 1987) is both a study and a celebration of queer family and tribal identity and has become something of a sacred text in its own right. The variety of male lifestyles that call themselves gay is described in Frank Browning, *The Culture of Desire: Paradox and Perversity in Gay Lives Today* (New York: Crown, 1993).

33. According to Steve Peskind, the question "Can I really be gay and Buddhist too?" was explicitly asked at the first meeting of the San Francisco Gay Buddhist Group in April 1980 (letter dated May 11, 1995).

34. Ernest Becker, *The Denial of Death* (New York: Free Press, 1973).

35. See John Erman's film *An Early Frost* (1985; RCA/Columbia) about a young gay couple facing the death of a partner from AIDS.

36. Joseph Acosta, "Straight Privilege," *White Crane Newsletter* no. 20 (1994): p. 17.

37. Jack Carroll, "Voices," *Turning Wheel* (fall 1992): 37.

38. Interview, San Francisco, August 18, 1994. Eric recommended Gavin Harrison, *In the Lap of the Buddha* (Boston: Shambhala, 1994), which deals with Buddhism as it relates to dysfunctional family and HIV-positive issues.

39. This was a precursor of the Buddhist AIDS Project, founded in fall of 1993 by Steve Peskind. Steve questions Eric Kolvig's assessment that the San Francisco queer community is experiencing *post*-traumatic stress syndrome—he would prefer to say there is an *ongoing* trauma (interview, San Francisco, June 22, 1995).

40. Gregg Cassin, "Break My Heart," *Turning Wheel* (fall 1992): 27.

41. Of the ten contributors to "Practicing Out of the Closet: Sexual Minorities Appreciating the Sangha," *Mountain Record* (fall 1991): 35–40, two explicitly mention "my own homophobia," one admits to the "denial" of his own homosexuality, and two refer to AIDS; all say that their practice helps them to deal with these problems.

42. Eric Kolvig, "Gay in the Dharma: Wisdom and Love," *Gay Buddhist Fellowship Newsletter*, March 1993.

43. Ibid.

44. Ibid.

45. *Mahāvagga* 25:3, I. B. Horner, trans., *The Book of the Discipline* (London: Luzac, 1951), 4:430. This story is often repeated in the queer Buddhist community of San Francisco, without attribution. For the exact reference I am indebted to Bruce Burrill (Internet posting to BUDDHA-L, Buddhist Academic Discussion Forum, October 6, 1995).

46. The distinction (which is almost axiomatic in Western counterculture, but which we may perhaps trace in some form back to Schleiermacher) between dogma and institutionalization (which is called religion) and, in Schleiermacher's words, "a sense and taste for the infinite" (which is called spirituality) was often made by my informants. Thus, it seemed that many people were attracted first to a spiritual community that accepted queer lifestyles and secondarily (albeit, if they stayed, quite genuinely) to Buddhism. Homophilic spiritual communities are therefore functioning, in America, as *upāya*.

47. I was fortunate to get a copy, via a member of the Gay Buddhist Fellowship (see later), of the first newsletter of the Seattle Gay Buddhist Fellowship.

48. David Schneider, *Street Zen: The Life and Work of Issan Dorsey* (Boston: Shambhala, 1993). Many informants commented that Schneider's biography is not funny enough and does not sufficiently bring out Issan's sense of the outrageous as, for example, when a disciple gravely asked him how he had been changed by his Zen practice, and Issan immediately replied, "Well, I no longer wear heels."

49. Ibid., p. 69.

50. Ibid., p. 76.

51. A summary history of Hartford Street Zen Center is given in the summer 1994 issue of its newsletter.

52. Interview at HSZC, August 5, 1994. Things are not always so silent at the "other places." Sojun Mel Weitsman, who recently retired as co-abbot of Zen Center, offhandedly made some explicitly homophobic remarks that led to an emergency meeting of the center in which he was asked to "explain" his remarks.

53. Interview, Zen Center, August 12, 1994.

54. The notion that Japanese are different from Caucasians was shared by a BCA

(Buddhist Churches of America) minister interviewed by Diane Ames: "Asked whether he knew any cases [of AIDS] in his congregation, he replied that no, everybody in this temple is Japanese-American." Diane Ames, "AIDS and the BCA," *Wheel of Dharma* (February 1995).

55. By "soft men" she may have meant feminine (but not necessarily effeminate) men: the term might, then, be a translation of *paṇḍaka.*

56. Charles Koren Baker and Joe Gallagher, "One Branch, No Separation"; Leavy Oliver, "On the Gay and Lesbian Retreat," *The Ten Directions* 15, no. 1 (spring–summer 1994): 39–40, 41.

57. Rob Gunn, "Identity Suffering," *Turning Wheel* (fall 1992): 23.

58. Announcement posted to BUDDHA-L, March 27, 1995. An enquiry for more general information on FWBO's stance on queer practitioners was answered by Greg Eichler, who declined to answer for the order but said, "On a personal level, I must say that I as a Gay man feel right at home and secure at the center" (E-mail, March 29, 1995).

59. Steve Peskind identifies the Dharma Sisters as "a second wave." He reports that the first lesbian group formed in the early 1980s in Oakland, California (across the bay from San Francisco), because the members did not find enough support in the gay men's meetings (telephone interview, March 17, 1995).

60. Steve Peskind reports that GBF at first did not want women members. The name change was intended to make GBF more inviting to women, but it has remained all male (telephone interview, March 17, 1995).

61. Discussion following sitting at David Sunseri's apartment in San Francisco, August 4, 1994.

62. Discussion following sitting at Hartford Street Zen Center, August 10, 1994. Indeed, far from marrying "a nice Jewish boy" Jackie vowed herself to partnership with Perri Franskoviak (see following note) in a "Wedding in the Dharma" on June 21, 1997, in St. Helena, California, with Vajracharya Lama Kunzang Palden officiating.

63. Perri Franskoviak, "Dharma Sisters Retreat Report," *Dharma Sisters Newsletter*, August 1994.

64. At the conclusion of the Dharma Sisters meeting on August 10, 1994, however, a member shared her fear on discovering that her lover had a uterine growth that might be cancerous. The fact that she could share such a fear, she said, was an important reason for her coming to the group.

65. Interview, San Francisco, August 1, 1994.

66. Tundra Wind, "Odyssey of a Zen Teacher," *White Crane Newsletter*, no. 14 (n.d. [c. 1992–93]).

67. Avalokiteśvara is the bodhisattva of compassion and Mañjuśrī is the bodhisattva of wisdom. Buddhism teaches that pure, or enlightened, mind manifests perfect wisdom and perfect compassion equally.

68. Letter January 29, 1994.

69. Dependent origination (or, as I prefer to call it, interdependent arising) is the fundamental teaching of Buddhism that everything is conditioned by, and in its turn conditions, everything else.

70. *Zen Wind*, no. 17 (n.d. [c. 1993]).

71. *Newsletter of the Seattle Gay Buddhist Fellowship*, no. 1.

Chapter 16: Responding to the Cries of the World

I thank Stephanie Kaza, Thich Minh Duc, Alan Senauke, Ken Tanaka, and Michael Zimmerman for their comments on earlier drafts. I also thank Ken Tanaka for invitations to give lectures in the Numata Lecture Series at the Institute of Buddhist Studies in Berkeley, California, in December 1994 and September 1995. This essay is based in large part on those two lectures.

In the chapter epigraph, D. T. Suzuki is giving a translation of part of the *Gaṇḍavyūha Sūtra*, in his *Essays in Zen Buddhism: Third Series* (London: Rider and Company, 1953), p. 129. The passage is found in *Entry into the Realm of Reality: The Text: A Translation of the Gandavyuha, the Final Book of the Avatamsaka Sutra*, trans. Thomas Cleary (Boston: Shambhala, 1989), p. 370.

1. Joanna Macy describes the theory and practice of such work in *Despair and Personal Power in the Nuclear Age* (Philadelphia: New Society Publishers, 1983). See also Joanna Macy, "Taking Heart: Spiritual Exercises for Social Activists," in Fred Eppsteiner, ed., *The Path of Compassion: Writings on Socially Engaged Buddhism*, 2d ed. (Berkeley: Parallax Press, 1988), pp. 203–13; and Joanna Macy, *World as Lover, World as Self* (Berkeley: Parallax Press, 1991).

2. This account has been reconstructed from Robert Joshin Althouse, "Diary of a Hungry Ghost," *Turning Wheel: Journal of the Buddhist Peace Fellowship* (spring 1994): 28–30. For accounts of the work of Glassman Rōshi and the Greyston Mandala, see Bernard Glassman and Rick Fields, *Instructions to the Cook: A Zen Master's Lessons in Living a Life that Matters* (New York: Bell Tower, 1996); Barbara Gates and Wes Nisker, "Street-Wise Zen: An Interview with Bernard Tetsugen Glassman," *Inquiring Mind* 12 (spring 1996): 10–11, 20; "Bernie Glassman Knows No Boundaries," *Shambhala Sun* 4 (May 1996): 42–48, 51, 55; David Rome, "Greyston: A Mandala of Caring," *Shambhala Sun* 4 (May 1996): 49; Susan Moon and Alan Senauke, "Monastery of the Streets: A Talk with Bernard Glassman," *Turning Wheel* (fall 1996): 22–25; Peter Cunningham, "Bearing Witness: Notes from Auschwitz," *Tricycle* (spring 1997): 35–39; and Susan Kaplow, "*Oswiecim* Means Enlightenment," *Turning Wheel* (summer 1997): 15–17.

3. See Thich Nhat Hanh, *Peace Is Every Step* (New York: Bantam Books, 1991), p. 91. The Tiep Hien Order (or "Order of Interbeing"), the organization that Nhat Hanh founded in 1964, has as its aim, according to its initial charter, "to study, experiment and apply Buddhism in an intelligent and effective way to modern life, both individual and societal." See Thich Nhat Hanh, *Interbeing: Commentaries on the Tiep Hien Precepts* (Berkeley: Parallax Press, 1987), p. 16.

4. See, for example, Raja Dharmapala, "Sri Lanka: The Dharmavedi Institute's Measures to End the Ethnic War," *Seeds of Peace* 9 (January–April 1993): 29–31. On Cambodia, see Liz Bernstein, Bob Maat, and Yeshua Moser, "A Moment of Peace, A Glimmer of Hope," *Turning Wheel* (summer 1993): 37–38; Liz Bernstein and Yeshua Moser, "Cambodia: Dhammayietra IV," *Seeds of Peace* 9 (September–December 1995): 31–32; Mahā Ghosananda, *Step by Step* (Berkeley: Parallax Press, 1992).

5. For a first-person account of the socially engaged Buddhist movement in Vietnam, see Chan Khong, *Learning True Love: How I Learned and Practiced Social Change in Vietnam* (Berkeley: Parallax Press, 1993). Some of the Dalai Lama's writings on Tibet are contained in *A Policy of Kindness: An Anthology of Writings by and about the*

Dalai Lama (Ithaca, N.Y.: Snow Lion Publications, 1990); see also José Cabezón, "Buddhist Principles in the Tibetan Liberation Movement," in Christopher Queen and Sallie King, eds., *Engaged Buddhism: Buddhist Liberation Movements in Asia* (Albany: State University of New York Press, 1996), pp. 295–320. For writings on Buddhist nonviolence and Burma, see Aung San Sui Kyi, *Freedom from Fear and Other Writings*, rev. ed. (London: Penguin Books, 1995). For Buddhist responses to the situation in the Chittagong Hill Tracts, see, for example, "Bimal Bhikkhu Addresses General Assembly of the United Nations," *Turning Wheel* (spring 1994): 15.

6. See George Bond, "A. T. Ariyaratne and the Sarvodaya Shramadana Movement in Sri Lanka," in Queen and King, *Engaged Buddhism*, pp. 121–46; and Joanna Macy, *Dharma and Development: Religion as Resource in the Sarvodaya Self-Help Movement* (West Hartford, Conn.: Kumarian Press, 1983).

7. See Santikharo Bhikkhu, "Planting Rice Together: Socially Engaged Monks in Thailand," *Turning Wheel* (summer 1996): 16–20.

8. See, for example, Susan Darlington, "Monks and Environmental Conservation: A Case Study in Nan Province," *Seeds of Peace* 9 (January–April 1993): 7–10; Andrew Getz, "A Natural Being: A Monk's Reforestation Project in Thailand," *Buddhist Peace Fellowship Newsletter* (winter 1991): 24–25.

9. See Alan Sponberg, "TBMSG: A Dhamma Revolution in Contemporary India," in Queen and King, *Engaged Buddhism*, pp. 73–120; and Terry Pilchick, *Jai Bhim! Dispatches from a Peaceful Revolution* (Berkeley: Parallax Press, 1988).

10. See Sulak Sivaraksa, *Seeds of Peace: A Buddhist Vision for Renewing Society* (Berkeley: Parallax Press, 1992); Sulak Sivaraksa, *Religion and Development* (Bangkok: Thai Inter-Religious Commission for Development, 1987); Donald Swearer, "Sulak Sivaraksa's Buddhist Vision for Renewing Society," in Queen and King, *Engaged Buddhism*, pp. 195–235; and Helena Norberg-Hodge, *Ancient Futures: Learning from Ladakh* (San Francisco: Sierra Club Books, 1992); Helena Norberg-Hodge, "Buddhist Engagement in the Global Economy," in Jonathan Watts, Alan Senauke, and Santikaro Bhikkhu, eds., *Entering the Realm of Reality: Towards Dhammic Societies* (Bangkok: International Network of Engaged Buddhists, 1997), pp. 219–40.

11. See Chatsumarn Kabilsingh, *Thai Women in Buddhism* (Berkeley: Parallax Press, 1991); and Nancy Barnes, "Buddhist Women and the Nuns' Order in Asia," in Queen and King, *Engaged Buddhism*, pp. 259–94. For an overview of Asian forms of socially engaged Buddhism, see Christopher Queen, "Introduction: The Shapes and Sources of Engaged Buddhism," in Queen and King, *Engaged Buddhism*, pp. 1–44; and Ken Jones, *The Social Face of Buddhism* (London: Wisdom Publications, 1989), pp. 227–80.

12. See Joe Gorin, *Choose Love: A Jewish Buddhist Human Rights Activist in Central America* (Berkeley: Parallax Press, 1993); Merrill Collett, "Patience and Pain in Colombia's Dirty War," *Turning Wheel* (fall 1995): 36–37; Ken MacLean, "What Does It Mean to Know?" (on Peace Brigades International), *Turning Wheel* (summer 1996): 25–26; and Terry Vandiver, "The Power of Presence," *Inquiring Mind* 12 (spring 1996): 12–13, 20.

13. Joanna Macy, "In League with the Beings of the Future," *Buddhist Peace Fellowship Newsletter* (winter 1991): 15–17; "The Nuclear Guardianship Project: For the Responsible Care of Radioactive Waste," *Buddhist Peace Fellowship Newsletter* (winter 1991): 17–18.

14. See Christopher Titmuss, "Interactivity: Sitting for Peace and Standing for Parliament," in Eppsteiner, *The Path of Compassion*, 2d ed. (Berkeley: Parallax Press, 1988), pp. 182–89.

15. Among the many books on women and contemporary Western Buddhist practice are Rita Gross, *Buddhism after Patriarchy: A Feminist History, Analysis, and Reconstruction of Buddhism* (Albany: State University of New York Press, 1993); Sandy Boucher, *Turning the Wheel: American Women Creating the New Buddhism*, rev. ed. (Boston: Beacon Press, 1993); Sandy Boucher, *Opening the Lotus: A Woman's Guide to Buddhism* (Boston: Beacon Press, 1997); Ellen Sidor, ed., *A Gathering of Spirit* (Cumberland, R.I.: Primary Point Press, 1987); and Deborah Hopkinson, Michele Hill, and Eileen Kiera, *Not Mixing Up Buddhism: Essays on Women and Buddhist Practice* (Fredonia, N.Y.: White Pine Press, 1986).

16. See Judith Stronach, "The Same Silence: Working towards Nonviolence in a Women's Penitentiary," *Turning Wheel* (summer 1994): 22–25; Melody Ermachild, "Patience," *Turning Wheel* (spring 1995): 13–16; Jarvis Masters, "Fruitcakes," *Turning Wheel* (spring 1995): 17–19; and Jarvis Masters, *Finding Freedom: Writings from Death Row* (Junction City, Calif.: Padma Publishing, 1997). The issue of *Turning Wheel* for winter 1992 was focused on work and life in prisons.

17. See Susan Davis, "Suhita Dharma in Richmond," *Buddhist Peace Fellowship Newsletter* (winter 1990): 32–33; Pamela Weiss, "An Appropriate Response: Maitri AIDS Hospice," *Turning Wheel* (spring 1994): 36–37.

18. For accounts of Glassman Rōshi's activities, see note 2. See also Adam Gopnik, "Livelihood," *Buddhist Peace Fellowship Newsletter* (summer 1989): 19–21. For anthologies of both Western and Asian approaches see Eppsteiner, *The Path of Compassion*; and Arnold Kotler, ed., *Engaged Buddhist Reader* (Berkeley: Parallax Press, 1996). Ken Jones gives an overview of the history and rationale for socially engaged Buddhism in *The Social Face of Buddhism*. Briefer overviews of socially engaged Buddhism can be found in several writings of Kenneth Kraft: "Prospects of a Socially Engaged Buddhism," in Kraft, ed., *Inner Peace, World Peace: Essays on Buddhism and Nonviolence* (Albany: State University of New York Press, 1992), pp. 11–30; "Meditation in Action: The Emergence of Engaged Buddhism," *Tricycle: The Buddhist Review* 2, no. 3 (spring 1993): 42–44, 46–48; "Practicing Peace: Social Engagement in Western Buddhism," *Journal of Buddhist Ethics* 2 (1995): 152–72 (the Internet address for the journal is http://jbe.la.psu.edu). Two journals have focused on documentation and reflection related to engaged Buddhism: *Turning Wheel: Journal of the Buddhist Peace Fellowship*, and *Seeds of Peace*.

19. For an overview of the history and work of the BPF, see Alan Senauke, "Buddhist Peace Fellowship: The Work and Network of Engaged Buddhism," *Inquiring Mind* 12 (spring 1996): 21–23.

20. See Sala Steinbach and Barbara Gates, eds., "The Colors of Buddhism: Six Explorations of Diversity," *Inquiring Mind* 12 (spring 1996): 14–19.

21. For some examples, see Donald Rothberg, "Buddhist Responses to Violence and War: Resources for a Socially Engaged Spirituality," *Journal of Humanistic Psychology* 32 (fall 1992): 41–75.

22. For sustained treatments of this issue, see Robert Sharf, "The Zen of Japanese Nationalism," in Donald Lopez, ed., *Curators of the Buddha: The Study of Buddhism under Colonialism* (Chicago: University of Chicago Press, 1995), pp. 107–60; James

Heisig and John Maraldo, eds., *Rude Awakenings: Zen, The Kyoto School, The Question of Nationalism* (Honolulu: University of Hawaii Press, 1995); and Brian Victoria, *Zen at War* (Trumbull, Conn.: Weatherhill, 1997).

23. Thich Nhat Hanh, *Being Peace* (Berkeley: Parallax Press, 1987), pp. 53–54.

24. Arnold Kotler, "Breathing and Smiling: Traveling with Thich Nhat Hanh," *Buddhist Peace Fellowship Newsletter* (summer 1989): 22, quoted in Kraft, "Prospects of a Socially Engaged Buddhism," p. 18.

25. This is the judgment of both Thich Minh Duc, an associate of Thich Nhat Hanh since the 1960s, and Arnold Kotler, also a long-time associate of Thich Nhat Hanh, and the editor and publisher of most of Nhat Hanh's English-language publications. Nhat Hanh, for example, was already speaking of "engagement" by the mid-1960s in his book on the Vietnamese war, *Vietnam: Lotus in a Sea of Fire* (New York: Hill and Wang, 1967).

26. My reconstructions of the history of Vietnamese engaged Buddhism are based on conversations with Thich Minh Duc in September 1995. Minh Duc has observed the engaged Buddhist movement since the early 1960s and remained in Vietnam until 1979. See also Stephen Batchelor, *The Awakening of the West: The Encounter of Buddhism and Western Culture* (Berkeley: Parallax Press, 1994), pp. 353–69; Chan Khong, *Learning True Love;* Sallie King, "Thich Nhat Hanh and the Unified Buddhist Church: Nondualism in Action," in Queen and King, *Engaged Buddhism,* pp. 321–63.

27. For further development of this interpretive approach, see Rothberg, "Buddhist Responses to Violence and War." For more detailed accounts of the traditional and doctrinal practice basis of engaged Buddhism, see the contributions in Kraft, *Inner Peace, World Peace;* Sallie King, "Conclusion: Buddhist Social Activism," in Queen and King, *Engaged Buddhism,* pp. 401–36; Jones, *The Social Face of Buddhism;* and Christopher Titmuss, *The Green Buddha,* ed. Gill Farrer-Halls (Totnes, Devon, England: Insight Books, 1985).

28. Nhat Hanh, *Being Peace,* p. 98. The basic Theravādin precepts are explained in Hammalawa Sadhatissa, *Buddhist Ethics: The Path to Nirvana* (London: Wisdom Publications, 1987).

29. See Robert Aitken, *The Mind of Clover: Essays in Zen Buddhist Ethics* (San Francisco: North Point Press, 1984), pp. 19–20; the quotation is from p. 20.

30. Sulak Sivaraksa, in Donald Rothberg, "A Thai Perspective on Socially Engaged Buddhism: A Conversation with Sulak Sivaraksa," *ReVision* 15 (winter 1993): 122. See also Sivaraksa, *Seeds of Peace,* pp. 73–79.

31. See Jones, *The Social Face of Buddhism,* p. 164. This development of a Buddhist social ethics, of an ethics guiding life among the complex systems of the contemporary world, is paralleled by many recent (and generally more articulated) developments within Western "applied" ethics. Here, the focus is on such themes as environmental ethics, medical ethics, professional ethics, famine and hunger, animal rights, capital punishment, and so forth. For a recent, religiously based attempt to approach many of these issues, see Ian Barbour, *Ethics in an Age of Technology: The Gifford Lectures, 1989–1991,* vol. 2 (San Francisco: HarperSanFrancisco, 1993). What is particularly promising about a Buddhist social ethics, in relation to this contemporary ethics, is that concern with complex systems can be linked to the close examination and transformation of individual experience, via Buddhist

practice. See, for example, David Loy, "Trying to Become Real: A Buddhist Critique of Some Secular Heresies," *International Philosophical Quarterly* 32 (December 1992): 403–25.

32. See, on this historical background, Walpola Rahula, "The Social Teachings of the Buddha," in Eppsteiner, *The Path of Compassion*, pp. 103–10; U. Chakravarti, *The Social Dimensions of Early Buddhism* (Delhi: Oxford University Press, 1987); Trevor Ling, *The Buddha: Buddhist Civilization in India and Ceylon* (New York: Charles Scribner's Sons, 1973); and Richard Gombrich, *Theravāda Buddhism: A Social History from Ancient Benares to Modern Colombo* (London: Routledge and Kegan Paul, 1988).

33. See, for example, Robert Aitken, *The Dragon Who Never Sleeps: Verses for Zen Buddhist Practice* (Berkeley: Parallax Press, 1992); Charlotte Joko Beck, *Everyday Zen: Love and Work*, ed. Steve Smith (San Francisco: Harper and Row, 1989); Jon Kabat-Zinn, *Wherever You Go, There You Are: Mindfulness Meditation in Everyday Life* (New York: Hyperion, 1994); Thich Nhat Hanh, *Present Moment, Wonderful Moment: Mindfulness Verses for Daily Living* (Berkeley: Parallax Press, 1990), and *Peace Is Every Step: The Path of Mindfulness in Everyday Life*, ed. Arnold Kotler (New York: Bantam Books, 1991).

34. See Stephen and Ondrea Levine, *Embracing the Beloved: Relationship as a Path of Awakening* (New York: Doubleday, 1995); John Welwood, *Journey of the Heart: Intimate Relationships and the Path of Love* (New York: HarperCollins, 1990); and Welwood, *Love and Awakening: Discovering the Sacred Path of Intimate Relationship* (New York: HarperCollins, 1996).

35. Recent *Turning Wheel* issues have been devoted, for example, to examining what Buddhist practice means in the context of families (winter 1996), communities (spring 1992), life in the city (fall 1997), and health care (winter 1998). See also Sandy Eastoak, *Dharma Family Treasures: Sharing Mindfulness with Children: An Anthology of Buddhist Writings* (Berkeley: North Atlantic Books, 1994); for an anthology on work and Buddhist practice, Claude Whitmyer, ed., *Mindfulness and Meaningful Work: Explorations in Right Livelihood* (Berkeley: Parallax Press, 1994); and, for an account of Buddhist practice in the context of urban decay and violence, Melody Chavis, *Altars in the Street: A Neighborhood Fights to Survive* (New York: Bell Tower, 1997).

36. See, for example, the work of Stephen Levine and Gavin Harrison on bringing mindfulness to illness, dying, and death: Stephen Levine, *Who Dies? An Investigation of Conscious Living and Conscious Dying* (New York: Anchor Books, 1982); Stephen Levine, *Healing into Life and Death* (New York: Anchor Books, 1987); Stephen Levine, *Guided Meditations, Explorations and Healings* (New York: Anchor Books, 1991); Gavin Harrison, *In the Lap of the Buddha* (Boston: Shambhala, 1994). See also the fall 1997 issue of *Tricycle*, focused on death and dying.

37. See Stephanie Kaza, "Conversations with Trees: Toward an Ecologically Grounded Spirituality," *ReVision* 15 (winter 1993): 128–36; and Stephanie Kaza, *The Attentive Heart: Conversations with Trees* (New York: Ballantine Press, 1993).

38. Other ecologically based practices developed by socially engaged Buddhists are outlined in Stephanie Kaza, "Acting with Compassion: Buddhism, Feminism, and the Environmental Crisis," in Carol Adams, ed., *Ecofeminism and the Sacred* (New York: Continuum, 1993), pp. 50–69; and Kenneth Kraft, "The Greening of Buddhist Practice," in Roger Gottlieb, ed., *This Sacred Earth: Religion, Nature, Environment*

(New York: Routledge, 1996), pp. 484–98. See also Allan Badiner, ed., *Dharma Gaia: A Harvest of Essays in Buddhism and Ecology* (Berkeley: Parallax Press, 1990); and Ken Jones, *Beyond Optimism: A Buddhist Political Ecology* (Oxford: Jon Carpenter Publishing, 1993).

39. See Peggy Wright, "Bringing Women's Voices to Transpersonal Theory," *ReVision* 17 (winter 1995): 3–10; and Jeanne Achterberg and Donald Rothberg, "Relationship as Spiritual Practice," in Donald Rothberg and Sean Kelly, eds., *Ken Wilber in Dialogue: Conversations with Leading Transpersonal Thinkers* (Wheaton, Ill.: Quest Books, 1998), pp. 259–74.

40. See the section "Immediate Family, Extended Family, Expanded Family: A Special Section on BPF's BASE Program," in *Turning Wheel* (winter 1996): 39–45, especially Donald Rothberg, "What Is to be Done? Small Groups and Engaged Buddhist Practice," pp. 43–45. See also Lewis Richmond, "Enlightenment Needs a Minyan," *Tricycle: The Buddhist Review* 5, no. 4 (summer 1996): 48–52.

41. This was a main theme in the second Western Buddhist Teachers' Conference, held in California in 1995. For some of the talks related to this theme, see John Tarrant, "Enlightenment and the Foundations of Teaching," *Blind Donkey* 15 (winter 1995): 4–7; and Michele McDonald, "Of Mud and Broken Windows: Teaching the Wounded Soul," *Blind Donkey* 15 (winter 1995): 12–15. See also Jack Kornfield, *A Path with Heart: A Guide through the Perils and Promises of Spiritual Life* (New York: Bantam Books, 1993), pp. 244–71. For further treatment of some of the underlying issues, see Greg Bogart, "The Use of Meditation in Psychotherapy: A Review of the Literature," *American Journal of Psychotherapy* 45 (1991): 383–412; Guy Claxton, ed., *Beyond Therapy: The Impact of Eastern Religions on Psychological Theory and Practice* (London: Wisdom, 1986); Mark Epstein, *Thoughts without a Thinker: Psychotherapy from a Buddhist Perspective* (New York: Basic Books, 1995); Donald Rothberg, "How Straight Is the Spiritual Path? Conversations with Buddhist Teachers Joseph Goldstein, Jack Kornfield, and Michele McDonald," *Revision* 19 (summer 1996): 25–40; Bruce Scotton, Allan Chinen, and John Battista, eds., *Textbook of Transpersonal Psychiatry and Psychology* (New York: Basic Books, 1996); Ken Wilber, John Engler, and Daniel Brown, *Transformations of Consciousness: Conventional and Contemplative Perspectives on Development* (Boston: Shambhala, 1986).

42. Titmuss, "Interactivity," p. 184.

43. Santikaro Bhikkhu, "The Four Noble Truths of Dhammic Socialism," in Watts et al., *Entering the Realm of Reality*, p. 92.

44. Ibid.

45. See Deena Metzger, "Personal Disarmament. Negotiating with the Inner Government," *ReVision* 12 (spring 1990): 3–9; Deena Metzger, "Personal Disarmament and the Nation-State Within," *Turning Wheel* (fall 1991): 21–22.

46. See Gene Knudsen-Hoffman, "Compassionate Listening: The First Step Toward Reconciliation," *Buddhist Peace Fellowship Newsletter* 12 (fall 1990): 9–10; David Grant, "Listening beyond Listening," *Turning Wheel* (summer 1996): 35–36; Fran Peavey, "Taming the Wildfire: The Anatomy of Social Hysteria," *Turning Wheel* (fall 1995): 32–35; Tova Green, "Dear Swallow: Albanians Resisting Non-Violently in Serbia," *Turning Wheel* (fall 1995): 38–39; Barbara Gates and Wes Nisker, "Thinking Like Water: An Interview with Tova Green and Fran Peavey," *Inquiring Mind* 4 (spring 1996): 7–9; David Grant, "Journey to Zaire: Studying Nonviolence with

Hutu Refugees," *Turning Wheel* (summer 1996): 21–22; David Grant, *Listening Project Training Manual* (Burnsville, N.C.: Rural Southern Voice for Peace, n.d.).

47. See especially John McConnell, *Mindful Mediation: A Handbook for Buddhist Peacemakers* (Bangkok: Mahachula Buddhist University; Spirit in Education Movement; Foundation for Children, 1995); Thubten Chodron, "Conflict Resolution and Buddhist Practice," *Turning Wheel* (fall 1991): 31–32.

48. Thich Nhat Hanh, *Touching Peace: Practicing the Art of Mindful Living* (Berkeley: Parallax Press, 1992), pp. 61–71; "Zen Reconciliation," *Buddhist Peace Fellowship Newsletter* 10 (spring 1988): 34–35.

49. See Paula Green, "If Jews and Germans Can Embrace at Auschwitz . . . Portraits of Reconciliation," *Turning Wheel* (spring 1995): 42–44; Paula Green, "To Share the Holy Land: Israelis and Palestinians in Dialogue," *Turning Wheel* (summer 1997): 43–44; and Paula Green, "Teaching Nonviolence in a Violence-Addicted World," *ReVision* 20 (fall 1997): 43–46.

50. Stephanie Kaza, "Emptiness as a Basis for an Environmental Ethic," *Buddhist Peace Fellowship Newsletter* 12 (spring 1990): 30–31.

51. See Donald Swearer, ed., *Me and Mine: Selected Essays of Bhikkhu Buddhadasa* (Albany: State University of New York Press, 1989), pp. 167–207; Sulak Sivaraksa, ed., *The Quest for a Just Society: The Legacy and Challenge of Buddhadasa Bhikkhu* (Bangkok: Thai Inter-Religious Commission for Development and Santi Pracha Dhamma Institute, 1994); Santikaro Bhikkhu, "Buddhadasa Bhikkhu: Life and Society through the Natural Eyes of Voidness," in Queen and King, *Engaged Buddhism*, pp. 147–93.

52. For two collections of essays on these themes, see Sulak Sivaraksa et al., eds., *Radical Conservatism: Buddhism in the Contemporary World* (Bangkok: Thai Inter-Religious Commission for Development and International Network of Engaged Buddhists, 1990); and Sulak Sivaraksa et al., eds., *Buddhist Perception for Desirable Societies in the Future: Papers Prepared for the United Nations University* (Bangkok: Thai Inter-Religious Commission for Development and Sathirakoses-Nagapradipa Foundation, 1993). See also Simon Zadek, "Towards a Progressive Buddhist Economics," in Watts et al., *Entering the Realm of Reality*, pp. 241–77. It should be said, however, that the links between basic Buddhist teachings and more detailed social analyses may be rather tenuous at times. Different (and possibly competing) interpretations may well be plausible, as is the case in examining social theories connected with other religious traditions.

53. Jim Wallis, *The Soul of Politics* (New York and Maryknoll, N.Y.: The New Press and Orbis Books, 1994), pp. xv, xvii.

54. Using the word *nonregressive* is shorthand for another important and complex discussion distinguishing socially engaged Buddhism and other related forms from what we might call "socially engaged" fundamentalism and other generally right-wing political movements. Many fundamentalists around the globe, after all, analyze the spiritual roots of contemporary issues and long for a social life suffused with spiritual values. As I suggested earlier, some examples of what could be seen to be socially engaged Buddhism in this century, for example in the case of Japanese Buddhism, have been aligned with militarism, aggression, and nationalism.

55. For references to many of the basic works in these areas, see Donald Roth-

berg, "The Crisis of Modernity and the Emergence of Socially Engaged Spirituality," *ReVision* 15 (winter 1993): 105–14.

56. For a general discussion of modernity and spirituality, see ibid.; for a more extended analysis of modern differentiation, see Jürgen Habermas, *The Theory of Communicative Action, Vol. 1: Reason and the Rationalization of Society,* trans. Thomas McCarthy (Boston: Beacon Press, 1984; originally published 1981).

57. This is the claim, for example, of Gary Snyder. See Catharine Ingram, Barbara Gates, and Wes Nisker, "Chan on Turtle Island: A Conversation with Gary Snyder," *Inquiring Mind* 4 (winter 1988): 1, 4–5, 25.

58. Recent works include Cornel West, *Beyond Eurocentrism and Multiculturalism, Vol. 1: Prophetic Thought in Postmodern Times* (Monroe, Me.: Common Courage Press, 1993); Rosemary Ruether, *Gaia and God: An Ecofeminist Theology of Earth Healing* (San Francisco: HarperSanFrancisco, 1992); Wallis, *The Soul of Politics;* Michael Lerner, *Jewish Renewal: A Path to Healing and Transformation* (New York: G. P. Putnam's Sons, 1994); Michael Lerner, *The Politics of Meaning: Restoring Hope and Possibility in an Age of Cynicism* (Reading, Mass.: Addison-Wesley, 1996). See also William Dean, *The Religious Critic in American Culture* (Albany: State University of New York Press, 1994).

59. The main essays from the conference were published in Watts et al., *Entering the Realm of Reality.*

60. The Think Sangha has developed a web page (http://www/bpf/think.html).

Epilogue

1. Other writers have noted similar themes. For example, Jack Kornfield identifies integration, democratization, and feminism in his piece in Don Morreale, ed., *Buddhist America: Centers, Retreats, Practices* (Santa Fe, N.M.: John Muir Publications, 1988), p. xv. Rick Fields in this volume cites six features: (1) is a largely lay movement, (2) is based on sitting meditation, (3) welcomes Western psychology, (4) is shaped by feminist insights, (5) harbors social action, and (6) contains democratic and "antihierarchical" sentiments.

2. See *Tricycle: The Buddhist Review* 1, no. 2 (winter 1991): 4. Helen Tworkov wrote in her editorial: "Asian-American Buddhists . . . so far . . . have not figured prominently in the development of something called American Buddhism." Ryo Imamura sent a rebuttal, and the controversy intensified when the rebuttal was not printed.

3. Ryo Imamura's letter in response to Helen Tworkov's editorial, and Tworkov's reply, are in the *Sangha Newsletter* (newsletter of the Wider Shin Buddhist Fellowship), no. 7 (summer 1994): 2–10; see the notes to Jan Nattier's essay in this volume for the location of this newsletter.

4. Kenneth K. Tanaka, "A Prospectus of the Buddhist Churches of America: The Role of Ethnicity," *The Pure Land* (December 1995): 130.

5. In his epoch-making book written two decades ago, Harvey Cox mentions meditation as one of the primary spiritual disciplines that attracted Americans to Eastern religions. *Turning East: The Promise and Peril of the New Orientalism* (New York: Simon and Schuster, 1977), p. 13.

6. Sitting, standing, walking, and lying are the four traditional forms of meditation.

7. Sogyal Rinpoche, *The Tibetan Book of Living and Dying* (San Francisco: HarperSanFrancisco, 1993). The copyright page states, "As of February 1994, 118,500 copies have been produced in twelve printings."

8. A study of nine accounts of socially and politically engaged Buddhist movements in contemporary Asia helped to dispel the standard perception. See Christopher S. Queen and Sallie B. King, eds., *Engaged Buddhism: Buddhist Liberation Movements in Asia* (Albany: State University of New York Press, 1996).

9. They gained approximately five hundred new members through a single 1995 mailing of the *Tricycle* subscriber list.

10. Rodger Kamenetz, *The Jew in the Lotus: A Poet's Rediscovery of Jewish Identity in Buddhist India* (San Francisco: HarperSanFrancisco, 1994), p. 7. See also Judith Linzer's *Torah and Dharma: Jewish Seekers in Eastern Religions* (Northvale, N.J.: Jason Aronson, 1996).

11. Gil Fronsdal, "The Treasures of the Theravāda," *Inquiring Mind* 12, no. 1 (fall 1995): 14–15. Diana Winston, in the same issue, expresses similar caution and doubt, though directed at American Buddhism in general (p. 12).

12. Thomas A. Tweed, *The American Encounter with Buddhism 1844–1912: Victorian Culture and the Limits of Dissent* (Bloomington: Indiana University Press, 1992), pp. 133–56.

13. Winthrop S. Hudson and John Corrigan, *Religions in America*, 5th ed. (New York: Macmillan, 1992), p. 405.

14. Ibid., p. 136: "Activism, as I have defined it, is the inclination to emphasize the spiritual significance of vigorous moral action in the world. It is the concern to uplift individuals, reform societies, and participate energetically in the political and economic spheres."

15. Ibid., p. 134: "They [proponents of optimism] emphasized the elevated capacities of persons, the positive elements of human life, the benevolent character of the universe, and the progressive development of history."

Selected Bibliography

Adam, Enid L., and Philip J. Hughes. *Religious Community Profiles: The Buddhists in Australia.* Canberra: Australian Government Publishing Service, 1996.

Akizuki, Ryōmin. *New Mahāyāna: Buddhism for a Post-Modern World.* Translated by James W. Heisig and Paul L. Swanson. Berkeley: Asian Humanities Press, 1990.

Almond, Philip C. *The British Discovery of Buddhism.* Cambridge: Cambridge University Press, 1988.

———. "The Buddha in the West: From Myth to History." *Religion* 16 (1986): 305–22.

Batchelor, Stephen. *The Awakening of the West: The Encounter of Buddhism and Western Culture.* Berkeley: Parallax Press, 1994.

Baumann, Martin. "Buddhism in the West: Phases, Orders and the Creation of an Integrative Buddhism." *Internationales Asienforum* 27, no. 3–4 (1996): 345–62.

———. "Creating a European Path to Buddhism: Historical and Contemporary Developments of Buddhism in Europe." *Journal of Contemporary Religion* 10, no. 1 (1995): 55–70.

———. "Culture Contact and Valuation: Early German Buddhists and the Creation of a 'Buddhism in Protestant Shape.' " *Numen* 44 (1997): 270–95.

———. *Deutsche Buddhisten: Geschichte und Gemeinschaften.* Marburg: Diagonal-Verlag, 1993 (2d updated and enlarged edition, 1995).

———. "The Transplantation of Buddhism to Germany: Processive Modes and Strategies of Adaptation." *Method and Theory in the Study of Religion* 6, no. 1 (1994): 35–61.

Becker, Carl. "Japanese Pure Land Buddhism in Christian America." *Buddhist-Christian Studies* 10 (1990): 143–56.

Bloom, Alfred. "The Unfolding of the Lotus: A Survey of Recent Developments in Shin Buddhism in the West." *Buddhist-Christian Studies* 10 (1990): 157–64.

Boucher, Sandy. *Turning the Wheel: American Women Creating the New Buddhism.* Updated and expanded edition. Boston: Beacon Press, 1993.

Buddhist Churches of America. *Buddhist Churches of America: Seventy-Five Year History, 1899–1974.* 2 volumes. Chicago: Nobart, 1974.

Butler, Katy. "Encountering the Shadow in Buddhist America." *Common Boundary* 8, no. 3 (1990): 14–22.

———. "Events Are the Teacher." *CoEvolution Quarterly* 40 (winter 1983): 112–23.

Conze, Edward. "Recent Progress in Buddhist Studies." In *Thirty Years of Buddhist Studies.* Oxford: Bruno Cassirer, 1967, pp. 1–32.

Cox, Harvey. *Turning East: The Promise and Peril of the New Orientalism.* New York: Simon and Schuster, 1977.

Croucher, Paul. *A History of Buddhism in Australia: 1848–1988.* Kensington, Australia: New South Wales University Press, 1989.

de Jong, J. W. *A Brief History of Buddhist Studies in Europe and America.* Bibliotheca Indo-Buddhica, No. 33. 2d revised edition. Delhi: Sri Satguru, 1987.

Dumoulin, Heinrich, and John Maraldo, eds. *The Cultural, Political, and Religious Significance of Buddhism in the Modern World.* New York: Collier Macmillan, 1976.

Ellwood, Robert S. *Alternative Altars: Unconventional and Eastern Spirituality in America.* Chicago: University of Chicago Press, 1979.

———. "Buddhism in the West." In Mircea Eliade, ed., *Encyclopedia of Religion* (New York: Macmillan, 1987), 2:436–39.

———. *The Eagle and the Rising Sun.* Philadelphia: Westminster Press, 1974.

Ellwood, Robert S., and Harry B. Partin. *Religious and Spiritual Groups in Modern America.* 2d edition. Englewood Cliffs, N.J.: Prentice-Hall, 1988.

Eppsteiner, Fred, ed. *The Path of Compassion: Writings on Socially Engaged Buddhism.* Berkeley: Parallax Press, 1988.

Farber, Don, and Rick Fields. *Taking Refuge in L.A.: Life in a Vietnamese Buddhist Temple.* New York: Aperture Foundation, 1987.

Farkas, Mary, ed. *The Zen Eye: A Collection of Zen Talks by Sokei-an.* Tokyo: Weatherhill, 1993.

Fields, Rick. "Confessions of a White Buddhist." *Tricycle: The Buddhist Review* 4, no. 1 (1994): 54–56.

———. "The Future of American Buddhism." *Vajradhatu Sun* 9, no. 1 (1987): 1, 22, 24–26.

———. *How the Swans Came to the Lake: A Narrative History of Buddhism in America.* 3d edition. Boston: Shambhala, 1992.

Finney, Henry C. "American Zen's 'Japan Connection': A Critical Case Study of Zen Buddhism's Diffusion to the West." *Sociological Analysis* 52, no. 4 (1991): 379–96.

Friedman, Lenore. *Meetings with Remarkable Women: Buddhist Teachers in America.* Boston: Shambhala, 1987.

Gross, Rita. *Buddhism after Patriarchy: A Feminist History, Analysis, and Reconstruction of Buddhism.* Albany: State University of New York Press, 1993.

Gunter-Jones, Roger. *Buddhism and the West.* London: Lindsay Press, 1973.

Hecker, Hellmuth. *Buddhismus in Deutschland: Eine Chronik.* 3d edition. Plochingen: Deutsche Buddhistische Union, 1985.

———. *Lebensbilder deutscher Buddhisten: Ein bio-bibliographisches Handbuch.* 2 volumes. Konstanz: University of Konstanz, 1990 and 1992.

Henderson, Harold. *Catalyst for Controversy: Paul Carus of Open Court.* Carbondale: Southern Illinois University Press, 1993.

Hing, Bill Ong. *Making and Remaking Asian America through Immigration Policy, 1850–1990.* Stanford: Stanford University Press, 1993.

Hori, G. Victor Sōgen. "Sweet-and-Sour Buddhism." *Tricycle: The Buddhist Review* 4, no. 1 (1994): 48–52.

Horimouchi, Isao. "Americanized Buddhism: A Sociological Analysis of a Protestantized Japanese Religion." Ph.D. dissertation, University of California, Davis, 1973.

Humphreys, Christmas. *The Development of Buddhism in England.* London: The Buddhist Lodge, 1937.

———. *Sixty Years of Buddhism in England (1907–1967).* London: The Buddhist Society, 1968.

———. *Zen Comes West: The Present and Future of Zen Buddhism in Britain.* London: George Allen and Unwin, 1960.

Hunter, Louise. *Buddhism in Hawaii.* Honolulu: University of Hawaii Press, 1971.

Hurst, Jane. *Nichiren Shoshu Buddhism and the Soka Gakkai in America: The Ethos of a New Religious Movement.* New York: Garland Press, 1992.

Imamura, Ryo. "A Comparative Study of Temple and Non-Temple Buddhist Ministers of the Jōdo Shin Sect Using Jungian Psychological Types." Ed. D. dissertation, University of San Francisco, 1986.

Jackson, Carl T. "The Influence of Asian upon American Thought: A Bibliographical Essay." *American Studies International* 22 (1984): 3–31.

———. "The Meeting of East and West: The Case of Paul Carus." *Journal of the History of Ideas* 29 (1968): 73–92.

———. *The Oriental Religions and American Thought.* Westport, Conn.: Greenwood Press, 1981.

Jones, Ken. *The Social Face of Buddhism: An Approach to Political and Social Activism.* London: Wisdom Publications, 1989.

Kashima, Tetsuden. *Buddhism in America.* Westport, Conn.: Greenwood Press, 1977.

———. "The Buddhist Churches of America: Challenges for Change in the 21st Century." *The Pacific World* 6 (1990): 28–49.

Kitagawa, Joseph T. "Appendix: Buddhism in America." In Joseph T. Kitagawa, *On Understanding Japanese Religion.* Princeton: Princeton University Press, 1987, pp. 311–28.

———. "Buddhism in America, with Special Reference to Zen." *Japanese Religions* 5 (1967): 32–57.

Kraft, Kenneth. "Recent Developments in North American Zen." In Kenneth Kraft, ed., *Zen: Tradition and Transition.* New York: Grove Press, 1988, pp. 178–98.

Lachs, Stuart. "A Slice of Zen in America." *New Ch'an Forum* 10 (1994): 12–20.

Lancaster, Lewis R. "Buddhism in the United States: The Untold and Unfinished Story." *Shambhala Review* 5, no. 1–2 (1976): 23–25.

Layman, Emma. *Buddhism in America.* Chicago: Nelson-Hall, 1976.

Lin, Irene. "Journey to the Far West: Chinese Buddhism in America." *Amerasia Journal* 22, no. 1 (1996): 107–32.

Linzer, Judith. *Torah and Dharma: Jewish Seekers in Eastern Religions.* Northvale, N.J., and London: Jason Aronson, 1996.

López, Donald S., Jr., ed. *Curators of the Buddha.* Chicago: University of Chicago Press, 1995.

Mann, Robert. *Buddhism in a Foreign Land: Essays on Meditation.* Bradford-on-Avon: Aukana, 1996.

Mellor, Philip A. "Protestant Buddhism? The Cultural Translation of Buddhism in England." *Religion* 21 (1991): 73–92.

Metraux, Daniel. *The History and Theology of Soka Gakkai: A Japanese New Religion.* Lewiston, N.Y.: Edwin Mellen Press, 1988.

Morreale, Don, ed. *Buddhist America.* Santa Fe, N.M.: John Muir Publications, 1988.

Mortland, Carol A. "Khmer Buddhists in the United States: Ultimate Questions." In May M. Ebihara and Judy Ledgerwood, eds., *Cambodian Culture since 1975.* Ithaca, N.Y.: Cornell University Press, 1984.

Nattier, Jan. "Visible and Invisible." *Tricycle: The Buddhist Review* 5, no. 1 (1995): 42–49.

Needleman, Jacob. *The New Religions.* New York: E. P. Dutton, 1977.

Needleman, Jacob, and George Baker, eds. *Understanding the New Religions.* New York: Seabury Press, 1978.

Notz, Klaus-Josef. *Der Buddhismus in Deutschland in seinen Selbstdarstellungen: Eine Religionswissenschaftliche Untersuchung zur Religiösen Akkulturationproblematik.* Frankfurt am Main: Peter Lang, 1984.

Numrich, Paul. *Old Wisdom in the New World: Americanization in Two Immigrant Theravada Buddhist Temples.* Knoxville: University of Tennessee Press, 1996.

———. "*Vinaya* in Theravāda Temples in the United States." *Journal of Buddhist Ethics* 1 (1994): 23–32.

Oliver, Ian P. *Buddhism in Britain.* London: Rider, 1979.

Peiris, William. *The Western Contribution to Buddhism.* Delhi: Motilal Banarsidass, 1973.

Prebish, Charles. "The Academic Study of Buddhism in the United States: A Current Analysis." *Religion* 24 (1994): 271–78.

———. *American Buddhism.* North Scituate, Mass.: Duxbury Press, 1979.

———. "Buddhism." In Charles H. Lippy and Peter W. Williams, eds., *Encyclopedia of the American Religious Experience: Studies of Traditions and Movements.* New York: Scribner's, 1988.

———. "Karma and Rebirth in the Land of the Earth-Eaters." In Ronald W. Neufeldt, ed., *Karma and Rebirth: Post Classical Development.* Albany: State University of New York Press, 1986.

———. "Two Buddhisms Reconsidered." *Buddhist Studies Review* 10 (1993): 187–206.

Prothero, Stephen. *The White Buddhist: The Asian Odyssey of Henry Steel Olcott.* Bloomington: Indiana University Press, 1996.

Sangharakshita, Bhikshu. *New Currents in Western Buddhism.* Glasgow: Windhorse Publications, 1990.

Schneider, David. *Street Zen: The Life and Work of Issan Dorsey.* Boston: Shambhala, 1993.

Seager, Richard H. *The World's Parliament of Religions: The East-West Encounter, Chicago, 1893.* Bloomington: Indiana University Press, 1995.

Sidor, Ellen S., ed. *A Gathering of Spirit: Women Teaching in American Buddhism.* Cumberland, R.I.: Primary Point Press, 1987.

Snelling, John. *Buddhism in Russia: The Story of Agvan Dorzhiev, Lhasa's Emissary to the Tsar.* Rockport, Mass.: Element, 1993.

———. *The Buddhist Handbook.* Rochester, Vt.: Inner Traditions, 1991. See especially "Buddhism Comes West," pp. 194–256.

Sponberg, Alan. "Green Buddhism and the Hierarchy of Compassion." *Western Buddhist Review* 1 (December 1994): 131–55.

Subhuti, Dharmacari (Alex Kennedy). *Buddhism for Today: A Portrait of a New Buddhist Movement.* 2d enlarged edition. Glasgow: Windhorse Publications, 1988.

———. *Sangharakshita: A New Voice in the Buddhist Tradition.* Glasgow: Windhorse Publications, 1994.

Tamney, Joseph B. *American Society in the Buddhist Mirror.* New York: Garland Publishing, 1992.

Tanaka, Kenneth. *Ocean: An Introduction to Jōdo-Shinshū Buddhism in America.* Berkeley: WisdomOcean Publications, 1997.

Tonkinson, Carole, ed. *Big Sky Mind: Buddhism and the Beat Generation.* New York: Riverhead Books, 1995.

Tsomo, Karma Lekshe, ed. *Buddhism through American Women's Eyes.* Ithaca, N.Y.: Snow Lion, 1995.

Tuck, Donald. *Buddhist Churches of America: Jōdo Shinshū.* Lewiston, N.Y.: Edwin Mellen Press, 1987.

Tweed, Thomas. *The American Encounter with Buddhism 1844–1912: Victorian Culture and the Limits of Dissent.* Bloomington: Indiana University Press, 1992.

Tworkov, Helen. *Zen in America.* New edition. New York: Kodansha America, 1994.

van Gemert, Victor. *Boeddhisme in Nederland: oversicht van boeddhistische stromingen in Nederland en Belgie.* Nijmegen: Zen-uitgeverij Theresiahoeve, 1990 (updated 1993).

Vessantara, Dharmachari. *The Friends of the Western Buddhist Order.* Glasgow: Windhorse Publications, 1988.

Wells, Mariann Kaye. *Chinese Temples in California.* Berkeley: University of California Press, 1962.

Williams, Duncan Ryūken, and Christopher S. Queen, eds. *American Buddhism: Methods and Findings in Recent Scholarship.* Surrey, UK: Curzon Press, 1998.

Wilson, Bryan, and Karel Dobbelaere. *A Time to Chant: the Soka Gakkai Buddhists in Britain.* Oxford: Clarendon Press, 1994.

Wratten, Darrel. *Buddhism in South Africa: From Textual Imagination to Contextual Innovation.* Cape Town: Cape Town University Press, 1997.

Illustrations

All photographs are by Don Farber and are reproduced by permission.

Chapter 1: For the 1988 opening of Hsi Lai Temple in Hacienda Heights, California, several hundred monks and nuns from Fo Kuan Shan Temple in Taiwan joined monks and nuns from various countries. After the opening ceremonies, they participated in a two-week training session led by Master Hsin Yun. During the training, these nuns pray before having lunch.

Chapter 2: At Senshin Buddhist Temple, part of the Buddhist Churches of America, temple members light candles in remembrance of their deceased loved ones during the Japanese Buddhist holiday Obon, Los Angeles, 1991.

Chapter 3: Japanese Zen master Joshu Sazaki Roshi gives a dharma talk during a meditation retreat at Rinzai-Ji Zen Center. At the right is poet and songwriter Leonard Cohen, longtime student and friend of Sazaki Roshi, Los Angeles, 1996.

Chapter 4: The Los Angeles Buddhist Church Federation holds their annual Hanamatsuri (Buddha's Birthday) ceremony and festival in Los Angeles's Little Tokyo. Representatives of Nichiren Shoshu pay their respects to the Buddha, 1992.

Chapter 5: A recently arrived Tibetan monk from Ganden Shartse Monastery in South India visits a toy shop in a shopping mall, Santa Monica, California, 1992.

Chapter 6: Three pioneers of Buddhism in America: (*left to right*) the late Vietnamese Zen master Thich Thien-An, Korean Zen master Seung Sahn, and the late Japanese Zen master Taizan Maezumi Roshi. These three Zen masters were friends and regularly attended Buddha's Birthday celebrations together. Behind them is one of Maezumi Roshi's dharma successors, Glassman Roshi, Zen Center of Los Angeles, 1979.

Chapter 7: In 1979, during the height of the boat people exodus, Vietnamese Zen master Thich Thien-An holds a ceremony on a boat in Los Angeles harbor for the boat people who died at sea. His Western and Vietnamese disciples participate in the service.

Chapter 8: American Theravāda monk Venerable Yogavacara Rahula stands with a monk from Sri Lanka, outside the International Buddhist Meditation Center, Los Angeles, 1979.

Chapter 9: Shinzen Young (*second from right*) leads a meditation retreat. Community Meditation Center, Los Angeles, 1982.

Contributors

A. W. BARBER is Associate Professor of Religious Studies at the University of Calgary, having completed his Ph.D. in Buddhist Studies at the University of Wisconsin–Madison. Prior to his Calgary appointment, he taught at Fo Kuang Shan Buddhist Institute and the Chung Hwa Institute of Buddhist Studies, both in Taiwan. He is the editor-in-chief of the *Journal of Buddhist and Tibetan Studies*, and served as editor for the seventy-two-volume set of *The Tibetan Tripiṭaka: Taipei Edition* (Taipei: Southern Material Center Publishing, 1991).

ALFRED BLOOM is Professor Emeritus at the University of Hawaii, specializing in Jōdo Shinshū Buddhism and Japanese religions. He also served as Dean and Head Professor at the Institute of Buddhist Studies in Berkeley, California. In addition to his numerous articles on Japanese Buddhism, his books include *Shinran's Gospel of Pure Grace, Life of Shinran: Journey to Self Acceptance*, and *Shoshinge: Heart of Shin Buddhism Strategies for Modern Living: A Commentary with Text of the Tannisho*. He is an active participant in the Jōdo Shinshū community in Hawaii.

STUART CHANDLER is a doctoral candidate in the Committee on the Study of Religion at Harvard University. He is writing his dissertation on Master Hsing Yun and Fo Kuang Buddhism. While at Harvard, he has also been involved in the Pluralism Project, a multiyear enterprise tracking the emergence of Buddhist, Hindu, Sikh, Jain, Islamic, and other religious communities in the United States.

ROGER CORLESS is Professor of Religion at Duke University. Born in England in 1938, he read Theology at King's College, University of London (B.D., 1961), moving to the United States in 1962, where he studied Buddhism at the University of Wisconsin (Ph.D., 1970) and History of Religions at the University of Chicago. He is a specialist in Pure Land Buddhism and a cofounder of the Society for Buddhist-Christian Studies. He has published four books, including *The Vision of Buddhism* (New York: Paragon House, 1989), and over fifty articles.

RICK FIELDS is the editor-in-chief of *Yoga Journal* and is also currently a contributing editor to *Tricycle: The Buddhist Review*. He is past editor of *The Vajradhatu Sun*, and his well-known volume *How the Swans Came to the Lake: A Narrative History of Buddhism in America* remains one of the most popular and influential volumes on the subject. His other books include *The Turquoise Bee: The Tantric Lovesongs of the Sixth Dalai Lama*, with Brian Cutillo; *The Code of the Warrior in History, Myth and Everyday Life*; and *Taking Refuge in L.A.: Life in a Vietnamese Buddhist Temple*. He was an early member of the faculty at The Naropa Institute in Boulder, Colorado, and was a long-time student of Chōgyam Trungpa.

GIL FRONSDAL received a Ph.D. in Buddhist Studies from Stanford University. He has been a student of *vipassanā* meditation in both the United States and in Southeast Asia, where he was ordained as a monk. He currently teaches *vipassanā* in California and is affiliated with Spirit Rock Center. He is coeditor (with Jack Kornfield) of *The Teachings of the Buddha*.

RITA M. GROSS is Professor of Comparative Studies in Religion at the University of Wisconsin–Eau Claire, where she has served since 1973. She earned her Ph.D. from the University of Chicago in 1975. Author of numerous essays and articles, she has also edited *Beyond Androcentrism: New Essays on Women and Religion* and *Unspoken Worlds: Women's Religious Lives* (with Nancy Falk). Her recent book *Buddhism after Patriarchy: A Feminist History, Analysis, and Reconstruction of Buddhism* was selected by *Choice* as an Outstanding Academic Book in its 1994 listing. Her newest book, *Feminism and Religion: An Introduction*, was recently published by Beacon Press. Since 1995, she has served as coeditor of the journal *Buddhist-Christian Studies*.

G. VICTOR SŌGEN HORI went to Japan in 1970 on a Mombushō (Ministry of Education) Fellowship to study Japanese philosophy. After receiving his Ph.D. from Stanford University in 1976, he was ordained and trained as a monk in the Zen monastery system for thirteen years. Since 1990, he has been the Numata Visiting Professor of Buddhist Studies at both the University of Toronto and Harvard University. Currently, he is working on a translation of the *Zenrin Kushū* while teaching Asian religions in the Faculty of Religious Studies at McGill University. At seven o'clock every morning during the school term, he can be found leading a small meditation group in the campus chapel.

JANE HURST is Professor of Philosophy and Religion at Gallaudet University, where she has taught these subjects simultaneously in voice and sign language for fifteen years. Dr. Hurst has been conducting field research on Nichiren Shōshū and the Sōka Gakkai since 1972. She is the author of *Nichiren Shoshu Buddhism and the Soka Gakkai in America: The Ethos of a New Religious Movement*.

RYO IMAMURA belongs to an eighteen-generation family lineage of Buddhist priests of the Jōdo Shinshū sect. He received his undergraduate degree in Mathematics, a master's degree in Counseling, and his doctorate in Counseling and Educational Psychology. He is Professor of Psychology at the Evergreen State College in Olympia, Washington. The focus of his work is East-West Psychology with an emphasis on Buddhist thought and practice. He is also a psychotherapist and cofounder of the East-West Counseling Center.

AMY LAVINE is a doctoral candidate in the History of Religions area at the University of Chicago. She is currently conducting fieldwork among the Tibetan refugee population in the New York City area for a project concerning collective memory and the role nostalgia plays in the Tibetan diaspora.

JAN NATTIER teaches Buddhist Studies at Indiana University. She is the author of *Once Upon a Future Time: Studies in a Buddhist Prophecy of Decline,* "The Heart Sūtra: A Chinese Apocryphal Text?" and various studies on Buddhism in Central Asia. Her current project is a study and translation of *The Inquiry of Ugra,* an early Mahāyāna text. She is also a past cochair of the Buddhism Section of the American Academy of Religion and the editor of a new journal entitled *Buddhist Literature* devoted to translation of Buddhist texts.

CUONG TU NGUYEN received his Ph.D. from Harvard University (specializing in Indian Buddhism). His works on Vietnamese Buddhism include "Rethinking Vietnamese Buddhist History: Is the *Thien Uyen Tap Anh* a 'Transmission of the Lamp Text'?" "Tran Thai Tong and the Khoa Hu Luc: A Study of Syncretic Ch'an in 13th Century Vietnam" (forthcoming), and *Zen in Medieval Vietnam.* He is Assistant Professor in the Department of Philosophy and Religious Studies at George Mason University.

PAUL DAVID NUMRICH received his Ph.D. from Northwestern University. His book, *Old Wisdom in the New World: Americanization in Two Immigrant Theravada Buddhist Temples* (University of Tennessee Press, 1996), examines the growing presence of immigrant Theravāda temples in the United States, focusing on established temples in Chicago and Los Angeles. Numrich serves as a Research Associate in the Religion in Urban America Program at the University of Illinois at Chicago.

CHARLES S. PREBISH received his Ph.D. from the University of Wisconsin–Madison (1971), where he served as research assistant to Richard H. Robinson. He is a professor in the Religious Studies Program at Pennsylvania State University. He has published nine books, including *Buddhist Monastic Discipline; Historical Dictionary of Buddhism;* and *A Survey of Vinaya Literature.* His volume *American Buddhism* (1979) is one of the first monographs to appear on this topic. He is a past officer in the International Association of Buddhist Studies, a former cochair of the Buddhism Group of the American Academy of Religion, and a founding coeditor of the electronic *Journal of Buddhist Ethics.*

DONALD ROTHBERG is on the faculty of the Saybrook Graduate School in San Francisco. He has taught philosophy at the University of Kentucky and Kenyon College, and is a coeditor of the journal *ReVision.* He has published many articles on socially engaged Buddhism (and socially engaged spirituality in general), epistemology and spiritual inquiry, transpersonal psychology, and critical social theory, and is the coeditor (with Sean Kelly) of *Ken Wilber in Dialogue: Conversations with Leading Transpersonal Thinkers* (1998). A long-time student of *vipassanā,* he has worked for many years with the Buddhist Peace Fellowship, presently serves on the board, and has led many groups and workshops on spirituality, everyday life, and social action.

MU SOENG is currently the director and a member of the teaching staff at the Barre Center for Buddhist Studies in Barre, Massachusetts. He was an ordained monk for eleven years in the Korean Zen tradition under Master Seung Sahn Sunim. He is the author of *Thousand Peaks: Korean Zen—Tradition and Teachers* and *Heart Sūtra: Ancient Buddhist Wisdom in the Light of Quantum Reality*.

KENNETH K. TANAKA received his Ph.D. in Buddhist Studies from the University of California, Berkeley, in 1986 and is the Reverend Yoshitaka Tamai Professor of Jōdo Shinshū Buddhist Studies at the Institute of Buddhist Studies, Graduate Theological Union, Berkeley, California. His writings include *The Dawn of Chinese Pure Land Buddhist Doctrine* and *Ocean: An Introduction to Jōdo Shinshū Buddhism in America*. He is an active participant in wider Buddhist and interreligious activities.

MARTIN J. VERHOEVEN graduated with distinction from the University of Wisconsin–Madison with a master's degree in History (1971). A University Fellow at Wisconsin, he later was awarded a postgraduate Ford Fellowship and went on to earn a Ph.D. in Buddhist Studies from Dharma Realm Buddhist University (1980). He was a Buddhist monk for eighteen years (as Heng Chau), and recently completed a second Ph.D. at the University of Wisconsin–Madison specializing in the American encounter with Asian religions. He is currently an Associate Research Professor at the Institute for World Religions in Berkeley, California. He is coauthor (with Heng Sure) of *With One Heart Bowing* (1979).

Index

Designer: Nola Burger
Compositor: Binghamton Valley Composition
Text: 10/12 Baskerville
Display: Weiss
Printer and binder: Maple-Vail Book Manufacturing Group